In this first full-length study of race and colonialism in
the works of James Joyce, Vincent J. Cheng argues that
Joyce wrote insistently from the perspective of a
colonial subject of an oppressive empire, and that
Joyce's representations of "race" in its relationship to
imperialism constitute a trenchant and significant
political commentary, not only on British imperialism
in Ireland, but on colonial discourses and imperial
ideologies in general. Exploring the interdisciplinary
space afforded by postcolonial theory, minority discourse, and cultural studies, and articulating his own
cross-cultural perspective on racial and cultural liminality, Professor Cheng offers a ground-breaking study
of the century's most internationally influential fiction
writer, and of his suggestive and powerful representations of the cultural dynamics of race, power, and
empire.

Cultural Margins 3

Joyce, race, and empire

Cultural Margins

General editor
Abdul JanMohamed
Department of English, University of California, Berkeley

The series **Cultural Margins** originates in response to the rapidly increasing interest in postcolonial and minority discourses among literary and humanist scholars in the US, Europe, and elsewhere. The aim of the series is to investigate the complex cultural zone within and through which dominant and minority societies interact and negotiate their differences.

Studies published in the series will range from examinations of the debilitating effects of cultural marginalization, to analyses of the forms of power found at the margins of culture, to books which map the varied and complex components involved in the relations of domination and subversion. This is an international series, addressing questions crucial to the deconstruction and reconstruction of cultural identity in the late-twentieth-century world.

Joyce, race, and empire

Vincent J. Cheng
University of Southern California

Published by the Press Syndicate of the University of Cambridge
The Pitt Building, Trumpington Street, Cambridge CB2 1RP
40 West 20th Street, New York, NY 10011–4211, USA
10 Stamford Road, Oakleigh, Victoria 3166, Australia

First published 1995

Printed in Great Britain at the University Press, Cambridge

A catalogue record for this book is available from the British Library

Library of Congress cataloguing in publication data

Cheng, Vincent John, 1951–
Joyce, race, and empire / Vincent, J. Cheng.
    p.   cm.
Includes bibliographical references (p.) and index.
ISBN 0 521 43118 2. – ISBN 0 521 47859 6 (pbk.)
1. Joyce, James, 1882–1941 – Political and social views.
2. Political fiction, English – Irish authors – History and criticism.
3. Politics and literature – Ireland – History – 20th century.
4. Imperialism in literature. 5. Colonies in literature.
6. Ireland – In literature. 7. Race in literature. I. Title.
PR6019.09Z52644   1995
823′.912 – dc20   94 30319
CIP

ISBN 0 521 43118 2 hardback
ISBN 0 521 47859 6 paperback

CE

Contents

Contents

Finnegans Wake: forays

viii

Illustrations

List of illustrations

Foreword

by Derek Attridge

During his boyhood in the ebbing nineteenth century, James Joyce breathed in politics with the Dublin air. In Ireland, as in many other countries dominated by a European power and torn internally by different responses to that dominating fact of existence, politics was inseparable from family life, friendship, religion, and vocation. The blazing quarrel at young Stephen Dedalus's first Christmas dinner in *A Portrait of the Artist as a Young Man* is perhaps the best known and the most vivid of Joyce's depictions of politics at work in the interstices of Dublin domesticity, and it is ironic that one of the issues at stake is precisely the separateness of politics from religion and from the family. Mr. Casey and Mr. Dedalus complain that the priests are delivering election addresses from the pulpit, while Dante Riordan insists that what the two men call "politics" is in fact religion. Mrs. Dedalus tries in vain to put a stop to the conversation: "For pity's sake and for pity sake let us have no political discussion on this day of all days in the year." Although we are given little overt indication of Stephen's reaction to the argument and the fierce emotions it arouses, the very highlighting of the scene – related in minute detail over about a dozen pages – testifies to its importance in Joyce's carefully-drawn "portrait of the artist."

The artist that James Joyce grew into cherished no illusions that politics could be walled off in a domain of its own. All his major work – and much of his minor work – documents the effects upon the citizens of Dublin of their country's status as a subject nation, and bears witness to the terrible history of that subjection. After Joyce's move to the Continent, that specific Irish history is more and more often seen as paralleling other colonial experiences of oppression and resistance. However, while Joyce's work was appearing, the peculiar

xi

challenge to cultural orthodoxy that it presented lay much more obviously in its formal innovations and its exploration of personal intimacies (of mind and body) than in its political dimension. T. S. Eliot made much of Joyce's "mythic method," while Ezra Pound revelled in his handling of language and convention (at least until *Finnegans Wake*). Moreover, the critical traditions which dominated institutions of higher education from the forties to the sixties and which played a major role in the metamorphosis of James Joyce from a scandalous literary extremist to a pillar of the modernist edifice, although they carried out a great deal of invaluable interpretative work, focused on the formal and the stylistic at the expense of the political. It is true that politics was amply documented by critics and biographers as a presence in Joyce's writing and life, but the page-by-page engagement with the political in his fiction was not analyzed – partly because there existed no critical framework within which such an activity could be undertaken. Where there was an emphasis on the ethical dimension of his work, it was more likely to be in terms of individual freedom and compassion than the politics of colonialism and anti-colonialism.

In recent years, however, a great deal of attention has been given to the particular cultural practices that arise in the varied contexts that can be labeled "colonial" and "postcolonial." However reductive these labels, the work of scholars such as Homi Bhabha, David Lloyd, Lisa Lowe, Edward Said, Gayatri Spivak, and Robert Young has been richly productive in questioning the tendency to give an automatic privilege to the metropolitan view of the world, in developing theoretical tools to make possible alternative understandings of the relation between the metropolitan and the peripheral, and in exploring the role of art within the struggle against national and racial oppression. In *Joyce, race, and empire*, Vincent Cheng has given us the first book devoted to these issues as they arise in Joyce's writing, drawing on both empirical and theoretical studies of race and empire as well as on studies of Joyce's own political allusions and interests, and deploying his considerable skill and experience as a reader of Joyce to argue a compelling case for the significance of the political in all his work.

He has gone further than this, however: one might say that not only has he demonstrated the importance of politics to Joyce, he has also demonstrated the importance of Joyce to politics. To trace the political as it manifests itself, writ large or small, throughout Joyce's oeuvre, is a valuable activity, but it leaves unanswered some of the most central questions. What part do, or can, Joyce's writings play in the political contest they so minutely engage with? Can Joyce be said to be a "political writer" not only in the sense that his work is shot through with political references and arguments, but in the sense that his work carries weight in the realm of the political? Professor Cheng suffers from no delusion as to the uselessness of Joyce's books as weapons in any particular political struggle, except perhaps as weighty and sharp-edged missiles; but he advances the more interesting argument that they contribute to the political *as works of literature*. They do this in the only way that literature can have an effect on human lives when it functions not as history, documentary, propaganda, sermon, treatise, or exemplum but as literature: by opening up new spaces of thought and feeling for those readers who let themselves be challenged and changed by what they encounter in a text. Thus Professor Cheng shows how Joyce's writing both acknowledges the current potency and the miserable legacy of binary thinking in the politics of race and empire and seeks continually for ways of breaching the oppositional logic upon which such thinking relies. The figure or the notion of the Other is a constant preoccupation in Joyce's work, from the Oriental fantasies of "Araby" to the "dark horse" in *Ulysses* and *Finnegans Wake*; and Cheng shows that his writing consistently reveals both the basic incoherence of these figurings and their enormous human cost. Moreover, as this book demonstrates, every deployment of a representation of otherness has a bearing on the Irish predicament that remained at the heart of Joyce's concerns, since the Irish have for centuries suffered as objects of just this kind of stereotyping prejudice.

One interesting result of this reading is that contrary to the common view that Joyce's work becomes less politically engaged as it becomes more formally innovative, the later writings emerge as the most politically committed of all. In particular, *Finnegans Wake*, with its finely detailed, and uproariously funny, attack on binaries of all kinds is seen to be engaged in the demolition – by excess, by outrage, by comedy – of those cherished modes of thought upon which racism and imperialism have always depended. Vincent Cheng has invited us to reread Joyce once more, from the brilliant beginnings to the exorbitant end, not just for the sake of familiar pleasures but to experience for ourselves the exposure and the shattering of the rigid, and rigidifying, oppositions by which we are all constrained.

Preface

A number of critics and scholars have particularly influenced, directly or indirectly, the nature of my arguments and analyses in this study. The ones I am most conscious of, in terms of general approaches and philosophical assumptions, are Jacques Derrida, M. M. Bakhtin, and Edward Said; in terms of specific influences, the writings of race theorists Michael Banton and L. P. Curtis, Jr. (among others); in terms of useful political models, Antonio Gramsci and Benedict Anderson, most especially; and in terms of writers on colonialism and postcolonialism, Frantz Fanon, Edward Said, Homi Bhabha, and Gayatri Spivak, among others. Of course, I am (as I have long been) very indebted to the preceding work of a number of fine Joycean colleagues and scholars.

Each of the chapters of this book focuses on particular issues within a particular Joycean text, employing what seemed to me the most fruitful methodological approaches and combinations in each instance. Chapter 2, "Catching the conscience of a race," is a study of the discursive construction of the "Irish race" as posited by the English during the nineteenth century in the prevalent discourses (scientific, cultural, political, literary, and artistic) of the time; of the Irish response to such a racialized construction and discourse; and of Joyce's negotiations (particularly in his essays) between such binary positions and racializations, issues which he will take up again most fully in *Ulysses*. My approaches here draw particularly on the work of contemporary race theorists (such as Banton and Curtis); of several Irish scholars, especially Seamus Deane, Luke Gibbons, and David Lloyd; and of cultural critics such as Said, James Clifford, Mary Pratt, Lisa Lowe, Gayatri Spivak, and Robert Young.

Chapters 3, 4, and 5 form a triad on the symptomatics and pathology of Irish colonialism as depicted in Joyce's *Dubliners*. Chapter 3, tracing the subtle trail of "The exoticized and Orientalized Other" as found in the collection's first three stories, depends for its methodological anchors on Said's work on "Orientalism," Bakhtin's cultural and narrative dialogics, and Lisa Lowe's negotiations of the relationship between Orientalism and feminism. Chapter 4, "The gratefully oppressed: Joyce's *Dubliners*," presents the colonialist symptomatics in the *Dubliners* stories within the colonial dynamics articulated by Fanon, within the cultural/political models articulated by Gramsci, and within the intersections of the two as articulated by Said and by Stuart Hall. Chapter 5, "Empire and patriarchy in 'The Dead'," is a study of the conjoined dynamics of empire and sexual colonization – as a case study of the issues of modernist and academic canonicity; and of the conjunctions between minority discourse, colonial politics, and sexual politics. This chapter is particularly indebted to Dominic Manganiello's work on Joyce's politics, to Margot Norris's essays on *Dubliners*, and to Spivak's negotiations of the intersections between sexual and colonial dynamics.

The three chapters (6, 7, 8) in the section (collectively titled "Imagining selves and nations") about *Ulysses* – which Fredric Jameson has called "the epic of the metropolis under imperialism" ("*Ulysses* in History," 134) – were originally conceived and written as a single (and very long) chapter. Chapter 6 ("Imagining selves") is particularly indebted to anthropological approaches to minority studies (e.g., Clifford, Pratt, Gerald Vizenor, Virginia-Lee Webb) in its depiction of the ethnography of Irishness and of perspectives of racial and ethnic otherness within *Ulysses*. Chapter 7 ("Imagining nations") discusses Joyce's representation of Irish Nationalism within discourses of Irishness and of Irish nationhood; this chapter draws centrally on the writings on nationalism by Benedict Anderson, Homi Bhabha, and Frantz Fanon. Chapter 8 ("Imagining futures: nations, narratives, selves") depicts the anti-essentialist alternatives represented by Joyce's texts and by some of Leopold Bloom's ideas in the context of the above studies of nationalism, and in terms of Abdul JanMohamed and David Lloyd's understandings and vision of "minority discourse."

The section on *Finnegans Wake* ("Forays") contains two case-studies for the kind of analyses which the *Wake*, as a work steeped in the very texture and colors of racial and colonial dynamics, encourages us to explore. Chapter 9, "White horse, dark horse:

Joyce's allhorse of another color," is a theoretically broad study of
the issues of essentialism and racism, and of their philosophical and
linguistic implications – within an illustrative analysis of a single set
of tropes (horses/races) as played out thematically in Joyce's texts,
particularly the *Wake*; Derrida's understandings of Western logocentrism and Bakhtin's articulations both of dialogism and of the
carnivalesque are basic touchstones for this chapter. Chapter 10,
"The general and the sepoy: imperialism and power in the Museyroom," focuses on a single short passage, the "Museyroom" – as a
case study of colonial/racial power politics and of the responses that
such politics engender from the colonial cultures on the margins of
empire. Drawing on the postcolonial theories articulated by Bhabha
and Spivak, this chapter also illustrates the dense texture of colonial/
racial issues, page by page, in the *Wake*; and of the sort of resonant
analyses rewarded by such detailed investigations and close readings
of the Wakean text. Finally, Chapter 11 concludes with a brief
discussion about the nature and effectiveness of Joyce's interventions
and articulations on race and empire.

Acknowledgments

I would like, first of all, to thank the Guggenheim Foundation for the generous fellowship that helped launch this project. I received further support and encouragement from my own institution, the University of Southern California, as well as from the University of California Humanities Research Institute; as a fellow in the latter's 1991–92 Fellowship Program in Minority Discourse, I also learned much from my colleagues in that fellowship group.

Earlier versions of three sections of this book first appeared elsewhere: a version of chapter 9 appeared in *Joyce Studies Annual 1991*, ed. Thomas F. Staley (Austin: University of Texas Press, 1991); a version of chapter 10 appeared in *Critical Essays on "Finnegans Wake,"* ed. Patrick A. McCarthy (New York: G. K. Hall, 1992); and a version of chapter 5 appeared in *Joyce Studies Annual 1993*, ed. Thomas F. Staley (Austin: University of Texas Press, 1993). I would like to thank the above for their permissions to reprint parts of those earlier essays.

A number of friends and colleagues have been immensely helpful and encouraging. Providing particularly insightful suggestions were John Bishop, Margot Norris, Kim Devlin, Fritz Senn, Ira Nadel, and especially Derek Attridge. I would further like to thank Richard Yarborough, Allan Casson, Maeera Shreiber, and the members of the Southern California *Finnegans Wake* Group for their very helpful suggestions and warm support.

Finally, I would like to thank Abdul JanMohamed for his encouragement as series editor of the "Cultural Margins" series with Cambridge University Press – and to thank, at the Press, Josie Dixon, Joanna Palmer, and especially Kevin Taylor who has supported this study with encouragement and advice from its inception. To all of the above, my gratitude.

Abbreviations

Quotations from the following works are cited in the text through these abbreviations:

CW   Joyce, James. *The Critical Writings of James Joyce*. Ed. Ellsworth Mason and Richard Ellmann. New York: Viking, 1959.

D   Joyce, James. *Dubliners*. New York: Viking, 1967.

D: Text   Joyce, James. *"Dubliners": Text, Criticism, and Notes*. Ed. Robert Scholes and A. Walton Litz. New York: Viking, 1969.

E   Joyce, James. *Exiles*. New York: Penguin, 1973.

FW   Joyce, James. *Finnegans Wake*. New York: Viking, 1939.

JJ*I*   Ellmann, Richard. *James Joyce*. First edition. New York: Oxford University Press, 1959.

JJ*II*   Ellmann, Richard. *James Joyce*. Revised edition. New York: Oxford University Press, 1982.

Letters   Joyce, James. *Letters of James Joyce*, volumes II and III. Ed.
II, III   Richard Ellmann. New York: Viking, 1966.

P   Joyce, James. *A Portrait of the Artist as a Young Man*. New York: Viking, 1964.
      Joyce, James. *"A Portrait of the Artist as a Young Man": Text, Criticism, and Notes*. Ed. Chester G. Anderson. New York: Viking, 1968.

SH   Joyce, James. *Stephen Hero*. Ed. John J. Slocum and Herbert Cahoon. New York: New Directions, 1959.

U   Joyce, James. *Ulysses: The Corrected Text*. Ed. Hans Walter Gabler with Wolfhard Steppe and Claus Melchior. New York: Random House, 1986.

Passages from *Ulysses* are identified by episode and line number. Quotations from *Finnegans Wake* are identified by page and line number. Citations from the other texts above are identified by page number. These conventions generally follow the format prescribed by the *James Joyce Quarterly*.

Introduction

In *Celtic Revivals: Essays in Modern Irish Literature* Seamus Deane writes in an essay on "Joyce and Nationalism":

> It is well known that Joyce, like Stephen Dedalus, considered himself to be the slave of two masters, one British and one Roman. It is equally well known that he repudiated the Irish Literary Revival ... Repudiating British and Roman imperialism and rejecting Irish nationalism and Irish literature which seemed to be in the service to that cause, he turned away from his early commitment to socialism and devoted himself instead to a highly apolitical and wonderfully arcane practice of writing. Such, in brief, is the received wisdom about Joyce and his relationship to the major political issues of his time. Although some revision of this estimate has recently begun, it remains as one of the more secure assumptions about his life and work.
>
> (*Celtic Revivals*, 92)

This certainly has been the longstanding view of the canonized Joyce: the great Modernist writer whose stylistic and aesthetic innovations revolutionized modern prose style, but who remained steadfastly apolitical. Or, as Dominic Manganiello remarks in *Joyce's Politics*, "The tenor of innumerable critical statements about Joyce is that he was indifferent to politics" (Manganiello, 1). But, as Deane goes on to comment about such "secure assumptions about [Joyce's] life and work": "It is, however, seriously misleading to view Joyce in this way" (*Celtic Revivals*, 92). For, as Manganiello has convincingly documented, "Joyce's work as an Italian journalist bears witness to the contrary. Not only did he keep abreast of the Irish political scene, but Joyce staunchly defended Griffith's [Arthur Griffith, founder of Sinn Fein] line of argument on key issues" (139); in November 1906 he had written to his brother Stanislaus that "If the Irish programme did not insist on the Irish language I suppose I could call myself a nationalist" (*Letters* II, 187).

This entrenched view, however, of an apolitical Joyce as the great modernist stylist, is certainly one that has been convenient and attractive to High Modernist aestheticism, with its canonization of stylistic innovation and intricacy as the highest values and determinants of modern literary art. As Fredric Jameson and other critics of Modernism have argued, this aesthetic approach to Modernism substitutes "style" as a red herring ("'style' is then the substitution of a spatial or perceptual 'meaning')" for material and historicized substance ("Modernism," 55). One effect, however, of this canonization – of the elevation of an Irish-Catholic colonial writer like Joyce into the pantheon of the Modernist greats – is hardly innocent but rather insidious: for it shifts attention away from the manifestly political content and ideological discourse of Joyce's works onto his unarguably potent role and influence in stylistic revolution. Several generations of readers and scholars have now (in large measure) focused their investigations onto Joyce's styles and away from the ideological discussions contained in the Joycean texts, secure in their assumptions that these works were apolitical and essentially non-ideological in nature. The net effect is to neutralize the ideological potency of Joyce's texts, to defang the bite of Joyce's politics. Perhaps only in this way could an Irishman whose works bristle with bitter resentment against the imperiums of State, Church, and Academy be somehow appropriated and rendered acceptable, even revered, as a High Modernist icon of the Great *English* Literary Canon.

After all, Ireland at the turn of the century – devastated by centuries of famine, poverty, and rule by English landlords – was virtually a Third World country under British domination; as Deane reminds us, "Ireland is the only Western European country that has had both an early and a late colonial experience ... a process of radical dispossession. A colonized people is without a specific history and even, as in Ireland and other cases, without a specific language" ("Introduction," 3, 11). To regard Joyce merely as another icon in the Great Tradition of English Literature, without paying significant attention to the specific historical contexts and ideological contents of his work, is to act as if there were no difference between an Irish-Catholic writer from Dublin who (it is ironic to recall) spent much of his artistic energy trying to debunk both English "history" and English literature (not to speak of dogmatic religious authority) – and, say, Lord Tennyson or Matthew Arnold. The irony is that

Joyce devoted much of his life (and his writing) to thumbing his nose at such institutional authorities and canonizing processes; the writer who was condemned, marginalized, and censored as obscene, vulgar, and *déclassé* during most of his lifetime has been subsequently canonized by an Academy that has chosen to construct a sanitized "Joyce" whose contributions are now to be measured only by the standards of canonical High Modernism. To assume that Joyce is an apolitical (or even regressive), aestheticizing, privileged white male writer in the Great Anglocentric Tradition, then, is willingly to buy into what the High Modernist academic canonizing processes would have us believe. It is also necessarily and consequently to occlude and ignore the specific nature of Joyce's texts and the ideological issues contained in such radical texts – as they were certainly considered then, both ideologically and stylistically – written by a colonial Irish–Catholic consciousness searching for alternatives to both a stifling nationalism and an oppressive British imperialism, subjected to press censorship in most of the English-speaking world.

By centering Joyce as a canonical figure in the traditional lineage of Spenser, Shakespeare, Milton, and Tennyson, are we not, indeed, effectively muting and blunting (even ignoring) the power of the key motivations behind his writings, which were most frequently attempts to resist and defy the authorized centrality of canons, empires (especially England), and totalizing structures? In canonizing the radically experimental and avant-garde Joyce, there is danger of failing to contextualize his polyglot linguistic talents in the light of his historical dispossession from a "native" national language that allowed him neither to retrieve Gaelic as an Irish native tongue, nor to feel at home in an English inflected by Empire and domination.[1]

Since the literary tradition of Shakespeare and Milton was, for Joyce, the imperial tradition of the English oppressor, he was deprived of any comfortably viable artistic models including those of a comic Irish tradition he himself construed as "court jesters" to the British masters. His de-classed status as a poor, urban Irish Catholic, that is, his failure in British class terms to be "a gentleman," obliged him both to seek other textual models (such as Irish literature, pop culture, and advertising; Flaubert, Ibsen, and other non-English writers) and avenues of publication for his works, as well as to challenge the censors and authorities by writing texts that threatened (and debunked) traditional, "centered," and dominant notions of art and culture.[2] Many of the revolutionary qualities of Joyce's stylistic, linguistic, and literary innovations can thus be persuasively traced to, and grounded in, his sense of ideological, ethnic, and colonial dispossession.

In recent years a number of Joyce scholars have begun a revision of this High Modernist acceptance of an apolitical Joyce.[3] This study, too, joins that effort toward reclaiming the power of Joyce's texts (as engagedly political and ideologically progressive) from a canonizing process that has, in large measure, managed to negate or neutralize that power by constructing "Joyce" as an apolitical stylistic innovator. The chapter on "Empire and patriarchy in 'The Dead'" (chapter 5) provides an especially suggestive case study of the clash between the Academy's institutional, canonizing practices and an ideological recuperation of Joyce's works, for "The Dead" is a favorite and model text in the Modernist canon.

In *The Consciousness of Joyce*, Richard Ellmann argues convincingly that by 1906 (at the time when Joyce was conceiving "The Dead") Joyce had been won over by the non-extremist brand of nationalism espoused by Arthur Griffith, founder of Sinn Fein, and "approved Griffith's moderate programme" (*Consciousness*, 86–88). Stanislaus claimed that Joyce read Griffith's newspaper, the *United Irishman*, every week; and Joyce himself wrote that Griffith's was the only policy of any benefit to Ireland (*Letters* II, 158; Manganiello, 118). Both Ellmann and Manganiello further document not only Joyce's own Irish Nationalist leanings at this time, but his intense interest and readings in socialism and his identification of himself as a "socialist" (he had written in 1905 that "my political opinions are those ... of a socialistic artist"; *Letters* II, 89). Ellmann argues that "Joyce's politics and aesthetics were one. For him, the act of writing was also, and indissolubly, an act of liberating" (*Consciousness*, 90); and Manganiello demonstrates that Joyce's writings, fiction and non-fiction, argue a significant political ideology shaped by such contemporary politics.

For Joyce was hardly an apolitical writer as he began his career as a writer. A quick glance through the essays, speeches and newspaper articles he wrote as a young man reveals an intellect intensely concerned and pointedly thoughtful about the Irish "race," the "Irish Question," and imperial England, voicing political arguments and consistently iterated positions on those topics that – as I will argue in this study – Joyce represented, developed, and further nuanced in his fiction for the rest of his life. A few suggestive examples from these essays, culled from many possible such quotations in the *Critical Writings*:

[If one should feel] that England does not have many crimes to expiate in Ireland, now and in the future, he is very much mistaken. When a victorious country tyrannizes over another, it cannot logically be considered wrong for that other to rebel ... no one who is not deceived by self-interest or ingenuousness will believe, in this day and age, that a colonial country is motivated by purely Christian motives. These are forgotten when foreign shores are invaded, even if the missionary and the pocket Bible precede, by a few months, as a routine matter, the arrival of the soldiers and the uplifters.

(CW 163).

For so many centuries the Englishman has done in Ireland only what the Belgian is doing today in the Congo Free State ... She enkindled its factions and took over its treasury. By the introduction of a new system of agriculture, she reduced the power of the native leaders and gave great estates to her soldiers. She persecuted the Roman church when it was rebellious and stopped when it became an effective instrument of subjugation. Her principal preoccupation was to keep the country divided, and if a Liberal English government that enjoyed the full confidence of the English voters were to grant a measure of autonomy to Ireland tomorrow, the conservative press of England would immediately begin to incite the province of Ulster against the authority in Dublin ... [England] was as cruel as she was cunning. Her weapons were, and still are, the battering ram, the club, and the rope.

(CW 166)

Nor is it any harder to understand why the Irish citizen is a reactionary and a Catholic, and why he mingles the names of Cromwell and Satan when he curses. For him, the great Protector of civil rights is a savage beast who came to Ireland to propagate his faith by fire and sword. He does not forget the sack of Drogheda and Waterford, nor the bands of men and women hunted down in the furthermost islands by the Puritan ... How could he forget? Can the back of a slave forget the rod?

(CW 168)

The new Fenians are joined in a party which is called Sinn Fein (We Ourselves). They aim to make Ireland a bi-lingual Republic, and to this end they have established a direct steamship service between Ireland and France. They practise boycotts against English goods; they refuse to become soldiers or to take the oath of loyalty to the English crown; they are trying to develop industries throughout the entire Ireland; and instead of paying out a million and a quarter annually for the maintenance of eighty representatives in the English parliament, they want a consular service in the principal ports of the world for the purpose of selling their industrial products without the intervention of England.

(CW 191)

[Now] the English Liberal ministry introduces a measure of devolution which does not go beyond the proposals made by the imperialist Chamberlain in 1885 ... Probably the Lords will kill the measure, since this is their trade, but if they are wise, they will hesitate to alienate the sympathy of the Irish for constitutional agitation; especially now that India and Egypt are in an uproar and the overseas colonies are asking for an imperial federation. From their point of view, it would not be advisable to provoke by an obstinate veto the reaction of a people who, poor in everything else and rich only in political ideas, have perfected the strategy of obstructionism and made the word "boycott" an international war-cry.

(*CW* 194)

In fact, the Irish question is not solved even today, after six centuries of armed occupation and more than a hundred years of English legislation, which has reduced the population of the unhappy island from eight to four million, quadrupled the taxes, and twisted the agrarian problem into many more knots.

(*CW* 199)

[The English are reluctant in] proceeding with the reform of their medieval laws, with the reform of their pompous and hypocritical literature, with the reform of their monstrous judicial system.

(*CW* 212)

These are hardly the thoughts of an apolitical colonial author.

In the "Cyclops" episode of *Ulysses*, Leopold Bloom finds himself in a pub, surrounded by xenophobic white Irish males who mock Bloom's religion, his racial heritage, and his manhood. Historically situated in an anti-Semitic Ireland itself politically impotent through its colonization by the English empire, Bloom is an Irishman particularly conscious of his own doubly marginalized status as a Jew within his country's marginalized status as a victim of English imperialism. In the "Circe" episode later that evening, Bloom fantasizes a New Jerusalem in which he would rule, the "New Bloomusalem"; this idealistic, utopian fantasy includes in its political agenda:

New worlds for old. Union of all, jew, moslem and gentile ... General amnesty, weekly carnival with masked license, bonuses for all, esperanto the universal language with universal brotherhood. No more patriotism of barspongers and dropsical impostors ... Mixed races and mixed marriage.

(*U* 15.1686–99)

Bloom's fantasy is one that Joyce would play out more fully in *Finnegans Wake*, that subversive book full of dark insurgencies

6

challenging the clear authority of white, Eurocentric empire – a night world/text which defies and decenters the authorized grammars of language, psyche, systems, power, empires, and daytime consciousness. Colin MacCabe has even suggested that *"Finnegans Wake*, with its sustained dismemberment of the English linguistic and literary heritage, is perhaps best understood in relation to the struggle against imperialism" ("Finnegans," 4). Yet Joyce's other, earlier narrative works – *Dubliners, Stephen Hero, A Portrait of the Artist as a Young Man, Ulysses* – had also been centrally concerned with the relation of race/ethnicity to an imperial power; and with the relationships between race, ethnicity, imperialism, colonialism, nationalism, and the structures of power – explored within the Joycean parameters and discourses of otherness, marginality, and exile. Such explorations of racial difference within the discourses of power and empire characterize all of Joyce's fiction, both in terms of a culturally constructed otherness ("Orientalism") and as an analogy for the Irish condition: from the images of "Araby" in *Dubliners* to the explorations of Irishness as a race (and the Irish as colonials) in "The Dead" and *A Portrait*; from Bloom as a marginalized Jew and a "dark horse," symbolic of those "throwaway" races on the margins of empire, to the images in *Ulysses* of Near Eastern exoticism, black American slaves, Africans, and so on; finally, to *Finnegans Wake*'s all-encompassing, multiplicitous, and heterogeneous nature – so full of plurabilities of difference-as-sameness – such as its ubiquitous Egyptology, its use of Chinese and Japanese pidgin and of Malay dialects, and its analogical equation of imperialistic situations: colonial India, black American slavery, the Israelites under Pharoah, and an Ireland denied Home Rule.

A writer who opposed anti-Semitism, racism, blind nationalism, male aggression, imperialism; who explored the nature of female consciousness; and who, as an exile and cosmopolite, lived his life in cities with culturally mixed populations (Trieste, Paris, Zurich) – Joyce repeatedly gave voice in his works to those silenced and exiled to the margins of dominant cultures, in an attempt to universalize the colonial relationship and struggle between an Ireland without Home Rule and the ruling British Empire. In this sense, many of Joyce's works can be viewed as, in part, attempts to explore the alternatives – alternatives to the discursive and hegemonic constructions of a dominant culture – available to the silenced voices on the margins of dominant and centralized authorities. Perhaps not coincidentally, Joyce has been a shaping influence for numerous contemporary

7

writers as inter-nationally and ethnically diverse as (to name a few) William Faulkner, Ralph Ellison, Gabriel Garcia Marquez, Maxine Hong Kingston, and Salman Rushdie (who wrote prophetically that many great writers "have been forced into silence, exile, or submission" at a time when "the Joycean option of cunning seems unavailable at present" ["Book," 26]).

I began this project as an exploration of Joyce's texts in terms of issues of "race" and ethnicity. In the Irish context, the issues of "race" and Irishness are so inextricably involved with issues of empire and colonialism (and English constructions of Irishness) that it very quickly became obvious that in fact this would have to be a study of the relationships between Joyce, race, and *empire*. Chapter 2 ("Catching the conscience of a race") discusses in culturally and historically specific detail the ways in which I am using the term "race" in this study, within its precise applications to the "Irish Question," English–Irish relationships, and the specific, relevant contexts and aspects of the Irish experience of colonialism within the English empire.

In this study, the first book-length treatment of race and colonialism in Joyce's works, I investigate not only Joyce's depictions and representations of "race" in its relationship to imperialism, but also how these treatments constitute a significant and sustained commentary on Joyce's part concerning such issues. Furthermore, I explore and discuss the implications of Joyce's depictions and critiques of these topics – both the progressive and enabling possibilities Joyce affords us for thinking about such charged issues and the problematic implications of his treatments and representations in those same terms. For example, one might consider the arguable effectiveness of Joyce's mode of ideological resistance, as in Colin MacCabe's rueful conclusion that *Finnegans Wake* is "a primer for a failed revolution, one that would have allied Ireland to Europe rather than simply separating twenty-six counties from Britain" ("Finnegans," 5). And, in a different context, one should certainly be alert to Seamus Deane's telling warning about Joyce's tendency to equate the Irish experience with universal analogies of otherness, thus potentially erasing racial (and other modes of) difference altogether:

The pluralism of [Joyce's] styles and languages, the absorbent nature of his controlling myths and systems, finally gives a certain harmony to varied experience. But, it could be argued, it is the harmony of

8

indifference, one in which everything is a version of something else, where sameness rules over diversity, where contradiction is finally and disquietingly written out.

(*Heroic*, 15)

I would argue that Joyce's works house, in carefully constructed intent, a symptomatic representation of the various ideological positions on these issues in turn-of-century Ireland – in very specific, cultural and historical detail and accuracy – and thus collectively can be seen as a dialogic locus for the many particular, historically based voices of the variant social discourses within the various levels of both hegemony and resistance. I see Joyce's works as forming, *in toto*, both a trenchant analysis and a potent critique of certain such ideological discourses (in the racialization and colonization of the Irish) and of the resultant colonial pathologies; these are Joycean critiques and positions which, as we shall see, were voiced consistently and insistently throughout his works – with increasing refinement, complexity, and nuance in the highly textured layerings of his later styles; as I will argue, these are, furthermore, representations that are sensitive to (and answer to) the sociopolitical theories of writers as different as Antonio Gramsci, Edward Said, and Frantz Fanon. As part of these critiques, Joyce articulates some philosophical, psychological, and linguistic implications involved in a racialized essence of imperial Self and colonized Other in terms of the broad dangers of philosophical essentialism; the psychic slippages and repressions involved in positing selves and others (I use "Other" to indicate the absolute difference/otherness constructed by racist discourses, as distinguished from the broad and heterogeneous range of actual [lower-case] "others"); and the linguistic indeterminacy revealed by the deconstruction of logocentric assumptions about the essential nature of language itself. Finally, I would argue that – within the consistency of Joyce's critiques (even if in parody or fantasy) – lies the artistic representation of some alternative approaches to such cultural problems; these collectively constitute, if not a utopian model (nor a purely linguistic "revolution"), at least a set of Joycean arguments for a desired alternative to the hopeless and destructive pathology of the racialized colonialism (and of the specific Irish responses to it) that Joyce depicts in his writings.

Obviously a study of this nature involves issues of, at once, literary criticism, modern philosophy, psychoanalysis, cultural history, political economy, anthropology, social history, race theory, linguistics, ethnic studies, postcolonial theory, and so on. In order to pursue such a complex project, it was both desirable and necessary for me to take on a cross-disciplinary approach, attempting to negotiate as well as I can a simultaneous sensitivity to a number of relevant and intersecting methodologies. In order to do so, I was fortunate to have been awarded both a Guggenheim Fellowship and a University of California Humanities Research Institute Fellowship, which together allowed me to continue intensive pursuit of my own longstanding commitment to and interest in what we now call cultural studies and minority discourse, two large and related intellectual subject-areas that encompass (under their broad umbrellas) the social/cultural relationships between these various disciplines. My involvement as a Fellow in the University of California Humanities Research Institute's 1991-92 Fellowship Program on "Dependency and Autonomy: The Relation of Minority Discourses to Dominant Culture" (led by Abdul JanMohamed) was especially illuminating in bringing me into constructive, interdisciplinary interaction with leading scholars from a number of different fields (anthropology, law, political science, ethnic studies, history, cultural studies), each working on issues of race and minority discourse; this resulted in, for me, a significant widening and deepening of the perspectives and critical tools available to me in my attempts to investigate and situate Joyce's work within the context of contemporary interdisciplinary discourses and studies of race, colonialism, and imperialism. This study, in consequence, was conceived as a literary analysis of broad and interdisciplinary interest for the humanities and for cultural criticism: a study not only of the century's most internationally influential fiction writer, but also of his suggestive and powerful representations of the cultural dynamics of race, power, and empire.

A study of "Joyce, race, and empire" can be written in many ways, from many different perspectives. To begin with, it could have allied itself to a particular intellectual discipline from among the various ones I name above; my own choice was to employ my training in literary criticism within the broad multidisciplinary interests of minority discourse studies and cultural criticism. In parallel fashion, I have, from the start, opted to approach these issues with a cross-cultural, internationalist perspective on race and on Irishness – as opposed to a deep immersion in either academic Irish Studies or in a particular nationalist politics.

Indeed, one might well ask the question of whether such a study as this were not better done by an Irish native, blessed not only with the insider's knowledge of native customs, language, history, and so on, but also with the specific cultural experience unknowable to the outsider. There is certainly some truth to this – although, to be sure, careful and judicious research can make up for some of the lack of "insider" knowledge, tempered with the outsider's advantage of being perhaps more receptive to a number of different perspectives with a greater degree of open-mindedness. Nevertheless, I have often envied the knowledge and experience of cultural and historical specificities available to Irish-born scholars whose work I admire and have learned much from – a list that includes the various perspectives and works of Seamus Deane, David Lloyd, Luke Gibbons, Denis Donoghue, Declan Kiberd, Emer Nolan, Augustine Martin, David Norris, and Fionnula Flanagan, among others. Studies about race, empire, and Joyce would look significantly different coming from each of them, and indeed a number of different scholars (both Irish and otherwise) are working on this subject currently; their individual studies will each provide particular approaches and interests quite different from mine, and I look forward to learning from these.

But (as will become quite obvious in this book) part of my argument and conviction is that a national, ethnic, or cultural identity (whether "Irish" or "Chinese" or whatever) is, to a large degree, itself a cultural construction that is not very easy to characterize; and this study of Joyce is engaged in the services of the larger cultural project of deconstructing the very notions of an essentialist (and suspiciously convenient) distinction between insider and outsider, between native and foreigner, between Self and Other (and other such analogously simplistic tags and labels). Indeed, it is possible that, in steeping oneself in the study of Irish history and culture, an outsider may end up having more specific knowledge about "Irishness" than many Irish-born natives living in Ireland ("insiders"). Furthermore, Irish natives are themselves hardly homogeneous in character or essence: although they certainly share some very real and specific cultural experiences, nevertheless a study of "Joyce, race, and empire" written by one Irish person is likely to differ very significantly from those written by other Irish natives – and these (hypothetical) studies might well differ much more from each other than any single one of them might from my own study. Finally, it would seem that the concern that anyone not "Irish" (whatever one may mean by that term) would necessarily be less qualified (careful research and scholarly rigor notwithstanding) to write or speak about Irishness and Irish topics is, in essence, a position little different, in its unexamined implications, from the insidious argument that only English people should be allowed to teach Shakespeare or that I, being Asian, should have become an engineer (rather than a professor of "English").

Indeed, it seems to me that there is at once a specific advantage to being Irish in a study of Irishness, and an equally important and specific advantage to *not* being Irish. It is the latter which I have precisely tried to benefit from (having little choice in the matter). In other words, this study is one (from the many possible and potentially illuminating studies hypothetically imaginable on this topic) that focuses on the cross-cultural constructions of difference, the nature of cultural and national identities, and the porousness of national/cultural definitions and "borders" (in the broadest sense); this study is argued from a particular, subjective position (my own) of cultural liminality – one different from, but perhaps not unrelated to, some of the experiences of cultural liminality which led Joyce to argue for his own internationalist perspective on the English–Irish question and on international politics. Consequently, this study is an attempt to look at the issues of "race" and "empire" (within the specific Irish contexts for those terms) in Joyce's texts – from a position not only interdisciplinary, but cross-cultural and international.

For these purposes, my own cultural background may indeed serve as a specific advantage, in part by affording a perspective free of the particular "nightmare of history" inherited necessarily by Irish natives. My happily mongrel background has both afforded and necessitated cross-cultural breadth and outlook. As a longstanding Joyce scholar and a native Asian, my engagement with this topic thus stems from both my literary interest in Joyce's works and my intense personal interest in issues of racial and national identities. Indeed, the two of them (my professional and personal interests) merge when it comes to this topic, and I would admit to an extreme *interestedness* (as opposed to "disinterestedness" or detachment) on issues of cultural identity: for my background is that of an internationalist childhood, spent – like that of Joyce, Nora, Giorgio, and Lucia – peripatetically wandering from country to country; and I too was brought up by Roman Catholic priests and nuns (in my case, Polish missionaries in Mexico and Brazil), steeped in the cosmology of traditional Catholicism. As a native Chinese speaker born in

Taiwan to two Chinese diplomats from the provinces of Canton and Hupei, I grew up living in many different countries and racially varied cultures (in Asia, Latin America, North America, Africa), especially Mexico, Brazil, the US, Canada, and Swaziland. Thus, the pursuit of a stable identity – whether national, racial, cultural, personal or otherwise – was for me a very complicated, perhaps doomed, proposition from early on.

For me, being "Chinese" was not only a birthright (we spoke Mandarin at home, celebrated Chinese cultural traditions, ate Chinese food) but also a highly problematic notion: it was a racial distinction of absolute difference/otherness by which some chose to mark me and thus render me invisible within their particular social hierarchies and constellations; it repeatedly marked me as a "foreigner" even though I was able to adapt myself to each specific culture and language enough to pass as a native speaker, and even though I at times felt myself to be as "Mexican" or "American" (or whatever) as I felt "Chinese"; it rendered me nonetheless indelibly "Chinese" in the eyes of many, in spite of the fact that I had left Taiwan at the age of four and had lived as long or longer in each "foreign" country than I had in "China." Indeed, the notion of an essential "Chinese" identity had already, early in my life, been deconstructed for me by the very fact that, since early childhood, our family dinner table conversations were obsessively charged with political discussions concerning the "real China," within a binary Taipei/Peking dialectic that was mutually exclusive and antagonistic: wasn't the Nationalist government in Taipei the "real" Chinese government?; could the Communist regime in Peking really speak for China?; surely *both* of them could not be simultaneously called "China"; but surely the native Taiwanese islanders and aborigines had no claim at all to being "really" Chinese; and so on.

I have grown to realize that all of these elements – my multinational background, my consequent fluency and interest in different languages and literatures, my devout Catholic upbringing – have made my "interest" (in every sense) in and affinity for Joyce seem not only quite natural, but perhaps even overdetermined. Similarly, my own professional history has been logically comparatist and multi-literary in nature. Professionally trained in "English" studies within the literary academy of the United States, my previous books have included an investigation of the complex relationship between the exiled Irish Joyce (whose writings defied and scandalized centralized, canonical authorities) and that most canonical writer of all, Shakespeare, the national poet of the English empire Joyce so resented; and a study (and English verse translation) of France's most beloved national drama, Corneille's *Le Cid* (a tale of great significance to both French and Spanish national histories), exploring the play's Spanish and French sources and its interpretations, especially in light of the Anglo-Saxon poetic tradition.[4]

Thus, my interests – both as professional *métier* and as personal history – in the issues of racial, ethnic, cultural, literary, and national identity/difference/marginality, all merge in the texts of James Joyce, a writer with an insistently internationalist perspective. As a multiculturally trained literary scholar teaching in the Anglo-American academy, I am writing from the interdisciplinary space afforded by minority discourse, cultural studies, and postcolonial theory – and from the exciting vantage point these areas have opened up for our expanding understandings of the dynamics of race, culture, colonialism, and power.

2

Catching the conscience of a race

This chapter is a study of the meanings and place of "race" as a concept in England and Ireland during the Victorian era and early twentieth century – especially in terms of an English–Irish discourse about "race" that, as we shall see, was inseparable from the "Irish Question" and issues of Empire and Home Rule. Thus, this chapter means to foreground and illuminate the contexts behind Joyce's usage and conception of the word "race"; the implications of the racial discourses of Joyce's time and place; and Joyce's response to and reappropriation of such implications.

I have little space here to go beyond the particular focuses of the present study, but the larger topic of nineteenth-century scientific racism, as well as its specific applications to the Irish "race," constitute, as I have discovered, a fascinating area of investigation. Readers may wish to refer to several studies that I have found especially helpful and illuminating, and to which this chapter is greatly indebted: Michael Banton's *Racial Theories* (1987), L. P. Curtis's *Anglo-Saxons and Celts: A Study of Anti-Irish Prejudice in Victorian England* (1968) and *Apes and Angels: The Irishman in Victorian Caricature* (1971), Patrick O'Farrell's *England and Ireland Since 1800* (1975), and Luke Gibbons's essay "Race Against Time: Racial Discourse and Irish History" (1991).

"Race" in popular usage

When, at the age of sixteen, Joyce wrote an essay on "Force" at University College, Dublin, he referred to certain dying animal species: "and then their race dies out as the bison of America is dying"; two paragraphs later he discussed the "subjugation ... of race over race. Among human families the white man is the predestined conqueror. The negro has given way before him, and the red men have been driven by him out of their lands and homes" (*CW* 20–21). Not only is it clear that at sixteen Joyce was very much a product of the racist discourse of nineteenth-century white, European cultures, but that Joyce was also typical of those cultures in the imprecision and malleability of his usage of the term "race," equally applicable in his essay to distinctions of species and of human skin color (the latter being our own more dominant, contemporary application of the term).

Michael Banton, in his comprehensive study *Racial Theories*, has detailed the complex, varied, and inconsistent theories and conceptions of race in Western history and science – in which "race" could variously be confused with issues of sociology, biology, ethnicity, nationality, genetics, lineage, physical typology, animal species, social class, status, and so on – often backed by the scientific or pseudo-scientific *imprimatur* of the most educated circles of the time. Even as they were proclaiming white, Aryan racial superiority based on notions of racial determinism (linking physiology, anatomy, and skull size with issues such as intelligence, national character, and race), Western race theorists could differ widely as to what the word exactly meant. Arthur de Gobineau, for example, could argue in 1853 that "all civilizations derive from the white race, that none can exist without its help" – while a year later Josiah Clark Nott could write that "The higher castes of what are termed Caucasian races [in the plural] ... have been assigned, in all ages, the largest brains and the most powerful intellect; *theirs* is the mission of extending and perfecting civilization" (Banton, 48, 43).

Furthermore, when it came to discussing the Irish or Celtic "race," the English conception of race usually became synonymous with religion (since in Victorian England the words Irish and Catholic were virtually inseparable as pejoratives) and with social class; as L. P. Curtis writes in *Anglo-Saxons and Celts*:

the lowly social and occupational status of the mass of Irish immigrants in Britain served to enhance their reputation of inferiority among respectable Englishmen ... The intimate relationship between class and race consciousness is borne out by the fact that the word race was also used throughout the century as a synonym for class. The "double dose of original sin" with which some Englishmen discredited the Irish referred as much to their inferior social position as to their racial and cultural inferiority.

(24)

16

In short, given the confusions between issues of biology, sociology, lineage, class, and so on, "race" as a term has been virtually a Rorschach test, a hopelessly unspecific term that serves as a blank screen or cypher upon which to encode a culture's or an individual's own unacknowledged preoccupations. As Curtis points out, "the word race always seems to cry out for definition, if only because those who use it so rarely bother to explain their meaning" (*Anglo-Saxons*, 2); as Banton concludes: "Were it not that so many members of the general public still thought in terms of race, it would by this time have been possible to dispense with the word" (96). Thus, in order to understand the "racial" issues of a particular past moment, it is crucial to locate as one's historical context the particular conjunction of meanings and discursive formations that shape the prevalent discourse of "race" at that particular time and place, in its scientific as well as popular usages. As Banton writes: "'Race' cannot be translated so easily because in English and some other tongues it is a folk concept, a word in popular use with a significance deriving from popular understanding and varying from one historical period to another" (xiii).

In the nineteenth century, as Banton demonstrates, the imprecision in the use of the word "was assisted by the upsurge in European nationalism and the readiness to see that sentiment as an expression of race, so that race was often equated with nation as well as type" (xiv). This was indeed how Joyce and his contemporaries largely understood the word and how Joyce used it in his writing – as a term that was interchangeable with the concepts of both nation and ethnicity. Yeats, for example, claimed in "The Fisherman" that he aimed (much like Stephen Dedalus) "To write for my own race." Joyce himself used the word "race" eleven times in *A Portrait of the Artist as a Young Man* – each time referring specifically to the Irish people as a race: "We are an unfortunate priestridden race" (37), "A priestridden Godforsaken race!" (37), "a priestridden race" (38), "a type of her race and his own" (183), "the soul of your race" (193), "This race and this country" (203), "the secret of her race" (221), "a race less ignoble than their own" (238), "the thoughts and desires of the race to which he belonged" (238), "A race of clodhoppers!" (249), and of course the famous formulation "the uncreated conscience of my race" (253). The book's one instance of the word in the plural refers similarly to the "entrenched and marshalled races" of Europe (167). This is a usage that has continued well into our century: in 1944, Seumas MacManus wrote *The Story of the Irish Race: A Popular*

History of Ireland, an influential and successful book reprinted five times between 1944 and 1966.

Joyce used the term similarly in his non-fiction. For example, in "The Day of the Rabblement" (1901) he had referred to the Irish as "the most belated race in Europe" (*CW* 70); and in his essays on the Irish poet James Clarence Mangan he had said that "Mangan is the type of his race," with "all the energy of his race" and "the great traditions of the race" (*CW* 81, 183, 186). Similarly, Joyce described Oscar Wilde as having "distinctive qualities, the qualities, perhaps, of his race" (*CW* 204). And, in "Ireland, Island of Saints and Sages," Joyce wrote about the "new Celtic race" which arose from the various ethnic mixes in Irish history to join together in "the cause of the new Irish nation against the British tyranny" (*CW* 161); near the end of the essay Joyce wonders "what might be the effects on our civilization of a revival of this race" from its downtrodden subservience, in a utopian vision of "the appearance of a rival island near England, a bilingual, republican, self-centred, and enterprising island with its own commercial fleet, and its own consuls in every port of the world" (*CW* 173).

As these last two examples illustrate, the word "race," when applied to the Irish in the nineteenth century, almost always assumed, as its inevitable if sometimes unspoken context, a binary dialectic and opposition between the Irish race and the English race; the Irish as a race were usually conceived and defined in terms of their relationship with the English as a race. Thus, the discourse of race as it pertained to Ireland also inevitably shaded into the discourse of Empire – of colonial issues, and of course of the "Irish Question" and Home Rule. After all, this connection between race and empire as issues was also logically fostered by the nature of nineteenth-century scientific racism (or racial typology, the term Banton prefers). As Edward Said points out, the racial classifications by such as Cuvier, Gobineau, and Knox, along with second-order Darwinism, all "seemed to accentuate the 'scientific' validity of the division of races into advanced and backward, or European–Aryan and Oriental–African. Thus the whole question of imperialism, as it was debated in the late nineteenth century by pro-imperialists and anti-imperialists alike, carried forward the binary typology of advanced and backward (or subject) races, cultures, and societies" (*Orientalism*, 206). The relationship between racial and imperial attitudes was a self-sustaining cycle, for "Popular beliefs in white superiority were probably conditioned by the success of Britain and other European countries in extending their influence over so much of the world" (Banton, *Racial Theories*, 77).

The European belief in white racial superiority reached its peak in the two decades preceding the First World War (Banton, 76) – that is, at about the time Joyce began to write. In 1895 (when Joyce was thirteen), Joseph Chamberlain, as the British Secretary of State for the Colonies, could proclaim his belief that "the British race is the greatest governing race that the world has ever seen"; as Banton points out, whereas the notion of a British "race" was highly questionable (Britain being composed of numerous "races"), Chamberlain and others "talked of race in the context of empire" and "regarded race as a synonym for nation" (Banton, 76). Race and empire were inseparably associated in the Victorian mind; as Curtis writes:

The period of most intense Anglo-Saxonism in England, which runs from the 1860's to the early 1890's, represented the apogee of British power and influence in the world ... the conviction that the *Pax Britannica* really did serve the best interests of the rest of the world [...] tended to reinforce ethnocentric assumptions about the genius of the Anglo-Saxon people for ordering their lives and those of other people ... all other races, in particular the Celts, required highly centralized or authoritarian institutions in order to prevent violent political and social upheaval.

(*Anglo-Saxons*, 31–32).

This was the context of "race" at the time Joyce began writing, near the turn of the century, as the English feelings of Anglo-Saxon racial superiority (especially over the Irish) and of pride in the British Empire were both at their highest point and, unhappily, coincided – in a mutually-reinforcing discourse of race and empire.

"White negroes"

Joyce opens his essay on "Ireland, Island of Saints and Sages" thus (*CW* 154):

Nations have their ego, just like individuals. The case of a people who like to attribute to themselves qualities and glories foreign to other people has not been entirely unknown in history, from the time of our ancestors, who called themselves Aryans and nobles, or that of the Greeks, who called all those who lived outside the sacrosanct land of Hellas barbarians.

Even as early as 1907, when this essay was written, Joyce was aware that nations participate in the activities of the Ego/Self, and in the consequent dynamics of Self and Other – in which the Self attributes to itself qualities "foreign to other people" who are thus labeled "barbarians." At the national and ethnic levels, these are discursive processes that participate in the dynamics of "othering" which create and consolidate an imagined national "character," a sovereign Self – most usually by defining "others" in terms of clearly defined essences and comfortable, essentialized stereotypes (of "barbarians"). For example, in 1836 Benjamin Disraeli railed about the Irish, who, he claimed,

hate our free and fertile isle. They hate our order, our civilization, our enterprising industry, our sustained courage, our decorous liberty, our pure religion. This wild, reckless, indolent, uncertain, and superstitious race have no sympathy with the English character. Their fair ideal of human felicity is an alternation of clannish broils and coarse idolatry. Their history describes an unbroken circle of bigotry and blood.

(cited in Curtis, *Anglo-Saxons*, 51)

Disraeli's description is classic in what it reveals – which is that "they" are everything that "we" are not (or at least prefer to think that we are not): subservient, disorderly, uncivilized, unenterprising, cowardly, indecorous, and so on. In fact, then, as Joyce's comments on the national "ego" also suggest, the nature of what one formulates as "other" and "barbarian" tells us much more about the Self than about the Other. As Curtis puts it, what the English "called 'Irish national character' ... presented a striking contrast and antithesis to the picture they had formed of their own national character" (*Anglo-Saxons*, 5):

Stated simply, this consensus amounted to an assumption or a conviction that the "native Irish" were alien in race and inferior in culture to the Anglo-Saxons ... The preference of many Englishmen for a racial explanation of Irish behavior tells us much more about the people who accepted stereotypes of Irish or Celtic behavior than it does about the actual condition of Irish society.

It was the prevalent Victorian Anglo-Saxonist belief that the Anglo-Saxon "race" was distinguished above all others, especially in its love for liberty and its ability to govern well and efficiently, thus explaining the rise of their empire; "Conversely, [they] tried to explain the failure of other nations and people to match that achievement by the absence of those same racial traits or features" (*Anglo-Saxons*, 8). In particular the "Irishman" – an expression that Conor Cruise O'Brien has referred to as the "pejorative singular" – was endowed by Anglo-Saxonists with those traits most feared or despised in respectable English society.[1] This process of course was basically similar to the way the English formed their images of Africans and Orientals, too, mixing "small fragments of reality with large amounts of what they wanted to believe about the indigenous people in order to arrive at a foregone conclusion based on their particular needs at the time" (*Anglo-Saxons*, 34) – homogenizing all "others" and their specific differences within a universalized, all-encompassing essentialism of the "Other" as primitive, barbaric, and uncivilized/uncivilizable.

The image of the Irishman as a barbarian was a consolidated tradition (the "wild Irish") in England and Scotland by the nineteenth century. In 1797 the Scottish historian John Pinkerton had written that the Irish Celts were "savages, have been savages since the world began, and will be forever savages; mere radical savages, not yet advanced even to a state of barbarism" (see Curtis, *Apes*, 95). As Curtis notes, "Adjectives like 'savage' and 'wild' recur" in descriptions of the Irish; "In an age when the manners and mores of primitive tribes were being studied with greater care, the Irish had to endure comparisons with aboriginal peoples in Africa, the antipodes, and the Orient" (*Anglo-Saxons*, 58) – peoples such as the Chinese, Hottentots, Maoris, Aborigines, Sudanese, and other supposedly "barbarian" peoples (*Apes*, 2). Charles Darwin himself, in his chapter on the extinction of races in *The Descent of Man* (544–45), had compared New Zealand's Maoris with Irish peasants. One particular tradition since the discovery of the New World was to compare the Irish to Native American Indians in terms of their relative primitiveness and savagery – a habit recently traced and analysed by Luke Gibbons in his essay on "Race Against Time: Racial Discourse and Irish History"; for example, in 1839 Gustave de Beaumont, having been to the New World, visited Ireland and found that the Irish peasants lived in even greater poverty and squalor than the noble savages of America (Gibbons, "Race Against Time," 98).

In "Ireland, Island of Saints and Sages" Joyce expresses his awareness of such stereotyping mechanisms, in which "The English now disparage the Irish because they are Catholic, poor, and ignorant" whereas in fact "Ireland is poor because English laws ruined the country's industries"; and in which Ireland has been made into "the everlasting caricature of the serious world." But, as Joyce goes on to point out about such English stereotypes, "That the Irish are really the unabalanced, helpless idiots about whom we read in the lead articles of the *Standard* and the *Morning Post* is denied by

the names of the three greatest translators in English literature –
FitzGerald, translator of the *Rubaiyat* of the Persian poet Omar
Khayyam, Burton, translator of the Arabian masterpieces, and Cary,
the classic translator of the *Divine Comedy*" (CW 167, 168, 171).
Significantly, Joyce's examples were able to prove themselves by
going *outside* the English/Irish cultural borders into broader, international cultural perspectives, through acts of cultural "translation."

In any event, such derogatory images of "other" cultures conjoin
in what Said calls an "essentialist universalism" (Young, *White
Mythologies*, 11) in which the Other is constructed to seem unchanging, unalterable, and universal along essentialized stereotypes
– as exemplified by the racial theorist Robert Knox's claim in his
study of *The Races of Men* (1850) about the despicable Irish
"character": "that character which I now know to be common to all
the Celtic race, wherever found ... under every circumstance ... is
precisely the same, unaltered and unalterable" (213). This serves to
consolidate a comfortable Us/Them binary and distinction that
operates along similar lines, as Curtis points out, to Freud's concept
of projection (*Anglo-Saxons*, 64):

The psychological importance of Paddy [as the stereotyped Irishman]
can best be explained in terms of the defense mechanism known as
projection. The almost mechanical way in which Anglo-Saxonists
assigned to Irishmen those very traits which were most deplored or
despised among the respectable middle and upper classes in Victorian
England leaves little room for doubt that the gentlemen who relied upon
this stereotype were merely projecting onto an assumedly inferior group
all those emotions which lay buried within themselves and which the
English social system encouraged – and at times compelled – them to
repress.[2]

This projection, Curtis notes elsewhere, is a "refracted image" which
"worked to enhance the self-esteem of the beholder at the expense of
those being stereotyped" (*Apes*, 14) – so much like Virginia Woolf's
depiction (in *A Room of One's Own*) of the female as a mirror which
allows the male to see himself as twice his actual size.

What are the effects and implications of such essentializing of a
universal primitivism? To begin with, these racial stereotypes create
comfortably, securely, clearly defined boundaries between the Self
and the Other, within the dynamics of what Derrida has taught us to
recognize as Western logocentrism. This construction of a universal
primitivism creates a clearly demarcated Us/Them binary and
difference which functions to reify the dominant Western culture's

sense of itself as civilized and rational by contrast – while repressing or occluding the knowledge that the qualities of primitive otherness are already contained (but repressed) within the self; in this way, Anglo-Saxonists could proclaim with Chamberlain, in all good conscience (or at least in all good "conscious"), that "the British race is the greatest governing race the world has ever seen."

The effects and implications of such static identity and essential-izing are important: (1) obviously, they maintain the savage versus civilized (Self versus Other) distinction intact, allowing for the continuation of a comfortable Us/Them binarity that serves to consolidate the imperial European subject as a sovereign self. (2) "Primitive" peoples are thus functioned within what ethnohistorian William Simmons calls "anthropological fictions": "the purist notions that native cultures resist history, or that they disappear in its presence" ("Culture Theory," 7). Statically and universally repre-sented by dominant cultures based on modes of synchronic analysis as essentially primitive, such native cultures appear beyond history, beyond temporality and diachronic development, doomed to vanish in the presence of history and civilization. Their only chance at survival, such logic would maintain, is to be ruled by those who have history and civilization on their side. (3) With a synchronic identity of universal static primitivism, the "native" culture gets functioned as a dying culture – not a living culture whose members may learn to control their own destinies, affecting and influencing not only their own futures but also the cultural systems of the dominant culture. Rather, the primitive other can only be represented (whatever its historical and continuing, specific actualities may be) as external to the self, and different – and not as either an integral part of the self or as having any influence or relationship with the self. All of these implications collude to construct the European sovereignty of self in what James Clifford calls "Master narratives of cultural disappearance" ("Four," 214).

It would then seem to logically follow that the primitive society cannot effectively rule itself, and must be governed properly to insure its own survival. Thus, the stereotyping of the Irish as a primitive, backwards "race" has a very direct effect on the political arena of Home Rule: the Irish Celt is deemed unfit for self-government (they cannot rule themselves; they must be ruled). As Curtis documents: "What both the [Home Rule] debates of 1886 and 1893–94 proved was that a majority of Englishmen, and especially those with education, property, and position in society, refused to change their minds about the ingredients of Irish national character. What really killed Home Rule in 1886 was the Anglo-Saxon stereotype of the Irish Celt" (*Anglo-Saxons*, 103).

As our own contemporary studies of race have repeatedly found, the stereotyping of the Other often functions, simultaneously and in parallel, on both racialized and gendered axes. Curtis notes that "There was another curiously persistent and revealing label, namely [Irish] characterization as a feminine race of people, while Anglo-Saxons were virile"; the parallel implications suggest an unconscious collusion between patriarchy and empire:

The relevance lies in the assumed connection between femininity and unfitness for self government. The habit of assigning sexual genders to various races and nations ... in a period when demands for female suffrage were being resisted by the overwhelming majority of Parliament, when the very idea of female emancipation aroused deep fears among the male members of the population, the assignment of feminine traits of mind to a people like the Irish certainly did not enhance their claim for political emancipation inherent in Home Rule ... the self-consciously mature and virile Anglo-Saxon had no intention of conferring his sophisticated institutions upon the childlike and feminine Irish Celt, as also on women and children.

(*Anglo-Saxons*, 61–62).

All of this would seem to suggest that the popular English conception of the Irish as a backwards Celtic race had attained the broad cultural force behind it consistent with the Gramscian notion of hegemony or the Foucaultian notion of "discourse" and discursive formations, along the lines of Said's concept of Orientalism: "such [Orientalist] texts can *create* not only knowledge but also the very reality they appear to describe. In time such knowledge and reality produce a tradition, or what Michel Foucault calls a discourse, whose material presence or weight, not the originality of a given author, is really responsible for the texts produced out of it. This kind of text is composed out of those pre-existing units of information ... in the catalogue of *idées reçues*" (*Orientalism*, 94).

So also the tradition of scientific racism – Thierry, Edwards, Renan, Gobineau, Michelet, and other scholars, scientists, historians, and explorers (some of whom Joyce had read[3]) – created a tradition of fascination with primitive peoples and savage societies in which, whether the treatise was one of pure fantasy or of conscientious study, repeatedly "White races were, needless to say, far superior to the others, especially in intelligence and the instinct of order" (Curtis, *Anglo-Saxons*, 38). The Victorian conception of the Celtic race formed just such a discourse: "Most educated Victorians determined their image of Ireland and the Irish either from limited contact with the Irish in Britain or from fiction, memoirs, history books, government reports, 'expert' accounts written by political economists and social reformers, and pure hearsay" (*Anglo-Saxons*, 34). The weight and power of this discourse of Irishness (one might call it Hibernianism) were such that when John Ruskin in 1861 visited Ireland for the very first time, he could at once label Dublin "far the melancholiest place" he had ever seen, and immediately add:

What I have seen of the Irish themselves in just the two hours after landing ... will, I suppose, remain as the permanent impression. I had no conception the stories of Ireland were so true. I had fancied all were violent exaggeration. But it is impossible to exaggerate.

(vol. 36:383; see *Anglo-Saxons*, 50)

Such is the force of a "discourse" that it can, as Said puts it, create its own reality.

Literature, too, both reflected and contributed to this discourse. In Elizabethan times, for example, Spenser had pronounced the "wild Irish" to be barbarous; later Milton wrote that they were "indocile and averse from all civility and amendment" (see O'Brien, *Concise History*, 55, 69). In the nineteenth century one could cite any number of respected English authors, from Ruskin to Kipling to Mrs. Gaskell. Carlyle characterized the Irish with "wild Milesian features, looking false ingenuity, restlessness, unreason, misery and mockery" (*Works*, 29:134–44; see Curtis, *Anglo-Saxons*, 132); Tennyson devoted a stanza of *In Memoriam* to "the blind hysterics of the Celt" (see *Anglo-Saxons*, 54). Even the philosopher David Hume had been earlier led to essentialize:

As the rudeness and ignorance of the Irish were extreme ... The ancient supersititions, the practices and observances of their fathers, mingled and polluted with many wild opinions, still maintained an unshaken empire over them, and the example alone of the English was sufficient to render the reformation odious to the prejudices of the discontented Irish ... The subduing and civilizing of that country seemed to become every day more difficult and impracticable.

(Hume, *History*, 397–98; see Gibbons, "Race Against Time," 101)

While Hume wrote this in 1796, such a discursive practice has not died out even in our own century; in fact, Joyce himself has been its victim – for, as Luke Gibbons has pointed out, it was the Unionist Provost of Trinity College, J. P. Mahaffy, who had assserted that "James Joyce is a living argument in favour of my contention that it

was a mistake to establish a separate university for the aborigines of
this island – for the corner boys who spit in the Liffey" (Gibbons,
113).

And in *Lady Chatterley's Lover* D. H. Lawrence could write:

He was a young Irishman … he had the silent enduring beauty of a
carved negro mask, with its rather full eyes, and the strong queerly-
arched brows, the immobile, compressed mouth: that momentary but
revealed immobility, an immobility, a timelessness which the Buddha
aims at, and which negroes express sometimes without ever aiming at it;
something old, old, and acquiescent in the race! Aeons of acquiescence in
race destiny, instead of our individual resistance. And thus a swimming
through, like rats in a dark river.

(quoted in Gibbons, "Race Against Time," 95)

Lawrence's contribution to the discourse of Irishness as a backward
race functions the Irish as being *like* the "negro"; but, in the
nineteenth century, the racializing of Irishness – within those
comfortably demarcated boundaries and fixed essences of a universal
primitivism – meant that the Irish/Celtic race was repeatedly related
to the black race not merely in terms of tropes, but insistently as *fact*,
as literal and biological relatives, both Celtic and "Negro" races
being positioned lower on the hierarchical ladder of racial superiority; finally, during the height of Celtophobia (late in the nineteenth
century), the Irish would eventually be assigned a non-human
position and relegated to a species of ape.

In 1880, two years before Joyce's birth, the Belgian political
economist and essayist Gustave de Molinari reported that English
newspapers "allow no occasion to escape them of treating the Irish
as an inferior race – as a kind of white negroes [sic] – and a glance at
Punch is sufficient to show the difference they establish between the
plump and robust personification of John Bull and the wretched
figure of lean and bony Pat" (quoted in Curtis, *Apes*, 1). This
observation about the Irish as "white negroes" suggests the prevalent
English attitude and discursive formation concerning the Irish; it is in
this historical context and discursive background that Joyce's
references to blacks and to other races operate, in which the Irish are
functioned as being "Europe's blacks" (as they were also recently
described in the popular film *The Commitments*[4]).

Of course, given the universalizing essentialism of the "primitive"
Other by a white European Self engaged in a world-wide project of
empire building, the Irish were naturally compared to and analogized with other races. In his racist and imperialist study of *Greater*

Britain (1868), Charles Dilke – in discussing what he called the "cheaper" races – had described the Chinese as the Irish of the Orient (*Anglo-Saxons*, 46). Respected figures like Bishop Stubbs could write that "If the Jews are on their way back to Palestine, could not the Irish be prevailed on *antiquam exquierer matrem* and emigrate in search of Scota, Pharoah's daughter?" (quoted in *Anglo-Saxons*, 82); historiographer John Richard Green affirmed what he called the "Ishmaelitish character" of the Celtic race. There had already been, as we have seen, a habit for three centuries of comparing the "wild Irish" to the savage natives of the New World.[5] Indeed, as Curtis notes, "educated Victorians" were in the habit of constructing "mutually derogatory comparisons between Irishmen and the Chinese, Hottentots, Maoris, Aborigines, Sudanese, and other 'barbarians'" (*Apes*, 2). In *Ulysses* and *Finnegans Wake*, Joyce would turn these derogatory comparisons on their head, by making Jewishness, Orientalness, and otherness redeeming concepts and comparisons. Joyce, as we shall see in later chapters of this study, rejects and reverses all these derogatory analogies to other races by using them in a positive, vital, and enabling manner; analogizing and equating the Irish with other races and colonized peoples by accenting the flattering aspects of such comparisons and by suggesting a solidarity of the marginalized and othered.

But the racial comparison most frequently and insistently made about the Irish during the latter half of the nineteenth century was with "negroes," especially with Bushmen and Hottentots, generally perceived as the lowest rungs on the scale of human races, just barely above the apes (see attached morphological tree). In a scientific discourse about race propelled by respected scientists and theorists such as Cuvier, Gobineau, and Nott, notions of Aryan superiority seemed incontestable, and were supported by "scientific" evidence arising from cranial measurements and other such questionable practices. In stereotyping the Irish, the English resorted to arguing that the Celtic race was closer to Bushmen and Hottentots on the human tree or ladder. For example, while European whites argued that Negro slaves "must be treated like neglected and badly brought up children" (Banton, *Racial Theories*, 60), so also English people such as Edith Balfour, upon visiting Ireland, would write about the natives that "They are like children still listening to old fairy stories ... They are like children who are afraid to walk alone, who play with fire, who are helpless; like children who will not grow up" (Curtis, *Anglo-Saxons*, 53). As with the feminizing of the Irish race,

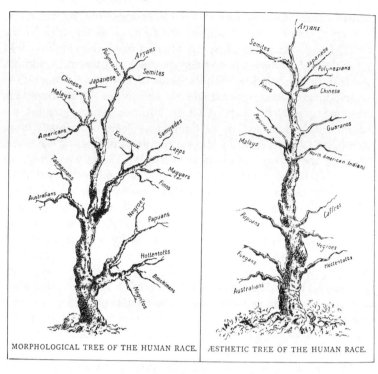

MORPHOLOGICAL TREE OF THE HUMAN RACE. | ÆSTHETIC TREE OF THE HUMAN RACE.

1. *Mantegazza's Racial Trees.* Paolo Mantegazza's ideas about a hierarchical taxonomy of different "races" was presented through the visual analogy of trees (he had "morphological," "aesthetic," and "intellectual" trees), with the supposedly more advanced races occupying the higher branches. (From Paolo Mantegazza, *Physiognomy and Expression*, London: 1904, plates 2 and 4, pp. 312, 314.)

the infantilizing of the Irish had an ulterior political motive that was hardly innocent (however unacknowledged): "Irishmen thus shared with virtually all the non-white peoples of the empire the label of childish, and the remedy for unruly children in most Victorian households was a proper 'licking'" (*Anglo-Saxons*, 54). The stereotyping of "Paddy" made it easy and even conscionable to reject Home Rule for the Irish; while Paddy supposedly was, as Curtis enumerates, "childish, emotionally unstable, ignorant, indolent, superstitious, primitive or semi-civilized, dirty, vengeful, and violent," the English believed that the Anglo-Saxon race "possessed traits exactly opposite to those that made the Irish

28

Celt so unfit for the management of his own affairs" (*Anglo-Saxons*, 53).

The case of Robert Knox, MD, serves as a particularly illuminating case study of the racializing of Irishness; in 1850 Knox published his study of *The Races of Men*, a comprehensive evaluation and classification of all known human races. Knox was an English anatomist and a popular lecturer about race who believed, like most Europeans of the time, that race was the greatest determinant of behavior and character, in his words that "Race is everything: literature, science, art, in a word, civilization, depend on it" (7); like other scientists of the time, he engaged in pseudo-scientific speculations about cranial measurements and the superiority of white races over darker races. But he seemed to have particular phobias about the Jewish and the Irish "races." His anti-Semitism, like his Celtophobia, repeatedly and illogically mistakes physical circumstances and history for inherent essences: "two hundred years at least before Christ [the Jews] were perambulating Italy and Europe precisely as they do now, following the same occupations – that is, no occupation at all"; "Wanderers, then, by nature – unwarlike – they never could acquire a fixed home or abode. Literature, science, and art they possess not. It is against their nature – they never seem to have had a country, nor have they any yet"; conveniently, Knox concludes that "they are becoming extinct" (131, 138, 140). The power of his essentialized image of an unalterable "Jewishness" is such that it can produce such astonishing reasoning as this: "in the long list of names of distinguished persons whom Mr. Disraeli has described as of Jewish descent, I have not met with a single Jewish trait in their countenance, in so far as I can discover; *and, therefore, they are not Jews*, nor of Jewish origin" (140; Knox's emphasis).

But it is "the barbarous Celt" who most discomfits Knox:

the Celtic race does not, and never could be made to comprehend the meaning of the word liberty ... I appeal to the Saxon men of all countries whether I am right or not in my estimate of the Celtic character. Furious fanaticism; a love of war and disorder; a hatred for order and patient industry; no accumulative habits; restless, treacherous, uncertain: look at Ireland.

(27)

Once again, such logic leads inevitably to a justification for refusing the Irish the right of self-government: "As a Saxon, I abhor all dynasties, monarchies, and bayonet governments, but this latter seems to be the only one suitable for the Celtic man" (27).

In asserting that the Irish are the lowest form of "what is called civilized man" ("Civilized man cannot sink lower than at Derrynane"), Knox makes the same insupportable claim about the Irish that he did about the Jews: "As a race, the Celt has no literature, nor any printed books in his original language ... There never was any Celtic literature, nor science, nor arts" (218). Finally, there is this astounding passage of Celtophobia:

the source of all evil lies in *the race*, the Celtic race of Ireland. There is no getting over *historical facts* ... The race must be forced from the soil; by fair means, if possible; still they must leave. England's safety requires it. I speak not of the justice of the cause; nations must ever act as Machiavelli advised: look to yourself. The Orange club of Ireland is a Saxon confederation for the clearing the land of all papists and jacobites; this means Celts.

(253–54)

This is nothing short of a recipe and justification for racial genocide. Knox's book and ideas are such that we are tempted today to dismiss them as the radical quackeries of a racist madman; unfortunately, the frightening reality is that his book (reprinted in 1866) and his theories were among the most respected and influential of the century, helping shape contemporary understandings of race; as Banton acknowledges: "Previous to his time, little or nothing was heard about Race in the medical schools: he changed all this by his Saturday's lectures, and Race became as familiar as household words to his students, through whom some of his novel ideas became disseminated far and wide" (59).

The widely disseminated power of such an insidious discourse and cultural construction is reflected in the hegemonic dominance these ideas had over even well-meaning and liberal-minded English people. For example, even socialists as progressive and committed to liberal causes as Sidney and Beatrice Webb could write during a visit to Dublin in 1892: "We will tell you about Ireland when we come back. The people are charming but we detest them, as we should the Hottentots – for their very virtues. Home Rule is an absolute necessity *in order to depopulate the country of this detestable race*" (quoted in Curtis, *Anglo-Saxons*, 63). Carlyle had an equally peremptory and racialized answer to the "Irish Question": "Black-lead them and put them over with the niggers" (see Gibbons, "Race Against Time," 96). Perhaps the most famous case of such Negrization was the infamous remark made by Lord Salisbury (who is mentioned in *U* 7.558), the Opposition leader during the Home Rule debates of

1886: "You would not confide free representative institutions to the Hottentots for instance." In the process, Salisbury also disqualified the Oriental nations and the Russians, concluding that only the "Teutonic race" was suited to self-government. However, as Curtis remarks, "his audience and posterity remembered only the Hottentot allusion": "Although he had not actually called Irishmen Hottentots, as most Home Rulers charged, he had drawn a painfully close analogy, and the friends of Irish nationalism rushed to join in the outcry against this racialist slur. In the resultant hue and cry no one seemed to care about the aspersion cast on the Hottentots, or on the Russians and Chinese" (*Anglo-Saxons*, 103).

Another influential race theorist was John Beddoe, president of the Royal Anthropological Institute, Fellow of the Royal Society, Fellow of the Royal College of Physicians, and respected author of *The Races of Britain* (1885). Beddoe believed that hair and eye color were keys to ethnic and racial identity, and he developed a specious formula he called the "index of nigrescence," which supposedly quantified the amount of melanin in skin, eyes, and hair – in the process assuming that one end of the nigrescence scale was clearly preferable to the other. He used this index of nigrescence to "prove" that the Irish were darker and more Negroid than the English. As Curtis relates: "Just how white-skinned were Irishmen? Who were the so-called 'black Irish,' and where did they come from? How close was a prognathous and nigrescent Celt to a Negro? Such questions were implicit and at times explicit in Beddoe's work; and the implicit answer was that not all men in the British Isles were equally white or equal" (*Anglo-Saxons*, 72). Speculating on the African genesis of what he called "Africanoid" Celts, Beddoe's index of nigrescence provided the scientific justification for racial hatred of the Irish as an inferior race. It was but the logical next step in such racist/ethnocentric reasoning to consider the Irish as subhuman apes.

This in fact had already been happening; by the 1860s the popular image of the Irishman in both popular cartoons and in written discourse was an anthropoid ape. L. P. Curtis's *Apes and Angels: The Irishman in Victorian Caricature* (1971) convincingly documents how Victorian cartoons and illustrations transformed "peasant Paddy into an ape-man or simianized Caliban ... by the 1860s and 1870s, when for various reasons it became necessary for a number of Victorians to assign Irishmen to a place closer to the apes than the angels" (2). The English, of course, reserved the designation of angels for themselves, frequently punning on angels, Angles, and Anglo-Saxons. Joyce comments ironically on such contrasts and puns when, in *Exiles*, Richard Rowan asks Robert Hand if he found Richard's son to be a child or an angel, and Robert answers, "Neither an angel nor an Anglo-Saxon" (*E* 81). Earlier, in *Stephen Hero*, Joyce had problematized the possibility of either race being angelic by having Stephen Daedalus respond to a question by Madden thus:

[Madden:] – You want our peasants to *ape* the gross materialism of the Yorkshire peasant?
[Stephen:] – One would imagine the country was inhabited by *cherubim*.

(*SH* 54, my emphases)

The timing of this culturally created image (of Irish apes) was again not accidental, for it was when the Irish turned to political activism and agitation in their demands for Home Rule that *Punch* and other periodicals began to "picture the Irish political outrage-mongering peasant as a cross between a garrotter and a gorilla" (Curtis, *Apes*, 31). Furthermore, the choice of the ape to represent a derogatory bestiality now politically convenient to assign to the Irish was most likely suggested by the coincidence of Fenian agitation with the debate over Darwin's *Origin of Species*, and fueled by the specters Fenianism conjured up for the English, such as mob rule, "Rome rule," republicanism, anarchism, and revolution against the Empire.

Bolstered by such scientific, anthropological reasoning as Beddoe's nigrescent and "Africanoid" Celts and Daniel Mackintosh's data claiming that the heads of Irish people were characterized by absent chins, receding foreheads, large mouths, thick lips, melanous and prognathous features,[6] it was inevitable that Anglo-Saxonist racism would turn the "white Negro" into a simian Celt. As Curtis argues:

The price paid by Irishmen for increasing political activity and agrarian protest was the substitution of epithets like Caliban, Frankenstein, Yahoo and gorilla for Paddy ... By the 1860s no respectable reader of comic weeklies – and most of their readers were respectable – could possibly mistake the simous nose, long upper lip, huge projecting mouth, and jutting lower jaw as well as sloping forehead for any other category of undesirable or dangerous human being that that known as Irish.

(*Apes* 22, 29)

The simianization of the Irish was part of the larger racialized discourse behind the "Irish Question," and was not just limited to the visual media of cartoon and caricature. An 1860 visit to Sligo provoked a troubled Charles Kingsley to write:

I am haunted by the human chimpanzees I saw along that hundred miles of horrible country. I don't believe they are our fault. I believe ... that they are happier, better, more comfortably fed and lodged under our rule than they ever were. But to see white chimpanzees is dreadful; if they were black, one would not feel it so much, but their skins, except where tanned by exposure, are as white as ours.

(see Gibbons, "Race Against Time," 95 and Curtis, *Anglo-Saxons*, 84)

Historian James Anthony Froude had already, in 1845, described the people in Catholic Ireland as "more like tribes of squalid apes than human beings" (Curtis, *Anglo-Saxons*, 85); Anglo-Irish novelist Edith Somerville could now replicate the hegemonic demotion of Irish Catholics to apes in her fiction, referring to "The Wild Irish – as who, in later days, should say The Gorillas" (Curtis, *Apes*, ix). And *Punch* could depict characters such as "Mr. MacSimius," a hirsute Irishman, saying: "Well, Oi don't profess to be a particularly cultivated man meself; but at laste me progenitors were all educated in the hoigher branches!" (*Apes*, 57).

But the most prevalent manifestations of the equation of the Irish Celt with an ape appeared in the popular cartoons of the day, in English periodicals such as *Punch* and *Judy*, in which any character with a prognathous jaw and simian features was readily recognized as representing an Irishman without any need for further identification. Joyce reveals his pained awareness of such derogatory stereotyping in *Stephen Hero*, when Madden (Davin in *Portrait*) speaks of those "old stale libels – the drunken Irishman, the baboon-faced Irishman that we see in *Punch*" (*SH* 64). To illustrate Madden's point, I have included a small but striking selection of such cartoons here (selected from L. P. Curtis's *Anglo-Saxons*, 60; and from his *Apes*, 41, 42, 43, 59, 60, 66, 67, 63). They depict Anarchy as an Irish agitator with repellent features evoking simianness (figures 2 and 3); an "Irish Frankenstein" described by *Punch* as a bestial *"Caliban* in revolt" (figure 4); St. Patrick's Day as a stereotyped "shindy" or "donnybrook" involving Irish-Americans in the form of gorillas bashing each others' heads (figure 5); a cartoon in *Harper's Weekly* balancing (as equal in weight) black slaves in the South with simian Irish-Americans (figure 6); a degenerate "Simian Irish Celt" doing a jig while John Bull and Uncle Sam look on disapprovingly (figure 7). The last example (figure 8) is perhaps the most striking: Paddy and Bridget, as the essentialized Irish pair, are portrayed as living in their native habitat, a shanty; the rather Wakean title of "The King of A-Shantee" connects the Irish Celt with the African Ashanti, and Paddy's clearly ape-like features imply that he may be the "missing

PUNCH, OR THE LONDON CHARIVARI.—October 29, 1881.

TWO FORCES.

2. *"Two Forces": Britannia vs. Anarchy.* John Tenniel's illustration in *Punch* underscored the manichean, colonialist images of good and evil: a frightened, vulnerable, and feminized Hibernia has to be protected from the savage, stone-wielding Irish male, representing Anarchy; her protector is none other than a majestic Britannia, wielding the sword of The Law and standing upon the lawless banner of the Irish Land League. (*Punch*, October 29, 1881.)

3. *Anarchy: detail from "Two Forces."* The close-up underscores how Paddy, as the stereotyped Irishman, had been fully simianized as a repellent Irish agitator with ape-like nose, lips, jaws, and teeth. (*Punch*, October 29, 1881.)

THE IRISH FRANKENSTEIN.

"The baneful and blood-stained Monster * * * yet was it not my Master to the very extent that it was my Creature ? * * * Had I not breathed into it my own spirit ?" * * * (*Extract from the Works of* C. S. P-RN-LL, M.P.

4.   *"The Irish Frankenstein."* Tenniel's stereotype of the Irish assassin appeared in *Punch* just two weeks after the Phoenix Park Murders, in which two English emissaries were assassinated in Phoenix Park. The prognathous jaw and simous nose of this monster/assassin – carrying pistol and bloodied dagger, standing over its maker in the form of a respectable and law-abiding English gentleman – were features which the English considered distinctly Irish. *Punch* described this Frankenstein as a Celtic Caliban: "Hideous, blood-stained, bestial, ruthless in its rage, implacable in its revengefulness, cynical in its contemptuous challenge of my authority, it seemed another and a fouler *Caliban* in revolt, and successful revolt, against the framer and fosterer of its maleficent existence." (*Punch*, May 20, 1882, pp. 234–35.)

36

5. *"The Day We Celebrate: St. Patrick's Day, 1867."* St.
Patrick's Day is depicted by Thomas Nast in *Harper's
Weekly* as a stereotyped "shindy" or "donnybrook"
involving Irish-Americans in the form of gorillas beating
up policemen and law-abiding citizens. (*Harper's Weekly*,
April 6, 1867.)

link" in the evolution between the lower species of apes and
Africans.

This "missing link" between "anthropoid apes" (a term Stephen
Dedalus uses in *U* 15.2590) and the Irish was spelled out in 1862 by
Punch, in a narrative fantasy titled "The Missing Link":

A gulf, certainly, does appear to yawn between the Gorilla and the
Negro. The woods and wilds of Africa do not exhibit an example of any
intermediate animal. But in this, as in many other cases, philosophers go
vainly searching abroad for that which they would readily find if they
sought for it at home. A creature manifestly between the Gorilla and the
Negro is to be met with in some of the lowest districts of London and
Liverpool by adventurous explorers. It comes from Ireland, whence it
has contrived to migrate; it belongs in fact to a tribe of Irish savages: the
lowest species of the Irish Yahoo. When conversing with its kind it talks
a sort of gibberish. It is, moreover, a climbing animal, and may
sometimes be seen ascending a ladder laden with a hod of bricks.

(*Punch*, October 18, 1862; the latter description brings to mind Tim
Finnegan)

6. *"The Ignorant Vote: Honors are Easy"* (Black Slaves and White Apes). Nast's cartoon in *Harper's Weekly* suggests that emancipated Southern slaves were equivalent in weight to the brutish Irish-American voters in the North, characterized by simian features and by the identifying clay pipe and hat of the stereotypical Irishman. (*Harper's Weekly*, December 9, 1876.)

7.   *"An Irish Jig."* James A. Wales's cartoon in *Puck* of "An Irish Jig" shows both John Bull and Uncle Sam unable to tame the wildness of the Irish ape, fattened on English and American food supplies (and also on "Drugs") and sporting distinctly ape-like features (as well as Celtic clay pipe and hat). (*Puck*, November 3, 1880, p. 150.)

8.   *"The King of A-Shantee."* In Frederick B. Opper's cartoon for
Puck, titled "The King of A-Shantee," Paddy and Bridget are
portrayed as the stereotypical Irish peasant couple, living in
their lowly shanty; the Irishman is connected through the pun
of "A-Shantee" with the African Ashanti, just as his
prognathous, simian features suggest that he may be the
theorized "missing link" in the evolution between apes and
black Africans. (*Puck*, February 15, 1882, p. 378.)

Such offensive racial typing, however fanciful and whimsical, suggests an ethnocentric pathology within the dominant culture of the English empire. As Curtis rightly and incisively concludes:

> It was comforting for some Englishmen to believe – on the basis of the best scientific authority in the Anthropological Society of London – that their own facial angles and orthognathous features were as far removed from those of apes, Irishmen, and Negroes as was humanly possible ... The simianizing of Paddy in the 1860s thus emanated from the convergence of deep, powerful emotions about the nature of man, the security of property, and the preservation of privilege ... Englishmen who celebrated the genius of the Anglo-Saxon race tended to see themselves as modern Athenians, endowed with Grecian noses and facial angles ... these men thought that the common Catholic Irishman was the antithesis of all these desirable qualities: Paddy was a wild, melancholic, indolent, unstable and prognathous Caliban ... After the outbreak of Fenian violence in the mid-1860s, Paddy descended further to find himself a niche somewhere between the "white Negro" and the anthropoid apes.
>
> (*Apes*, 103, 105, 107)

Breaking the binary trap

This, then, was the context of "race" – of racialized discourse and racial *idées reçues* – at the end of the nineteenth century: a discourse racialized along a binary axis that posited the English "race" as one pole (the positive) and the Irish as the other (the negative), in which "Irish" was defined as everything not desirably "English." Thus, the conception of an essentialized and racialized Irishness *depended*, for its very definition and formulation, on the English ideal of English-ness, a national ego-ideal (assuming that "Nations have their ego, just like individuals"). Furthermore, given the dependency of Irish-ness (as a racial concept) on the English–Irish opposition, any discussion of the Irish race inevitably carried with it the weight and associations of Empire (and its corollaries, the "Irish Question" and Home Rule).

Joyce was certainly very aware of and very sensitive to such stereotyping and essentializing. Having denied "that the Irish are really the unbalanced, helpless idiots about whom we read in the lead articles of the *Standard* and the *Morning Post*," Joyce argues (in "Ireland, Island of Saints and Sages") that these stereotypes have their origin in the oppressive conditions of an Irish environment long suffering under the cruel Penal Laws (which forbade Irish Catholics to vote, become government employees, practice a trade or profession, sit in parliament, own land, keep a horse, and so on) imposed until recently by England (see *CW* 168–71); but, as he goes on to note about the constructed stereotypes, "this pejorative conception of Ireland is given the lie by the fact that when the Irishman is found outside of Ireland in another environment, he very often becomes a respected man. The economic and intellectual conditions that prevail in his own country do not permit the development of individuality" (*CW* 171).

That same year (1907) Joyce wrote a brief essay for *Il Piccolo della Sera* in Trieste titled "Ireland at the Bar," in which he narrated a very suggestive story (which I quote at length):

Several years ago a sensational trial was held in Ireland. In a lonely place in a western province, called Maamtrasna, a murder was committed. Four or five townsmen, all belonging to the ancient tribe of the Joyces, were arrested. The oldest of them, the seventy year old Myles Joyce, was the prime suspect. Public opinion at the time thought him innocent and today considers him a martyr. Neither the old man nor the others accused knew English. The court had to resort to the services of an interpreter. The questioning, conducted through the interpreter, was at times comic and at times tragic. On one side was the excessively ceremonious interpreter, on the other the patriarch of a miserable tribe unused to civilized customs, who seemed stupefied by all the judicial ceremony. The magistrate said:

"Ask the accused if he saw the lady that night." The question was referred to him in Irish, and the old man broke out into an involved explanation, gesticulating, appealing to the others accused and to heaven. Then he quieted down, worn out by his effort, and the interpeter turned to the magistrate and said:

"He says no, 'your worship.'"

"Ask him if he was in that neighbourhood at that hour." The old man again began to talk, to protest, to shout, almost beside himself with the anguish of being unable to understand or to make himself understood, weeping in anger and terror. And the interpreter, again, dryly:

"He says no, 'your worship.'"

When the questioning was over, the guilt of the poor old man was declared proved, and he was remanded to a superior court which condemned him to the noose. On the day the sentence was executed, the square in front of the prison was jammed full of kneeling people shouting prayers in Irish for the repose of Myles Joyce's soul. The story was told that the executioner, unable to make the victim understand him, kicked at the miserable man's head in anger to shove it into the noose.

(*CW* 197–98)

In December of 1882 an old man named Myles Joyce had indeed been hanged, along with two other men, in County Galway for murder; he "was generally considered to be an innocent victim of public indignation" (*CW* 197). Joyce's telling of the tale emphasizes the fact that, as a Gaelic-speaking Irish Celt, Myles Joyce was allowed no voice of his own in an English-speaking forum. The story serves as an allegory of the Irish "race" under English domination. As Gayatri Spivak has asked, *can* the subaltern speak? Or must we conclude, along with Karl Marx, that "they cannot represent themselves; they must be represented"? If so, that representation is often, as in this story, distorted and peremptory, resulting in public execution or personal self-destruction. As Spivak has argued about the subaltern woman under imperialism, she is allowed no subject position from which to speak: "there is no space from where the subaltern (sexed) subject can speak" (Young, *White Mythologies*, 163); thus everyone else speaks for her but herself. And if the racialized and colonized Irish subalterns "must be represented," *how* can they be represented? How can *Joyce* represent them, and thus create/ represent the uncreated/unrepresented conscience of his race? Should he speak as an Irishman, or must he use the language and cultural systems of the oppressors? (As Stephen Dedalus thinks about the English dean of studies in *A Portrait*: "How different are the words *home, Christ, ale, master*, on his lips and on mine! ... His language, so familiar and so foreign, will always be for me an acquired speech" [*P* 189]). To speak as an Irishman means that, like Myles Joyce, one will not be heard: surely it did not escape Joyce's linguistic sensitivity that the de-speeched subaltern here has the same name as himself and is of "the ancient tribe of the Joyces."[7]

Joyce's own comment after telling this story is revealing precisely along these lines:

The figure of this dumbfounded old man, a remnant of a civilization not ours, deaf and dumb before his judge, is a symbol of the Irish nation at the bar of public opinion. Like him, she is unable to appeal to the modern conscience of England and other countries. The English journalists act as interpreters between Ireland and the English electorate ... Skimming over the dispatches from London (which, though they lack pungency, have something of the laconic quality of the interpreter mentioned above), the public conceives of the Irish as highwaymen with distorted faces, roaming the night with the object of taking the hide of every Unionist.

(*CW* 198)

Joyce is aware that being-spoken-for ("interpreted" and represented) results in the essentialized negative stereotypes of the race ("the Irish

No. 1.—This is little Chalks sent over by the London Illustrated Smudge to furnish truthful sketches of Irish character.

No. 2.—This is his model.

No. 3.—And this is the sketch he furnishes.

9. *"Setting Down in Malice."* The cartoonist of *Pat* suggests the typical and distorted representation of Irish features and character by the English press, in which an English reporter "Chalks" (no. 1) portrays a handsome and respectable Irishman (no. 2) as a bestial and vampiric gorilla instead (no. 3). (*Pat*, new series, 1:2, January 22, 1881.)

as highwaymen with distorted faces, roaming the night"). Unable to speak, Ireland is "unable to appeal to the modern conscience of England and other countries." Along with Joyce, Ireland herself was acutely aware of the trap involved in this pattern of being "represented" and essentialized – as illustrated in a telling Irish political cartoon ("Pat"; see illustration 9), in which an English journalist sent to Ireland to "furnish truthful sketches of Irish character" encounters a handsome and respectable-looking Irish gentleman – and draws/represents him instead as a frighteningly bestial and vampiric gorilla. As Joyce has Madden point out in *Stephen Hero*, the Irish Celt is labeled/libeled as "the baboon-faced Irishman that we see in *Punch*" (*SH* 64). How can one break this pattern and represent oneself and one's own "race" and conscience?

For this binary pattern is a trap that essentializes and limits representation to precisely its own terms, terms one must play by if one accepts the binary oppositions. In other words, if you try to prove that you aren't what "they" say you are, you are judging/arguing by the same rules/categories "they" are and so you end up reifying/maintaining those categories in place as functional realities; for example, if you try to prove that you are more angel than ape, that you aren't a Hottentot or Maori, then you are only reinforcing and reinscribing the terms of a hierarchy that places angels (and Anglos) at the top and "Negroes" and Orientals near the bottom. A textbook example of the dangers of such totalizing binaries is the case of Benjamin Disraeli, who, as an English Jew trying to exculpate Jews from English and European anti-Semitism, proved more English than the English and more racist than the Anglo-Saxonist. John Tenniel's cartoon (see illustration 10) in *Punch* of Disraeli masquerading as an angel brilliantly underscores the racial suprema-cist's motivating fear and anxiety of being seen or represented as an ape instead (Curtis, *Apes*, 106). In Curtis's analysis, Disraeli was "among the leading apostles of race consciousness in England" and "espoused the deterministic meaning of race because he wished to establish the fact that the Jews were a supremely gifted people who were head and shoulders above the other races of the world in all important cultural respects" (*Anglo-Saxons*, 30). In needing to prove that one is more angelic and less ape-like than others, one ends up buying into the very terms of a binary hierarchy of Self and Other that needs to label and denigrate the Other (whether "Negro," Oriental, or Irish) as barbaric and subhuman in order to assert the Self's own unquestionably civilized "culture" and humanity by

PUNCH, OR THE LONDON CHARIVARI.—December 10, 1864.

DRESSING FOR AN OXFORD BAL MASQUÉ.

"THE QUESTION IS, IS MAN AN APE OR AN ANGEL? (*A Laugh.*) NOW, I AM ON THE SIDE OF THE ANGELS. (*Cheers.*)"—Mr. Disraeli's *Oxford Speech, Friday, November* 25.

10. *"Dressing for an Oxford Bal Masqué."* In Tenniel's cartoon, Disraeli's masquerade as an Oxonian angel underscores the central fear by racial supremacists of being thought of as an ape rather than as an angel. (*Punch*, December 10, 1864.)

46

contrast. Consequently, Disraeli's attitudes towards "other" races were, in spite of his own marginalized/othered status, essentialist and prejudicial, resulting, as we have seen, in his opinion that the Irish are a "wild, reckless, indolent, uncertain, and supersititious race" who "hate our order, our civilization, our enterprising industry, our sustained courage, our decorous liberty, our pure religion" (*Anglo-Saxons*, 51; one wonders which "pure religion" Disraeli meant).

Is it possible to break this pattern, to step outside its functions? Joyce, as is well known and as his essays exemplify, "tells his compatriots that they must cease to be provincial and folklorist and mere Irish" (*CW* 8); he rejected the limitations of a narrow and provincial nationalism in order to speak to a wider, international (and not purely "English") forum, advocating internationalism over provincialism, advising the Irish to look towards Europe and the international community as its "bar of public opinion," rather than trying to define itself within English constructions of empire, race, and nationhood. (See also the coda to this chapter, on Stephen Dedalus.) Joyce's logic might be seen as a choice not to play by the same terms as the binary system which would function him as a primitive and racialized Celtic other, but to "play along" with such terms and racial comparisons – by re-functioning them and activating them in an enabling (rather than disabling) fashion. As Banton has noted about attitudes towards racial difference and sameness, "Ideas about race have mostly been used to exclude people from privilege while ideas about shared ethnicity have been used to create bonds of belonging together" (*Racial Theories*, 126); in *Ulysses* and *Finnegans Wake*, Joyce repeatedly, as we shall see, turns the racialized, derogatory analogies of the Irish as racial others into enabling bonds of shared ethnicity. If the Irish were depicted as other races, Joyce shows that being like (or just being) other races is a positive thing. As early as 1907, he was arguing that the Celtic race in Ireland had Oriental roots: "This language [Gaelic] is oriental in origin, and has been identified by many philologists with the ancient language of the Phoenicians," a racialized analogy clearly meant to be positive rather than pejorative, since the Phoenicians were "an adventurous people, who had a monopoly of the sea" and were "the originators of trade and navigation, according to historians." "The language that the Latin writer of comedy, Plautus, put in the mouth of Phoenicians in his comedy *Poenulus* is almost the same language that the Irish peasants speak today," Joyce asserts, and likewise "the religion and civilization of this ancient people, later known by the name of Druidism, were Egyptian" – a Druidism which was transplanted to Ireland (*CW* 156). A few pages later Joyce points out that Irish civilization is "almost as old as the Chinese" (dating back "to a time when England was an uncivilized country"): "If an appeal to the past in this manner were valid, the fellahin of Cairo would have all the right in the world to disdain to act as porters for English tourists. Ancient Ireland is dead just as ancient Egypt is dead" (*CW* 173; as Professor MacHugh says in *Ulysses*, "Kingdoms of this world. The masters of the Mediterranean are fellaheen today" [*U* 7.911]). The Orientalist comparison had already provided the Irish with the enabling analogy of themselves as Israelites (led by Parnell as another Moses) searching for freedom from a tyrannical Egyptian empire, an analogy Joyce would play with in the "Aeolus" episode of *Ulysses* and which he first evoked in his 1912 essay on "The Shade of Parnell," who "like another Moses, led a turbulent and unstable people from the house of shame to the verge of the Promised Land" (*CW* 225). None of these equations/analogies between the Irish and other "races" has derogatory implications for the peoples being compared; rather, they argue that the Irish share in and participate in the strengths and glories of these other civilizations. Joyce is able to employ the racialized analogies positively, even if only by suggesting a solidarity of the marginalized – as when he warns that the English, "if they are wise, ... will hesitate to alienate the sympathy of the Irish for constitutional agitation; especially now that India and Egypt are in an uproar and the overseas colonies are asking for an imperial federation" (*CW* 194).

By the time Joyce came to write *Ulysses* he would equate the Irish with the Greeks as well as with the Phoenicians and the Jews (and, as we shall see, with many other races and peoples), citing Victor Bérard's arguments about Homer in *Les Phéniciens et l'Odysseé*; as Richard Ellmann has pointed out: "In Bérard's view, Homer was a Hellene, Ulysses a Phoenician rover. Joyce could conveniently assume that all Semites were alike, Phoenicians and Hebrews being for his purposes ... interchangeable, and so he could claim Bérard's authority for that climactic encounter in *Ulysses* when 'jewgreek meets greekjew'"; after all, as Ellmann reasons, "Bérard suggested that Homer may have worked with an Egyptian epic based upon a Phoenician sailing manual. In other words, the whole Middle East played its part" (*Consciousness*, 27). Which is to say that the very conception of *Ulysses* is based on an implied equation of otherness with the self, of Oriental/Jew with West/Greek, denying the comfort and clarity of binary distinctions based on an essentialized (and fetishized) notion of inherent difference.

To base a nationalist response upon the terms of these essentializing binary distinctions is to play by the same rules of that binarity and thus to take on the same hierarchical assumptions. Thus, as Gibbons argues, "many of the conceptions requisitioned by nationalist propagandists in defence of Irish culture are, in fact, an extension of colonialism, rather than a repudiation of it. The racial concept of an Irish national character is a case in point" ("Race Against Time," 104). By positing a countering notion of Irish racial/ national character to combat the English stereotype, Irish nationalists were themselves performing an act of static stereotyping; "the 'Celt,' and by implication the Celtic revival, owed as much to the benevolent colonialism of Matthew Arnold as it did to the inner recesses of hidden Ireland" (104).[8]

Such binary logic is predicated on an Us/Them distinction that argues for racial purity and superiority, Us always being valued above Them. Buying into those terms means simply reversing the terms, and claiming that, "No, it's *we* who are better than *you*" – in an act of reverse racism. Irish Nationalism and the Celtic Revival, what Curtis calls Celticism, were in large measure just this sort of response; thus, for example, Arthur Griffith could (much like Disraeli), while arguing for Irish autonomy and freedom, be so otherwise bigoted as to approve of black slavery (see Gibbons, "Race Against Time," 104). As Curtis argues:

The very ethnocentrism of those men who administered the new British empire in the nineteenth century had the effect of awakening or reactivating counter-ethnocentric impulses among their colonial subjects, not least because these "natives" had to endure constant reminders of their own inferiority in the eyes of the Anglo-Saxonists whose orders and edicts they were supposed to obey.

The irony, at times, futility, of Anglo-Saxonist attitudes towards Ireland is that they drove a number of Irish men and women to fabricate their own mythology of racial and cultural superiority.

(*Anglo-Saxons*, 120)

Celticism or Irish Nationalism tried to do for the "Irish race" what Anglo-Saxonist racism had done for the "English race," by exalting the Self's own proclaimed racial and cultural superiority in comparison to all other races/cultures. Thus, Irish scholars involved in the Celtic Revival during the latter decades of the nineteenth century argued that they were "the direct descendants of a pure and holy race, composed of Firbolgs, Tuatha de Dananns, and Milesians, whose ancient institutions, veneration for learning, and religious zeal made Saxon culture ... look nothing less than barbarian"; as Curtis concludes, "ethnocentric Irish men and women sought to combat heavy doses of Anglo-Saxonist venom with a Celticist serum of their own making" (*Anglo-Saxons*, 15), seeking to provoke patriotic fervor by being "racy of the soil." Ernest Renan's (whom Stephen cites three times in *Stephen Hero*) lyrical and ecstatic views of the Celtic race in his *La Poésie des Races Celtiques*, arguing that the Celts were unmatched in the world in both their purity of blood and their strength of character, were sounded by the Gaelic League and the Irish Literary Revival; similarly Irish apologists like Charles Gavan Duffy had already proclaimed that "The history of Ireland abounded in noble lessons, and had the unity and purpose of an epic poem" (see Lloyd, *Nationalism*, 68). The collusion and mirrored quality of such ethnocentrisms is suggested by the fact that the same logic and the same stereotypes were invoked by both sides: Matthew Arnold's analyses of the distinctive character of the Irish genius (such as that "he is truly sentimental") were in fact largely derived from Renan, which also explains why the Arnoldian image should have so appealed to the Irish Literary Revival. The ease with which Irish apologists could accept "the Arnoldian stereotype as benign – in fact, as not a stereotype at all – explains how it could be taken to heart by Irish revivalists," as Gibbons (104) suggests.

In fact, the very notion that there was still a pure and distinct Celtic race living in Ireland was an essentialist construction that, ironically enough, was equally acceptable (in fact essential) to *both* the Irish Nationalist and to the Anglo-Saxon imperialist, for both depended (emotionally and psychologically) on the notion of themselves as a race pure and distinct from others. Thus, the Celticist response was a mirror image of Anglo-Saxonist racism; Curtis writes:

There was a good deal of ancestor worship and racial mythology in Celticism, just as much, in fact, as in Anglo-Saxonism. Rare was the meeting of a branch of the Gaelic League, the Gaelic Athletic Association, or the Ancient Order of Hibernians at which there was no allusion to the purity and the antiquity of the Irish race. Whether labeled Celtic, Gaelic, Goidelic, Milesian, or plain Irish, that race possessed qualities and virtues far superior to those of Anglo-Saxons.

(*Anglo-Saxons*, 109)

In 1892 Douglas Hyde delivered in Dublin his powerful and influential lecture on "The Necessity for De-Anglicising Ireland," advocating that the noble Celtic race should divest itself of the despicable culture of the "bloody brutal Sassenachs" and return to Irish cultural purity by studying Gaelic, "our once great national tongue."[9] This nationalist nostalgia for origins argues for the same kind of cultural purity and superiority as the Anglo-Saxonist supremacists had long done for the English "race"; in spite of all the bloody invasions, settlements, and migrations in Irish history – Celts, Romans, Danes, Normans, Saxons, and so on – the Irish were somehow still held up as being pure of blood; arguments were even made by Celticist enthusiasts that America had been discovered in 545 AD by St. Brendan or that Shakespeare had been a Celt (suggestions Joyce roundly mocks and parodies in the "Cyclops" episode of *Ulysses*). Such Celtic ethnocentrism was most fervently embraced by the Fenians (whose very name reflects a commitment to Celtic mythology and militarism), espousing an ancient mythology that seemed to justify war, bloodshed, and heroic death, adding the likes of Shane O'Neill, Wolfe Tone, and Robert Emmet to the mythological pantheon of Cuchulain and Finn MacCool.[10] Joyce, who found Emmet's "foolish uprising" and the Young Ireland movement to risk pointless spilling of blood (*CW* 189), would have none of this Celtic ethnocentrism, blood cult, and originary nostalgia – and refused to be involved in the Revival or in the public activities of Irish Nationalism (see also coda to this chapter, on Stephen D[a]edalus's response, in *Stephen Hero* and *A Portrait*, to Celticism). His parody of Fenian Celticism in the "Cyclops" chapter of *Ulysses* skewers (as we shall see in chapter 7) such blindly racist logic as that espoused by the "Citizen," modeled on Michael Cusack, Treasurer of The Gaelic Union (see pamphlet in illustration 11) and founder of the Gaelic Athletic Association. For the pacifist, exiled, and multilingual Joyce, the "spiritual liberation" of Ireland and the creation of the "conscience of my race" involved getting out of the binary structure and into an internationalist, multilingual, and multiculturalist perspective. Unfortunately, on the Emerald Isle itself the "Irish Question" is even today still very much the "English Question"; as Curtis concludes ruefully, "The idea of the racial purity or homogeneity of the Irish people lives on in Ireland ... because the emotional investment in that myth continues to serve some of the same functions today that it did in pre-independence Ireland" (*Anglo-Saxons*, 118).

The Gaelic Union.

Under the Patronage of

HIS GRACE, MOST REV. T. W. CROKE, ABP. OF CASHEL;

Founded March 17th, 1880,

For the Preservation and Cultivation of the Irish Language.

President—The Right Honble. The O'Conor Don. P.C., D.L., M.R.I.A.

Treasurer—Michael Cusack, Esq.

Honorary Secretaries, {Rev. J. E. Nolan, O.D.C. {R. J. O'Mulrennin, Esq.

Address—No. 19 Kildare Street, Dublin. Meetings—Every Saturday at 4 p.m.: The Mansion House.

Means.

To publish cheap books from which to learn Irish.
To give prizes and premiums to students of Irish.
To promote the teaching of Irish in schools.

Membership, 10s. annually, which entitles a Member to "The Gaelic Journal," post free for the year.
The Gaelic Journal (Irish and English), 6d. a number; Annually, 5s.; by post, 6s.
List of Publications, Pamphlets, and Reports, post free, on application, by letter only.

"THE CARE OF THE NATIONAL LANGUAGE IS A SACRED TRUST."—Schlegel.

To encourage the study of our Native Language, I will give to every Member of the Gaelic Union, and to every Subscriber to "The Gaelic Journal," ONE Copy of St. Patrick's Prayer Book, at half published price; if by Post, one penny extra. The order must be filled in on this form, and returned to address at foot.

Dear Sir,

Please forward One Copy of St Patrick's Prayer Book to

Name,_____

Address,_____

Nearest Post Town,_____

Enclosed find _____ shil _____ pen

To

REV. J. E. NOLAN, O.D.C.,
St. Teresa's, Clarendon-st., Dublin.

11. "The Gaelic Union." Pamphlet put out by The Gaelic Union "to encourage the study of our Native Language," an activity it refers to (citing Schlegel) as "a sacred trust." Michael Cusack is listed as Treasurer. (My thanks to Theresa O'Connor for providing a copy of this pamphlet.)

What Joyce grew increasingly to understand is that, whereas racism and ethnocentrism depend on static essences and absolute difference, peoples and populations contain multiplicitous and heterogeneous characteristics of both individual and cultural difference that cannot be so conveniently (and logocentrically) named and labeled. In such binary operations both Self and Other get conveniently and comfortably demarcated (and *bordered*, by an essentialist Pale): as Curtis writes about the English view of the English/Irish dyad,

Where the Celt was child-like, the Anglo-Saxon was mature; instead of emotional instability, he could boast of self-control; he was energetic not lazy, rational not superstitious, civilized not primitive, clean not dirty, ready to forgive not vengeful, and prepared to live under the rule of law. This temperamental antithesis was all-embracing: it left no loophole for the Irish to share much in common with their English rulers.

(Anglo-Saxons, 53)

Such binary oppositions are based on a totalizing (and Manichean) mechanics of absolute difference which allows neither for shared traits nor for heterogeneity within each individual group characterized.[11] As Banton points out in regard to the anthropological and evolutionary logics behind nineteenth-century racial typologies, "Those who operated with essentialist concepts assumed that all individual members of a species were fundamentally similar, whereas every animal breeder knew well that no two animals were identical" (Banton, *Racial Theories*, 69). Instead, such dualisms lead the oppressed group within the dyad also, as we have seen, to reinscribe the same patterns, logic, and distinctions as the dominant group's; to play by the rules and terms of the oppressor, thus reaffirming the values valorized within such dualistic oppositions. As Lisa Lowe writes in *Critical Terrains: French and British Orientalisms* (1991), in arguing "against the recuperation of any binary version of difference": "binary constructions of difference – whether Occident and Orient, male and female, or a static concept of dominant and emergent – embody a logic that gives priority to the first term of the dyad while subordinating the second" (24).

As we have seen, the result is a form of reverse ethnocentrism in which the racialized and colonized subaltern group (Ireland) searches for its own native origins and cultural superiority in order to proclaim a racial purity with which to match and mirror the claims of its imperial oppressor. In *White Mythologies: Writing History and the West* (1990), Robert Young points out that "those who evoke the 'nativist' position through a nostalgia for a lost or repressed culture idealize the possibility of that lost origin being recoverable in all its former plenitude without allowing for the fact that the figure of the lost origin, the 'other' that the colonizer has repressed, has itself been constructed in terms of the colonizer's own self-image" (168). As Spivak has argued and as the Celticist case illustrates, such a "nativist" position merely mirrors the hierarchical fantasies of the colonizer's culture now projected onto the fantasized originary culture of the "Other," and that all such arguments, from either side, employ the terms and logic constructed by the dominant, colonizing culture (see, for example, "Rani" and "Subaltern"). As Frantz Fanon elaborates in *Wretched of the Earth* (163):

Western bourgeois racial prejudice as regards the nigger and the Arab is a racism of contempt; it is a racism which minimises what it hates. Bourgeois ideology, however, ... manages to appear logical in its own eyes by inviting the sub-men to become human, and to take as their prototype Western humanity as incarnated in the Western bourgeoisie.[12]

One of the colonizer's rules/terms by which both sides of such a binary dialectic play is a "purer than thou" racial claim, arguing the purity and essence of one's own racial group. Lowe reminds us that "When we maintain a static dualism of identity and difference, and uphold the logic of the dualism as the means of explaining how a discourse expresses domination and subordination, we fail to account for the differences inherent in each term"; she notes that a binary opposition of Self and Other, like Occident and Orient (or British and Irish), is "a misleading perception which serves to suppress the specific heterogeneities, inconstancies, and slippages of each individual notion" (*Critical Terrains*, 7). Thus, arguments for either an Anglo-Saxon racial essence/purity or a Celtic racial essence/purity are but wishful thinking. As early as 1895 William D. Babington had written *Fallacies of Race Theories as Applied to National Character*, in which he refuted the theory that either the English or the Irish were separate races, noting that the concept of "the English race" itself willfully ignored the fluid mixture of races in Britain over many centuries, as well as suggesting the irony that the existence of a distinct Celtic race in Ireland was a concept agreeable "alike to the Irish patriot and to the English apologist for English rule"; Babington reasonably argued that there were no such things as inherently Celtic (or English) virtues or vices, and that the specific differences between cultures resulted from social and environmental influences (see

Curtis, *Anglo-Saxons*, 104). During the same period, as Gibbons points out, the translator and scholar George Sigerson (mentioned by Joyce in *Ulysses* 9.309) had similarly "sought to remove the racial epithet 'Celtic' entirely from the cultural canon, arguing that Irishness incorporated the residue of several cultural or 'racial' strains, as befitted a country exposed to successive waves of invasion and internal strife over the centuries" ("Race Against Time," 105).

Instead of a pure lineage of cultural inheritance, composite cultures might more fruitfully be theorized not on a notion of difference based on rigid binarisms but on a heterogeneity resulting from porous borders and live spheres of influence and interaction, on what Lowe calls "heterotopicality": "A condition of multiple and interpenetrating positions and practices – what we might call *heterotopicality* – is one way of describing the dynamic through which discursive conditions are transformed"; this term suggests "multiplicity and interpenetration – the continual yet uneven overlappings, intersections, and collusions of discursive articulations" (*Critical Terrains*, 15). After all, the very activities and characteristics which the Self would expel and represent as primitive and Other in fact shape the Self's own culture and constitution. What is occluded is not only the actual heterogeneous specificities of different cultures, but also the presence of the other within the self, the willingness to acknowledge that not only does the other-within shape the self, but that in very real ways it *is* the self. What is denied is an awareness of the fluid and reciprocal nature of influence and cultural formation in which the self both acts and is acted on. As James Clifford puts it in his essay on "Traveling Cultures," "what's elided is the wider global world of intercultural import–export in which [the encounter with the other] is always already enmeshed" (100). The physical as well as figural *topos* of a conquered culture (as also of the conqueror's culture) is already what Mary Pratt calls a "contact zone," composed of porous or fluid "borders" which blur and deny any clear markers of absolute difference (in this sense, Gloria Anzaldúa's figuration of "borderlands" functions similarly).[13]

This was a reality Joyce was well aware of in his choice to reject the Celticism within Irish Nationalism, founded as it was on this binary trap. As I have suggested, his argument that the Irish should look beyond their narrow provincialism and their affairs with England and develop a more international consciousness was an attempt to break out of such constricting dynamics and terms, in which an Irish essence could be defined only on the conqueror's terms (such as those posited by Arnold) and in reaction/response to English claims. For Joyce rejected wholesale the Celticist argument for racial purity and national characteristics, which he found to be as specious as the English stereotyping of the Irish character as the "baboon-faced figures" (*SH* 64) and "the unbalanced helpless idiots we read about" (*CW* 171) in the English papers and magazines. Like Babington and Sigerson, we find him (in "Ireland, Island of Saints and Sages") reminding us that "the Celtic race" was "compounded of the old Celtic stock and the Scandinavian, Anglo-Saxon and Norman races ... with the various elements mingling and renewing the ancient body." The Irish, Joyce argues, are in fact a very mixed race – "Do we not see that in Ireland the Danes, the Firbolgs, the Milesians from Spain, the Norman invaders, and the Anglo-Saxon settlers have united to form a new entity?" (*CW* 166) – including many Irish patriots such as Parnell "in whose veins there was not even a drop of Celtic blood" (*CW* 161–62; the present mayor of Dublin, Mr. Nannetti, he informs his Triestine audience, is Italian). Joyce's representation of the Irish "race," cogently articulated in a significant passage, is very much a vision of a complex mix of racial and cultural strains operating within a fluid "contact zone":

Our civilization is a vast fabric, in which the most diverse elements are mingled, in which nordic aggressiveness and Roman law, the new bourgeois conventions and the remnant of a Syriac religion [Christianity] are reconciled. In such a fabric, it is useless to look for a thread that may have remained pure and virgin without having undergone the influence of a neighbouring thread. What race, or what language ... can boast of being pure today? And no race has less right to utter such a boast than the race now living in Ireland.

(*CW* 165–66)

In rejecting the argument that the "race now living in Ireland" has somehow remained "pure and virgin," Joyce is rejecting the ideological foundation behind the Citizen's, the Gaelic League's, and the Literary Revival's motivations. In arguing that in Irish civilization "the most diverse elements are mingled," Joyce is acknowledging the hybridity and collaboration of discursive influences and cultural formations. His works, as we shall see, become increasingly informed by his sensitivity towards the nature of the hybridity, ambivalences, and interpenetrations involved in hegemonic and discursive formations. This is, of course, the understanding of discourses that Foucault advanced in *The Order of Things* when he suggested that the histories of the Same (Self) and the Other were inextricably implicated and interpenetrated: "the history of the order imposed on things would be the history of the Same – of that which, for a given culture, is both dispersed and related" (xxiv); as Shem/ Mercius would say to Shaun/Justius in *Finnegans Wake*, "the days of youyouth are evermixed mimine" (*FW* 194.04). Having acknowledged that the other is always already inside, Foucault went on in the *History of Sexuality* to, in Robert Young's words, "formulate[] the structures of power in exactly the same way, so that the forces of domination and resistance are caught up, sometimes indistinguishably, within each other" (*White Mythologies*, 86). The structures of colonial power and racial discourse should likewise not be premised upon comfortable binary hierarchies that occlude heterogeneity and difference by positing oppositional and essentialized extremes, but rather envisioned as composed of heterogeneous multiplicities spanning a whole spectrum of difference. As Banton points out about those genetic and biological differences repeatedly used to justify racial essences and typologies: "Physical variation is continuous. It is human societies which rather arbitrarily draw distinctions and use them to create and reinforce social discontinuities" (*Racial Theories*, 128). The creation of such demarcated and consolidated borders and arbitrary discontinuities has much to do with related issues of nominalism, essentialism, and logocentrism – which are the subject of later chapters, about Joyce's self-conscious blurring (especially in *Ulysses* and *Finnegans Wake*) of the racialized demarcations of difference inherent in the concepts of "dark horse" and "white horse" as symbols of a racial other and an imperial self, within a pluralistic vision and continuous spectrum of different colorings, horses of an-Other color(s). For Joyce was consciously rejecting the rigid simplicity of the reflected racial arguments and characters posited by both Anglo-Saxonism and Celticism, as he attempted more fruitfully to engage in the "spiritual liberation of my country" and to "create the uncreated conscience of my race" by representing Ireland in "my nicely polished looking-glass" instead – a representation mirrored not in the haze of a Celtic twilight but, in Seamus Deane's phrase, by a "mirror held up to Culture" ("Joyce the Irishman," 41).

Coda: the case of Stephen D(a)edalus

Both the *Stephen Hero* manuscript (probably written 1904–06) and its later, much compressed version *A Portrait of the Artist as a Young Man* (published 1916) feature at their centers a young man discovering his artistic vocation, Stephen Dedalus (spelled Daedalus in *Stephen Hero*). The two texts contain many of the same fictional characters, often based closely on real persons in Joyce's acquaintance. I am including this extended "coda" as part of the current chapter (rather than as a separate chapter) because it quarries these two Joycean texts for their detailed representations and illustrations of the theoretical and ideological issues of race and Irishness, as discussed earlier in this chapter. For fundamental to both *Stephen Hero* and *A Portrait* are the depictions of the Irish Nationalist movement popular in Joyce's youth – as exemplified by the Daniels household which young Stephen frequents and by his companions at University College Dublin – and of Stephen's responses to such Celticism, within the binary dialectics of Irishness and Englishness.

For the young Stephen Dedalus, the various and constraining structures of authority and institutional power are imperial in that they have empire over him, they deny him personal autonomy and personal home rule. What he is concerned with most, by the end of both texts, is the development of his personal liberty and artistic freedom; any force that would constrict such development is suspect, including the Nationalist movement: "The programme of the patriots filled him with very reasonable doubts; its articles could obtain no intellectual assent from him. He knew, moreover, that concordance with it would mean for him a submission of everything else in its interest ... He refused therefore to set out for any task if he had first to prejudice his success by oaths to his patria" (*SH* 76–77).

In *A Portrait* Stephen declares his *non serviam* against the "nets" that would entrap him and which together constitute the institutions of hegemonic authority over him: "nationality, language, religion" (*P* 203) – along with their familial corollaries, collaborating in "Home Rule" issues in every sense of the word "home." Nationality includes not only "patria" and the nightmare of Irish history that have created a colonized Ireland enslaved to England, but also the consequent pressures to participate in the current popular Celticist fervor for the fatherland – a movement whose familial presence began with Stephen's own father, the Parnellite whose tears shed over the Chief move young Stephen at the Christmas dinner in Bray early in the novel, and who continue to berate "the Bantry gang" (which included Tim Healy) even near the end of the novel (*P* 228). Religion includes not only the Roman Catholic Church whose "fathers" ruled over Stephen's education and career, but their familial counterparts in the devout Dante and in his mother who wishes him to make his Easter duty. Language includes not only the language of the English oppressors which Stephen uses but always with an outsider's consciousness –

How different are the words *home, Christ, ale, master* on [the English-man's] lips than on mine! I cannot speak or write these words without unrest of spirit. His language, so familiar and so foreign, will always be for me an acquired speech. I have not made or accepted its words. My voice holds them at bay. My soul frets in the shadow of his language.
(*P* 189)

– but also the "native" Gaelic tongue of the Irish past which the Celticist movement advocates, but which is no more native nor natural (nor familiar/familial) to Stephen than English. Rather, Stephen ultimately chooses to look linguistically and politically beyond the English/Irish binary opposition towards Europe and towards a more internationalist perspective based on multiplicity and difference.

While the role in his works of what Joyce thought of as the "imperium of Rome" is too large a topic in itself for the already capacious scope of this study, nevertheless it is important to keep in mind that Joyce did see religion as inseparable from the politics of nationalism and empire in Ireland. For Stephen, too, religion is a very major element within the hegemonic powers of institutional authority which would hold sway and empire over him – not only because of the Church's direct role in Irish politics (as in the Parnell affair) and in betraying the Irish cause, as delineated angrily by Mr. Casey at the Christmas dinner:

– Didn't the bishops of Ireland betray us in the time of the union when bishop Lanigan presented an address of loyalty to the Marquess Cornwallis? Didn't the bishops and priests sell the aspirations of their country in 1829 in return for catholic emancipation? Didn't they denounce the fenian movement from the pulpit and in the confes-sionbox? And didn't they dishonour the ashes of Terence Bellew MacManus?
(*P* 38)

– but also because the Church represents for Stephen a generalized authority and empire over his mind and person. He explains his refusal to do his Easter duty thus: "I fear ... the chemical action which would be set up in my soul by a false homage to a symbol behind which are massed twenty centuries of authority and venera-tion" (*P* 243; Cranly's subsequent question about whether Stephen would have done the same "in the penal days" serves to remind the reader of the intricate connections between imperial English rule and religion, since the longstanding Elizabethan penal code was used to subjugate Catholics only). As Stephen says in *Stephen Hero* (53), "The Roman, not the Sassenach, was for him the tyrant of the islanders." His responses to Irish Nationalism have been in part shaped by its hand-in-glove collusion with Catholicism under the auspices of a generalized "authority and veneration" from which Stephen wishes to declare his independence; thinking of his fellow students seduced by Irish Nationalism, Stephen remarks that they "respected spiritual and temporal authorities, the spiritual authorities of Catholicism and patriotism, and the temporal authorities of the hierarchy and the government. The memory of Terence MacManus was not less revered by them than the memory of Cardinal Cullen" (*SH* 173). The hegemonic structures of hierarchy exist as much in religious institutions as in the secular world, as Stephen remarks about the Jesuit monastery he visits: "The toy life which the Jesuits permit these docile young men to live is what I call a stationary march" (*SH* 187).

In fact, Stephen thinks of the Church precisely in terms of militaristic and imperial rule (as in "stationary march"): "He spurned from before him the stale maxims of the Jesuits and he swore an oath that they should never establish over him an ascendancy" (*SH* 38); to an Irish reader the word "ascendancy" could not but suggest the Protestant Ascendancy over Catholic Ireland, suggesting a similarity between the English political tyranny over the Irish body and the Catholic spiritual tyranny over the Irish soul. The specific spiritual tyranny Stephen is subjected to in *Stephen Hero* is the censorship of his paper on Ibsen – censorship by Dr. Dillon, the President of the College, who as a figure of hierarchical tyranny and suppression, is appropriately both an Englishman and a Catholic priest. To Stephen, the Jesuit monastery resembles the militaristic mentality associated with conquest and empire: "He recognised at once the martial mind of the Irish Church in the style of this ecclesiastical barracks" (*SH* 73).

This ecclesiastical militarism of the soldiers of God was, of course, also literally implicated in the spread of European empires and foreign colonies. Stephen recalls hearing "his godfather explain to a more rustic proprietor the nature of the work done by the missionary fathers in civilising the Chinese people. He [Stephen's godfather] sustained the propositions that the Church is also the chief repository of secular culture ... He saw in the pride of the Church the only refuge of men against a threatening democracy and said that Aquinas had anticipated all the discoveries of the modern world" (*SH* 241). The militaristic role of "conquest" by the Church is made even more explicit by the rector in *A Portrait*, urging the boys (during the religious retreat in chapter III) to consider a missionary vocation by invoking the college's patron Saint Francis Xavier, who had been

sent by saint Ignatius to preach to the Indians. He is called, as you know, the apostle of the Indies. He went from country to country in the east, from Africa to India, from India to Japan, baptising the people ... He wished then to go to China to win still more souls for God but he died of fever on the island of Sancian. A great saint, saint Francis Xavier! A great soldier of God! ... Ten thousand souls won for God in a single month! That is a true conqueror ...

(*P* 107–8)

The "apostle of the Indies" here, as a "great soldier" and "true conqueror" "winning" over country after country, is hardly to be distinguished in his activities from Napoleon in Egypt or Wellington in India – and thus the Jesuit Belvedere College begins to meld into the playing fields of Eton.

The collusion between imperialism and religion in the conquest of foreign colonies and their subsequent economic exploitation (*India mittit ebur*, as Stephen later recalls [*P* 179; India sends ivory]) is also suggested in the story of Dante, the religious zealot Mrs. Riordan. During the Christmas dinner scene we learn that Stephen "had heard his father say that she was a spoiled nun and that she had come out of the convent in the Alleghanies when her brother had got the money from the savages for the trinkets and the chainies" (*P* 35). As Ellmann points out, the real Dante Conway in Joyce's childhood similarly "had been on the verge of becoming a nun in America when her brother, who had made a fortune out of trading with African natives, died and left her 30,000 pounds" (*JJI*, 24). In other words, Dante's sanctimonious religiosity and high moral tone are belied by her complicity – one shared by the missionary sects in foreign colonies – with colonial exploitation (*India mittit ebur*) and the African trade, which have funded her freedom and social position.

The Church's role in encouraging Irish Nationalism also makes Stephen suspicious. In both *Stephen Hero* and *A Portrait*, Stephen experiences the call of Celticism, a "voice [which] had bidden him be true to his country and help to raise up her fallen language and tradition" (*P* 84). In the nationalistic Daniels household and at

University College, this Celticist voice hails Stephen and makes its appeal, in simultaneity with the priestly pressure hailing him with a religious calling; both voices pitch interpellated "vocations" which he distrusts. ("He himself was the greatest sceptic concerning the perfervid enthusiasms of the patriots" [*SH* 204].) The depiction of Mr. Hughes, the teacher of the Irish language class, is Joyce's portrait of the Celticist enthusiast (*SH* 59–60):

He spoke in a high-pitched voice with a cutting Northern accent. He never lost an opportunity of sneering at seoninism ["West Britonism," derived from Seon/John, esp. John Bull] and at those who would not learn their native tongue. He said that Beurla [English] was the language of commerce and Irish the speech of the soul ... He scoffed very much at Trinity College and the Irish Parliamentary party. He could not regard as patriots men who had taken oaths of allegiance to the Queen of England and he could not regard as a national university an institution which did not express the religious convictions of the majority of the Irish people ... Hughes, who was the son of a Nationalist solicitor in Armagh, was a law-student at the King's Inns.

Stephen's own response and critique of Nationalism are in part colored by the role of the Church. To begin with, Stephen argues that the priests are disingenuous in their encouragement of Gaelicist practices, encouraging (in our contemporary phrase) a nostalgia for lost origins, as a means by which to solidify the faith and their control over the believers: " – Do you not see, said Stephen, that they encourage the study of Irish that their flocks may be more safely protected from the wolves of disbelief; they consider it is an opportunity to withdraw the people into a past of literal, implicit faith?" (*SH* 54). Stephen recognizes that the emphasis on Irish language and culture is a misdirected nostalgia for a glorious Celtic past and purity which may have never really existed, based – as we have seen – on the reaction of the oppressed group within a binary logic and structure imposed by the oppressors; this pure Celtic glory and Firbolg/Milesian origin is no more real than the vaunted Anglo-Saxon racial purity erected by the other side. Nevertheless, the Celticist logic is a binarity that seeks to deny/demean anything English and glorify everything Irish – as in Hughes's essentializing characterizations of English/Beurla as "the language of commerce and Irish [as] the speech of the soul."

The result of such logic is a romantic sentimentalization of all things Celtic and a consequent chauvinistic blindness to the specific permutations of actual conditions and social realities. In *A Portrait*,

Stephen recalls the hostile Nationalistic audience's boos and catcalls during the infamous debut of Yeats's *The Countess Cathleen* at the Abbey Theatre: "A libel on Ireland!" "Made in Germany!" "Blasphemy!" "We never sold our faith!" "No Irish woman ever did it!" "We want no amateur atheists." "We want no budding buddhists" (*P* 226). Joyce, who *was* an amateur atheist and Buddhist sympathizer (more on that later), was himself in the audience and, unlike the hissers and booers, "clapped vigorously" (*JJI*, 68–69) – refusing to see the world only through shamrock-tinted glasses which would deny any possibility of Irish immorality or even imperfection.

When in *Stephen Hero* Stephen's friend Madden (Davin in *A Portrait*), the ardent Nationalist peasant, tells him that " – We want an Irish Ireland" and then asks: " – And don't you think that every Irishman worthy of the name should be able to speak his native tongue? ... and don't you think that we as a race have a right to be free?" (*SH* 54, 56) – Stephen's response refuses to be lured by the circular logic of the binarity: " – It seems to me you do not care what banality a man expresses so long as he expresses it in Irish." When Madden argues that "I do not entirely agree with your modern notions. We want to have nothing of this English civilisation ... You want our peasants to ape the gross materialism of the Yorkshire peasant?" – Stephen refuses to engage in the essentializing of either culture as apes or angels: " – One would imagine the country was inhabited by cherubim" (*SH* 54). Rather than get sucked into a mirrored binarity, Stephen is willing to acknowledge the cultural relativism implicit in different cultures and multiple perspectives, as he later tells Cranly: "What we symbolise in black the Chinaman may symbolise in yellow: each has his own tradition. Greek beauty laughs at Coptic beauty and the American Indian derides them both" (*SH* 212; in *A Portrait* 208 he reiterates that "The Greek, the Turk, the Chinese, the Copt, the Hottentot ... all admire a different type of female beauty").

Stephen's young Nationalist friend Madden/Davin (based on Joyce's friend George Clancy), however, is trapped inside the powerful, binary logic of Celticism. In *A Portrait* Stephen describes Davin as "the young peasant worshipp[ing] the sorrowful legend of Ireland ... His nurse had taught him Irish and shaped his rude imagination by the broken lights of Irish myth ... [with] the attitude of a dullwitted loyal serf"; as a result, "Whatsoever of thought or of feeling came to him from England or by way of English culture his mind stood armed against in obedience to a password: and of the world that lay beyond England he knew only the foreign legion of France in which he spoke of serving" (*P* 181). In effect, such a closed system is trapped within the oscillation of an English/Irish dialectic, in which everything is still defined around Englishness.

Stephen at one point thinks of Davin affectionately as a "rude Firbolg mind" with a "delight in rude bodily skill – for Davin had sat at the feet of Michael Cusack, the Gael" (*P* 180). Davin is an athlete and a sports enthusiast, disciple of Michael Cusack, the real-life founder of the Gaelic Athletic Association (and model for the xenophobic Citizen in *Ulysses*), whose championing of Irish sport was a central force in the Celticist movement. At the Irish language classes in *Stephen Hero*, Cusack, "A very stout black-bearded citizen ... was a constant figure at these meetings" (*SH* 61), along with Madden/Davin "who was the captain of a club of hurley-players" as well as Arthur Griffith, "the editor of the weekly journal of the irreconcilable party" (*The United Irishman*). Stephen, who is not an athlete, perceives some relation between the movement's emphasis on sport/play and its liberationist ethos: "The liberty they desired for themselves was mainly a liberty of costume and vocabulary ... here he saw people playing at being free" (*SH* 62). Stephen cites as an example the case of Hungary, a nation which the Celticists glorify as a "long-suffering minority, entitled by every right of race and justice to a separate freedom," but which has managed to emancipate itself; "In emulation of that achievement bodies of young Gaels conflicted murderously in the Phoenix Park with whacking hurley-sticks" (*SH* 62). Stephen's ironic observation to Madden/Davin about such emulative play: " – I suppose these hurley matches and walking tours are preparations for the great event." Hurley, or hurling, the Irish Nationalist sport, is a very rough and brutal sport with similarities to football, rugby, hockey, and lacrosse; as Chester Anderson notes, "Hurley ... is still associated with Irish nationalism and the Irish language" (*P: Text* 524). In *A Portrait*, Stephen, after first quoting ironically from the Fenian drill book (" – Long pace, fianna! Right incline, fianna! Fianna, by numbers, salute, one, two!"), then comments to Davin/Madden about the relations between Fenian drills, revolutions, and hurley: " – When you make the next rebellion with hurleysticks ... and want the indispensable informer, tell me. I can find you a few in this college" (*P* 202).

Stephen goes on to deride the nationalist zealot Hughes, the law student with the barrister father: " – One of these days he will be a barrister, a Q.C., perhaps a judge – and yet he sneers at the Parliamentary Party because they take an oath of allegiance ... I do not quite follow the distinction you make between administering English law and administering English bullets: there is the same oath of allegiance for both professions." When Madden suggests that "Better be a barrister than a redcoat," the pacifist Stephen reminds him of the militaristic nature of hurley clubs: " – You consider the profession of arms a disreputable one. Why then have you Sarsfield Clubs, Hugh O'Neill Clubs, Red Hugh Clubs?" (*SH* 63; all named after legendary Irish warriors). The logic of a Celtic xenophobia constructed as a mirror image of English racial/national chauvinism results in such mirror images of aggressive, martial behavior (as was so even, say, with the York and Lancaster "teams" which Stephen's class in Clongowes had been divided into). As an older Stephen would again reflect later in *Ulysses*, listening to the bellicose sounds of the schoolboys' hockey game in "Nestor," there is a direct correlation between war/combat and the playing fields of Eton or Clongowes: "Jousts. Time shocked rebounds, shock by shock. Jousts, slush and uproar of battles, the frozen deathspew of the slain, a shout of spearspikes baited with men's bloodied guts" (*U* 2.316–8).

As Stephen later notes, "Renan's Jesus is a trifle Buddhistic but the fierce eaters and drinkers of the western world would never worship such a figure. Blood will have blood" (*SH* 190). These words of Stephen's bring to mind Joyce's review in 1903 of a book about Buddhism, in which his sympathy with Buddhist methods of non-aggression and pacifism is clear. After pointing out that "Five things are the five supreme evils for [Buddhists] – fire, water, storms, robbers, and rulers" (note that water, storms, and rulers are things that Stephen fears, too), Joyce goes on to characterize Western values as bellicose and bloodthirsty by contrast: "Our civilization, be-queathed to us by fierce adventurers, eaters of meat and hunters, is so full of hurry and combat, so busy about many things which perhaps are of no importance, that it cannot but see something feeble in a civilization which smiles as it refuses to make the battlefield the test of excellence" (*CW* 94). There is an echo in these thoughts of Stephen, whose only "arms" will be silence, exile, and cunning, and of Joyce, who would – even through two World Wars – steadily refuse to grant the battlefield any validity as a test of worth.

The narrowness of Celticist logic, based on the closed system of a binary, mirrored English/Irish dialectic, results in a narrow-minded provincialism which Joyce depicts in *Stephen Hero* and *A Portrait* as part of Stephen's critique of Celticist Irish Nationalism. When Stephen's mother admits to never having heard of Ibsen, Stephen takes the occasion to point out that "in Ireland people don't know much about what is going on out in Europe" (*SH* 84). When the President of the College, as the Censor, tries to suppress Stephen's paper on Ibsen, he admits (when questioned by Stephen) to never having read a word of Ibsen (*SH* 93). And the general response to Stephen's paper, when he does deliver it, is that it is "a reproduction of the decadent literary opinions of exhausted European capitals" (*SH* 102). Hughes's response to the paper is emblematic:

He declared in ringing Northern accents that the moral welfare of the Irish people was menaced by such theories. They wanted no foreign filth. Mr Daedalus might read what authors he liked, of course, but the Irish people had their own glorious literature where they could always find fresh ideals to spur them on to new patriotic endeavours. Mr Daedalus was himself a renegade from the Nationalist ranks: he professed cosmopolitism. But a man that was of all countries was of no country – you must have a nation before you have art.

(*SH* 103)

Stephen would certainly have agreed with part of Hughes's assessment, since, like Joyce, he was indeed a renegade from the Nationalist ranks and a professed cosmopolitist; for Joyce, it was in fact desirable to be of all countries rather than of a single country, to put art before nation rather than to render art subservient to nation as "The cracked lookingglass of a servant" (*U* 1.146). Responses like Hughes's, refusing to acknowledge other, more internationalist and cosmopolitan perspectives in favor of a narrow nationalistic one, are only a willed version of the provincialness of the ignorant Irish peasant, exemplified by that old Irish peasant's comment on hearing about things outside his ken, quoted (with slight variation) in both *Stephen Hero* and *A Portrait* – "Aw, there must be terrible quare craythurs at the latther ind of the world" (*SH* 243; *P* 251).

Stephen, as an artist seeking to create the "uncreated conscience" of the Irish race, realizes that it is with this old man, the personified figure of Irish provincial narrowness, that he must battle in seeking a spiritual liberation for Ireland that looks to a wider, internationalist perspective: "I fear him. I fear his redrimmed horny eyes. It is with him I must struggle all through this night till day come" (*P* 252). For as yet Ireland was only what Stephen calls "the afterthought of Europe" (*SH* 53: in Joyce's own notes on the corresponding manuscript page appear the words "Ireland – an afterthought of Europe"), physically and spiritually "at the farthest remove from the centre of European culture, marooned on an island in the ocean" (*SH* 194); and Ireland needs to become a part of Europe, to "take her place among the nations of the earth," not existing only in relation to England: as Joyce had articulated it, "a bilingual, republican, self-centred, and enterprising island with its own commercial fleet, and its own consuls in every port of the world" (*CW* 173). When Madden suggests to Stephen that the Irish have nothing to gain from the English literature and language, Stephen reminds him that "English is the medium for the Continent" (*SH* 54). As Robert Hand would say to Richard Rowan in *Exiles*: "If Ireland is to become a new Ireland she must first become European. And that is what you are here for, Richard. Some day we shall have to choose between England and Europe" (*E* 51). Choosing Europe and the internationalist perspective of a world community would allow Joyce and Ireland to break free from the binary operations of a closed system of English/Irish, Saxon/Celtic opposition, in which the rules have already been constructed always to favor the first of the two terms in each set of oppositions.

While Stephen appears to be, like Joyce, a pacifist and a cosmpolitist, it is also clear in these two texts that Stephen is not quite Joyce, but a "young man" with ideas and with rather arrogant pretensions to being an artist. This is perhaps clearer in *Stephen Hero* than in *A Portrait*, for the earlier work contains frequent qualifications (not yet revised/refined out of existence) of Stephen as a "perturbed young Celt" (*SH* 40) with an "ineradicable egoism" (*SH* 34) and a self-important need for the "flavour of the heroic" (*SH* 29), and so on. A pacifist who refuses to sign the Tsar's petition for universal peace, Stephen (like the younger Joyce) is prone to couch his serious arguments in arrogance and egotism: "I care nothing for these principles of nationalism ... My own mind is more interesting to me than the entire country" (*SH* 247–48).

The limitations of Stephen's attitudes towards his country are also tested by Joyce in these two texts by his two Nationalist friends, the characters Madden/Davin and MacCann ("McCann" in *Stephen Hero*), both of whom are treated relatively affectionately in the texts. For example, Madden accuses Stephen that "No West-Briton could speak worse of his countrymen" (*SH* 64). Especially probing are the conversations between Stephen and McCann, "a serious young feminist" (*SH* 39) modeled directly on Francis Skeffington, whom Joyce had called the cleverest man in University College, after himself (*JJ1*, 63).

In *A Portrait* the seemingly good-natured MacCann speaks quite frankly to Stephen: "Dedalus, you're an antisocial being, wrapped up in yourself. I'm not. I'm a democrat: and I'll work and act for social liberty and equality among all classes and sexes in the United States of the Europe of the future" (*P* 177). While Joyce shared Stephen's distrusts of Irish Nationalism, he might well have also agreed with MacCann's assessment of Stephen; and "equality among all classes and sexes in the United States of the Europe of the future" is not that different from the internationalist political agenda which Joyce would develop in the less demagogic medium of his subsequent fiction (and in his own beliefs), an agenda which would be presented in *Ulysses* through the utopian visions of Leopold Bloom. MacCann's blend of political idealism and pragmatism, while derided by Stephen, is an activist version of at least some of the pacifist and internationalist views which Joyce would try to promote through his fiction, especially *Ulysses* and *Finnegans Wake*:

MacCann began to speak with fluent energy of the Csar's rescript, of Stead, of general disarmament, arbitration in cases of international disputes, of the signs of the times, of the new humanity and the new gospel of life which would make it the business of the community to secure as cheaply as possible the greatest possible happiness of the greatest possible number ...
– Three cheers for universal brotherhood!

(*P* 196)

In *Ulysses* Leopold Bloom's pacifist/utopian visions of a universal brotherhood will be even more comically parodied and mocked than MacCann's are here by Stephen, without necessarily being rendered any less genuine or powerful.

MacCann jibes back at Stephen: "Minor poets, I suppose, are above such trivial questions as the question of universal peace" (*P* 197); even if Stephen was, Joyce was certainly not above such questions – for he would deal with the question of universal peace in his fiction for the rest of his life. But MacCann proceeds to comment good-naturedly: " – Dedalus, ... I believe you're a good fellow but you have yet to learn the dignity of altruism and the responsibility of the human individual" (*P* 199; also *SH* 52). This observation is not that different from Stephen's mother's prayer at the end of *A Portrait* that he "may learn ... what the heart is and what it feels" (*P* 252), a wish that Stephen takes seriously enough that he will later struggle over his mother's words and meaning throughout *Ulysses*. It is something that Joyce may well have expected the reader to agree with, too.

Likewise, the much simpler-minded Nationalist Davin/Madden, whom Stephen treats most affectionately among his university companions, urges Stephen to "Try to be one of us ... In your heart you are an Irishman but your pride is too powerful" (*P* 203) – another observation that the reader (and Joyce himself) might wish to agree with. Speaking of Irish patriots like Tone and Parnell (who were, after all, heroes of Stephen and of Joyce, too), Davin observes that "They died for their ideals, Stevie ... Our day will come yet, believe me" (*P* 203). The poignant irony of Davin's comment – in a quite different retrospective coloring – must have given Joyce pause in later life: for, as with Tone and Parnell, their day would indeed come to die for their ideals. Among Joyce's patriot friends, both MacCann and Davin/Madden would become Irish martyrs: MacCann/Skeffington would be killed by the British in the Easter Rebellion (1916 – the same year *A Portrait* was published), and George Clancy (Davin/Madden), after becoming mayor of Limerick, would be murdered in his own house and in front of his family by the English Black and Tans (see editor's notes in *P: Text* 522–23). As Joyce had predicted, the hurleystick rebellions would prove no match for British military power, giving birth instead only to Yeats's "terrible beauty."

In chapter v of *A Portrait*, Stephen's rejection of Irish Nationalism and his decision to go abroad to Europe are paralleled by his simultaneous rejection of "E. C.," the young lady whom he is nevertheless very clearly attracted to. The connections between this personal/romantic denial and his artistic/political stance are suggested more clearly in the earlier *Stephen Hero*, where "Emma Clery" is depicted (and named) much more fully. Stephen first meets Emma at the nationalistic Daniels household (based on the Sheehy family in Joyce's own youth):

A dark full-figured girl was standing before him ... he found out that she was studying in the same college with the Miss Daniels and that she always signed her name in Irish. She said Stephen should learn Irish too and join the League. A young man of the company ... spoke with her across Stephen addressing her familiarly by her Irish name. Stephen therefore spoke very formally and always addressed her as "Miss Clery." She seemed on her part to include him in the general scheme of her nationalising charm.

(*SH* 46)

As the dark temptress whose "nationalising charm" invites him to "learn Irish too and join the League," Emma is here portrayed much more clearly than in *A Portrait* as a feminine embodiment of Irish Nationalism, whose feminine lures clearly attract Stephen (who goes on immediately to enroll in a Gaelic class). Her position as an emblem of the Irish Nationalist cause, hailing Stephen to her/its side, clarifies an important dimension to her role as the "Temptress" of the Villanelle and to the (otherwise murky and misogynistic) reasons behind Stephen's portrayal of her in *A Portrait*'s chapter v as the dark embodiment of the "batlike race" of Ireland which Stephen needs to reject and leave behind.

Thus, Emma's interests in Stephen as a Nationalist convert also connect her with the West of Ireland (and with the Celticist enthusiasm of Miss Ivors in "The Dead"), as he learns at one point that "Emma had gone away to the Isles of Aran with a Gaelic party" (*SH* 162). In *A Portrait* Stephen recalls Davin's story about his long walk back after a hurling match (in the countryside near Limerick) when "there was a mass meeting that same day over in Castletownroche" (presumably a Land League agitation meeting); a half-dressed peasant woman in a lonely farmhouse along the road offered Davin a glass of milk and invited him to stay the night with her. Stephen goes on to think of this woman as "a type of her race and his own, a batlike soul waking to the consciousness of itself in darkness and secrecy and loneliness and, through the eyes and voice and gesture of a woman without guile, calling the stranger to her bed" (*P* 183). At that moment Stephen is accosted by a young girl trying to sell him flowers: "He left her quickly, fearing that her intimacy might turn to gibing and wishing to be out of the way before she offered her ware to another, a tourist from England or a student of Trinity" (*P* 184). Interestingly, the images of these three figures – Emma, the half-dressed woman offering Davin milk, and the flowergirl – combine in chapter v with the old milkwoman in the first episode of *Ulysses* into a feminized embodiment, for Stephen, of Ireland and her provincialness. The flowergirl will instead sell her wares to "a tourist from England or a student of Trinity" – just as the old milkwoman will play up to Haines and Mulligan, an English tourist and a Trinity medical student, her imperialist and shoneen exploiters (Trinity as the Royal University for the ruling classes), and not recognize in Stephen the true conscience of her race: "She bows her old head to a voice that speaks to her loudly ... me she slights" (*U* 1.418–19). So also the half-dressed peasant woman offers her milk and her self to strangers. Stephen thinks of Emma similarly as a representation of Ireland, unable to recognize in him (rather than in the Celticist enthusiasts) her own personal alternative and liberation – and so it is she who finally embodies for Stephen the seductive, bloodsucking, batlike soul of Ireland and its race:

> perhaps the secret of her race lay behind those dark eyes … a batlike soul waking to the consciousness of itself … [with] a priested peasant, with a brother a policeman in Dublin … To him she would unveil her soul's shy nakedness, to one who was but schooled in the discharging of a formal rite rather than to him, a priest of eternal imagination, transmuting the daily bread of experience into the radiant body of everliving life.
>
> *(P 221)*

Emma's familiarity with the young priest (Father Moran) and with her policeman brother suggests to Stephen an emblematic collusion of the Irish race with the religious and secular institutions that constitute the authorities and hierarchies that oppress it (and him); as Ireland embodied, she seems to him more willing to unveil her body and sell her soul to those authorities and strangers who would exploit her, than to recognize in Stephen the artist/priest of her imagination seeking to liberate her – favoring, like the flowergirl or old milkwoman, her exploiters rather than her artists. To Stephen, justly or not, Emma *is* Hibernia (he is of course misogynistically essentializing Irish womanhood with the pejorative image of a "batlike soul"); significantly, while Stephen desires her, he feels that he must scorn and leave her. In such a context and in view of Stephen's mythopoetic mentality, his rejection of Emma (after imaginatively functioning her as the seductive lure of Ireland and Irish Nationalism) seems somewhat more comprehensible; his leaving Ireland for Europe not only parallels his rejection of Emma, but in a sense they are the very same act, since she has grown to represent to Stephen the very Irish Nationalist mind-set he must put aside.

Thinking of Emma as someone who "could love some clean athlete who washed himself every morning to the waist and had black hair on his chest" *(P 234)* but who would not love a scruffy but independent young artist, Stephen arrogantly wonders how he might be able to liberate the conscience of the Irish race: "How could he hit their conscience or how cast his shadow over the imaginations of their daughters, before their squires begat upon them, that they might breed a race less ignoble than their own?" *(P 238)*. While

Stephen's "ineradicable egoism" might declare its *non serviam* in arrogant ways, the novel portrays Stephen as trying to learn how to liberate Ireland in a new and different way, trying to be an Irish patriot through means other than a provincial Nationalism and armed rebellion, through his art and a revolution of the word.[14]

Indeed, we learn that Stephen's artistic calling had its first roots in the politics of national liberation. Immediately after the highly-charged political discussion at the Christmas dinner scene, culminating in Mr. Casey's and Simon Dedalus's tears over "Poor Parnell! My dead king!" (*P* 39), young Stephen, we learn, had tried to write his first poem: "sitting at his table in Bray the morning after the discussion at the Christmas dinner table, trying to write a poem about Parnell on the back of one of his father's second moiety notices" (*P* 71; Joyce himself had as a young boy written a first poem about Parnell, titled "Et Tu, Healy"). Similarly, his understandings of politics ("He wondered if they were arguing at home about that. That was called politics" [16]) were conceived in concert with his aesthetic appreciation of visual beauty: colors were associated with both beauty and political factions – maroon and green for Davitt and Parnell; York and Lancaster as symbolised by white and red roses. Stephen, significantly, is on the York side of his Clongowes class – that is, on the Irish side (the Irish had backed York against Lancaster); but he wonders: "White roses and red roses: those were beautiful colours to think of ... But you could not have a green rose. But perhaps somewhere in the world you could" (*P* 12). Young Stephen's aesthetic musings here have suggestive political implications – since red and white are the colors of England, can one even have a "green rose" "perhaps somewhere in the world"? – in terms of the very possibility of Irish nationhood within the world community, independent of the colors of England.

As a young, fledgling artist, Stephen passes his leisure time "in the company of subversive writers whose gibes and violence of speech set up a ferment in his brain" (*P* 78). Joyce provides Stephen – in the latter's growing sense of himself as a revolutionary of the word, searching for national liberation through the conscience of his race – with a personal lineage of Irish patriots very much like Joyce's own. Not only is Stephen's father a former disciple of Parnell's who bequeaths his nationalistic fervor to his son (recall not only the Christmas dinner but memories such as Simon taking Stephen to the laying of a stone memorial to Wolfe Tone on Grafton Street [*P* 184]), but Mr. Casey (based on the Joyce family friend John Kelly) is a patriot who got "three cramped fingers making a birthday present for Queen Victoria" (*P* 28). As Ellmann explains: "Kelly was in prison several times for Land League agitation, and John Joyce regularly invited him to recuperate from imprisonment ... at the house in Bray. In jail three fingers of his left hand had become permanetly cramped from picking oakum, and he would tell the children that they had become so while he was making a birthday present for Queen Victoria" (*JJI*, 24). Stephen himself is descended from a line of patriots: "his father had told him that ... his granduncle had presented an address to the liberator there fifty years before" (*P* 26); Joyce's own grand-uncle was John O'Connell, father of William O'Connell ("Uncle Charles" in *A Portrait*) and a distant relative of Daniel O'Connell, the Liberator who successfully repealed the Act of Union. On his own side of the family, Simon Dedalus can point to the portrait of his grandfather on the wall: "Do you see that old chap up there, John? ... He was a good Irishman when there was no money in the job. He was condemned to death as a whiteboy" (*P* 38). Ellmann confirms that there was such a personage in the Joyce family, part of the "ancient tribe of the Joyces" (*CW* 197): "The great-grandfather bequeathed a zeal for nationalism ... in the life of the writer. As a young man this Ur-James Joyce joined the 'White-boys,' or Catholic agitators against landlords, and was condemned to death, though the sentence was not carried out" (*JJI*, 10).

In *Exiles*, the Irish journalist Robert Hand considers Richard Rowan – an exiled Irish writer based on Joyce himself – a patriot and calls him "The descendant of Archibald Hamilton Rowan" (*E* 53), although Rowan himself denies the lineage. In *A Portrait*, young Stephen at Clongowes had "wondered from which window Hamilton Rowan had thrown his hat on the haha" (*P* 10). The Irish patriot Hamilton Rowan was a friend of Wolfe Tone who had escaped to Clongowes Castle after being convicted in 1794 for sedition: "He shut its door just as the soldiers were shooting, so that their bullets entered the door; then he threw his hat on the haha [a sunken hedge or wall] as a decoy, and let himself through a secret door into a tower room. His pursuers were fooled, thinking he had left, and he was able afterwards to make good his escape to France" (*JJI*, 29). While, like Richard Rowan, Stephen is not related to Hamilton Rowan, his first youthful success at defying oppressive authority is linked to Rowan's own heroism at Clongowes, for, as he courageously walks towards the rector's quarters after the unjust pandybatting by Father Dolan, we are told that "He came out on the landing above the entrance hall and looked about him. That was where Hamilton Rowan had passed and the marks of the soldiers' slugs were there" (*P* 56) – allying Stephen's own fledgling act of resistance against injustice with the marks of heroic, patriotic resistance to imperial tyranny and authority.

By the time he is at University College, Stephen has realized that national zeal and heroism for him would take place not through physical combat but in a different arena of revolutionary activism, that of spiritual and artistic liberation: as he tells Madden in *Stephen Hero* about his paper on Ibsen (titled significantly "Art and Life"), "This is the first of my explosives" (*SH* 81). Stephen – whose weapons are neither bombs nor hurleysticks,[15] but the arms of his literary art (silence, exile, and most of all cunning) – certainly runs the risk of an apolitical aestheticism (such as Joyce has been accused of) in his concerns with an Aristotelian/Thomistic aesthetic theory based on "nominal definitions, essential definitions" (*P* 178), as he chooses to turn away from the political discussion with Davin (in which he has rejected Ireland as "the old sow that eats her farrow" [*P* 203]) to matters of aesthetics with Lynch, to the definitions and logocentrism of an essentialist *claritas*: "Aristotle has not defined pity and terror. I have" (*P* 204; this danger will be the topic of chapter 9). But at least Stephen, in doing so, is aware that, in his attempt to fashion a spiritual liberation for his "race," he must get out of the Celticist vicious cycle, in which a provincial Ireland is narrowly locked in an inescapable struggle with England within a closed binary system:

> 3 April: Met Davin at the cigar shop ... He was in a black sweater and had a hurleystick. Asked me was it true I was going away and why. Told him the shortest way to Tara was *via* Holyhead.
>
> (*P* 250)

Stephen's cryptic response to Davin's question suggests his conviction that the road to Irish freedom (the traditional Irish seat at Tara) was to be found not through the hurleystick of Irish Nationalism carried by Davin, but via Holyhead, the closest port outside Ireland on the way to the Continent. It is there that Stephen hopes to "discover the mode of life or of art whereby [his] spirit could express itself in unfettered freedom" (*P* 246) – so as "to forge in the smithy of my soul the uncreated conscience of my race" (*P* 253).

Dubliners: colonialist symptomatics

3

Dubliners: The exoticized and Orientalized Other

Joyce claimed that "My intention [in *Dubliners*] was to write a chapter of the moral history of my country," and that in so doing "I have taken the first step towards the spiritual liberation of my country" (Letters to Constantine Curran, August 1904, and Grant Richards, May 20, 1906). If an *intentional/authorial* reading of *Dubliners* thus demands a moral history of the city as "the centre of paralysis" (Letter to Grant Richards, May 5, 1906), the stories in *Dubliners* nevertheless provide us with a *symptomatic* reading of the cultural and political histories and tensions of Dublin at the turn of the century – as we shall see repeatedly in looking at these stories. One cultural symptom of the desire for spiritual liberation manifested itself in the various and deeply embedded cultural representations and encodings of such desire within the appropriated images of an exotic Other, especially the Orient; these are the cultural *idées reçues* best depicted by Edward Said's compelling deconstruction of "Orientalism" as "the corporate institution for dealing with the Orient ... Orientalism as a Western style for dominating, restructuring, and having authority over the Orient" (*Orientalism*, 3).

A crucial aspect of Orientalism is that the Orient and the exotic other provide for the European self both a *topos* and a *tropos* for "spiritual liberation," for imagined rebellion, freedom, escape, and license (even licentiousness) – as a hidden self that was purportedly other, and which resisted the sociopolitical encodings of a known and repressive cultural system and hegemony, allowing for an exploration (both in geographic actuality and in the mind's eye) of the unknown and mysterious heart of darkness: as Said notes further, "European culture gained in strength and identity by setting itself off against the Orient as a sort of surrogate and even

77

underground self" (3). As Homi Bhabha points out: "[Orientalism] is, on the one hand, a topic of learning, discovery, practice; on the other, it is the site of dreams, images, fantasies, myths, obsessions and requirements" ("Difference," 199); a discipline of learning and power, on the one hand, but also a fantasy of the Other. The Orient and the racialized exotic Other thus became a culturally constructed repository (what V. G. Kiernan called "Europe's collective day-dream of the Orient" [Said, *Orientalism*, 52]) for the occidental self's drive for difference, mystery, subversion, irrationality, and otherness: "Orientalism was ultimately a political vision of reality whose structure promoted the difference between the familiar (Europe, the West, 'us') and the strange (the Orient, the East, 'them')" (Said, *Orientalism*, 43). Joyce's texts, as we shall see, are at once deeply interwoven with received representations of the romance of the Orient, of the Orient/Other/Exotic as a site of imaginative "othering" – as well as simultaneously participating in an evolving, genetic scrutiny and critique of such processes of othering and essentializing.

It should be clear at this point that this chapter has introduced a concept of otherness and of the "other" that varies somewhat from, but is also fundamentally related to and dependent on, the idea of the "other" explored in the previous chapter. That chapter had analyzed the other as the constructed product of an imagined and absolute *difference* from the self, a discursive repository of all that is repugnant to the self, and whose very presence *within* the self is denied and repressed in order to construct the self's own self-image and subjectivity; such a process repeatedly figures the other as primitive, barbaric, bestial, sexually rapacious, stupid, and so on – in the manner in which the English constructed and represented the Irish (as well as other "races") during the nineteenth century. The current chapter elaborates a somewhat different "other" – that product of unacknowledged, unauthorized *desire* (beyond the accep-table bounds of the culture's norms): not so much what the self cannot acknowledge as what it cannot have. Thus, for example, the Orientalized Other becomes the imagined locus for the exotic, voluptuousness, *jouissance*, excess, sexual license, and so on. These two versions of otherness, while obviously differing, are not at all at odds, but merely respond to the various discursive needs of the culture. Since the imagined other is always a construction of the self, it is always *different*, always a result of (and a response to) the specific situation of the imagining subject or self (or culture) that is producing it. Each of these constructions (otherness as difference, otherness as desire) serves different needs within the cultural discourse, but they are not fully distinct from each other; rather, they not only reinforce each other but – both being based on an imagined difference – repeatedly collapse into each other; both are products of a racist ideology and both are central to the discourses of imperialism. Indeed, a main focus in this chapter is to suggest how – in the specific Irish case as represented in *Dubliners* – each of these versions of otherness is always already contaminated by and dependent on the other one. As Said has amply demonstrated, not only had Orientalism "kept intact the separateness of the Orient, its eccentricity, its backwardness" within the West's "division of races into advanced and backward ... or European–Aryan and Oriental–African" (*Orientalism*, 206), but, furthermore, such a division of absolute difference went cheek by jowl with the cultural imagining that constructed the Orient as the arena of untold *luxe et volupté*. It is these connections, and their implications, that the current chapter pursues.

For the romantic young narrators in the opening stories of *Dubliners*, the Orient stands for what it had already represented to Schlegel in 1800: "It is in the Orient that we must search for the highest Romanticism"; thus, as a place of romantic exoticism and licentiousness, it becomes, in Said's words, "a living tableau of queerness" (*Orientalism*, 103). Each of these imaginative young narrators (or arguably the same narrator for the first three stories) desires for escape (both literal and spiritual), in each case conjuring an exoticized representation of otherness as the spiritually liberating alternative to a stifling paralysis; but in each case the conjured alternative also evokes disillusion. Joyce certainly seems to be suggesting, as most commentators have argued, that the external environment and its hemiplegia/paralysis crush individual romantic sensibilities, encouraging even the more sensitive Irish children to accept and internalize paralysis. But the stories themselves also further dramatize the revelation, as we shall see, that it is in part also the inherent "queerness" of the exoticized alternative itself which terrifies and disillusions. For, as Robert Young puts it in *White Mythologies*, "Orientalism represents the West's own internal dislocation, misrepresented as an external dualism between East and West" (140).

For the sensitive and the imaginative, the exotic Other is an alternative escape into the regions of the uncanny, the mysterious, the imagination. One key into this otherworld is language, as the young narrator in "The Sisters" intuits in his nightly intonation (much like the "awesome holy" of the Latin Catholic liturgy) of the exotic-sounding words *paralysis, gnomon,* and *simony* – for they conjure and evince a gothic fascination, an attraction/repulsion for both the beauty and the darkness of the mysterious unknown, in a projection of fearful symmetry: "But now it sounded to me like the name of some maleficent and sinful being. It filled me with fear, and yet I longed to be nearer to it and to look upon its deadly work" (*D* 9).

The young boy chafes at the claustrophobic paralysis of a life enclosed within the limited confines of such types as Old Cotter (the "tiresome old red-nosed imbecile"), the boy's uncle and aunts, and Father Flynn's ignorant sisters. His uncle's admonition to "Let him learn to box his corner. That's what I'm always saying to that Rosicrucian there: take exercise" (*D* 11) urges him towards a life of cultural normalcy defined both by the prescribed cultural male expectations (exercise/fitness, boxing, machismo) and by the unconscious phenomenology of enclosure, entrapment, and paralysis ("cornered" in a "box" or coffin). In contrast lurks the socially undesirable danger of queerness and otherness: the Rosicrucian sect as the realm of the mysterious, the mystical, the Oriental. As Robert Scholes and A. Walton Litz note, this mystical order was founded by Father Rosenkreuz: "a legendary figure who was reputed to have found the secret wisdom of the East while on a pilgrimage in the 15th century. By extension, the term became a slang description of anyone given to dreamy or unwordly behavior. The study of Roscrucianism and other esoteric systems was popular with Dublin intellectuals at the turn of the century" (*D: Text*, 464).

If the "Rosicrucian" boy is "given to dreamy or unworldly behavior," it is perhaps because Father Flynn had provided for the boy an outlet from the drabness of his daily life through the incantatory mystery of words and rituals involved in such things as Latin, stories about the catacombs, the "complex and mysterious" (*D* 13) rituals of the Church, the sacredness of the Eucharist, and so on. These are, of course, also the realms of literature, the imagination, the visionary, and dreams. Now that the old priest is dead, the boy's window of escape into the irrational Other seems gone – except perhaps through dreams and the visionary. Appropriately enough, his dream of Father Flynn evokes an ambivalent site of fearful symmetry: "I felt my soul receding into some pleasant and vicious region" (*D* 11). This pleasant and vicious region is at once the realm of the imagination/Other and the Orient itself (Said and others have documented how the Orient has been depicted by the West as simultaneously a picture of indescribable seductiveness and of unspeakable degradation), for the two become the same in the boy's mind: "[I] tried to remember what had happened afterwards in the dream. I remembered that I had noticed long velvet curtains and a swinging lamp of antique fashion. I felt that I had been very far away, in some land where the customs were strange – in Persia, I thought" (*D* 13–14). This imagined Persia of the mind is also the Orientalized and feminized self of the Western imagination (but named/repressed as "other"). The velvet curtains (suggestive of veils, purdah, and harems) and antique swinging lamps (suggestive of incense, Aladdin's lamp, and the Arabian tales) are but slight hints that the young boy has already assimilated the collective cultural discourse of the East – a discourse much more fully developed later in the mind of the boy in "Araby." But this dream of Persia as the metaphysical site for the "pleasant and vicious region" of the imagination is only the first of many instances in Joyce's works of the repeated investment of one's dreams with the exoticism of the Orient – for this Persian dream is a dream of an entire culture ("Europe's collective day-dream of the Orient") which we will see played out later on in the minds of the boy in Araby, in Stephen Dedalus and Leopold Bloom's shared dream of the previous night in *Ulysses*, in Molly Bloom's streaming of consciousness, and in the collective unconscious of the Wakean dreambook.

If the East reflects here a psychic need to escape (in Jungian terms, to search for the *anima*, one's other half or self), it is a drive/ desire occasioned by a cultural lack: a search for a spiritual life and liberation somewhere out there, by the individual soul enclosed in an Irish labyrinth entrapping and suffocating it. But within the very representation of this fearful symmetry is encoded a binary opposition which – like the Westernized construction of Orientalism itself (so heavily fraught with sexual licentiousness and degeneracy) – pre-structures a hierarchical relationship that always already functions the Oriental as Other (defined not in terms of its own actual specificities but only in terms of, and in contrast to, the Self) and thus as inferior and fearsome.[1] For that dream of Persian escape, the lure of the distant music of dulcimers and the smells of incense, is at once pleasant and vicious: at once the desired realm of the imaginary, and the fearful realm of untold perversion and corruption; at once beauty and strangeness.[2] The boy has internalized both the cultural construction of the Orient as Desire and its corollary construction as degeneracy/evil: for the exotic world of Father Flynn and of the East is also construed by the culture as the world of corruption and perversion ("there was something queer ... there was something uncanny about him," the boy is told [D 10]). This prescription results in the boy's dream imagining spittle on Father Flynn's lips while the priest's grey face wishes "to confess something"; in the "crime" of the broken chalice and "the special odour of corruption" and disease which also seems to hang around the old priest; and finally in madness, as the priest is pictured "sitting up by himself in the dark in his confession-box, wide-awake and laughing softly to himself" (D 18). In the end, the Western imagination's construction of the Orient carries within its binary opposition the inevitable rejection of the Other for seeming unacceptably different, marginal, even mad; such "Rosicrucian" behavior can only be interpreted by the culture and finally by the boy himself as "something gone wrong with him." So long as the Other only exists as a *trope* (rather than a literal *site*), as an essentialized amalgam of indescribable (literally unrepresentable) beauty and unspeakable (literally unimaginable) degeneracy, what Said calls a "tableau of queerness" – that is, so long as it only exists as Other, as the definition of absence/lack in contrast to the Self's presence – it is already caught in a binary opposition that (always already) contains within itself the seeds of its own rejection as abnormal, marginal, unacceptable, or corrupt. For the Orient as a site of desire reflects a deep and systemic ambivalence towards, in Homi Bhabha's words, "that 'otherness' which is at once an object of desire and derision" ("The Other Question," 19).

This point is further underscored in the collection's second story, "An Encounter" – a story of childhood experience that on the surface would seem to have no relevance to a study of race or Orientalism. But it is a story of thwarted escape fashioned along some of the same parameters as its more obviously relevant neighbors, "The Sisters" and "Araby." The young boy who narrates is a *reader* – and reading, especially for those who can't literally or physically travel or escape, functions as a mode of mental voyaging and exploration through the imagination – just as, conversely, Orientalism involves an exploration/colonization of foreign lands through the mental faculties of imagination and desire: "I wanted real adventures to happen to myself. But real adventures, I reflected, do not happen to people who remain at home; they must be sought abroad" (*D* 21). The young narrator is the first of Joyce's many characters, who, like Joyce himself, wishes for a literal escape from the paralysis of the Irish labyrinth through "exile" to a foreign land. Two stories later, Eveline will face that very alternative as a *real* possibility.

For this young boy, however, the escape can still only be achieved through the imagination, via the mediation of texts. What this boy reads is escapist literature from the popular boys' magazines: "It was Joe Dillon who introduced the Wild West to us. He had a little library made up of old numbers of *The Union Jack, Pluck*, and *The Halfpenny Marvel*. Every evening after school we met in his back garden and arranged Indian battles" (*D* 19). To an Irish boy, Indians in the Wild West and their alien languages ("– Ya! yaka, yaka, yaka!") represent – like the words *gnomon* and *simony* and the Orientalized images of Persia – an alien and exotic mystery, an Otherness to escape to away from one's own drab life, an Otherness which boys like the narrator and his buddy Mahony were inducted into by an older boy named Joe Dillon. "Everyone was incredulous when it was reported that he had a vocation for the priesthood. Nevertheless it was true" (*D* 19). The cruel irony of the surprise here is a telling foreshadowing of what happens even to the most independent and imaginative boys, like Joe Dillon: his rebellious, independent instincts get crushed, and he eventually becomes a priest, serving the imperium of Rome. Joe Dillon stands as a cautionary tale about how co-option and acquiescence to the hegemonic imperiums are already encoded within even the seemingly independent individual subjectivity, a perhaps inevitable paralysis already foreshadowed (as we saw) in "The Sisters" by the young boy's (and the culture's) construction of the Other as inescapably degenerate and deviant.

But Joe Dillon's legacy to the younger boys is, as we learn, "a spirit of unruliness" (*D* 20). This striking formulation stands in direct opposition to paralysis, for "unruliness" suggests motion, energy, activity, insurgency: defiance of rule and order, in rebellious opposition to paralyzed conformity and hierarchical rigor; the spirit of anarchy and the Bakhtinian carnivalesque (what Stephen Dedalus would call in *A Portrait* "the misrule and confusion of my father's house"), that liberating spirit that suspends the rule of authority and under the aegis of which people can slough off their hierarchical preconceptions and biases. As the young narrator says about this spirit of unruliness, "under its influence differences of culture and constitution were waived" (*D* 20): this spirit is a decentering or destabilizing of traditional order and authority, of rule and ruliness, which allows for differences of culture and constitution to be waived and suspended, for people to accept each other as separate and different and free, and not as hierarchically overdetermined. Bakhtin could not have put it better.

As a "reluctant Indian," the young boy admits that "The adventures related in the literature of the Wild West were remote from my nature but, at least, they opened the doors of escape" (*D* 20). A cultural irony layered behind the young boys' indulging their spirit of unruliness by playing at being Indians in the Wild West, by "othering" the exotic Indians, is a European history of cultural analogies between the Indians and the Irish in which the Irish themselves were functioned as the Indian/Oriental Other. As Luke Gibbons has demonstrated (see also chapter 2, on the racialization of Irishness), "This type of comparison between the subject populations of both colonies [America and Ireland] established a network of affinities that was to recur in descriptions of both the Irish and the Indians" ("Race Against Time," 98) from the seventeenth century to the present. The Irish were represented as similar to native American Indians in terms of a range of customs, personal habits, physical features, primitive wildness and resistance to civilizing. This last feature suggests an independence and subversion of the structures of authority and conformity which especially appeals to the young boys in their identification with the exotic Indians and in their consequent "othering" of their own selves, opening up "the doors of escape."

Reading, imagination, and the spirit of unruliness result in a desire to escape; the counter-forces here are the structures of authority and rule/ruliness, which try to impose order and conformity and thus stifle the imagination. As Father Butler, their schoolteacher, says upon discovering the boys reading these Wild West stories: "– What is this rubbish? he said. *The Apache Chief!* Is this what you read instead of studying your Roman History? Let me not find any more of this wretched stuff in this college. The man who wrote it, I suppose, was some wretched scribbler that writes these things for a drink. I'm surprised at boys like you, educated, reading such stuff" (*D* 20). In strikingly emblematic and symptomatic poles, stories about rebellious native warriors (such as Geronimo, the Apache chief) are deemed inappropriate and uncanonical, in direct contradistinction to the prescribed canon for young schoolboys, exemplified here by Roman history (such as Caesar's *Gallic Wars*) as the model text of a Eurocentric Western academic imperium. Just as Joyce's own works would for decades be considered "rubbish" and "wretched stuff" concocted by "some wretched scribbler that writes these things for a drink," vulgar and unfit for consumption by a civilized and "educated" culture, so also they embody a spirit of unruliness which has both appealed to the subversive reading imagination and been seen as a threat by the institutions of both state and academy. (Unfortunately, unlike Joyce's now-canonical texts, tales by and about Indians are all too often still relegated to a marginalized space beyond the canonical pale.)

Under such strict cultural governance, the boys are driven from culture to anarchy for their intellectual stimulation and escape: "I began to hunger again for wild sensations, for the escape which those chronicles of disorder alone seemed to offer me" (*D* 21). "Chronicles of disorder" is another memorable phrase which forecasts Stephen Dedalus's later choice of "the misrule and confusion of his father's house" (the Dedalus household; and the world: Our Father's house) over the regulated life of the Jesuit "order" (as opposed to "disorder" and the subversive chaos of the real world).[3] In a sense, one might well argue that all of Joyce's works manifest the "spirit of unruliness" and "chronicles of disorder." Notice how even at the verbal and linguistic level, Joyce's works (especially but not only *Finnegans Wake*) reflect that spirit: the pun, the word play, the portmanteau word – as play, as excess of signification, as doubleness/ambiguity and supplementarity – decenter the authority of a unitary, essentializing signification. Joyce's language evinces a progressive movement towards linguistic anarchy, defying wholeness and presence and the authority invested in a unified subject. Thus the Joycean text has proved itself a hospitable field of play for poststructuralist theorists, as a model of *différance*, of linguistic rioting against the authorized unitary subject within a continuous process of deferring, crossing out, and reconstructing meaning.

Searching for adventures like those in the "chronicles of disorder" in their reading, the boys play hooky, "a day's miching" (*D* 21). Significantly, they go to the docks and look at the sea and the big ships – both of which repeatedly in *Dubliners* evoke the potential of escape into an alien other: "Mahony said it would be right skit to run away to sea on one of those big ships and even I, looking at the high masts, saw, or imagined, the geography which had been scantily dosed to me at school gradually taking substance under my eyes. School and home seemed to recede from us and their influences upon us seemed to wane" (D 23).

But their day of escape is neither particularly successful nor exciting. Instead, they end up meeting a seedy man dressed in green, carrying a stick. At first he seems appealing to the narrator, for he seems liberal, sensitive, and well-read, praising the poetry and novels of romance/adventure by such as Scott and Lytton. He seems to understand love, speaking about the soft nice hair and hands of girls. But then he walks away for a few minutes – and presumably masturbates (according to Joyce's letters to Stanislaus). When he returns, his former sensitivity about love and desire, and his seeming affection for girls with "nice white hands" and "beautiful soft hair," have been replaced by "a compulsive fantasy about the whipping of boys" (Senn, "An Encounter," 30), building up to a verbal-sadistic crescendo: "he would give him such a whipping as no boy ever got in this world ... He described to me how he would whip such a boy as if he were unfolding some elaborate mystery. He would love that, he said, better than anything in this world" (D 27).

As Fritz Senn writes: "Here love has been turned, *per-verted* [literally 'turned around'] into its opposite. Since love is a door of escape from isolation [and from, one might add, paralysis], a vitalizing contact with another being, the closing of this door is especially pathetic. This man, too, was probably stirred in his youth by the spirit of unruliness. Now he belongs to those who are ranged against it: 'When a boy was rough and *unruly* there was nothing would do him any good but a good sound whipping' [27]" (Senn, "An Encounter," 30–31; my emphasis). Love, desire, and the search for the other are all unruly activities that break bounds and participate in a spirit/chronicle of disorder; but finally the strange man seems aligned with the spirit of rule and conformity. The queer old josser seems, finally, an even more dramatic and pathetic example of capitulating to a systemic conformity than Joe Dillon, who became a priest; of the eventual and seemingly inescapable stifling of imagination and the spirit of unruliness, a per-version of the spirit of carnivalesque liberality, turned around eventually into a sadistic version of authoritarian rule and conformity. As such, this man with green eyes and green clothes becomes almost a figure for Irish adulthood, perverting the rambunctious fancy and imagination of youth (traits they, adults, apparently also once had but lost) into decadence and paralysis.

The story's title perhaps suggests that the encounter with adventure is also a child's first encounter with perversion, with the discovery that mystery and adventure can also be tinged with decadence and corruption – the wages, as it were, of the spirit of unruliness and disorder. Consequently the young boy is disillusioned, and finds himself at the end happy and relieved to return to the good-old-boy normalcy of his less imaginative friend Mahony. But any positing of an enabling epiphany here is very ambiguous and troubled. To begin with, as with "The Sisters," the window of escape into the mysterious Other ends up seemingly inevitably stained with decadence and evil: the aura of disease and corruption hovering around Father Flynn now erupts in "The Encounter" as overt action. However, as with "The Sisters," that disillusion is already prescribed and inscribed into a binary system of othering/Orientalizing that posits disorder, unruliness, and otherness as absences which exist only in terms of their opposites: thus, the experience of the queer old josser cannot be accepted or interpreted by the boy as simply something unusual or strange and nothing more – that is, as a mark of heterogeneous difference within a spectrum of possibilities and multiple others – but can only be viewed as the inevitable other term (within a binary opposition) to the authorized Self and hegemonic authority from which he is wishing to escape. Thus, as a result of this encounter, the entire search for adventure and desiring for the Other becomes invested and tainted with such "corruption" – for in such a system the Other can only exist in a homogenized and essentialized form that is defined as the unauthorized, the licentiously unlicensed, the unacceptable. The boy is thus driven by the fearful half of the "fearful symmetry" (fearful of evil and perversion) to interpret his own urge to break boundaries, his own desire to search for otherness, as dangerous and evil – instead of allowing that his own drives might take their own potentially different and heterogeneous forms, different from either Father Butler or the queer old josser and not allied to either one. Since the latter possibility does not exist in the created binary system of Self and Other (in which one term is always valorized over the other; in which the Other is already pre-inscribed with the degeneracy that is the repressed and expelled part of the Self labeled "Other"), our protagonist is driven by fear of the josser/Other back to the safety of the known and canonized. In discovering that this search for adventure and escape from Father Butler results instead in an encounter with a perverted version of authority even worse than Father Butler, a queer old josser carrying a whipping stick – like an unauthorized version of *A Portrait*'s Father Dolan who whips Stephen Dedalus with his pandybat and is young Stephen's personal bugaboo for institutional, conventional, and religious patriarchal authority – our young narrator here interprets this disillusioning discovery as the inevitable result of the spirit of unruliness, according to the one-dimensional track of options available within the binary logic of the Orientalized other. Thus, the story's pathos lies in the *self*-stifling of one's drive to break boundaries, for – frightened by the "tableau of queerness" by which the Other has been exoticized and Orientalized – the young boy is driven at the end of the story (in its last paragraph), in fear and disillusion, to suppress his own spirit of unruliness and to seek instead the safe normalcy of his less sensitive, more conventional, more "normal," masculist buddies: this is the first step towards becoming the adult Irishman we will see repeatedly in Joyce's works, boxed in his corner and drowning out his sorrows and evading his problems in the male conviviality of drunkenness and braggadocio in the public house.

"Araby" begins with the information that "North Richmond Street, being blind, was a quiet street ... The other houses of the street ... gazed at one another with brown imperturbable faces" (*D* 29). These are the same brown houses which are described in *Stephen Hero* as "those brown brick houses which seem the very incarnation of Irish paralysis" (*SH* 211). While the brown houses "gaze" at one another imperturbably, their inability to see beyond their own paralysis is suggested in the metonymic invocation of "blindness" attached to North Richmond Street – and, in fact, in the atmosphere of Joyce's own childhood spent in such paralysis. For in 1894 the Joyces were living at 17 Richmond Street North, in the very house described in the story. During May 14 to May 19 of that year, the "Araby Bazaar" came to Dublin – an event well and carefully documented by a number of previous studies of *Dubliners* and which I will not recapitulate in detail here.[4] The event had been advertised by a large commercial poster announcing "Araby in Dublin" (in large, exotic lettering) as a "Grand Oriental Fete"; the poster pictures an Arab riding a camel, lists the entrance fee as one shilling, and mentions the Jervis Street Hospital (presumably as a charity beneficiary; see Ellmann, *JJII*, plate 3, for a reproduction of this poster). This is the bazaar referred to in Joyce's story.

This traveling bazaar was a local manifestation of the widespread Orientalist interest in "Araby" prevalent in popular Western culture of the time. For example, a year earlier, the 1893 World Exhibition in Chicago featured something called the "Midway Plaisance": it was, as Luther Luedtke has documented, "a teeming bazaar ... out of the *Thousand and One Nights*. When President Grover Cleveland inaugurated the Exhibition on May 1, 1893, it is reported that Algerian and Egyptian belly-dancers dropped their veils along the parade route in tribute. If much was revealed, even more was suggested. The 'Street in Cairo' became famous before the Fair was a week old ... " ("Julian," 3).

The young boy narrating "Araby" is much like the narrators of the first two stories, a romantic and sensitive boy who likes to read, especially stories of romance and adventure such as *The Abbot* (by Sir Walter Scott), *The Devout Communicant* and *The Memoirs of Vidocq* (*D* 29); his romantic, Gothic tastes are revealed by his admission that he liked the last of these three books best "because its leaves were yellow" (*D* 29). Yellow leaves also suggest fall; and an impending Fall from grace and loss of Edenic innocence are prefigured by his immediate description, at this point, of "the wild garden behind the house [which] contained a central apple-tree" (*D* 29).

The object of the boy's romantic obsessions is his friend Mangan's sister, whose sensuality bewitches him: "Her dress swung as she moved her body and the soft rope of her hair tossed from side to side ... I kept her brown figure always in my eye ... I had never spoken to her, except for a few casual words, and yet her name was like a summons to all my foolish blood" (*D* 30). Mangan's sister induces in the boy a rapturous ecstasy of chivalric romance and religious adoration, as he imagines her even while he wanders through the noise of city streets and markets and "the shrill litanies of shop-boys":

Her image accompanied me even in places the most hostile to romance ... These [street] noises converged in a single sensation of life for me: I imagined that I bore my chalice safely through a throng of foes. Her name sprang to my lips at moments in strange prayers and praises which I myself did not understand ...

(*D* 31)

In detailing what the boy calls "my confused adoration" with a Christian diction involving "litanies," "chalice," and "strange prayers and praises," Joyce partakes in the language of the Holy Grail and of religious quests/crusades to the Holy Land. These mark a convergence between religious adoration of a feminine goddess/

89

Madonna (the sacred cup/chalice/grail as mythical image for the feminine) as the adoration of Our Lady, and the medieval/chivalric courtly tradition of romantic Love as the neo-religious adoration of one's own Lady. The boy partakes in the female idolization and deification that is part of both the Romance tradition of courtly love and the Christian essentializing of woman around the desired figure of the Virgin (as one term in the Madonna/Whore binary; more on that later). In so doing, the boy appropriates Mangan's flesh-and-blood sister and objectifies her into an essentialized image of the Madonna, the functional inspiration and Holy Grail ("Her image accompanied me ... [as] I imagined that I bore my chalice safely through a throng of foes") by which the ego images its own desire as a projected and objectified Other; this moment is a prototype for the traditional essentializing of Woman in Western Christian patriarchy.

Appropriately, the adolescent male desire for a feminine Other here is intertwined in the story itself with the exotic and mysterious East: "When she addressed the first words to me I was so confused that I did not know what to answer. She asked me was I going to *Araby*. I forget whether I answered yes or no. It would be a splendid bazaar, she said; she would love to go" (*D* 31). "Going to Araby" is precisely the literal as well as figurative curve of the young boy's desire, and the link between Woman and Araby is predetermined in a patriarchal Christian, Western society. For "Desire," in its broadest sense, can be thought of as a longing for a personal, sexual, or cultural otherness, for difference, for a union with the exotic, the alien, the strange: to get at, to quest and find, to become one with, something outside of the self – that "pleasant and vicious region" which is the Persia of the mind. Indeed, the "Orient" (whatever that amorphous word may mean) has always served that function for the Western imagination – which has for centuries pictured the East as the mysterious Other, the inscrutable Orient, a feminized entity to be desired, seduced, explored, and conquered – in what Chandra Mohanty ("Under Western Eyes," 352) terms the "Western ideological and political project [of humanism] which involves the necessary recuperation of the 'East' and 'Woman' as Others".[5] As Lisa Lowe points out in *Critical Terrains: French and British Orientalisms*: "Such associations of orientalism with romanticism are not coincidental, for the two situations of desire – the occidental fascination with the Orient and the male lover's passion for his female beloved – are structurally similar. Both depend on a structure that locates an Other – as woman, as oriental scene – as inaccessible, different, beyond" (2).

In describing his response to what he calls the "magical name" (*D* 34) of Araby, our young boy almost seems in part aware of the dynamics of such Orientalized "othering" grafted onto sexual/ romantic "othering" and desire: "At night in my bedroom and by day in the classroom her image came between me and the page I strove to read. The syllables of the word *Araby* were called to me through the silence in which my soul luxuriated and cast an Eastern enchantment over me ... I had hardly any patience with the serious work of life which ... stood between me and my *desire*" (*D* 32; my emphasis). As with the boy's dream of Persia in "The Sisters," the fabulous Arabia here is that magical place associated with the exotic, the mysterious, the lush East: the distant lands of untold wealth and unimaginably sensual entertainments, of the *Thousand and One Nights*, of Scheherazade, the Caliph of Baghdad, the *Rubáiyát*, the land of the Phoenix and mysterious rituals, harems, houris, and Grand Oriental Fetes. The bazaar itself probably took its name from a popular song at the time, "I'll Sing Thee Songs of Araby," which participated in just such exoticization and othering of the mysterious East (*D: Text*, 468):

> I'll sing thee songs of Araby,
> And tales of far Cashmere,
> Wild tales to cheat thee of a sigh,
> Or charm thee to a tear ...

In both religious history and in this boy's personal story, Araby is the site of a "holy" quest which masks con-quest (and desire) under the guise of religious zeal. Commentators have noted how Joyce puns on the boy's "beginning to idle" in his idolatry of Mangan's sister. Such is the nature of both Orientalist and feminine "othering"; Said notes that Orientalism was "a reconstructed religious impulse, a naturalized supernaturalism" (*Orientalism*, 127); "the Orient was a place of pilgrimage" based on "the Romantic idea of restorative reconstruction (natural supernaturalism)" (168).

While "Araby" is a "magical name" for the boy, Mangan's sister is given no name of her own in the story – for she functions as a female blank page awaiting his male inscription. As Hélène Cixous points out: "what is called 'other' ... is the other in a hierarchically organized relationship in which the same [the self] is what rules, *names,* defines, and assigns 'its' other ... the reduction of a 'person' to a 'nobody' to the position of 'other' – the inexorable plot of racism" (*Newly,* 70–71; my emphasis). What identity Mangan's sister has is linked with the name of her brother Mangan and, in Joyce's mind, with the Irish poet James Clarence Mangan, a favorite of Joyce's. One of Mangan's best-known poems, and one of Joyce's favorites, is "Dark Rosaleen," about a young girl who figures for Ireland herself (Dark Rosaleen is a traditional name for Ireland). Thus, Joyce invites us to see Mangan's nameless sister, who is described only as a "brown figure" (*D* 30), as a cipher or figure for Ireland herself in a nationalized extension of feminine "othering."

In 1902 Joyce wrote an essay on "James Clarence Mangan," which he then reworked in 1907 into a lecture with the same title, delivered at the Università Popolare in Trieste. In the latter, he calls Mangan "the most significant poet of the modern Celtic world, and one of the most inspired singers that ever used the lyric form in any country" (*CW* 179; significantly, he links the dead Mangan with the Irish/ English question by suggesting that "Mangan will be accepted by the Irish as their national poet on the day when the conflict will be decided between my native land and the foreign powers"). Mangan was a Romantic poet who claimed that many of his poems were translations from the Arabic (Joyce wrote that "it appears that he had some knowledge of oriental languages, probably some Sanskrit and Arabic"; *CW* 178). Significantly, Joyce associates Mangan's Irish romanticism with both the Middle East and with religious–chivalric– romantic questing:

East and West meet in that personality (we know how), images interweave there like soft, luminous scarves, the words shine and ring like the links in a coat of mail, and whether he sings of Ireland or of Istamboul, his prayer is always the same, that peace may come to her who has lost it, the pearl of his soul, as he calls her, Ameen [a name from Mangan's poem "The Last Words of Al-Hassan"].

This figure which he adores recalls the spiritual yearnings and the imaginary loves of the Middle Ages, and Mangan has placed his lady in a world full of melody, of lights and perfumes, a world that grows fatally to frame every face that the eyes of a poet have gazed on with love. There is only one chivalrous idea, only one male devotion, that lights up the faces of Vittoria Colonna, Laura and Beatrice, just as the bitter disillusion and the self-disdain that end the chapter are one and the same. But the world in which Mangan wishes his lady to dwell ... is a wild world, a world of night in the orient.

(*CW* 182-83)

In the 1902 version, Joyce had added to the list of Vittoria, Laura, and Beatrice: "Mona Lisa – [they all] embody one chivalrous idea, which is no mortal thing, bearing it bravely above the accidents of lust and faithlessness and weariness; and she whose white and holy hands have the virtue of enchanted hands, his virgin flower, and flower of flowers, is no less than these an embodiment of that idea" (*CW* 79). In these striking and accumulated lines from his two essays on Mangan, Joyce unpacks the medieval–Christian "othering" of woman as the mysterious virgin Other, the Mona in the Madonna, within the trope of the Orient as Other. Perhaps equally striking is his description of "the chivalrous idea" as something one "bear[s] ... bravely above the accidents of lust and faithlessness and weariness" (compare "bore my chalice through a throng of foes") and which involves "the bitter disillusion and the self-disdain that end the chapter" – for in these lines Joyce could have equally well been describing his own tale of "Araby."

Having boldly promised Mangan's sister (as she turned her silver bracelet around her wrist) that "If I go ... I will bring you something" (*D* 32), our young narrator awaits impatiently the night of the bazaar. That night he has to contend with his late-returning uncle – unpleasant, selfish, drunk (like so many father-figures in Joyce's texts) – a figure for the paralysis the boy wishes to escape. As the boy is finally allowed to leave, his uncle begins to recite *The Arab's Farewell to his Steed* (more on that later). Clutching "a florin tightly in my hand" (*D* 34), the boy takes a train ride towards the bazaar. This symbolic journey to Araby is, at once, a desired escape from the labyrinth of Irish paralysis, and a pilgrimage in quest of the feminine and the Oriental Other as the anticipated destination of male desire.

The well-known epiphany which concludes the story involves the boy finding the bazaar nearly deserted, then hearing men "counting money on a salver" and listening "to the fall of the coins"; finally, he overhears a banal and mundane conversation, between two young gentlemen and a young lady with English accents – a conversation which illustrates one of Joyce's descriptions of "epiphany" in *Stephen Hero* as "the vulgarity of speech" (*SH* 211). The disappointing reality of the bazaar, its cheap commercialism and drab conversation, seem to cheapen the secret world of dreams and desire the boy had constructed in his mind, deflating the loftiness of his adoration of Mangan's sister. In the final paragraph, the truth of his disillusion "shines forth" to reveal to him his own blindness and the vanity of his dreams and romantic illusions, in an epiphanic fall from grace and innocence: "Gazing up into the darkness I saw myself as a creature driven and derided by vanity; and my eyes burned with anguish and anger" (D 35; recall Joyce's discussion of Mangan's chivalry as "the bitter disillusion and the self-disdain that end the chapter").

On this last page of the story, the word "fall" occurs twice (both in relation to the "fall of coins"), for the progress of this story is one of *lapsus*. However, "the bitter disillusion and the self-disdain that end the chapter" are, in a very problematic sense, always already overdetermined and inevitable – just as the very first paragraph of the story already foreshadows, with its "yellow leaves" and its image of a "wild garden" containing "a central apple-tree" (D 29), the eventual "fall" into an awareness of vulgarity, materialism, and a debased romanticism. For the story dramatizes, from one perspective, the inescapable results and problematics built into the dynamics of "othering" within a system (Western and Christian) of essential-ized/Orientalized binaries, the dynamics of Self and Other.

To begin with, the Orientalizing/othering urge essentializes all the heterogeneous manifestations of difference (in nationality, race, ethnicity, culture, and so on) within the notion of a unitary, definable, knowable Other; this voracious concept colonizes all alien cultures and ethnicities under the banner of a homogeneous "Orient" (or, here, "Araby"). As Said states: "The actualities of the modern Orient were systematically excluded" (*Orientalism*, 177).[6] As Lowe (*Critical Terrains*, 7) argues: "The binary opposition of Occident and Orient is thus a misleading perception which serves to suppress the specific heterogeneity, inconstancies, and slippages of each indivi-dual notion." For example, the "Midway Plaisance," the Araby bazaar featured in the 1893 World Exhibition in Chicago, was "a teeming bazaar of romantic faces, colors, nationalities, and seduc-tions out of the *Thousand and One Nights*" with "Algerian and Egyptian belly-dancers"; a "Street in Cairo"; "a village of Algeria and Tunis, with Arab tents – nearby a Turkish Village and Indian bazaar"; "in the harem of a Moorish palace bare-breasted dancing girls held statuesque poses. Beautiful young women of Algiers, Tunis, Tripoli, Morocco, Egypt, Palestine, Persia, Siam, Burmah, China, and Japan presented themselves somewhat more discreetly" (Luedtke, "Julian," 2–3). The totalizing exhibition strategy mirrors the Orientalist impulse to equate all "others" into a single, grand Other.[7] The account by Julian Hawthorne (son of Nathaniel) of the "Midway Plaisance" both partakes in and describes the exhibition's stereotyping of the mysterious and ineffable Orient: "a concentration of Oriental gorgeousness, glowing with color, and such colors as we would not dare to even think of in our own aesthetic moments; and yet nothing is in other than perfect taste and harmony" (Luedtke, "Julian," 6).

One problem with such an all-encompassing, essentializing discourse is that every term within its extended system of binary oppositions (Self and Other; holy and evil; virgin and whore; and so on) already contains its binary opposite, since the essentialized Other already contains (but cannot recognize or distinguish between) such disparate heterogeneities. As Young puts it, "There may indeed be other knowledges, but they would take different, multifarious forms – unlike the Western creation of the Orient as a generalized 'other' which is constituted as the same everywhere and for all time (there could be no clearer instance, perhaps, of how the other is turned into the same)" (127); "the creation of the Orient, if it does not really represent the East, signifies the West's own dislocation from itself, something inside that is presented, narrativized, as being outside" (*White Mythologies*, 139) within an ambivalence of desire which Bhabha calls "that 'otherness' which is at once an object of desire and derision" ("The Other Question," 19). Thus, the grail-like spirituality of one's desire and questing can all too easily be turned over/into the sensuality of "fleshpots of Egypt," for both notions are already contained within the essence of an Orientalized Other; what sounds like the muezzin's call in the holy temple is revealed to be the enchanting siren song of harem or houri. As Harry Stone pointed out in a seminal essay on "'Araby' and the Writings of James Joyce," the boy in the story "makes his journey, but it is a journey to Egypt, to Araby, to the market place, not back to the Holy Land" (364). As R. B. Kershner points out, "for the Victorians ... the most important role of the East in the popular imagination was as a locale of sexual license and perversion within a context of sensual wealth – the original arena of *luxe et volupté*" (*Ulysses*/Orient, 13).[8] As Said has thoroughly documented, "everything about the Orient ... exuded dangerous sex" so that "in time, 'Oriental sex' was as standard a commodity as any other available in the mass culture, with the result that writers and readers could have it, if they wished, without necessarily going to the Orient" (*Orientalism*, 167, 190). Thus, Julian Hawthorne's cultural raptures inevitably lead him to the "underbelly" of Orientalism: "the slender tremulous scream of the Algerian dancing girls"; "the female abdomen execut[ing] such feats as never before entered your wildest and most unrestrained imagination"; "a laughing, languishing, roguish glance from a pair of Oriental eyes, and an invitation from a pair of lips that are fit to make a Musselman's Paradise" (Luedtke, "Julian," 6; Luedtke's comment on the popular commercialization and material commodification of the exotic Orient is at one with the substance of the boy's epiphany in Joyce's story: "Each Oriental rapture ends, characteristically, with the clink of coins and price of admission"). As Said notes, finally "The Orient becomes a living tableau of queerness" (*Orientalism*, 103). Thus, the deconstruction of the holy quest as sin and luxury, as sensualist (and even as materialist and commercialized) indulgence, is already built into the binary structure of the object-ified essentialism; Desire as holy quest is also desire as sexual con-quest.

In exact complementarity, the "othering" of women in Christian patriarchy results in a similarly binary opposition as the othering of the Orient. For if, in the scheme of essentialized Woman, Woman is Madonna, she is also Whore; Our Lady is also the temptress Eve; the Virgin Mary is also Mary Magdalen (so also Joyce's letters reveal his tendency to configure Nora as both beatific inspiration and libidinous motivator, as the essence of all forms of Desire). This overdetermined encoding within the romantic–religious cult of female idolatry is suggested in the very nature of the young boy's reading (both secular and religious), in the very contents of our cultural production: thus his disillusion is already inscribed into his desire. For, as Stone has pointedly illustrated, Scott's *The Abbot* is a romance

with a religious title that obscures the fact that it is the secular celebration of a worldly queen, Mary Queen of Scots, a queen enshrined in history as saint and harlot ... an idolized Catholic queen by the name of Mary ... a "harlot queen," a passionate thrice-married woman who was regarded by many of her contemporaries as the "Whore of Babylon," as a murderess who murdered to satisfy her lust.

(350)

That the boy reads a book by Scott romanticizing as an unblemished heroine a Queen Mary who was generally considered a harlot (the queen as quean; Mary as Magdalen) and associated with Babylon as a figure of Orientalized luxury, already pre-scribes the curve of Joyce's story and epiphany and reveals the overdetermined disillusion that comes with romanticism, the fall lurking behind a rise. Thus, Stone's nickname for Mangan's sister – the "Madonna of the Silver Bracelet" ("'Araby,'"353) – appropriately suggests the disillusion of commercialism and prostitution inscribed into the figure of essentialized Woman. So also, we recall that inscribed into the popular culture's very siren call of desire, that illustrated poster for the Dublin "Araby Bazaar" in 1894, is already a commodified blend of the lure of the exotic East and blatant commercialism: "For one shilling, as the program put it, one could visit 'Araby in Dublin' and at the same time aid the Jervis Street Hospital" (Stone, "'Araby'," 346).

To summarize thus far: our young male narrator projects his personal desire onto a religiously worshipped and feminized icon/idol; he does so, as the patriarchal Christian history of the West has also done, by othering/Orientalizing the figure of Woman; as with the West, he figures Woman and Desire by con-figuring them with an essentialized Orient/Araby. Kershner has argued that "the portrayal of woman as Other in *Ulysses* is in constant dialogical relationship with the portrayal of the Orient as Other" (*Ulysses*/Orient, 27); we have seen that this dialogical relationship between female othering and Orientalism is already present in Joyce's works as early as "Araby." The analogy may have been inevitable, for (as Said notes) "Orientalism also encouraged a peculiarly (not to say invidiously) male conception of the world" which figured the Orient as female, with "its feminine penetrability, its supine malleability" (*Orientalism*, 206-8).

Furthermore, Said also argues that "the scope of Orientalism exactly matched the scope of empire" (*Orientalism*, 104); after all, "the whole question of imperialism, as it was debated in the late nineteenth century ... carried forward the binary typology of advanced and backward (or subject) races, cultures, and societies" (*Orientalism*, 206). This, too, is a relationship that Joyce's "Araby" excavates, in what is perhaps the story's most striking double-take. At the end, the young boy's epiphany presumably concerns his new awareness of the sordid materiality and vulgar commercialization behind the stuff of his dreams, that is, the inevitable disillusion behind his romantic othering. But ironically the construction of his epiphany shifts that romanticized othering of the Other into an othering of the Self: for in describing himself as "a creature driven and derided by vanity" whose "eyes burned with anguish and anger," the boy is melodramatizing his own specific experience into a romanticized and essentialized grand passion. This shift (the self as other) perhaps serves as the transition for what is a possible (and certainly deeply underscored) separate epiphany by the *reader*: the

Irish/colonized Self as feminized and Orientalized Other. Within the complex analogies and dense patterns of figuration woven into this story's texture, especially as they concern Orient and empire, the title of "Araby" contains a sharp irony: for this is finally a parable about Ireland as much as about an Orientalized Other. Nor should this be surprising: after all, the same binary dynamics of othering and essentialism we have been discussing are also built into the English/Irish relationship (see chapter 2).

Nor was this a new concept and cultural premise for Joyce. As Kershner has shown, there was a cultural tradition "through which the Irish themselves were cast as Orientals, long before Joyce's time" (*Ulysses*/Orient, 17): for example, William Collins's 1742 collection of poems titled *Persian Eclogues* was retitled by Collins himself as his "Irish Eclogues"; Lord Byron, himself an influential Orientalist, wrote in the dedication of Thomas Moore's *The Corsair*: "Collins, when he denominated his Oriental his Irish Eclogues, was not aware of how true, at least, was a part of his parallel ... wildness, tenderness, and originality, are part of your national claim of oriental descent, to which you have thus far proved your title"; Irish explorer Richard Burton, in writing about the Arabian tales, likened "imaginative races like the Kelts, and especially Orientals, who imbibe supernaturalism with their mother's milk"; Moore himself wrote *Lalla Rookh*, a book about the Orient, without ever having been to the East, by merely reconfiguring it as another Ireland (*Ulysses*/Orient, 17–18, 24).

Joyce, in using Mangan's mix of Irish romanticism, medieval romance and chivalry, and Orientalism (Mangan wrote Arabic "translations" though he was probably quite ignorant of the language), was participating in a similar tactic: for the invocation of Mangan and of a character called "Mangan's sister," within the popular associations of "Araby", would likely evoke in Joyce's Irish readers a resonant ambivalence between Woman as Orient and Woman as Ireland/Dark Rosaleen. Joyce's own vision of Mangan as poet asserts this very conflation within the context of imperial domination and dispossession, for he had earlier written about the works of Mangan, in whom "East and West meet": "whether the song is of Ireland or of Istambol it has the same refrain, a prayer that peace may come again to her who has lost her peace, the moonwhite pearl of his soul, Ameen" (*CW* 78). Joyce saw Mangan as a national poet ("Mangan is the type of his race"), for "He, too, cries out, in his life and in his mournful verses, against the injustice of despoilers" (*CW* 81).

In Joyce's story the young boy's discovery of the tawdriness of reality in contrast to his idealized romantic dream world occurs in the context of an Ireland presented as a center of paralysis: where the ineffectiveness of a potentially redeeming religious and spiritual authority is suggested on the opening page by the death of the priest who lived on North Richmond Street (*D* 29), replaced instead by sordid materialism and hucksterism in "the flaring streets" full of "drunken men and bargaining women" and "the shrill litanies of shop-boys who stood on guard by the barrels of pigs' cheeks": this is a commercialized Ireland that has been prostituted to Mammon, peopled by such as Mrs. Mercer (with her mercenary echo), the pawnbroker's wife. The bazaar itself is a tawdry commercial affair in which the narrator's sacred quest is simply to *buy* something. Significantly, he carries a florin as his mode of passage and transaction – the coin of the English invader, a "silver coin minted by the English with a head of Queen Victoria on one side and the Queen's coat of arms (including the conquered harp of Ireland) on the other" and which Irish Catholics found offensive (Stone, "'Araby'," 359). Appropriately, the bazaar is exemplified by a shabby stall presided over by vulgar English accents – "the accents of the ruling race, the foreign conquerors" (Stone, "'Araby'," 363) – supervising a postlapsarian fall, "the fall of the coins" (*D* 35). All of these details underscore the fact that "Araby" is but a figure for Ireland (and that Mangan's sister is Dark Rosaleen), an Ireland whose soul and self have been debased and prostituted to political and economic imperialism.

The story's invoked but unquoted poem, *The Arab's Farewell to His Steed*, has a poignant significance in Joyce's scheme, for it too is a story of betrayal and disillusion, in which a beautiful and beloved possession (the Arab's horse) is sold for money to a stranger, in an image that conflates the dark horse of Araby with the image of Ireland as Dark Rosaleen prostituted to the English:

> My beautiful, my beautiful! that standeth meekly by,
> With thy proudly arched and glossy neck, and dark and fiery eye!
> Fret not to roam the desert now with all thy winged speed;
> I may not mount on thee again! – thou'rt sold, my Arab steed!
>
> The stranger hath thy bridle-rein, thy master hath his gold;
> Fleet-limbed and beautiful, farewell! – thou'rt sold, my steed, thou'rt sold!

Harry Stone has persuasively deciphered the resonant allusiveness and functional appropriateness of Joyce's invocation of this poem, written by Caroline Norton, a vaunted Irish beauty who was sued for divorce by her husband for having committed adultery with Lord Melbourne, the English Prime Minister; the notorious divorce trial then unmasked the scandalous reality that it had been the husband himself who had instigated the adulterous union as a mode of self-advancement. As Stone (358) argues:

That an Irish woman as beautiful as Caroline Norton should have been sold by her husband for English preferments; that she should have been sold to the man who, in effect, was the English ruler of Ireland; that she, in turn, should have been party to such a sale; that this very woman, writing desperately for money, should compose a sentimental poem celebrating the traitorous sale of a beautiful and supposedly loved creature; and that this poem should later be cherished by the Irish (the uncle's recitation is in character, the poem was a popular recitation piece, it appears in almost every anthology of Irish poetry) – all this is patently and ironically appropriate to what Joyce is saying.[9]

Thus, in Joyce's densely textured story about "Araby" we have a parallel set of orientalisms: the religious adoration and othering of Our Lady; the romantic idol-ization by the male of his Lady; the quest – in Western history as well as Western romantic literature – for a feminized and essentialized Orient. All these tropes – religious, masculist, racialist – are finally figures for (or mirrors of) Ireland's colonial relation to imperial England – within the always-already corrupted and debased binarity of othering that functions the Other (Ireland) as a debased harlot/houri prostituted to England. Such is the consistent and inevitable logic of essentialist binarism: in which the soul's adoration of the Madonna is degraded into a young seductress with a silver bracelet; in which the chalice of a holy grail is but a cheap porcelain vase the boy almost buys for his Madonna of the Silver Bracelet; and in which the temple of the exotic and idolized Other turns out to be nothing but a cheap marketplace presided over by the English oppressors. Araby and the Persia of the mind, that "pleasant and vicious region" of one's Desire, are finally tropes for Ireland's relationship to England; in Joyce's vision of a debased and colonized Ireland, Dark Rosaleen is not a Gaelic Madonna but a cheap flirt selling her wares and her self for the coins of strangers.

4

The gratefully oppressed: Joyce's Dubliners

Like the young male narrator in "Araby," Joyce's "Eveline" lives in
one of those "little brown houses" (D 36) which for Joyce embody
Dublin as "the centre of paralysis"; she, too, like the young lads in
the first three stories, is suffocating in such an atmosphere, as she
continually breathes "the odour of dusty cretonne" (D 36). The
pervasive dust in the story becomes a correlative for the stagnation
and decay of a living paralysis, in which everything settles; in which
golden lads and girls all must, as chimney sweepers, come to dust.
   Like the lads in the first three stories, she too wishes to escape. Her
need to escape is, if anything, greater – for both her gender and her
age have resulted in much more desperately, materially confining
manifestations of paralytic entrapment: she is "over nineteen" and as
yet unmarried, living with and taking care of (since her mother's
death) a drunkard of a father who brutalizes her (there is perhaps
even a threat of sexual violence): "she sometimes felt in danger of her
father's violence. She knew it was that that had given her the
palpitations ... latterly he had begun to threaten her and say what he
would do to her only for her dead mother's sake. And now she had
nobody to protect her" (D 38). Hers is an all too frequent reality for
women under patriarchy: "She had hard work to keep the house
together and see that the two young children who had been left to
her charge went to school regularly and got their meals regularly. It
was hard work – a hard life" (D 38).
   Understandably, Eveline, like the young male narrators, both
needs and desires escape. Like them, she fantasizes the appeal of the
Other, embodied for her in the possibility of running off to sea (new
life, baptism) on a ship with Frank, in quest of the exotic and alien
destination of "Buenos Ayres" – literally and appropriately the

"good airs" of a liberating site of otherness, in contrast to the dust of "Dear Dirty Dublin." Just as the young male narrators had found a key to such otherness through words, books, and language, Eveline's fantasies center symbolically around music as the text of otherness. Significantly, the harmonium in her own home has been broken (*D* 37), but Frank, who is "awfully fond of music" (*D* 39), entices her with the lure of a new life in unknown countries by taking her to see *The Bohemian Girl*, a popular musical of the time, and by singing "about the lass that loves a sailor" and (like Othello to Desdemona) telling "tales of distant countries" (*D* 39). Furthermore, the last night that her mother was alive, an organ-grinder outside had played "a melancholy air of Italy" (the exotic Mediterranean site to which Joyce himself had escaped and where he was now writing this story). But, significantly, her father had ordered the organ-player away: "Damned Italians!" (*D* 40). Once more, the "Father" figure embodies the suppression of that "spirit of unruliness" which seeks escape, otherness, and "distant music" (*D* 210).

Unlike the boys in the first three stories, however, Eveline is presented with a *literal* (rather than fantasized) escape, a chance to leave for "a distant unknown country" (*D* 37) – as Joyce and Nora had done in 1904. Unfortunately, her ability to dream and imagine such difference is severely hampered by her limited imagination, so manifestly controlled (as with Gerty MacDowell) by the sentimental and the cliché:

> She was about to explore another life with Frank. Frank was very kind, manly, open-hearted ... He took her to see *The Bohemian Girl* and she felt elated as she sat in an unaccustomed part of the theatre with him. He was awfully fond of music and sang a little. People knew that they were courting and, when he sang about the lass that loves a sailor, she always felt pleasantly confused. He used to call her Poppens out of fun. First of all it had been excitement for her to have a fellow and then she had begun to like him.
>
> (*D* 38–39)

Eveline can only picture Frank, like Gerty, in cliché terms; she *listens* to his songs and to his stories, but does not herself sing, read, imagine, or seek. Eveline is hardly a risk-taker, hardly a free-thinking "bohemian" girl herself.[1]

And so the reader is perhaps not surprised that, confronted with the real possibility of leaving, Eveline gives in to the security of the known and familiar in her fear of the unknown: "but now that she was about to leave it she did not find it a wholly undesirable life"

(*D* 38). For the unknown other is always both attractive and fearful, a pleasant and vicious region in the mind. Like Hamlet, Eveline chooses to remain mired in paralysis: "But that the dread of ... / The undiscovered country, from whose bourn / No traveller returns, puzzles the will, / And makes us rather bear those ills we have, / Than fly to others that we know not of" (*Hamlet* III.1.78–82).

Puzzled in will, Eveline succumbs first to a revisionist nostalgia ("Her father was becoming old lately ... he would miss her. Sometimes he could be very nice"; *D* 39) and then to the memory of the promise she made her mother "to keep the home together as long as she could" (*D* 40). In Joyce's works, the dead, the past, and history inevitably refuse to stay dead – and continue to be "nets" (to use Stephen Dedalus's term) of entrapment one must try to fly by. For a moment the memory of her mother's fate and eventual madness – "that life of commonplace sacrifices closing in final craziness" – frightens Eveline back into the impulse to "Escape! She must escape!" (*D* 40). After all, Eveline is faced with the prospect of reinscribing for herself the same exact fate as her mother's, within what are arguably a woman's two worst archetypal fears: to become one's mother; and to be the madwoman in the attic.

And so she rushes to the "North Wall" (*D* 40) to meet Frank and run away with him – that North Wall, next to all the ships, that was the scene of so many migrations (including that of Joyce and Nora) by so many wild geese choosing exile or escape from Dublin for a better life. But Eveline, one of the few characters in *Dubliners* offered a literal chance to escape, is finally not adventurous or bohemian enough: afraid to take risks, she cannot embrace the spirit of unruliness, and instead suffers what is for Joyce an important failure of moral courage. Unable to choose action over paralysis, she condemns herself to the prison of her dust-filled little brown house, eschewing the freedom of potentially "good air" for the hard life and crazed fate of her own mother. It is a story with devastating feminist resonances.

"After the Race" is of course a story about a race, about a sporting competition; it is also a story about races, about the competition between races (in the popular usage at the time of "race" as frequently synonymous with both ethnicity and nation). This is perhaps the first instance in Joyce's works in which issues of race and empire are suggested through allusions to the activity of "racing"; such references will, as we shall see, be much more frequent in the later works, usually in terms of horse races. But this particular story is about car racing, in part because Joyce had interviewed for the *Irish Times* in 1903 (an interview published April 7, 1903) a French driver named Henri Fournier who was preparing for the second James Gordon Bennett Cup race (*CW* 106). Fournier, one of the best racing drivers of the time, served as the model for the character of Segouin in "After the Race," which Joyce wrote only a few months after the interview (*D: Text*, 473). The interview itself is sketchy and suggestive; but, as Richard Ellmann and Ellsworth Mason point out in reference to that "conflict of native and exotic" they find at the heart of "After the Race," "A Little Cloud," and "The Dead": "underneath the ironical plainness of [Joyce's] interview with Fournier it is not difficult to see in embryo something of the same conflict" (*CW* 106).

After Fournier describes himself as "one of the three [competitors] selected to represent France" in the Gordon Bennett Cup race, Joyce asks Fournier if he will also compete for "the Madrid prize" and then queries: "Which of the races comes first – the Irish race or the Madrid race?" (*CW* 107). The question seems especially ironic in view of the fact that Joyce's short story about Fournier/Segouin would involve a competition between people from a number of different "races" (French, English, Irish, German, Belgian, Hungarian, American); and also in view of Joyce's subsequent question to Fournier – "which nation do you fear most?" – which the Frenchman answers thus: "I fear them all – Germans, Americans, and English. They are all to be feared" (*CW* 108). Since "After the Race" is finally a story about foreigners who come to Ireland to exploit it and take its money and then leave, the following interview exchange – evoking the title of Joyce's subsequent story – also seems ironically charged and suggestive:

> [Joyce]:   "Will you remain any time in Ireland?"
> [Fournier]: "After the race?"
> [Joyce]:   "Yes."
> [Fournier]: "I'm afraid not … "

> (*CW* 108)

Joyce's story begins with Irish crowds watching the race, as "the cars came scudding in towards Dublin"; the irony and contrast couldn't be more sharp in Joyce's description, for "through this channel of poverty and inaction the Continent sped its wealth and industry" (*D* 42). At the level of paralysis, the "inaction" of Dublin is contrasted to the speed and motion of England and of the Continent;

in like fashion, at the level of socio-economics, the "poverty" of Ireland is contrasted to "the wealth and industry" of the Continent. The irony lies in the fact that in actuality the two terms are related and interdependent, that the latter (the European powers) exploits (and depends on) this "channel of poverty and inaction" for much of its achieved speed, wealth, and industry – just as continental nations such as France, Germany, and Belgium, the three nations whose cars and drivers have just won top honors in the race, depend on the exploitation of their colonies for their power and racialized superiority. The even sharper irony lies in the fact that "the clumps of people" representing Irish poverty (in contrast to the sleek racing cars of the Continent) "raised the cheer of the gratefully oppressed" (*D* 42) as the cars went by: for here the colonized have internalized the values of the colonizer, cheering the activities of the colonial masters and becoming consensual slaves, "the gratefully oppressed." In these lines Joyce very subtly probes what could be described as a colonial version of Antonio Gramsci's important refinement of the concept of "hegemony" – as elaborated in his *Prison Notebooks* – not as a domination dependent solely on physical coercion but as a powerful set of social forces that manages through its accumulated discursive formations and authorities to obtain (in Stuart Hall's description of the Gramscian term) "the active consent of those over whom it rules ... in the construction of hegemony" ("Gramsci's Relevance," 19).[2] These "gratefully oppressed" can also be thought of, in terms of the spirit of unruliness, as "grateful dead" – for the suggested effect is precisely the spiritual death and quiescence that lie at the heart of *Dubliners* and which Joyce calls paralysis.

This process of hegemonic consent is exemplified by Jimmy Doyle's father, who – we are told – "had begun life as an advanced Nationalist" but "had modified his views early" (*D* 43). In other words, he had quickly curbed his political and rebellious fervor (and presumably his active support of Nationalist, anti-English policies) as a matter of pragmatics; as a result, he had been able to advance in the business world and "had become rich enough to be alluded to in the Dublin newspapers as a merchant prince" (*D* 43). As a businessman who made his money by collaborating with the oppressors, Jimmy Doyle's father prefigures – as we will see – Patrick Morkan in "The Dead." That he "had made his money as a butcher in Kingstown" (*D* 43; the choice of place name is itself perhaps not accidental) allies him with the mercantile rapaciousness of Mrs. Mooney in "The Boarding House," the butcher's daughter who "dealt with moral problems as a cleaver deals with meat" (*D* 63) and who prostitutes her own daughter (displaying her like "meat") for economic advantage; that "he had been fortunate enough to secure some of the police contracts" (*D* 43) further allies Mr. Doyle with the mercantile brutishness of Corley in "Two Gallants" who is the son of a police inspector. As a "shoneen" (popular term for English collaborator) seeking economic preferments from the authorities, Jimmy Doyle's father has passed on to Jimmy the mercantile values of the colonial sellout: because Segouin "was reputed to own some of the biggest hotels in France," "such a person (as his father agreed) was well worth knowing" (*D* 43). The Doyles themselves, as wealthy Irish merchants, aspire to ruling-class status and in so doing become part of the active hegemonic system itself: as Stuart Hall notes in his discussion of Gramscian hegemony, "within the [hegemonic] 'bloc' will be strata of the subaltern and dominated classes, who have been won over by specific concessions and compromises and who form part of the social constellation but in a subordinate role" (15).

The father's adopted "shoneen" values have been passed on to his son through a social process of education and cultural formation: for "He had sent his son to England to be educated" and "had afterwards sent him to Dublin University to study law"; "Then [Jimmy] had been sent to Cambridge to see a little life" (*D* 43). "Dublin University" was another name for Trinity, Dublin's Protestant university with close ties to its English counterparts. Appropriately, "it was at Cambridge that [Jimmy Doyle] had met Segouin" (*D* 43) as well as the latter's English friend Routh, and had been inducted into the fast, cosmopolitan crowd to which Jimmy is now a hanger-on, tolerated – it is clear – only because of his father's wealth.

Jimmy Doyle's English education reflects how shoneen values get inculcated in subaltern groups through processes of social formation and education: in Gramsci's words, the State is also "educative and formative"; this is, as Hall points out, "the point from which hegemony over society as a whole is ultimately exercised" (18). The State (which Gramsci defines as "hegemony armoured by coercion") is active in raising, to use Gramsci's own words (in *Selections from the Prison Notebooks*), "the great mass of the population to a particular cultural and moral level" through the "educative functions of such critical institutions as the school" (Gramsci, 263; Hall, 19). As Hall concludes: "These emphases bring a range of new institutions and arenas of struggle into the traditional conceptualization of the state and politics. It constitutes them as specific and strategic centres of struggle ... The impact on the very conception of politics itself is little short of electrifying" (19–20).

Within the discursive and social formations that actively maintain hegemony and that participate in this broadened conception of politics, then, are perhaps not only schools like Cambridge and their colonial imitators (like Trinity), but also the cultural institutions of sports (such as racing), of gambling (such as card games), and of social gatherings (such as dinner parties) – all of which are present in this brief story with significant political ramifications. The dinner party (hosted by Segouin) is a political arena which displays in microcosm the political agendas in the story. Mr. Doyle is interested in his son's companions, a wealthy and cosmopolitan crowd (consisting of two Frenchmen, a Hungarian, and an Englishman), for obvious self-advancement, for he is investing in Segouin's "motor establishment in Paris" (*D* 43): "it had been [Jimmy's] father who had first suggested the investment; money to be made in the motor business, pots of money" (*D* 45). In turn, Segouin and his friends are present in large part to exploit Mr. Doyle's financial resources: "Of course, the investment was a good one and Segouin had managed to give the impression that it was by a favour of friendship the mite of Irish money was to be included in the capital of the concern" (*D* 45). Jimmy himself – who, we are told, "had money and he was popular" (*D* 43), the latter quality being an implied consequence of the former – was excited today because "He had been seen by many of his friends that day in the company of these Continentals" (*D* 44). In fact, in aspiring to the values and company of the Continental "fast" set, Jimmy has inherited his father's aspiration to *become* a Continental: "Jimmy, too, looked very well when he was dressed and, as he stood in the hall giving a last equation to the bows of his dress tie, his father may have felt even commercially satisfied at having secured for his son qualities often unpurchasable" (*D* 45).

At a dinner table so brimming with covert political agendas, it is perhaps appropriate that the conversation should turn overtly to politics. However, when it does, a confrontation between Irishman and Englishman (in the person of Routh, Segouin's sidekick from Cambridge) erupts: "Jimmy, under generous[3] influences, felt the buried zeal of his father wake to life within him: he aroused the torpid Routh at last. The room grew doubly hot and ... there was even danger of personal spite" (*D* 46). In other words, Jimmy's own sentiments about his Irish "race" surface briefly here in the form of his father's "buried zeal" for Irish Nationalism, articulated through his resentment of the Englishman Routh; ironically, peace is restored when Jimmy himself "buries" that nationalistic zeal again by accepting Segouin's occlusion of the specific Irish experience of colonial domination within a toast to humanity at large: "The alert host at an opportunity lifted his glass to humanity and, when the toast had been drunk, he threw open a window significantly" (D 46).

The fires of his nationalist zeal having been quenched, Jimmy Doyle now succumbs fully to the lure of the oppressors, drowning himself in drink and carousing on the town with the foreigners, in what Jimmy's bourgeois aspirations convince him are the practices of the urbane ruling class to which he aspires: "What merriment! Jimmy took his part with a will; this was seeing life, at least ... They drank ... it was Bohemian" (D 47). Such bohemianism, however, works at the same level of illusion as with Eveline: a self-deluding appearance of subversion and risk-taking without any substance, wedded instead to a status quo of paralysis and subservience. Joined by an American named Farley, the carousing group "drank Ireland, England, France, Hungary, the United States of America" (D 47) in a seeming show of solidarity between races (after the race, after the morning's sportive competition between races). Jimmy's reactions are predictable: "What jovial fellows! What good company they were!" (D 48)

In the final scene, the competitive, political arena shifts to the card table – where a very drunk Jimmy Doyle ends up happily losing a lot of money all night long, especially in a very exciting last game played into the wee hours. However, much as we suspect that Segouin, Routh, and company only tolerate the Doyles for the Doyle money they wish to exploit, so also there is a hint here that the card game has been rigged to relieve Jimmy of some more of his Irish money. As Robert M. Adams has noted, there is "a suggestion of sharp practice" here ("A Study," 101). It seems likely that the two friends from Cambridge, Segouin and Routh, a Frenchman and an Englishman, may be exploiting Doyle through a concocted sting:

Jimmy did not know exactly who was winning but he knew that he was losing ... then some one proposed one great game for a finish.
... It was a terrible game. They stopped just before the end of it to drink for luck. Jimmy understood that the game lay between Routh and Segouin. What excitement! Jimmy was excited too; he would lose, of course ... Routh won. The cabin shook with the young men's cheering and the cards were bundled together ... Farley and Jimmy were the heaviest losers.

(D 48)

As Adams pointedly remarks: "The game of cards, which lies between Routh the Englishman and Segouin the Frenchman, and in which Farley the American and Doyle the Irishman are the heaviest losers, is a thumbnail sketch of Irish history. 'It was a terrible game,' thinks poor lost Jimmy Doyle. Indeed it was" ("A Study," 103).[4]

The grimmest irony of this "terrible game" lies in this: that not only is Jimmy Doyle fleeced by the sharp play of Continental cardsharps (the colonizer once again exploiting the colonized native), but that Jimmy is happy and grateful for the experience, enjoying the excitement and the privilege of their company, and – at the moment of his greatest loss and exploitation – himself raising the "cheer of the gratefully oppressed." In this way, "After the Race" seems very much an Irish parable of racial hegemony in the Gramscian sense. What Hall (27) concludes to be the importance of Gramsci's formulation of hegemony could also be applied to what Joyce's story illustrates in terms of consensual subservience and "grateful oppression" in Ireland:

[Gramsci] shows how the so-called "self" which underpins these ideological formations is not a unified but a contradictory subject and a social construction. He thus helps us to understand one of the most common, least explained features of "racism": the "subjection" of the victims of racism to the mystifications of the very racist ideologies which imprison and define them.

In such a perspective, the story's title *"After the Race"* seems particularly apt – for the actual car race is perhaps the least important form of "racing" in this story.

In *Orientalism* Edward Said defines the Orientalist/imperialistic project as one that functions within Western societies in accordance with the Gramscian concept of hegemony, which he elaborates thus:

Gramsci has made the useful analytic distinction between civil and political society in which the former is made up of voluntary (or at least rational and noncoercive) affiliations like schools, families, and unions, the latter of state institutions (the army, the police, the central bureaucracy) whose role in the polity is direct domination. Culture, of course, is to be found operating within civil society, where the influence of ideas, of institutions, and of other persons works not through domination but by what Gramsci calls consent. In any society not totalitarian, then, certain cultural forms predominate over others, just as certain ideas are more influential than others; the form of this cultural leadership is what Gramsci has identified as *hegemony*.

(7)

As Gramsci argued, "one might say that State = political society + civil society, in other words hegemony protected by the armour of coercion" (*Prison Notebooks*, 262–63); thus, this definition of the State (force plus hegemony) depends equally on discursive developments in civil society.[5] Hegemonic consent operates, in other words, through the willing adoption and internalization within *civil* society of the values and qualities espoused by *political* society and state institutions – just as Mr. Doyle replaced his nationalistic fervor with a zeal for commercial exploitation characteristic of those who rule Ireland (both foreigners and their native imitators and collaborators). These values get transmitted consensually and often unconsciously, so that the qualities, culture, and practices of the ruling class are in turn mimicked and deployed by individuals within the subaltern classes in their own behavior with each other. This being so, the behavior of individuals within a subaltern group will be frequently symptomatic of received hegemonic values and practices.

In "Araby" the boy narrator discovers to his shock that the notions of romance and gallantry have been corrupted and appropriated by the culture's commercial prostitution to England and to Mammon – that is, to the foreign oppressor and to the economic power by which it rules and exploits. In "After the Race," young Jimmy Doyle's illusion of romantic cosmopolitanism is revealed as debased by the hegemonic submission and prostitution by his father to the commercial values of the oppressor; the story shows us the process by which such "shoneen" values are transmitted within "civil society" through, as Said points out, affiliations such as schools (Cambridge, Trinity) and family (Jimmy's father), displacing the more independent and rebellious "buried zeal" that both Jimmy and his father once had. By the time we get to "Two Gallants" and "The Boarding House," the espousal of such youthful romantic ideals has been fully dispelled by a tawdry and pervasive atmosphere of human exploitation for personal and economic gain.

Whereas "After the Race" illustrated the transmission of debased hegemonic values through civil society (schools, family, and cultural institutions like literature, sports and gambling), "Two Gallants" illustrates how the *"political* society" of "state institutions," in Said's formulation ("the army, the police, the central bureaucracy"), transmits its militaristic values of aggressive conquest to the behavior of those it rules; these values are so internalized that they govern individual behavior patterns, even within the interpersonal dynamics of love and romance. Having observed that "The scope of Orientalism exactly matched the scope of empire" (*Orientalism*, 104), Said has shown that the orientalist/imperialist relationship is basically defined as sexual conquest (309). That imperial paradigm and trope of sexual domination/conquest, when assimilated hegemonically within the culture, ends up retransmitted as *literal* sexual conquest – at the individual, interpersonal level – in a literal manifestation of the intersection of imperial and sexual politics, what Gayatri Spivak calls "the masculist-imperialist ideological formation" ("Subaltern," 296). "Two Gallants" is a story of conquest working at the levels of both individuals (sexual conquest) and nations (imperial conquest).

Lenehan and Corley are our ironically designated "two gallants." Lenehan is "a leech" (*D* 50): at thirty-one years old, he is weary, cynical, jobless, and single, cunningly living off of loans and handouts from disreputable friends – "a sporting vagrant armed with a vast stock of stories, limericks, and riddles" (*D* 50; this description makes him hardly atypical of the single, male-masculist society so prevalent in Joyce's texts). Just as Jimmy Doyle tries to imitate the values and behavior of the foreign exploiters, so also Lenehan admires and envies the oppressive values and tactics of his exploitative companion Corley, even less "gallant" a creature than Lenehan: "rude" (*D* 49) and crude, "Corley had not a subtle mind" (*D* 52), for his vulgar values are broad *machismo*. His concerns seem to be focused purely on sexual conquest, and both his vocabulary ("fine tart," "in the family way," "on the turf," and so on) and his manner of speech are those of the patriarchal, monologic male ego: "He ... was fond of delivering final judgments. He spoke without listening to the speech of his companions. His conversation was mainly about himself" (*D* 51).

Significantly, Corley is the son of a police inspector – so that it is clear whence he got those brutish, militaristic values: "Corley was the son of an inspector of police and he had inherited his father's frame and gait ... He was often to be seen walking with policemen" (*D* 51). As representatives of Dublin Castle and the coercive power of the English colonial State, the police were very much in evidence; as Mark Wollaeger points out, "Dublin ... was the most heavily policed city in the United Kingdom, and both the Dublin Metropolitan Police (DMP) and the Royal Irish Constabulary (RIC), who patrolled the rest of Ireland, were administered from the central site of Dublin Castle. Lord Morely called Dublin Castle 'the best machine that has ever been invented for governing a country against its will'" ("Bloom's," 801). Joyce would also have had in mind "Ivy Day in the

Committee Room," which he had just completed a few months earlier – in which the Dublin election canvassers discuss the infamous "Major Sirr" (D 125): Henry Charles Sirr (1764–1841) was, like Corley, the son of a policeman and a symbol of Irish collaboration with the conquerors; "born in Dublin Castle, [Sirr] succeeded his father as chief of the Dublin police. He worked with the English in suppressing the rebellion of 1798, and became in the popular mind the type of the Irish turncoat" (D: *Text*, 491). In *Ulysses* Leopold Bloom similarly expresses to Stephen his opinion that "a lot of those policemen, whom he cordially disliked, were admittedly unscrupulous in the service of the Crown" (U 16.76–77); appropriately, at that very moment in "Eumaeus," Corley himself enters, "the eldest son of inspector Corley of the G division" (U 16.133). Corley's bulky frame and burly gait here seem but correlatives of his imperial self: "His bulk, his easy pace, and the solid sound of his boots had something of the conqueror in them" (D 55). In his macho aggressiveness and his police connections, there is a brutishly militaristic air, a conqueror's attitude, in Corley.

The epiphanic disillusion in "Araby" concerned the debased commercialization of romance and chivalry; here, gallantry serves only as an ironic mask for abuse and exploitation, for clearly neither Corley nor Lenehan is gallant, romantic, or chivalrous. The code of gallantry and chivalry was rooted in the soldierly, military traditions of Western medieval romance – as exemplified by such legendary warriors as the Cid, Lancelot, Lohengrin, the Chevalier Bayard, and so on. Somehow that tradition of European gallantry had become perverted into the *machismo* of its modern-day counterparts, Corley and Lenehan. Joyce's own statements about this story reveal that he intended from the first to mount an attack on that militaristic mentality, the macho need for conquest which defines Corley. Joyce wrote to Stanislaus on February 11, 1907 that reading Guglielmo Ferrero, a socialist journalist whose work in Trieste's *Il Piccolo della sera* Joyce had admired, had given him the idea for "Two Gallants" (*Letters* II, 212). According to Ellmann, Stannie believed that the story was "inspired by a reference in Guglielmo Ferrero's *Europa Giovane* to the relations between Porthos and the wife of a tradesman in *The Three Musketeers*" (*JJ*I, 228) – presumably, as Litz points out, "a reference to that episode in which Porthos uses his status as a 'gallant' to obtain money from the procurator's wife" ("Two Gallants," 371). Certainly such exploitation of one's militaristic gallantry for monetary and sexual advantage is precisely in keeping with Joyce's story. Joyce himself had condemned the English printer who had refused to handle Joyce's story by invoking both Dumas and Ferrero (in a letter to Grant Richards, *Letters* II, 132–33):

[The printer's] idea of gallantry has grown up in him (probably) during the reading of the novels of the elder Dumas ... I would strongly recommend to him the chapters wherein Ferrero examines the moral code of the soldier and (incidentally) of the gallant. But it would be useless for I am sure that in his heart of hearts he is a militarist.

Joyce's condemnation of the printer as a militarist suggests that the story is itself an attack on such a militaristic mentality. Dominic Manganiello delineates Ferrero's views on militarism (and his attack on its basic hypocrisy) thus:

In [Ferrero's] *L'Europa giovane* the moral code of the soldier consists in arousing men's "inert brutality." Ferrero associates this militaristic activity, which he considered typical of the Germanic races, with the art of gallantry ... Such "brutal" [sexual] encounters resemble the equally anonymous ones on the battlefield. The male lacks all patience regarding the art of "gallantry" because not love but biological need impels him to seek women. Ferrero's point is that sexual relations are adjusted to the brutality of the male rather than to the gallantry which the female might desire.

(Joyce's Politics, 50)

Thus, in Ferrero the debasement of romantic love to brutal sex is seen as an index of a militaristic national sensibility; in "Two Gallants" Joyce picks up on this notion and applies it to the Irish situation, once again delineating a connection and analogy between imperial politics, war, and sexual politics. As Manganiello suggests: "For Joyce, ... the brutalism of love and politics were interconnected. He strongly objected to militarism, and to whatever manner that militarism chose to express itself" *(Joyce's Politics, 52)*.

The hapless object of Corley's militaristic urge for conquest and exploitation, masked as "gallantry" and romance, is a "fine tart" who works as a "slavey in a house in Baggot Street" (D 50) – in other words, a maid working for a very wealthy family. The fact that "tart," "slavey," and "house" all contain echoes of prostitution is much to the point, for – although she is dressed in the Blessed Virgin Mary's colors of blue and white – she is but a debased version of female purity and Irish womanhood. In all likelihood, furthermore, the people she is a "slavey" to would be well-to-do Anglo-Irish landlords of the ruling class.

Corley's and Lenehan's locker-room language seems only able to depict women as whores or animals intended for male sexual gratification: the slavey whom Corley deceives and has under his thumb (bringing him cigars, stealing for him, all the while not even knowing his name) is a "fine tart" who is "up to the dodge" about not getting "in the family way" (D 51); a previous sexual conquest of his is "on the turf now" – i.e., a prostitute – and Lenehan supposes that "that's your doing" (D 53).[6] Love, in fact, can only be pictured as a transaction involving sex and money; even when he wearily imagines being able to marry and settle down, Lenehan thinks of it as a matter of financial gain: "He might yet be able to settle down in some snug corner and live happily if he could only come across some simple-minded girl with a little of the ready" (D 58). Just as Ireland finds itself commercially prostituted to England and to money – a point underscored by the ending of "Araby," by the values of Jimmy Doyle and his father in "After the Race," and by Mrs. Mooney's pandering of her own daughter Polly (as another symbol of debased young Irish womanhood) – so also such hegemonic models and values get internalized and symptomatically replicated within interpersonal relationships.

The prostitution of Ireland, its role as a slavey, is stunningly encapsulated in the story's poignant symbol of the harp being plucked at "heedlessly" by a street harpist:

His harp too, heedless that her covering had fallen about her knees, seemed weary alike of the eyes of strangers and of her master's hands. One hand played in the bass the melody of *Silent, O Moyle*, while the other hand careered in the treble ...

(D 54)

The harp, symbolizing Irish music and art (it was an important cultural element in the Celtic Revival), is also a traditional and feminized figure for Ireland itself, "a traditional emblem of Ireland's glorious past" (*D: Text*, 475).[7] In his personification of the harp as a weary woman, Joyce is thus suggesting Ireland's degradation and prostitution at the hands of strangers: having heedlessly dropped her clothes to her knees, she bares herself wearily to "the eyes of strangers" and to the caresses of "her master," whose hands – like a seducer or paying customer – fondle her in both her bass and her treble. Thus, the harp/Ireland is figured here as a prostitute wearily dropping her skirts and lying down ("on the turf") to serve the strangers and masters, her conquerors, in a monetary exchange – like a slavey or a whore, playing a tune at her master's hands. Combined, the parallel images of the harp and the slavey suggest that Ireland, its femininity, its art, and its religion (the Blessed Virgin Mary) have all prostituted themselves before the conqueror for money – a conqueror embodied within an internalized, domestic hegemony by the male, brutish, militaristic Corley.

Furthermore, the song being played on the harp, "Silent, O Moyle" (or "The Song of Fionnuala"), one of Thomas Moore's *Irish Melodies* and one of Joyce's favorite songs (see *Letters* III, 341, 348), is itself an apt gloss and commentary on the story. The song – which records the plight of Fionnuala, the daughter of Lir, transformed into a swan, telling her "tale of woes" and awaiting her release – grows to embody the plight of Ireland herself:

> Yet still in her darkness doth Erin lie sleeping,
>   Still doth the pure light its dawning delay.
> When will that day-star, mildly springing,
>   Warm our isle with peace and love?
> When will heaven, its sweet bell ringing,
>   Call my spirit to the fields above?
>
>   (Litz, "Two Gallants," 374)

As Litz concludes: "Clearly the young slavey and the harp in Kildare Street represent Ireland's contemporary subjugation, her lack of political independence and national pride" (375). Both suggest the literal embodiment and presence of imperial politics in the hegemonically shaped nature of a debased sexual politics.

As the story progresses, the reader is led to imagine that what Lenehan is waiting so eagerly to hear from Corley is the outcome of some new sexual or romantic exploit – only to discover in the story's last lines, like the boy in "Araby," that the controlling motif all along had been money, not romance: "A small gold coin shone in the palm" (*D* 60). As an epiphany, the gold coin is resonantly and strikingly appropriate, for, in a debased culture, it *is* the currency of romance, too – suggesting how the holy grail and quest of male gallantry, chivalry, and romance have been debased into vulgar avarice and greed. As Litz puts it: "The gold coin – probably stolen, like the cigars, from the servant girl's employer – is a final symbol of debased 'gallantry,' but it is also a fitting climax to the related motifs of Ireland's political, economic, and spiritual degradation. It is a true epiphany, a showing forth of hidden reality" (377).

The coin itself is also a final reminder that this story is a parable about empire and conquest, for the "small gold coin" is "presumably a sovereign, a twenty-shilling gold piece" (*D: Text*, 476) and a considerable sum of money at the time. Thus, the currency of exchange in this story of exploitation, prostitution, and sexual conquest is a coin whose very name suggests the power of Empire – that Empire whose very sovereignty over its Irish subjects prostitutes them to its coin, and robs them of their own sovereignty, of their own self-determining role as sovereign subjects in their own right. Thus, like the feminine harp and the slavey, the coin itself is one more rich symbol of British domination and of Irish prostitution, once more underscoring Joyce's (and Ferrero's) point that military conquest at the international level is matched by militaristic conquest at the interpersonal level, in corresponding manifestations of brutish male conquest. As with "The Dead" (as we shall see in the next chapter), "Two Gallants," then, is a story suggesting the conjunction of sexual and imperial politics, what Stephen Dedalus will later refer to as "the brutish empire" (*U* 15.4569–70). Ironically and poignantly, the internalization and adoption of these values of military conquest by members of the conquered class themselves, and their consequent conquest and exploitation of each other in precisely parallel terms, suggests an advanced stage in the fluid but consensual processes of social–discursive formations characteristic of hegemony, a "gratefully" suffered oppression which Joyce depicts as spiritual death.[8]

Frantz Fanon reminds us that the colonial native "never ceases to dream of putting himself in the place of the settler – not of becoming the settler but of substituting himself for the settler" (*Wretched*, 52). The wish to be not the victim but the victimizer thus often tends to reinscribe the colonial paradigm as a neocolonial (or later postcolonial) paradigm in which the colonized native can function as the "counterpart" of the former colonial settler, in systemic replications (however minute) of hierarchical domination and hegemony. Both "A Little Cloud" and "Counterparts" are stories about bullies and victims, and about "counterparts" within just such variously reproducible structures of oppression. Such structures are the products of hegemony in the Gramscian sense, of consensual internalization and adoption of the values and practices of the apparent "ruling class" – which can then be transmitted and replicated at all the various levels of social construction and formation. Gramsci points out that "the moment of 'hegemony'" creates "the hegemony of a fundamental social group over a series of subordinate groups"; there will be, associated with the ruling elements, what Stuart Hall describes as "strata of the subaltern and dominated classes, who have been won over by specific concessions and compromises and who form part of the social constellation but in a subordinate role" ("Gramsci's Relevance," 14–15). These form different but comparable, parallel levels and arenas of social contestation: the emblematic competition between races/nations at the card table in "After the Race" is replicated in these two stories as contests both between "races" and also *within* strata of the Irish "race" itself, due to the consensual, hegemonic adoption of the imperial model. At the level of the individual ego, this most frequently takes the form of what Freud would refer to as "the narcissism of minor differences" (*Future*, 13) – a narcissistic and unconscious manoeuver of the ego which allows an individual to tolerate and accept his/her own victimization (as one of the "gratefully oppressed") by focusing on minor distinctions that the narcissistic self can then use to feel a measure of superiority over others[9] – thus replicating the hierarchical domination and colonization of which one is oneself a victim (as in the case of, say, poor white laborers' disdain for black laborers just barely below them on the socio-economic ladder). Both of these *Dubliners* stories dramatize and symptomatize such dynamics and dilemmas, represented here at the levels of both social formation and individual psychology (even pathology).

"A Little Cloud" begins with Little Chandler recalling seeing Ignatius Gallaher off at the North Wall eight years ago, as the latter left for "the great city London where Gallaher [now] lived" and where he had become "a brilliant figure on the London Press" (*D* 70–71), while Chandler is still spinning his wheels in the Dublin "dust" (*D* 71). As Robert Scholes has noted, we have yet another Irish–English contestation: "Gallaher ... is related to Weathers in 'Counterparts,' representing an alien London world which challenges and in some sense defeats Dublin as the Englishman Routh defeats Jimmy Doyle at cards in 'After the Race'" ("Counterparts," 379). Chandler's indirect narrative discourse aches with envy for Gallaher and for Gallaher's London and European experiences over his own meagre Dublin existence. This is an existence spent "under the shadow of the gaunt spectral mansions in which the old nobility of Dublin had roistered" (*D* 71); until today "he had never been in Corless's" where people "eat oysters and drink liquers"; where waiters "spoke French and German"; where cabs brought "richly dressed ladies, escorted by cavaliers ... caught up their dresses, when they touched earth, like alarmed Atalantas" (*D* 72). Chandler finds himself acknowledging: "There was no doubt about it: if you wanted to succeed you had to go away" (*D* 73); he himself dreams of writing poetry that would be praised by "the English critics" (*D* 74). What we have here is a culturally constructed desire for "culture" – high culture in its Eurocentric cosmopolitan essence.

Craig Werner points out that, as he walks towards Corless's, Chandler "encounters signs that his own oppressed condition is typical of Dublin under British rule" (such as the "horde of grimy children ... like mice upon the thresholds" [*D* 71]), signs "recalling Charles Dickens's harsh portraits of industrial London." "Only dimly aware of his victimization," however, Chandler "ignores both the children and the 'gaunt spectral mansions,' historically resonant emblems of the 'old nobility of Dublin'" (Werner, *"Dubliners"*, 115) – daydreaming instead of Corless's as the desired (but inaccessible) site of "culture" and ruling-class privilege. Now that Little Chandler was going to go to Corless's to meet the great Ignatius Gallaher – both Corless's and Gallaher being metonymies in his mind for England, as "every step brought him nearer to London" (*D* 73) – he can engage in the "narcissism of minor differences": "for the first time in his life he felt himself superior to the people he passed" (*D* 73).

In his desire for cultural superiority over the madding crowd of Dublin, Chandler is in mind-set basically very little different from Ignatius Gallaher, who has seemingly achieved the position Chandler desires: both are products of a consensual acceptance of imperial hegemonic norms, values and hierarchies. Ignatius Gallaher exemplifies the paradigmatic figure Fanon calls "the townsman": he "dresses like a European; he speaks the European's language, works with him, sometimes even lives in the same district"; he is the latter party within the antagonism which exists "between the native who is excluded from the advantages of colonialism and his counterpart who manages to turn colonial exploitation to his account" (*Wretched*, 112). Both Gallaher and Chandler aspire to an imagined cultural privilege which Fanon describes as that of the "national bourgeoisie": "This bourgeoisie, expressing its mediocrity in its profits, its achievements, and in its thought tries to hide this mediocrity by buildings which have prestige value at the individual level, by chromium-plating on big American cars, by holidays on the Riviera and weekends in neon-lit nightclubs" (*Wretched*, 176) – so much like the flashy stories of Paris glitter and the Moulin Rouge by which Gallaher tries to assert his own "narcissism of minor differences." This is a "native bourgeoisie" which, under colonial hegemony, has, as Fanon goes on to note, "adopted unreservedly and with enthusiasm the ways of thinking characteristic of the mother country" (*Wretched*, 168).

That Gallaher has successfully taken on the values of the oppressor is underscored by Joyce, who twice emphasizes that Gallaher was wearing an "orange tie" (*D* 75, 81). Gallaher now uses those Eurocentric values and experiences, as marks of cosmopolitan superiority, to – in turn – victimize and patronize Chandler and his "dear dirty Dublin" (*D* 75) – condescendingly mocking Chandler's habit of mixing water in his whisky (*D* 75); his provincialism (*D* 76: "Have you never been anywhere, even for a trip? ... Go to London or Paris. Paris for choice. That'd do you good"); his limited sexual experience (*D* 76: "I've been to the Moulin Rouge, and I've been to all the Bohemian cafes. Hot stuff! Not for a pious chap like you, Tommy"); and so on. Terry Eagleton has noted that "The liberal humanist notion of Culture was constituted, among other things, to marginalize such peoples as the Irish, so that it is particularly intriguing to find this sectarian gesture being rehearsed by a few of the Irish themselves" ("Nationalism," 33); ironically, the hollowness of this particular "sectarian gesture" employed by Gallaher to flaunt his superiority over Chandler and Dublin, as England had for centuries over Ireland, is made clear by the fact that this supposed superiority consists only of such superficialities as drinking habits and sexual titillation, which for Joyce already constituted the marks of the male Dubliner's paralysis. Thus, it is not surprising that the more "refined" Gallaher seems, nevertheless, to have the same masculist rapaciousness and misogyny (and racism) as Corley in "Two Gallants": "I mean to marry money. She'll have a good fat account at the bank or she won't do for me ... There are hundreds – what am I saying? – thousands of rich Germans and Jews, rotten with money, that'd only be too glad ... " (*D* 81).

Although himself a victim of Gallaher's pretensions towards cultural superiority, the processes of consensual hegemony inculcate the same cultural desire and pretentiousness in Little Chandler, so that he not only envies (and wishes to be) Gallaher (*D* 83: "A dull resentment against his life awoke within him ... Could he go to London?"), but he begins to replicate the same dynamics of masculist rapaciousness (*D* 83: "He thought of what Gallaher had said about rich Jewesses. Those dark Oriental eyes, he thought, how full they are of passion, of voluptuous longing!") and narcissistic hierarchization, as he – in turn – tries to patronize Gallaher by contending that Gallaher will himself soon marry: "You'll put your head in the sack, repeated Little Chandler stoutly, like everyone else if you can find the girl" (*D* 81), thus putting Gallaher on the defensive. In a colonial hegemony, the gratefully oppressed become colonial "counterparts" who reproduce and reinscribe the colonial paradigm (and binary structure) within the dynamics and nuances of what Homi Bhabha has elaborated variously as "mimicry" and "ambivalence"; within the dialectic, once more (in Fanon's words), "between the native who is excluded from the advantages of colonialism and his counterpart who manages to turn colonial exploitation to his account." This point is made even clearer in the next story in *Dubliners*, appropriately titled "Counterparts."

As with "After the Race" and "A Little Cloud," "Counterparts" is a story of "racial" competition – between national ethnicities, and, hegemonically, at other levels of social contestations between both subaltern groups and individuals. This story, perhaps more directly than any other in *Dubliners*, reflects the pathology of victimization under colonial domination.

Mr. Alleyne, Farrington's boss, is a bully who victimizes the hapless Farrington. His "piercing North of Ireland accent" (*D* 86) clearly identifies him as representative of the imperial Ascendancy and aligns him with London as clearly as does Gallaher's orange tie. That Joyce means his victimization of Farrington to be read as emblematic of the ethnic struggle and resentment between Orange and Green factions is suggested by the fact that the two men's bad feeling for each other had its origin in "the day Mr Alleyne had overheard him mimicking his North of Ireland accent to amuse Higgins and Miss Parker" (*D* 92). That accent also connects this story to "Araby," "Two Gallants," and "After the Race" – for Farrington's occupational, financial, and spiritual enslavement to Alleyne echoes the repeated Joycean motif of Irish economic prostitution to England as suggested in the Araby bazaar with its English accents and coins; in the Irish prostitution to Ireland in "Two Gallants" as symbolized by the harp, the slavey, and the gold sovereign; and in the financial rape and swindle of Ireland suggested in Jimmy Doyle's card game with the Englishman Routh. Mr. Alleyne himself is but a less refined, bully-version of Ignatius Gallaher, for both imitate the colonialist superiority and domination they aspire to: both belong to what

Fanon calls the "national bourgeoisie" which identifies itself with the colonizer's bourgeoisie, "from whom it has learnt its lessons" so as "to take on the role of manager for [Western/colonialist] enterprise, and ... in practice set up its country as the brothel of Europe" (*Wretched*, 153–54).

The condition of colonial victimization and abuse, embodied in the person of Farrington, exhibits itself in a set of pathological symptoms. (1) First, there is the resort to drink, the opiate of the oppressed, as a mode of transference of personal and cultural rage: "A spasm of rage gripped his throat for a few moments and then passed, leaving after it a sharp sensation of thirst. [Farrington] recognized the sensation and felt that he must have a good night's drinking" (*D* 87); "The dark damp night was coming and he longed to spend it in the bars, drinking with his friends amid the glare of gas and the clatter of glasses" (*D* 89). (2) Secondly, women, money and othering combine in a rapacious fantasy (for Farrington) of sexual and economic power: "Miss Delacour was a middle-aged woman of Jewish appearance. Mr Alleyne was said to be sweet on her or on her money ... She was sitting beside his desk now in an aroma of perfumes, smoothing the handle of her umbrella and nodding the great black feather in her hat" (*D* 90); this description combines echoes of exoticized and Orientalized sex with both prostitution and financial enslavement in an escapist, masculist fantasy we have seen before in "Two Gallants" and "A Little Cloud." (3) However, neither drink nor erotic fantasy can fully blunt the accumulated rage resulting from victimization, and Farrington brims with barely controllable violence: "He longed to execrate aloud, to bring his fist down on something violently ... He felt strong enough to clear out the whole office single-handed. His body ached to do something, to rush out and revel in violence. All the indignities of his life enraged him ... He felt savage and thirsty and revengeful, annoyed with himself and with everyone else" (*D* 90, 92). This is a chain reaction of violence, violence bred from the violence suffered at the hands of his employer with the North of Ireland accent and that of a whole colonial system of oppression.

This violent anger finally surfaces as the evening progresses and Farrington drinks more and more. Appropriately, his drunken anger is first directed at the English: as he fails to catch the attentions of an attractive woman with "a London accent" (*D* 95), he brims with resentment at the Englishman Weathers who had kept ordering expensive drinks of "Irish and Appollinaris" at Farrington's expense (all the while "protesting that the hospitality was too Irish"): "If there was one thing that he hated it was a sponge. He was so angry that he lost count of the conversation of his friends" (*D* 95). Weathers is yet another figure in the Joycean gallery of English characters who, like Routh or Haines (in *Ulysses*), participate in the hegemonic prostitution of Ireland to England by "sponging" off of its resources.

Appropriately, Weathers and Farrington end up in an arm-wrestling match at the pub, symbolically a grudge match "to uphold the national honour" (*D* 95) – a wrestling match which Farrington loses, much as Jimmy Doyle had lost at cards to Routh. Having been forced to make an abject apology earlier to his employer Alleyne, an Orangeman, and having just been again personally and culturally emasculated by losing an arm-wrestling contest redolent of ethnic pride to Weathers, an Englishman, Farrington "was full of smouldering anger and revengefulness. He felt humiliated and discontented" (*D* 96). Caught in a cycle of violence between victimizer and victim, Farrington's anger requires for him – to use Fanon's terms – to become the "settler," to be the victimizer. And so, this story ends with the poignant, pathetic, and pathological circumstances of domestic violence – in which Farrington goes home and beats his own son – a domestic violence which is a sociologically engendered product of an imperial violence already replicated as economic oppression.[10]

For, in a hegemonic system in which the gratefully oppressed take on consensually the values of the oppressors, what results is a complex and nuanced hegemony in which the distinctions between rulers and ruled are blurred, in which the colonized yearn to imitate and replicate the colonizers in socially constructed forms of personal/cultural desire. In such cases, the colonial paradigms of domination and oppression are hegemonically reinscribed, replicated, and retransmitted within the dynamics of the subaltern culture itself. At the personal level, one result is the need to assert one's own individual "narcissism of minor differences" – exhibited, in varying degrees, by characters as ostensibly different as *Ulysses*'s Gerty MacDowell (see Shaffer, "Joyce and Freud"), Little Chandler, and Ignatius Gallaher. In the case of Farrington, bullied and victimized and defeated in every other arena on this day and evening, the only place in which his ego can feel somehow superior is at home – through the victimization of his son, in a reinscription of the corresponding "counterparts" of a viciously cyclic, Hegelian paradigm. This sad narrative goes a long way toward suggesting the causal linkages between colonial hegemony and social, economic, colonial, and domestic violence. As Fanon had remarked, "the last resort of the native is to defend his personality vis-a-vis his brother" (*Wretched*, 54). Or, in his introduction to *Wretched of the Earth*, Jean-Paul Sartre – as a European conscious of the related processes of oppression, hegemony, and pathology which Fanon so brilliantly dissects – reminds us that in such a system the colonized native "betrays his brothers and becomes our accomplice; his brothers do the same thing. The status of 'native' is a nervous condition introduced and maintained by the settler among colonized people *with their consent*" (21; Sartre's emphasis).

Fanon's depiction of the internecine conflict among the colonized, what Sartre refers to as the betrayal of one's brothers, was indelibly re-enacted in Ireland at the national level by the drama of Parnell. Before his betrayal and defeat, Parnell had been able to unite the disparate segments of colonial Ireland in collective alliance against English domination in the cause of Home Rule; as Joyce wrote in his own essay on "The Shade of Parnell," his was "the extraordinary personality of a leader who ... forced the greatest English politicians to carry out his orders; and, like another Moses, led a turbulent and unstable people from the house of shame to the verge of the Promised Land" (*CW* 225). However, when he was deposed in Committee Room number 15, Joyce writes, "Of his 83 representatives only 8 remained faithful to him" (*CW* 227); the clergy, the Irish press, the citizens of Castlecomer (who "threw quicklime in his eyes"), and so on, all hounded him to his demise. Parnell's downfall was brought about by the Irish themselves; as Joyce writes: "In his final desperate appeal to his countrymen, [Parnell] begged them not to throw him as a sop to the English wolves howling around them. It redounds to their honour that they did not fail this appeal. They did not throw him to the English wolves; they tore him to pieces themselves"[11] (*CW* 228).

The shade of Parnell, this background of internecine betrayal and the rhythms of Irish treason, forms the historically specific con-textual background to "Ivy Day in the Committee Room," a study of post-Parnellite, shoneen politics. On this day, October 6, the anniversary of Parnell's death, this particular committee room finds a gathering of canvassers for a local Dublin election. Their candidates are Colgan, a bricklayer, representing the radical United Irish League (see *D: Text*, 491), and Richard J. ("Tricky Dicky") Tierney, P. L. G., the representative of the more moderate Nationalists, the Irish Parliamentary Party. The Conservatives (Unionists), a minority party with English allegiances, have apparently thrown their backing to the Nationalist candidate rather than to the more radical Colgan (*D* 131).

In this story and in the wake of Parnell's death, the Nationalist zeal once focused under his leadership has been replaced in Irish citizens by a prostituted, shoneen politics that would sell its services to anyone willing to pay for them, regardless of political affiliation or ideology. An exception is Joe Hynes, a Colgan supporter, who still believes that his candidate ("a good honest bricklayer") stands for something: "Hasn't the working-man as good a right to be in the Corporation as anyone else – ay, and a better right than those shoneens that are always hat in hand before any fellow with a handle to his name? ... One man [Colgan] is a plain honest man with no hunker-sliding about him. He goes in to represent the labour classes. This fellow you're working for [i.e., Tierney] only wants to get some job or other" (*D* 121). Hynes expresses his disdain for "shoneens" who collaborate with the ruling class for personal gain – characters such as Jimmy Doyle's father, Ignatius Gallaher, and Tricky Dicky Tierney, who – as Craig Werner points out, "poses no threat to entrenched English interests" ("Dubliners," 106); after all, even the Conservatives can comfortably support Tierney. The spirit of Parnell has indeed been corrupted in a world where, as Thomas B. O'Grady points out, "one such as Tierney, a Poor Law Guardian ["P. L. G."] – that is, an administrator of the Poor Law Amendment Act of 1834, which often forced the Irish poor to leave their own parishes in search of work [and was generally associated with oppression of the Irish poor] – may run as a candidate in the Dublin Municipal elections on the ticket of the Nationalist party, a remnant of Parnell's party" ("Ivy," 132).

In contrast, Hynes represents the politics of "the working-man [who] is not looking for fat jobs for his sons and nephews and cousins. The working-man is not going to drag the honour of Dublin in the mud to please a German monarch ... Don't you know that they want to present an address of welcome to Edward Rex [Edward VII was descended from the German royal family] if he comes here next year? What do we want kowtowing to a foreign king?" (*D* 121–22) Hynes reminds them that if Parnell (who had opposed Edward VII's earlier visit as the Prince of Wales in 1885) were still alive, "we'd have no talk of an address of welcome" (*D* 122), but that now Tricky Dicky Tierney might well vote for the address. Even one of

Tierney's own men, Mat O'Connor, admits such a likelihood – but, like the rest of Tierney's men, is more concerned that he gets paid by Tierney than that Tierney's politics be justifiable: "By God! perhaps you're right, Joe, said Mr O'Connor. Anyway, I wish he'd turn up with the spondulics" (i.e., money; *D* 122). This is a truly prostituted Ireland, in which, as Werner (107) puts it, "None of the Nationalist workers shows any interest in anything other than getting paid. None evinces even a wistful hope that the political system offers any hope for change."

"How does he expect us to work for him if he won't stump up?" (*D* 123) is the repeated concern of Tierney's men; as O'Grady puts it, "it is this strict work-for-pay attitude which is the common denominator ... Money is the only incentive, it seems, for working for 'Tricky Dicky Tierney'" ("Ivy," 135). After all, Tierney's own men – such as Henchy – admit that "O, he's as tricky as they make 'em ... He hasn't got those little pigs' eyes for nothing" (*D* 123). Henchy himself is typical of the betrayal of the principles Parnell stood for: he welcomes the proposed visit of Edward VII for financial reasons (*D* 131: "The King's coming here will mean an influx of money into this country"), ignoring political principles. When he tries to excuse the English monarch's personal life – "He's fond of his glass of grog and he's a bit of a rake, perhaps, and he's a good sportsman. Damn it, can't we Irish play fair" (*D* 132) – and is then asked about Parnell's case, he refuses to see "the analogy between the two cases" (*D* 132); no doubt, as Werner puts it, "Joyce felt no further need to underscore the irony of this talk of fair play for the philandering English king from the political heirs of a leader driven from power because of an affair with a woman he ultimately married" ("Dubliners," 108).

In the wake of Parnell's betrayal by his own disciples, an attitude of internecine distrust, of betrayal amongst one's own brothers, pervades; in a world where one sells one's political soul to whoever would pay, everyone seems suspect. Thus, Hynes's suspicions about Tierney are echoed by Tierney's own men; Henchy in turn suspects that Colgan's party is composed of spies and of radical "hillsiders and fenians" ("Hillside men" was a term for Fenians), half of whom, he claims, "are in the pay of the Castle" (*D* 125; Dublin Castle was the headquarters of the English colonial rule). Such shoneens – including presumably their own candidate Tierney, whose corruptibility Henchy has just owned up to – are "lineal descendant[s]" of "Major Sirr": "That's a fellow now that'd sell his country for fourpence – ay – and go down on his bended knees and thank the Almighty Christ he had a country to sell" (*D* 125). As Scholes and Litz (491) point out: "Henry Charles Sirr (1764–1841), born in Dublin Castle, succeeded his father as chief of the Dublin police. He worked with the English in suppressing the rebellion of 1798, and became in the popular mind the type of the Irish turncoat." After the betrayal of Parnell, it seems, anything is possible and everyone is suspect.

However, in suspecting "these hillsiders and fenians" of being "Castle hacks," Henchy exempts Hynes himself: "I don't say Hynes ... No, damn it, I think he's a stroke above that" (*D* 126). By the end of the story we find out why – for Hynes was one (presumably unlike the rest of them) who had remained loyal to the Chief, and thus whose principles *could* be trusted: "There's one of them, anyhow, said Mr Henchy, that didn't renege him. By God, I'll say for you, Joe! No, by God, you stuck to him like a man!" (*D* 133) The others urge Hynes to recite the poem he wrote on Parnell's death, and he delivers a poor, mawkish, but heartfelt poem, patriotically praising Parnell and condemning those who "laid him low": "Shame on the coward caitiff hands / That ... Betrayed him to the rabble-rout" (*D* 134–35). His recital is met by warm applause; then "all the auditors drank from their bottles in silence" (*D* 135). This silence is the silence of complicit guilt, for – as Hynes's poem indirectly suggests and as the story has shown – all of them but Hynes have compromised and prostituted their political ideals, and thus all share in the betrayal of Parnell and the Nationalist principles for which he stood. All of them, as O'Grady puts it, "except Hynes are in the Committee Room, ultimately, in the hopes of getting paid for canvassing for a political candidate whom they neither like nor trust" ("Ivy," 139). When the Conservative Crofton, in the last lines of the story, is asked what he thinks of the poem, his only comment was "that it was a very fine piece of writing" (*D* 135). Since the poem is clearly anything but a fine piece of writing, however sincere, Crofton's answer seems to focus on a pseudo-aesthetic critique in order to occlude and evade the uncomfortable political critique implicit in the poem – curiously anticipating, as Werner (109) has pointed out, contemporary attacks on modernism's desire to separate aesthetics from ideology, with Crofton presenting "technical criticism as an evasion of all that, in a living political culture, the poem might mean." Only in this way can individual Dubliners rationalize putting their Nationalist political ideals up for sale.

From here it is only a small step to taking material advantage of Nationalist fervor and idealism for private profit and personal gain – which is what Mrs. Kearney tries to do in "A Mother": "When the Irish Revival began to be appreciable Mrs Kearney determined to take advantage of her daughter's name [Kathleen] and brought an Irish teacher to the house" (D 137). Having pushed her daughter into Nationalist circles and friendships, she then capitalizes on those connections to land a contract for her daughter to play the piano in a concert organized by the *Eire Abu* [Victory for Ireland] Society. This pathetic story in which a mother ruins a daughter's artistic career by her own obsession with financial gain is perhaps the nadir of Irish paralysis in terms of the prostitution of patriotic ideals and Nationalist fervor: by this point in the *Dubliners* stories, the Moyle seems truly silent, and the Irish harp seems very much a harlot who, before the eyes of strangers, has heedlessly, willingly, and even gratefully let her coverings fall to her knees.

5

Empire and patriarchy in "The Dead"

Preface: Joyce, politics, and the canon

This chapter on "The Dead" attempts to reclaim the power of this justly celebrated text as engagedly political and ideological – from a canonization process that has, in large measure, managed to defang and neutralize that power within Joyce's texts by constructing "Joyce" as an apolitical, stylistic innovator. "The Dead" provides an especially suggestive case study of the clash between the Academy's institutional, canonizing practices/powers and an ideological reclamation of Joyce's works, for surely "The Dead" is a model text in the Modernist canon, a familiar favorite and staple of every collection of "great" modern short fiction, one of the most frequently taught works in introductory college literature classes, perhaps the only Joycean text widely familiar to a general reading audience.

I first tested an early version of this chapter as a paper at the 1991 Joyce Conference (June 11–16, 1991 in Vancouver, Canada). Admittedly the essay was a risky venture involving some real ideological dangers (on which I wished to elicit constructive discussion and advice). To my surprise, I learned from the controversial response to this paper more about the nature of the risks one takes in trying to repoliticize a highly canonical work: while the younger scholars and graduate students found my reading exciting and attractive, the quite vocal response from a few of the more established scholars was troubled. "Very interesting and imaginative, but I'm afraid you are doing serious violence to the story" was the vexed response of one very senior scholar, whose work I admire very much. What, I wondered, was this thing being referred to, *"the* story" that I was supposedly doing violence to? Does not *"the* story" really mean "the way *I* have always been taught to read it, the way I have invested years of my own effort in teaching it"? If so, no wonder the graduate students and younger faculty weren't troubled: they had no major investment yet in *one* particular and exclusive way of reading the story, the "Authorized Version" of "The Dead." This traditional reading of the story focuses on the Morkans' Christmas party as a display of seasonal warmth and goodwill, Irish hospitality, high spirits, and the Irish gift of gab (all qualities of the essentialized stage-Irishman; the recent and popular John Huston movie followed suit). Gabriel Conroy, the main character, is portrayed in this standard reading as very sympathetic, as kind and sensitive – a bit of a wimp, perhaps, a bit overly self-reflective and overly hung up on being "civilized" and on the latest fashions from the Continent (such as goloshes), and so on – but who nevertheless in the end arrives at a deeply moving and universal, humanizing epiphany, a growth of personal self-awareness by his highly-refined individual (and unified) subjectivity occasioned by learning for the first time about an incident from his wife's past. Such is the aesthetically pleasing curve of this reassuringly sanitized and humanistic, canonized version of "The Dead." What I learned from delivering this paper was that years of personal investment in such readings can create within excellent and otherwise open-minded Joyce scholars a mono-lithic reification of such a reading as *"the* story," and a consequent resistance to radically different, especially overtly political, readings.

But Joyce was hardly an apolitical creature while he was living in Italy and composing *Dubliners.* He wrote to his brother Stanislaus in 1905 that "my political opinions ... are those of a socialistic artist" (*Letters* II, 89); repeatedly he asked his brother to send him articles and editorials on the Irish/English situation, so as to keep up with the politics at home. As early as 1903, Stannie had reported that "[Jim] is interesting himself in politics – in which he says [he has] original ideas ... He calls himself a socialist but attaches himself to no school of socialism" (Manganiello, *Joyce's Politics*, 42). Nor was Joyce's socialistic interest a purely nominal posturing: as Richard Ellmann first noted (in 1977), "Joyce's political awareness was based on considerable reading. His library in Trieste included especially books by socialists and anarchists. He had, for example, the first 173 Fabian tracts bound in one volume. Among other writers who interested him were notably the two anarchists, Kropotkin and Bakunin, and the social reformer, Proudhon" (Ellmann, *Conscious-ness*, 82). In fact, among the numerous political texts in Joyce's personal library in Trieste (see Ellmann, *Consciousness*, 97) were, notably, works by Michael Bakunin (*God and the State*), Henri Bergson (*The Meaning of the War*), John F. Boyle (*The Irish Rebellion of 1916*), the Irish patriot/martyr Roger Casement (*Britisches gegen Deutsches Imperium*), Joseph Conrad (*The Secret Agent*), Fenian revolutionary Michael Davitt (*The Fall of Feudalism in Ireland*), Paul Eltzbacher (*Anarchism*), the first 173 Fabian Tracts, Maxim Gorky (several volumes, including *I fasti della rivoluzione russa*), Arthur Griffith (*The Finance of the Home Rule Bill* and *The Home Rule Examined*), several books by Kropotkin, Mikhail Lermontov, Machiavelli, Marinetti, John Stuart Mill, Nietzsche, Sydney Olivier (*White Capital and Coloured Labour*), Charles Stewart Parnell, P. J. Proudhon, Bertrand Russell (*Principles of Social Reconstruction*), George Bernard Shaw (including *Socialism and Superior Brains*), Irish revolutionary James Stephens, Benjamin Tucker, Sidney Webb (*Socialism and Individualism*), and H. G. Wells (including *A Modern Utopia*). Manganiello further documents that Joyce's knowledge of socialist and anarchist literature was extensive, and that he was influenced by, among others, Malatesta, Stirner, Bakunin, Kropotkin, Elisee Reclus, Spencer, Tucker, Proudhon, Tolstoy, and Conrad (*Joyce's Politics*, 72).

The Trieste Joyce lived in while writing *Dubliners* was a colonized city, a largely Italian population under Austro-Hungarian imperial rule. The two political situations confronting Joyce were strikingly analogous: both Trieste and Dublin were occupied cities, the Austrians having ruled Trieste for almost as long as the British had Dublin; both peoples claimed a language different from that forced on them by their conquerors; both were Catholic cities ruled by a foreign empire. In fact, Joyce wrote essays for Trieste's major newspaper (*Il Piccolo della sera*) arguing the similarity between Italian irredentism and the Irish independence movement.

While one could cite from a number of different critical and journalistic essays Joyce wrote while in Trieste, I will focus on a single one for illustration, on what, for my purposes, is perhaps the most interesting of Joyce's Triestine writings: his lecture on Ireland, delivered in Italian to an Italian audience in 1907 at the Università Popolare – particularly since it was written at the same time he was beginning to conceive "The Dead." The forty-six page manuscript of "*Irlanda, Isola dei Santi e dei Savi*", translated into English under the title of "Ireland, Island of Saints and Sages" (*CW* 153–74), is a particularly interesting work to read in tandem with *Dubliners*, especially "The Dead," since it illuminates some of the issues and concerns which form the backdrop to the fictional story Joyce was in process of composing.

"Nations have their ego, just like individuals," Joyce begins – anticipating Freud's later argument (in *The Future of an Illusion* and *Civilization and its Discontents*) that civilizations and nations function (and can usefully be analyzed) like individual psychologies. It is also significant that Joyce begins by analogizing different forms of politics, here personal and inter-national politics. He had already argued the analogy between Triestine and Dublin politics in *Il Piccolo della sera*, and was very much taken by the Italian socialist Guglielmo Ferrero, a Dreyfusard journalist for the newspaper who included Ireland in his discussion of European affairs. Ferrero's book *L'Europa giovane* (1897) – a title which echoed Mazzini's "Young Europe" movement intending "to link the various European nations together in a common crusade" (Manganiello, *Joyce's Politics*, 48) – was mentioned often by Joyce in his letters to Stannie.[1] Ferrero's view on the relationship between militarism and sexual politics – that is, that the male tradition of militarism and bellicose chauvinism results in sexual relationships being dominated by the brutality of the male rather than by the gentility and gallantry desired by the female – influenced Joyce's depiction of sexual relationships in *Dubliners*, especially (as has been well documented) in "Two Gallants" but also (as I will argue) in "The Dead." Significantly, both Joyce and Ferrero make direct analogies between sexual and international politics; between imperial politics, war, and sexual relationships.

In his lecture Joyce goes on to correlate different manifestations of international imperialism: "for so many centuries the Englishman has done in Ireland only what the Belgian is doing today in the Congo Free State," and what, he goes on to note prophetically, the Japanese "will do tomorrow in other lands" (*CW* 166). Most notably, Joyce's view of British rule in Ireland is uncompromisingly clear in this public address, hardly neutral, detached, or apolitical:

[England] enkindled [Ireland's] factions and took over its treasury. By the introduction of a new system of agriculture, she reduced the power of the native leaders and gave great estates to her soldiers. She persecuted the Roman church when it was rebellious and stopped when it became an effective instrument of subjugation. Her principal preoccupation was to keep the country divided ...

She was as cruel as she was cunning. Her weapons were, and still are, the battering-ram, the club, and the rope; and if Parnell was a thorn in the English side, it was primarily because when he was a boy in Wicklow he heard stories of the English ferocity from his nurse . . .

The English now disparage the Irish because they are Catholic, poor, and ignorant; however, it will not be so easy to justify such disparagement to some people. Ireland is poor because English laws ruined the country's industries, especially the wool industry, because the neglect of the English government in the years of the potato famine allowed the best of the population to die from hunger, and because under the present administration, while Ireland is losing its population and crimes are almost non-existent, the judges receive the salary of a king, and governing officials and those in public service receive huge sums for doing little or nothing.

(CW 166–67)

Joyce argues that, under such subjugation, a colonized people is faced with some inevitable choices, in words that bring to mind Frantz Fanon's arguments in *Wretched of the Earth*:

When a victorious country tyrannizes over another, it cannot logically be considered wrong for that other to rebel. Men are made this way, and no one who is not deceived by self-interest or ingenuousness will believe, in this day and age, that a colonial country is motivated by purely Christian motives. These are forgotten when foreign shores are invaded, even if the missionary and the pocket Bible precede, by a few months, as a routine matter, the arrival of the soldiers and the uplifters . . .

Nor is it any harder to understand why the Irish citizen is a reactionary and a Catholic, and why he mingles the names of Cromwell and Satan when he curses. For him, the great Protector of civil rights is a savage beast who came to Ireland to propagate his faith by fire and sword. He does not forget the sack of Drogheda and Waterford, nor the bands of men and women hunted down in the furthermost islands by the Puritan, who said that they would go "into the ocean or into hell," nor the false oath that the English swore on the broken stone of Limerick. How could he forget? Can the back of a slave forget the rod?

(CW 163, 168)

While Joyce chafes against the racialized English stereotype of the Irish as "Catholic, poor, and ignorant" and as "the unbalanced, helpless idiots about whom we read in the lead articles of the *Standard* and the *Morning Post*" (CW 171), he is aware that neither is there any pure racial/ethnic Irish essence (or past) to posit as an alternative (whether real or nostalgic) to British influence – for a country with a longstanding history of invasions, subjugations and colonizations is irremediably now a *bricolage* of ethnically mixed diversities and shared cultures, exhibiting the multicultural characteristics of Mary Pratt's "contact zone" (33) or of Gloria Anzaldúa's "Borderlands":

Our [Irish] civilization is a vast fabric, in which the most diverse elements are mingled, in which nordic aggressiveness and Roman law, the new bourgeois conventions and the remnant of a Syriac religion [i.e., Christianity] are reconciled. In such a fabric, it is useless to look for a thread that may have remained pure and virgin without having undergone the influence of a neighbouring thread. What race, or what language (if we except the few whom a playful will seems to have preserved in ice, like the people of Iceland) can boast of being pure today? And no race has less right to utter such a boast than the race now living in Ireland.

(CW 165–66)

Joyce, however, does not entirely despair of the possibility of a non-nostalgic Irish revival ("that the Irish dream of a revival is not entirely an illusion"), engaging in a vision of a successful overthrow of imperial power and achievement of self-sufficient nationhood:

It would be interesting ... to see what might be the effects on our civilization of a revival of this race. The economic effects of the appearance of a rival island near England, a bilingual, republican, self-centred, and enterprising island with its own commercial fleet, and its own consuls in every port of the world. And the moral effects of the appearance in old Europe of the Irish artist and thinker ...

As Joyce points out: "If the Irishmen at home have not been able to do what their brothers have done in America, it does not mean that they never will" (CW 163).

These were Joyce's thoughts on Ireland and England around the time he began to write "The Dead."

Manganiello reminds us that "The first work Joyce ever wrote was political. This was the poem ... 'Et Tu, Healy,' which was composed at the age of nine shortly after Parnell's death" (*Joyce's Politics*, 3), lamenting Charles Stewart Parnell's betrayal by one of his own lieutenants, Timothy Healy. But one might well even refer to Joyce as a political writer if one takes on the meaning of the word "political," as I have been doing above, in the broader sense: "the whole of human relations in their real, social structure, in their power of making the world" as Roland Barthes defines the word (Ellmann, *Consciousness*, 73); or, in Robert Dahl's standard definition, "any pattern of human relationships that involves, to a significant extent, power, rule, or authority" (*Modern*, 6; Manganiello, *Joyce's Politics*, 8). Joyce himself, as we have already seen, exhibits a tendency to correlate and analogize similar forms of particular "politics" and the exercises of power.[2]

"The Dead" is, in this broader sense, profoundly political. For, as we shall see, it is a text that tries to analogize a number of forms of political and power relationships, suggesting and exploring their intersectionalities: imperial, racial, cultural, familial, and sexual politics. How is one to analogize or theorize similarities and differences of particular minority discourses, of particular marginalized voices? This is a question and a project that Joyce's texts take on, from the early *Dubliners* stories (as we have seen) to the later *Ulysses* and *Finnegans Wake* (with their much more complex and highly textured versions of sameness-within-difference). "The Dead"'s attempt to analogize different forms of oppression and of responses to such oppressions plays out (in a fictional field of play) some of the problems facing any study of "minority discourses": what issues do different minority discourses have in common, and how do they impinge on, intersect with, reinforce, or even cause, each other? How can we depict and theorize a potentially enabling harmony (or collectivity) of culturally-specific differences and experiences without obliterating, occluding, or homogenizing the specificity and particularity of individual difference and experience (in what Deane calls "the harmony of indifference" [*Heroic*, 16])? How can such an insistence on pluralistic difference, local specificity, and heterology be observed without resulting in fragmentation, quiescence, and loss of collective agency – thus ultimately reaffirming the hegemony of the dominant discourse? In these respects, this story can, at one level, be usefully examined in terms of Abdul R. JanMohamed and David Lloyd's vision of "the task of minority discourse, in the singular: to describe and define the common denominators that link various minority cultures," for these cultures "have certain shared experiences by virtue of their similar antagonistic relationship to the dominant culture, which seeks to marginalize them all" ("Minority Discourse," 1) – in an exploration of what might constitute "minority discourse."

Empire and patriarchy in "The Dead"

James Joyce's "The Dead" has elicited a great deal of fine criticism which illuminates our understandings of that story. This chapter does not aim at a comprehensive and coherently balanced interpretation of the story, but at a specialized reading from a particular angle of analysis, as a study of the conjoined dynamics of empire and sexual colonization, what Gayatri Spivak has referred to as "the masculist-imperialist ideological formation" ("Subaltern," 296).[3] This is a reading of Gabriel Conroy as a well-meaning patriarch who is *almost* a domestic tyrant (the "almost" here is an important qualification), a qualified representation by Joyce of a potentially oppressive patriarch in symbolic collaboration with the ruling masters of the English colonial empire – what Stephen Dedalus calls the "brutish empire" (*U* 15.4569–70). My intention is to draw parallel lines of mastery and colonization, of authority and marginalization, in terms of various and related forms of politics: imperial, racial, cultural, familial, and sexual.[4]

I would not wish to dispute that Gabriel Conroy is a quite sympathetic character, especially in contrast to all the other male rogues, drunkards, and failures who populate Joyce's gallery of *Dubliners*.[5] But he is no less sympathetic in spite of, or (as I would argue) because of, Joyce's scrupulously searing and unflattering portrayal of him. The very first direct impression we get of Gabriel is his voice, as he and Gretta arrive at the Morkans' annual dance, responding to Lily's relief at their arrival ("Miss Kate and Miss Julia thought you were never coming") by putting down his wife: " – I'll engage they did, said Gabriel, but they forget that my wife here takes three mortal hours to dress herself" (*D* 177).[6] This seemingly good-humored comment suggests, however, an essentializing of the female in a form of infantilization, similar to the affectionate attitude of the British Empire towards its colonies as incorrigible children (always unruly, always late) who can thus only be properly ruled by the parent empire. As Edward Said has thoroughly documented, English imperialist policies regarded their subjects (often their "little brown children") as "what is already evident: that they are a subject race, dominated by a race that knows them and what is good for them better than they could possibly know themselves" (*Orientalism*, 35).[7] The connection between imperial and sexual domination is perhaps unintentionally but appropriately (however speculatively on my part) suggested by Gabriel's very next words, " – Here I am as right as the mail, Aunt Kate!" – for the Royal Mail ("His Majesty's vermillion mailcars" [*U* 7.16]) was a notoriously imperial institution (often vandalized by colonial insurrectionists);[8] both the empire and the male ego are employed in the activity ("the masculist-imperialist ideological formation") of making judgments and hierarchical distinctions between what is central ("as *right* as the mail/male") and what is marginal, for domination involves the imposition of dominant order, structure, and distinctions – of gender, race, class, hierarchy, margins, and so on.[9] What Gabriel will learn tonight is how spurious and unstable those distinctions and marginalizations, the activities of the authorized Ego, are.

Gretta's own natural instinct and spirits are limited and controlled by the disapproving authority of a paterfamilias who infantilizes those instincts: " – But as for Gretta there, said Gabriel, she'd walk home in the snow if she were let" (*D* 180). Gabriel's rule and mastery extends also to the children, as Gretta reports to Aunt Kate: "He's really an awful bother, what with green shades for Tom's eyes at night and making him do the dumb-bells, and forcing Eva to eat the stirabout. The poor child! And she simply hates the sight of it!" (*D* 180) While the two aunts may laugh ("for Gabriel's solicitude was a standing joke with them"), the image drawn of Gabriel here is of a well-meaning domestic tyrant imposing the Law of the Father. Gretta's own resentment is only partially disguised (unlike Eva's) by her humorous banter: "O, but you'll never guess what he makes me wear now! ... Goloshes! ... Whenever it's wet underfoot I must put on my goloshes. To-night even he wanted me to put them on, but I wouldn't. The next thing he'll buy me will be a diving suit" (*D* 180).

To an uncomprehending Aunt Julia who has never heard of goloshes, Gretta explains that they are "Guttapercha things ... Gabriel says everyone wears them on the continent" (*D* 181). Julia's response (" – O, on the continent, murmured Aunt Julia, nodding her head slowly") suggests her *sotto voce* resentment of Gabriel's presumably continual attempts to impose a more "civilized," continental culture on their own (by implication) wild and backward colonial Irish mentalities. "Guttapercha," a rubbery material from Malaya, and "goloshes" ("Made of India rubber or the less elastic gutta-percha" [Gifford, *Joyce Annotated*, 114]) together suggest the role (in a product economy) which India, Malaya (like India, an English colony), and other imperial colonies played in the service and material comfort of the European masters: their highly refined and "civilized" European culture of goloshes and pianos (as highly "finished" end-products) depends on the gutta-percha and the ivory ripped out of colonial nations by the labor and sweat of the colonized natives.[10] No wonder, then, that the word goloshes "reminds [Gretta] of Christy Minstrels" (*D* 181), of blackface "Negro" minstrels out to entertain white audiences. Thus the wearing of goloshes becomes a correlative for a more "civilized" dominant European culture, whose very cultural superiority and refinement depended on the exploitation of its colonies – in contrast to the more primitive, unrestrained, and still uncolonized Irish free spirit allied symbolically to the West of Ireland and Gretta's roots in Galway.[11]

Similar dynamics seem to me at work in Gabriel's exchange, as he is removing his goloshes, with Lily the caretaker's daughter. Margot Norris suggests that Lily's retort – "The men that is now is only all palaver and what they can get out of you" – may be a response to a Gabriel who is flirting with her ("Stifled," 495). I would suggest, rather, that the sexual dynamics here are again a case of sexual infantilization, of Gabriel's insensitivity to the fact that Lily is no longer a child, but a woman with her own voice:

> – Tell me, Lily, he said in a friendly tone, do you still go to school?
> – O no, sir, she answered. I'm done schooling this year and more.
> – O, then, said Gabriel gaily, I suppose we'll be going to your wedding one of these fine days with your young man, eh?
>
> (*D* 178)

Such patronization and infantilization elicit from Lily an assertion ("with great bitterness") of her own, adult female voice: "The men that is now is only all palaver and what they can get out of you."

Her retort touches on one of the story's central concerns, the question of what is the proper male (or as Shaun asks about Shem in *Finnegans Wake*, "when is a man not a man?" [*FW* 170.05]). Gabriel is himself (as per Lily's accusation) a man of "all palaver," for he is, as a writer of book reviews and after-dinner speeches, a man of "words" – perhaps in contrast to his as-yet undiscovered counterpart, Michael Furey, the man of romantic "fury" from whom Gabriel will feel a challenge to his maleness.[12] Which of the two is "right as the male"? Man of action, man of words: this is a masculine dualism/distinction that would continue to engage Joyce, for the Royal Mail as a phallogocentric imperial institution is behind the creation of Shaun the Post as the macho and patriarchal twin ("right as the mail"), himself an active carrier of words ("letters"), in constant opposition and rivalry to his wordsmith brother Shem the Pen, like Gabriel a shaper of words ("*write* as the male").

Lily has rendered this moment awkward by challenging Gabriel's masculinity and his mastery, refusing to act as the child he expects of her.[13] Gabriel's flustered response is to thrust a coin into her hands, in spite of her protest that "I wouldn't take it" (he allows her no choice and walks off); in other words, he buys her off by imposing his dominance in a different field of mastery in which he can still hold sovereignty, that of relative wealth and power.[14] In the attempts by Gabriel's ego to gain a sense of control and mastery during the evening, we increasingly are provided with the dynamics of the imposition of *mastery*: of the mail/male, of wealth, power, class, empire, and continent – over the colonized but still unruly Irish spirit, identity, femininity, and homerule/autonomy.

Later in the party Gabriel has another unpleasant run-in with yet another Irish woman, his colleague Miss Ivors, the outspoken Irish Nationalist. By this point it may seem to us apt that Miss Ivors especially should so discomfit Gabriel, since she openly stands for something he fears and has repressed, denied, or sold out: his "Irishness", that unruly, romantic, wilder, less cultured, less civilized, and uncolonizable self which the authorized Ego wishes to deny and which seems to be represented here by Gretta and Michael Furey and the West of Ireland (and Joyce's own Galway-born wife Nora). This seems a fear and repression instilled in Gabriel in part by the class snobbery of his mother, who we learn had disapproved of Gretta's "country cute"-ness (*D* 187). Appropriately, "Gabriel himself had taken his degree in the Royal University" (*D* 187). This latter was a "degree-granting institution" which (according to Gifford, *Joyce Annotated*, 116) "reflected English (Protestant) academic standards and effectively determined the curricula of its member institutions (including Catholic University College, Dublin)" – in other words, a "shoneen" institution imposing the cultural values of the English masters (culture and education *à la* Matthew Arnold, whose *Culture and Anarchy* was in Joyce's personal library in Trieste).[15] And now we learn that Gabriel writes for *The Daily Express*, a conservative paper with royalist leanings, suggesting his own unconscious collusion with the Empire ("He wanted to say that literature was above politics" [*D* 188]), a discovery by Miss Ivors that leads to her teasing charge that he should be "ashamed of [him]self" for being a "West Briton" (*D* 187–88) – that is, a sellout and collaborator with the imperial masters.[16]

But Miss Ivors good-naturedly admits that she liked his review of Browning's poems in *The Daily Express*, and now invites him and Gretta to a group vacation in the West. Once again, Gabriel's snobbery is barely disguised, as he admits that his preference is to vacation "to France or Belgium or perhaps Germany" (*D* 189); all three were, we might note, powerful countries with imperial holdings and aspirations; like England, France and Belgium had extensive empires around the globe. Miss Ivors's unrelenting probing ("And why do you go to France and Belgium ... instead of visiting your own land? ... And haven't you got your own language to keep in touch with – Irish?") finally draws from Gabriel an exasperated response that " – O, to tell you the truth, ... I'm sick of my own country, sick of it!" (*D* 189)[17]

When a few moments later Gretta learns about the proposal for a vacation in the West and pleads with him, " – O, do go, Gabriel, she cried. I'd love to see Galway again", Gabriel's response once again is to assert his patriarchal mastery by closing off further discussion: " – You can go if you like, said Gabriel coldly" (Gretta can only complain in frustration to Mrs. Malins, " – There's a nice husband for you, Mrs Malins" [*D* 191]).

Stung by Miss Ivors's accusation that he is a West Briton, Gabriel twice fantasizes escaping to the snow outside (*D* 192 and *D* 202): in both cases, his mental picture of escape appropriately revolves around the Wellington Monument dominating the snow in Phoenix Park, that phallic obelisk symbolizing British imperial and patriarchal rule. He now decides to get back at Miss Ivors by inserting into his speech an intentional jab at her:

Ladies and Gentlemen, the generation which is now on the wane among us may have had its faults but for my part I think it had certain qualities of hospitality, of humour, of humanity, which the new and very serious and hypereducated generation that is growing up around us seems to me to lack. Very good: that was one for Miss Ivors. What did he care that his aunts were only two ignorant old women?

(*D* 191)

Only two ignorant old women?! The hypocrisy of Gabriel's speech and value judgments becomes apparent in his more pressing desire to attack Miss Ivors. This hypocrisy reveals a level of cultural snobbery already hinted at in his preference for things continental, such as goloshes and cycling in France or Belgium. Earlier he had wondered whether in his speech he should quote some lines from Browning: "for he feared they would be above the heads of his hearers. Some quotation that they could recognize from Shakespeare or from the Melodies would be better. The indelicate clacking of the men's heels and the shuffling of their soles reminded him that their grade of culture differed from his" (*D* 179). Cultural snobbery is an authoritarian tendency to marginalize others by making value-charged distinctions about difference.[18] Old ladies are worthless and not to be listened to (or old maids, as with Maria in "Clay" [Norris,

"Narration"]). So also drunks, like Freddy Malins, who are to be cared after like infants but not to be taken seriously.

Interestingly, however, it is perhaps Freddy who seems to have some real aesthetic culture and appreciation.[19] While Gabriel, despite his intellectual pretensions, cannot appreciate Mary Jane's piano performance of academic pieces because they lacked melody (*D* 186), it is Freddy who is able – perhaps with the clarity of vision shared by the dispossessed and marginalized – to see through (or ignore) Aunt Julia's old-maid exterior and to realize how wonderful her singing is tonight, for, as the narrator admits, "To follow the voice [Julia's], *without looking at the singer's face*, was to feel and share the excitement of swift and secure flight" (*D* 193, my emphasis). And so Freddy congratulates her effusively if a little drunkenly. Similarly, he is able and willing to admit that one of the finest tenor voices he has ever heard was that of a black man, "a negro chieftain singing in the second part of the Gaiety pantomime who had one of the finest tenor voices he had ever heard" (*D* 198), a comment everyone else chooses to ignore (after all, he is only a drunk): " – And why couldn't he have a voice too? asked Freddy Malins sharply. Is it because he's only a black?" (*D* 198; one recalls "without looking at the singer's face").

"And why couldn't he/she have a voice too?" is a Joycean question which, as we have seen, could be asked here about Gretta, Lily, Freddy, and Ireland herself, among others. And of course about Aunt Julia, who does have a real "voice," which she has exercised in a poignant performance of "Arrayed for the Bridal" – a very difficult soprano aria adapted from Bellini's *I Puritani*. Here I would refer you to Norris's compelling argument ("Stifled," 496–502) that Julia Morkan is repeatedly belittled, infantilized, and ignored in the story in spite of a brilliant performance that is likely the swan song to a frustrated career in subservience to a religious patriarchy which has, as Aunt Kate put it, "turn[ed] out the women out of the choirs that have slaved there all their lives and put little whipper-snappers of boys over their heads" (*D* 194) – for a papal edict in 1903 (*In Motu Proprio*, just months before the Morkans' Christmas party) had decreed that henceforward women were to be banished from church choirs. Julia's story is a painful and poignant one indeed; she is one of many voices, from the polylogic multivocality on the social and cultural margins of Dublin, which are suppressed and denied in *Dubliners*.

Even Gabriel's little jokes reveal unacknowledged cultural snobbery, as in: " – Now, if anyone wants a little more of what vulgar people call stuffing let him or her speak" (*D* 198). Most revealing, however, is the funny anecdote he tells late in the party about "the late lamented Patrick Morkan, our grandfather" and his horse named Johnny: "One fine day the old gentleman thought he'd like to drive out with the quality to a military review in the park" (*D* 207). These lines seem to suggest that, having made his money by owning and operating a starch mill, old Mr. Morkan developed pretensions to being "quality" and thus, co-opted by the economy of the empire, wished, like the "quality," to attend a "military review in the park," presumably a display of English military power. This buying-into the values of the oppressor is a trait of the grandfather which seems to have been inherited by both Gabriel's mother and by Gabriel himself.[20]

– Out from the mansion of his forefathers, continued Gabriel, he drove with Johnny. And everything went on beautifully until Johnny came in sight of King Billy's statue: and whether he fell in love with the horse King Billy sits on or whether he thought he was back again in the mill, anyhow he began to walk around the statue.
Gabriel paced in a circle round the hall in his goloshes amid the laughter of the others.

(*D* 208)

King Billy, of course, was William III, the Protestant prince of Orange, conqueror of Ireland at the Battle of the Boyne, and the scourge of Irish Catholics. This equestrian statue of King Billy on College Green was despised by Dubliners as a hated symbol of English domination and of the Irish defeat at the Boyne. As Adaline Glasheen points out (citing Gilbert's *History of Dublin*, III. 40–56): "In Dublin (before the Free State) the Ulstermen's brazen calf was a lead equestrian statue of King Billy on College Green which, on Williamite holy days, was painted white (a white horse in a fanlight is still a sign of Protestant sympathies) and decorated with orange lilies ... and green and white ribbons 'symbolically placed beneath its uplifted foot.' Catholics retorted by vandalizing the statue, tarring, etc., and in 1836 suceeded in blowing the figure of the king off the horse" (*Third Census*, 309). So that Gabriel, notably clad in his "civilized" goloshes, circling round and round the hall in imitation of Johnny circling King Billy's white horse, is unknowingly reinscribing the marks of an Irish cycle of paralysis, of satellitic subservience to (and co-option by) the Empire.[21]

141

It is at this point in the story that Gabriel looks up the stairwell to see his wife in a striking and attentive posture:

> He stood still in the gloom of the hall, trying to catch the air that the voice was singing and gazing up at his wife. There was grace and mystery in her attitude as if she were a symbol of something. He asked himself what is a woman standing on the stairs in the shadow, listening to distant music, a symbol of. If he were a painter he would paint her in that attitude. Her blue felt hat would show off the bronze of her hair against the darkness and the dark panels of her skirt would show off the light ones. *Distant Music* he would call the picture if he were a painter.
>
> (*D* 210)

In his mind's eye he *is* a painter, for, as a number of commentators have noted, Gabriel engages here, as the Western patriarchal tradition has for centuries, in the aesthetic objectification of women as art and symbol, as object rather than subject.[22] As these critics have noted (e.g., Norris in "Stifled," 486, 492), this moment should recall two previous intertextual references in the story to famous balcony scenes in literary history, *Romeo and Juliet* (*D* 186: "A picture of the balcony scene in *Romeo and Juliet* hung" over the piano) and "My Last Duchess" by Robert Browning (the poet who has been on Gabriel's mind and in his speech all evening). Recall that, in Browning's poem, the speaker (the Duke of Ferrara) is a domestic tyrant who domesticates (and presumably kills) his unacceptably high-spirited wife (too non-passive, too much a subject) by aestheticizing and literally objectifying her – that is, he turns her into a painting hanging above the stairwell – so that he may possess her as object and stifle her own emerging subjectivity. Browning's Duke is a ruthless patriarch engaging in an aggressively masculine colonization, aestheticization, and objectification of woman.

The song Gretta is listening to is a stunningly appropriate choice on Joyce's part, for "The Lass of Aughrim" is likewise a song about mastery, domination, and mistreatment (even rape) of a peasant woman by a patriarchal nobleman. "The Lass of Aughrim" is a version (among many, with many titles) of "Lord Gregory"; although the details differ from version to version, the version Joyce seems to have known[23] tells of Lord Gregory having forced himself sexually on the Lass ("Sorely against my will"), who then gets with child as a result; the song finds her standing in the rain outside the castle with her cold and dying child as she begs to be let in, only to be refused entrance and recognition by Lord Gregory (and in some versions also by his cruel mother).

Is Gretta Conroy a modern-day Lass of Aughrim? To begin with, Joyce's choice of this variant title/version ("The Lass of Aughrim") allies it with the West of Ireland, for the town of Aughrim is about thirty miles from Galway, the hometown of both Gretta and Nora Barnacle. Furthermore, as Ruth Bauerle points out, "The music's folk simplicity is at variance with the deliberately civilized, continental preferences of Gretta's husband Gabriel" (*Songbook*, 177). Note further parallels: like Michael Furey, Gretta (scorning goloshes) and the Lass both uninhibitedly stand in the rain; all three seem to suggest a primitive wildness as yet undomesticated. Gabriel, on the other hand, wears goloshes and retires to a nearby hotel to protect himself from rain and snow (just as Lord Gregory is sheltered from the rain in the warmth of his castle), and prefers the strictures of a "civilized" cultural code prescribed by Continental and English influences. Gabriel's mother had scorned Gretta's country-cuteness and low-bred backgrounds – just as Lord Gregory's mother scorns the abused Lass of Aughrim.

Furthermore, I would suggest that to Joyce and to his Irish readers the town of Aughrim should hold an even more potent symbolic value than has been heretofore noted in discussions of "The Dead" – for it is closely associated with the Battle of the Boyne and with the subjugation of Ireland by the English. The twelfth of July, known as "White Horse Day" (for "King Billy on White Horse"; McHugh, *Annotations*, 347) is celebrated by Ulster Protestants as the victory at the Boyne (in 1690) over the papists. But that date and that battle are also associated and frequently confused with another (and perhaps more historically significant) battle, the Battle of Aughrim. As the *Encyclopaedia Britannica* notes, although the Battle of the Boyne is celebrated on July 12, that date "is actually the old style date of the more decisive Battle of Aughrim in the following year," 1691. As R. F. Foster writes in *Modern Ireland 1600–1972*:

[I]t is uncertain whether [the Boyne] was the decisive battle of the war, though Protestants celebrate it still. Jacobites saw it as an indecisive engagement, Aughrim a year later being 'the great disaster' ... all hope went after Aughrim, where [the Irish forces] lost the day in a welter of heroics, confusion and alleged treachery: 'the most disastrous battle in Irish history' ... The losses were enormous, in what was to be the last great pitched battle in Irish history.

(148, 150)

It was the Irish defeat at Aughrim a year after the Boyne that finally and fully sealed English domination of Ireland. Aughrim, then, like Browning's murdered Duchess or the hapless Lass in the song, becomes itself a poignant symbol of domination and colonization by imperial patriarchs – that murdered Irish past, the dead, the bodies of, as Yeats wrote in his verse play *Purgatory*, "long ago / Men that had fought at Aughrim and the Boyne."

Thus, if we consider Gretta as a modern-day Lass of Aughrim, we find in Joyce's selection of this song heard on a stairwell a set of carefully designed parallels between conqueror and conquered, between imperial oppressor and colonized victim, in which Aughrim, its Lass, Gretta, and Michael Furey in the rain all merge into a composite image of the loss of the Irish soul and autonomy to the imperial masters: King Billy conquering the Irish at Aughrim and the Boyne; Protestant England dominating Catholic Ireland; Lord Gregory raping the helpless Lass of Aughrim, then letting her perish in the rain (as Michael Furey had perished) only to be eventually aestheticized in folksong; Browning's Duke tyrannizing, then murdering, and finally aestheticizing his last Duchess as a painting at the top of the stairwell; and Gabriel Conroy's attempt to master Gretta by infantilizing, then essentializing and objectifying her as art (as a stairwell painting titled *Distant Music*: "What is a woman standing on the stairs in the shadow, listening to distant music, a symbol of"). As Spivak has written in reference to subaltern women: "Between patriarchy and imperialism, subject-constitution and object-formation, the figure of the woman disappears" ("Subaltern," 296).

Even more sinister and disturbing is the fact that the subsequent scene between Gabriel and Gretta in the Gresham Hotel *almost* provokes not just an intellectual and aesthetic domination, but physical mastery and violation. For, as we have already seen in Gabriel's framing of *Distant Music*, it is the aestheticized *image* of Gretta, more than Gretta herself, which (like an erotic Venus or a *Playboy* centerfold) arouses Gabriel from his crisis of ego-confidence into brutal lust: "She had no longer any grace of attitude but Gabriel's eyes were still bright with happiness. The blood went bounding along his veins; and the thoughts went rioting through his brain, proud, joyful, tender, valorous" (D 213). Having been aroused by an objectified fantasy of his wife, Gabriel now first reviews his erotic memories of her, then fantasizes her undressing:

Like distant music these words that he had written years before were borne towards him from the past. He longed to be alone with her. When the others had gone away, when he and she were in their room in the hotel, then they would be alone together. He would call her softly:
– Gretta!
Perhaps she would not hear at once: she would be undressing. Then something in his voice would strike her. She would turn and look at him...

(*D* 214)

As they return to the hotel, Gabriel becomes more and more erotically aroused: "But now, after the kindling again of so many memories, the first touch of her body, musical and strange and perfumed, sent through him a keen pang of lust. Under cover of her silence he pressed her arm closely to his side" (*D* 215); "She mounted the stairs behind the porter, her head bowed in the ascent, her frail shoulders curved as with a burden, her skirt girt tightly about her. He could have flung his arms about her hips and held her still for his arms were trembling with desire to seize her and only the stress of his nails against the palms of his hands held the wild impulse of his body in check" (*D* 215).

When Gretta does not respond to his caresses as Gabriel would wish, his mental reaction is one of smoldering sexual anger:

He was trembling now with annoyance. Why did she seem so abstracted? He did not know how he could begin. Was she annoyed, too, about something? If she would only turn to him or come to him of her own accord! To take her as she was would be brutal. No, he must see some ardour in her eyes first. He longed to be master of her strange mood.

(*D* 217)

These are startling lines, in which Gabriel rejects "taking her as she was" as "too brutal," since he needs to "see some ardour in her eyes first" and to be "master of her strange mood." A few lines later we learn that "He longed to cry to her from his soul, to crush her body against his, to overmaster her ... He was in such a fever of rage and desire that he did not hear her come from the window" (*D* 217).

As Ruth Bauerle has suggested in her provocative essay titled "Date Rape, Mate Rape: A Liturgical Interpretation of 'The Dead,'" Gabriel and Gretta almost literally re-enact the date rape at the source of the story of Lord Gregory and the Lass of Aughrim.[24]

Should we then despise Gabriel Conroy as a version of Lord Gregory or of Browning's Duke? We might consider that Gabriel's situation is not atypical of heterosexual men in our society, and that the basic situation in the Conroys' hotel room is a common scene that has been reenacted in bedrooms at some time or other by every sexually-active couple in human history: one partner is sexually frustrated to discover that the other is not "in the mood," not as aroused as oneself. Too often, however, the result has been either physical violation or abuse, or, more frequently, passive acquies-cence by the female ("taking her as she was"). The crucial difference here is that Gabriel is checked by his own highly developed self-awareness (which has earlier [179] already led him to question his own mastery and male-ness as a failure in both his conversation with Lily and in the speech he had prepared), so that when Gretta now reveals that all along she was not getting similarly aroused (as he had thought) but rather was thinking of the young, dead Michael Furey, Gabriel is assailed by "a shameful consciousness of his own person" (*D* 219–20), seeing himself now as "a ludicrous figure, acting as a pennyboy for his aunts, a nervous well-meaning sentimentalist, orating to vulgarians and idealizing his own clownish lusts" (*D* 220). As his wife breaks into tears of passionate grief, Gabriel first "held her hand for a moment," and then, "shy of intruding on her grief, let it fall gently and walked quietly to the window" (*D* 222).

Gabriel's final epiphany, in this reading of the story, becomes, it seems to me, even more moving – for it is an act of emotional expansiveness, self-understanding, and generosity. The West and the snow in his final vision suggest all those repressed elements that Gabriel's ego has denied, sold out to, or been co-opted out of – including the uninhibited freedom of the Irish soul and of the marginalized others, in contrast to his patriarchal and imperialistic urge for mastery, dominion, colonization, and hierarchy. Gabriel's self-conscious willingness finally to grant Gretta a private space of her own, in which she can be her own emotional subject, inscribes a *possible* alternative by which to break free from the culturally-encoded male pattern prescribed by his mental framing of his wife as an aestheticized painting; and by the previous and parallel masculine matrixes suggested by the models of the British Empire over its far-flung colonies, King Billy at Aughrim and the Boyne, Lord Gregory over the Lass, and Browning's Duke over his late wife. Instead, Gabriel's final vision of the falling snow which "was general all over Ireland" attempts to break down the barriers of difference con-structed by the patriarchal ego he is so deeply (if unconsciously) implicated in, into at least a recognition of generosity and sameness, all shades of equal color, whether these "shades ... pass[ing] boldly into that other world" be Michael Furey, Aunt Julia, black opera singers, or himself: "One by one they were all becoming shades ... Generous tears filled Gabriel's eyes." (*D* 223) "Generosity" – a charged term in Joyce's personal vocabulary, suggesting a collective social conscience[25] – allows for the acceptance of others as subjects, breaking down the unified self into a consciousness of a shared or collective subjectivity, allowing the walls of the ego to dissolve and for identities to mix in a vision, however momentary or melodramatic on Gabriel's part, of uncompartmentalized, non-hierarchical sameness – as the snow falls faintly through the universe and faintly falling, equally and non-preferentially, over everyone, living and dead, usurper and usurped.

Ulysses: imagining selves and nations

6.

Imagining selves[1]

The Tower: ethnography, essence, and colonialism

The Irish, as we have seen in chapter 2, were discursively endowed by Anglo-Saxonists with those traits most feared or despised in respectable English society – in a process similar to the way in which the English formed their images of other races, too, in a universalized essentialism of the Other as primitive, barbaric, and uncivilized/ uncivilizable. Joyce's *Ulysses*, I would argue, is founded, from its very first moments at the Martello Tower, upon an acute awareness of precisely these discursive and anthropological dynamics.

The Introit which Buck Mulligan intones in the opening lines of *Ulysses* – "*Introibo ad altare Dei*" (*U* 1.5; I will go to the altar of God) – is, of course, the opening line of the Latin Mass. Its original source, however, although less well remembered, is no less significant: Psalm 43 (Vulgate 42), sung by the Hebrews in Babylonian exile. On the lips of an Irishman living in an Irish tower owned by the English, these words and context invoke a Hebraic history of displacement, diaspora, and struggle for one's homeland and for Home Rule – the first instance in Joyce's novel of a racialized, Jewish-Hebraic parallel to the "Irish Question." For "Telemachus," the opening chapter of *Ulysses*, provides us with a symptomatic re-presentation of the dynamics and tensions of a colonized people without Home Rule and of its resultant need to appease the whims of its colonizers.

In such a context, the Martello Tower becomes a figure and parable for Ireland itself; as a small part of Irish territory embodying the dilemma of the whole, the tower is a synecdoche for the Irish condition without Home Rule: it is "occupied" (in both domestic and imperial senses) by a British presence (Haines) and by a native collaborator, the latter having the treacherous qualities of the wooden-horse (Mulligan, "equine ... grained and hued like pale oak"). Stephen's very first words in the novel – "Tell me, Mulligan ... How long is Haines going to stay in this tower?" (*U* 1.47–49) – resonate with the Home Rule question and the longing for Irish autonomy from English occupation. The fact that this is an enforced, military occupation is suggested by the history of the Martello towers as military defences, by the repeated references to the tower's "round gunrest" (e.g., *U* 1.9), and by Mulligan's mock-military language (e.g., " – Back to barracks!" in *U* 1.19). Significantly, the Englishman Haines is himself a colonial presence who carries and brandishes a gun, an English sahib raving and moaning about shooting a black panther; later Stephen calls him a "panthersahib" (*U* 3.277), conscious of the parallel between Ireland and India as British colonies. Appropriately, Haines is the son of a man who, Buck tells us, made his fortune by colonial exploitation, "by selling jalap to Zulus or some bloody swindle or other" (*U* 1.156–57). Like father, like son: Haines has come to Ireland to profit from another form of colonialist exploitation, intending to make a collection of Irish folk sayings – much like anthropologists or ethnographers from European empires doing field work on tribal peoples in native colonies. In fact, I would like to suggest that one way to think about the dynamics of "Telemachus" is as an ethnographic encounter with a "native" population, in which the British anthropologist ventures out in the wilderness to study the primitive "wild Irish" and their folkways, in the presence of a willing native informant (Mulligan) and the latter's semi-willing specimen of study (Stephen).

Stephen's resentment at the English occupation of the tower for which he pays the rent is suggested, not only in his opening question to Mulligan, but again in his response to Mulligan's Wildean witticism about Stephen's face in the mirror being "The rage of Caliban at not seeing his face in a mirror" (*U* 1.143). While Buck may be willing to condone the English racialization and simianization of the Irish as a native "Caliban," the Irish response – as in the cartoon titled "Pat" (see figure 9) – was often the rage of the Irishman precisely at seeing his face represented in the English mirror *as* Caliban, and the parallel rage of not seeing in one's reflection oneself as one's own master. For Stephen's response to Buck is that the mirror is "a symbol of Irish art. The cracked lookingglass of a servant" (*U* 1.146), a comment which voices and reasserts the resentment of the Irish at being forced (and racialized) into the servitude of a Caliban.

Mulligan is delighted with Stephen's retort for a different reason:

– Cracked lookingglass of a servant! Tell that to the oxy chap downstairs and touch him for a guinea. He's stinking with money and thinks you're not a gentleman. His old fellow made his tin by selling jalap to Zulus or some bloody swindle or other. God, Kinch, if you and I could only work together we might do something for the island. Hellenise it.

(*U* 1.154–58)

This is the delighted response of the native informant who has discovered something else he can peddle to the ethnographer, something he knows the ethnographer will want – a touch of local color, a native witticism: "Tell that to the oxy chap downstairs and touch him for a guinea." As informant, Mulligan displays an understanding of the imperial ethnographer/explorer's Museum Mentality, searching for what the latter is already expecting to find (and later to exhibit), that "reality" already constructed by an Orientalized discourse (which can then be turned into marketable commodities – whether as collection of folk sayings or as museum object). As Native American writer Gerald Vizenor points out: "Tribal cultures have been transformed ... from mythic time into museum commodities ... colonial inventions, museum bound. Portrait painters, photographers, explorers, traders, and politicians have, with few exceptions, created a metasavage in perfect racist opposition to the theologies of the dominant culture" (*Crossbloods*, 85, 88). "For," in Benedict Anderson's words, "museums, and the museumizing imagination, are both profoundly political" (*Imagined*, 178). Haines's interest in Irish customs and folklore is but another version of his father's economic exploitation of the African colonies.[2]

Mulligan's reference to Haines as an "oxy chap" who thinks that Stephen "is not a gentleman" elicits in Stephen's mind the memory of "Clive Kempthorne's rooms" at Oxford (when Stephen visited Mulligan there): "Palefaces: they hold their ribs with laughter" (*U* 1.165–66). Stephen's memory of the young, privileged Oxonians uses Irish slang for the English, appropriately suggesting the self-consciously racialized discourse of the Irish as Native American Indians before their paleface conquerors (see Gibbons, "Race Against Time"), as well as an echo of the English "Pale" (the small coastal area around Dublin to which English rule was limited before the mid-seventeenth century); later in the day, Stephen again refers to some English tourists he notices as "palefaces" (*U* 10.341); and in his Shakespeare lecture will suggest a shared consciousness of cultural/colonial invasion between Irish and "American" Calibans: "The *Sea Venture* comes home from Bermudas and the play Renan admired is written with Patsy Caliban, our American cousin" (*U* 9.756–57). The "oxy chap" and "gentleman" references underscore Haines's class consciousness and superior airs (he is, appropriately, wearing a "tennis shirt" – lawn tennis was the sport of cultured English gentlemen, as Stephen is well aware when he later puns on "Lawn Tennyson, gentleman poet" in *U* 3.492): for Haines belongs to that genteel and gentlemanly Culture to which Stephen's own *déclassé* Irish Catholicism is considered but barbaric Anarchy. Even the "deaf gardener" at Oxford is, in Stephen's mind here, "masked with Matthew Arnold's face" (*U* 1.173); later in "Circe," Stephen will again drunkenly envision *two Oxford dons with lawnmowers ... masked with Matthew Arnold's face*" (*U* 15.2513–14), reinforcing the iconic evocations of Arnold, Oxford, and well-kept lawns (English gardens, tennis) as representations of English notions of culture. This first episode of *Ulysses* is, appropriately, textured with such references to Arnold and Arnoldian ideas about Hellenism, Hebraism, Culture and Anarchy.

Mulligan himself has clearly bought into the Arnoldian cultural discourse, for he takes onto himself the hegemonic role of interpreter of Hellenic culture and aesthetics to the Barbarian Calibans (and, through the episode's racialized analogies, to the presumed Hebraism of the islanders): "*Epi oinopa ponton.* Ah, Dedalus, the Greeks! I must teach you. You must read them in the original. *Thalatta! Thalatta!*" (*U* 1.78–80); "we might do something for the island. Hellenise it" (*U* 1.158). (Later, in "Oxen of the Sun," we are parodically told that Mulligan, trying to improve "the calibre of the race," prophesies that "Kallipedia [Greek for the contemplation of beauty] ... would soon be generally adopted and all the graces of life, genuinely good music, agreeable literature, light philosophy, instructive pictures, plastercast reproductions of the classical statues"; *U* 14.1250–53). Stephen's unspoken, internal response to Buck's call to Hellenism – "To ourselves ... new paganism ... *omphalos*" (*U* 1.176) – is quite different in tenor, combating Mulligan's hailing of Stephen as fellow Hellenist and cultured aesthete with a "new paganism" and with an echo of the Irish nationalist slogan *Sinn Fein* ("We ourselves"), celebrating his "Hebraic"/Irish/barbaric otherness like a quietly defiant Caliban.

Joyce further undercuts Mulligan's own shoneen pretensions to culture a page later by underscoring Mulligan's servitude (however self-conscious and witty) to the Saxon conquerors, as Mulligan scrambles to make breakfast because "The Sassenach wants his morning rashers" (*U* 1.232; "Sassenach" is Gaelic for "Saxon conqueror").

As native informant, Mulligan is at once manipulating Haines, as well as prostituting himself (and the image of his race that he thinks will sell), for English money; the ethnographic encounter inevitably involves a monetary transaction with those who control the financial resources: " – I told [Haines] your symbol of Irish art. He says it's very clever. Touch him for a quid, will you? A guinea, I mean" (*U* 1.290–91; Buck's internal emendation of "quid" to "guinea" subtly suggests his own need to privilege the more hegemonically "gentlemanly" sum and term). When Stephen points out that he will get paid this morning, Mulligan calls it "The school kip" (*U* 1.293, and again in 1.466); the slang meaning of "kip" as "brothel" is quite appropriately functional here, given that Stephen is prostituted to a job he doesn't like, working for an Ulsterman (Deasy) at a hegemonic school for privileged young boys in order to get money.[3] Stephen is reminded that he will be paid, in Buck's words, "Four shining sovereigns ... Four omnipotent sovereigns" (*U* 1.296–97): Buck's repeated word here underscores the reality that Stephen is literally a servant to an omnipotent master – a colonial subject to an imperial sovereign and thus himself a sovereign subject, paid in a currency that is linguistically the metonymic coin (sovereigns, crowns) for the royal English power. Mulligan turns the screw further at this point by singing a song about "Coronation day": "Coronation day" was not only a song celebrating Edward VII's coronation (sung by subjects about their sovereign), but appropriately also a slang term for payday, since one gets paid in "crowns" and "sovereigns" (Gifford, *"Ulysses" Annotated*, 19). The inescapable reminder is that the Irish are themselves subjects to crowns and sovereigns – both to English royalty and to the money that the Crown controls. No wonder that Stephen, remembering himself as a "server" of mass at Clongowes, now thinks of himself as "A server of a servant" (*U* 1.312).

Mulligan's own kip is that of native informant, prostituting his wit for Haines's approval now with a bawdy story about "old mother Grogan": " – That's folk, he said very earnestly, for your book, Haines. Five lines of text and ten pages of notes about the folk and the fishgods of Dundrum. Printed by the weird sisters in the year of the big wind" (*U* 1.365–67). Mulligan's own self-consciously non-sensical parody of Irish "folk" lore reflects his understanding of exactly what the ethnographic discourse is looking for: having trotted out some morose local color in the person of Stephen Dedalus, he now tells colorful stories about "fishgods" in "the year of the big wind" ("Can you recall, brother, is mother Grogan's tea and water pot spoken of in the Mabinogion?"), and finally he unveils his most promising local specimen, the old milkwoman.

The entire scene with the milkwoman is a wonderful parody of the ethnographic encounter with a tribal culture, seeking what Virginia-Lee Webb calls "manipulated images" of an essentialized (dead) tribal past, "images that were used to help construct pejorative myths that served colonial interests" ("Manipulated," 1–2), with the native informant acting as interpreter: " – The islanders, Mulligan said to Haines casually, speak frequently of the collector of prepuces" (*U* 1.393–94). Mulligan's self-consciously parodic orchestration and manipulation of the scene allows him to have his cake and to eat it, too – since he does actually manage to engage Haines's ethnographic interest in both Stephen's Irish wit and in the milkwoman as an essentialized specimen of Irish folksiness. What Mulligan knows Haines is looking for are the comfortably static images of an essentialized stage Irishness, such as colorful verbal wit (Stephen) and primitive, folksy backwardness (old milkwoman).[4] Such images are not only marketable commodities but in their more insidious implications "could be used to justify any aspect of the colonial enterprise" (Webb, "Manipulated," 5). For "primitive" peoples have been repeatedly functioned within what ethnohistorian William Simmons calls "anthropological fictions," "the purist notions that native cultures resist history, or that they disappear in its presence" ("Culture," 7) – in what ethnohistorian James Axtell describes sarcastically (in discussing Native American history) as "the short 'pathetic' story of the 'inevitable' triumph of a 'booming' white 'civilization' over a 'fragile' 'primitive' culture" (*European*, 7); all of these attempts to freeze a static backwardness onto a native culture collude to construct a European sovereignty of self in what James Clifford calls "master narratives of cultural disappearance" ("Four," 214).

Stephen, thinking of the milkwoman as "silk of the kine" and "poor old woman" – traditional terms for Ireland herself – realizes that, like the tower, she represents a figure for Ireland who is passively subject to exploitation by the colonizer and by his shoneen collaborator: "A wandering crone, lowly form of an immortal serving her conqueror and her gay betrayer, their common cuckquean" (*U* 1.404–05) – a female cuckold commonly exploited by Haines and Mulligan. While she prostitutes herself unknowingly to them, she ignores her real spokesman, the bard seeking to create the conscience of his race: "She bows her old head to a voice [Mulligan] that speaks to her loudly, her bonesetter, her medicineman: me she slights … and to the loud voice [Haines] that now bids her be silent" while he speaks to her in Gaelic. She does not understand, and thinks it is French: this is Joyce's ironic comment on an Ireland that has been constructed and essentialized as a dying, Gaelic, primitive otherness, when in reality Ireland herself no longer fits this Orientalized stereotype.[5] So that it is Mulligan and Haines who speak Gaelic, employing Irish colloquialisms like "Is there Gaelic on you?" (*U* 1.427), while the milkwoman (speaking English) thinks that it is Haines who is from the West of Ireland. Haines's opinion – "he thinks we ought to speak Irish in Ireland" (*U* 1.432) – smacks of the same hegemonic cultural need as the desire of white American culture to construct the "authentic" (Native American) Indian, to view the Indian (or Irish) other as Other, as quaint, primitive, "wild Irish" – as dead stereotype of an absolute difference. No wonder that Haines suddenly remembers – "That reminds me, Haines said, rising, that I have to visit your national library today" (*U* 1.469–70) – presumably to do ethnographic and folkloric research on the essentialized Irish, for he is more interested in the Irish as a dead culture constructed by academic and ethnographic discourse than as a living and changing culture; he is seeking to find what has already been constructed as the essential discourse of Irishness, rather than observing current realities, such as the fact that the old milkwoman speaks no Gaelic ("I'm told it's a grand language by them that knows"). So off he runs to a national library which was "identified with efforts to preserve records and keep the Irish language and culture alive" (Gifford, *"Ulysses" Annotated*, 22).

Later, in the library itself, Best remarks that Haines is "quite enthusiastic, don't you know, about Hyde's *Lovesongs of Connacht* … He's gone to Gill's to buy it" – to which comment Eglinton responds by pointing out that "The peatsmoke is going to his head" (*U* 9.93–100). The Irishmen are quite aware of Haines's ethnographic "enthusiasm" for a primitive Irish past and essence, seeking out the "lean unlovely English" of Douglas Hyde's collection of songs from the West (Connacht) with its reek of the peat used to heat peasant homes in the West.[6] In the "Oxen of the Sun" parodies, Haines thus wonderfully reappears as a ghost carrying a "portfolio full of Celtic literature in one hand" (that is, Hyde's *Lovesongs*) and speaking in Gaelic idiom: "This is the appearance is on me. Tare and ages, what way would I be resting at all, ... and I tramping Dublin this while back with my share of songs and himself after me the like of a soulth or a bullawurrus?" (*U* 14.1013–21).

Vizenor, in discussing Edward Curtis's romanticized photographs of Native American tribal people, demonstrates pointedly how such manipulated, command performances of a "tribal past" depend on a "structural opposition of savagism and civilization" – which, of course, functions to maintain the dominant culture's own constructed essence and sense of Self: "This obsession with the tribal past is not an innocent collection of arrowheads, not a crude map of public camp sites in sacred places, but rather a statement of academic power and control over tribal images, ... linguistic colonization of oral traditions and popular memories" (*Crossbloods*, 83, 86). As Vizenor ironically points out, dominant culture never gives us images of Indians "perched at pianos, dressed in machine stitched clothes, or writing letters to corrupt government agents" (85); no, they must remain primitives and savages, our recognizably "authentic" Indians.

Similarly, we might ask why Haines, in searching for the "real" Ireland (like Adela Quested in Forster's India), is so interested in Stephen's witty sayings and in the milkwoman's supposed primitive folksiness – but not in the Stephen who has traveled to Paris, and even less in the well-traveled, urbane, Oxonian Buck Mulligan, both examples of real contemporary Irishness. Clifford, in discussing "a problematic figure, the 'informant'," points out that these are usually "complex individuals routinely made to speak for 'cultural' knowledge" and yet who in actuality "have their own 'ethnographic' proclivities ... and have seldom been homebodies" ("Traveling," 97), but rather are themselves active agents in a variety of activities, most of which never get reported or represented by Western observers. Instead, anthropology has participated repeatedly in strategies for localizing "others" as "natives," confining or imprisoning them "through a process of representational essentializing, what [Arjun Appadurai] calls a 'metonymic freezing,' in which one part or aspect of peoples' lives come to epitomize them as a whole, constituting their theoretical niche in an anthropological taxonomy. India equals hierarchy, Melanesia equals exchange, and so forth" ("Traveling," 100). As Benedict Anderson (184) observes, the "museumizing imagination" creates "a totalizing classificatory grid" and "The effect of the grid was always to be able to say of anything that it was this, not that; it belonged here, not there. It was bounded, determinate, and therefore – in principle – countable" (one might add namable, essentializable, stereotypable). But in actuality, to quote Appadurai, "Natives, people confined to and by the places to which they belong, groups unsullied by contact with a larger world have probably never existed" (Clifford, "Traveling," 100). Haines's eagerness to find an Ireland frozen in primitive rituals and Gaelic language/culture is mocked both by the milkwoman's incomprehension of Gaelic and by Buck and Stephen's educated worldliness. As Clifford puts it, "What's elided is the wider global world of intercultural import–export in which the ethnographic encounter is always already enmeshed" ("Traveling," 100).

Knowing this, Mulligan, as informant, has cleverly dangled the lure of Stephen's wit as specimen of local color, and Haines now bites: "I intend to make a collection of your sayings if you will let me" (*U* 1.480). Unlike the milkwoman or Haines, however, Stephen – like Buck – understands that the point of the ethnographic encounter is not actual cultural accuracy but profit; his reply is thus unsettling to Haines precisely because he knows he is being exploited and prostituted, and so wants to get the most for it: "Would I make any money by it?" (*U* 1.490). Or, as he says to Mulligan: "The problem is to get money. From whom? From the milkwoman or from him. It's a toss up, I think ... I see little hope from her or from him" (*U* 1.497–501). For Stephen, who like Joyce wishes to get out of this binary dialectic, neither Ireland nor England can provide a satisfactory solution. Mulligan, though, can only complain that Stephen is ruining his ethnographic pimping: "What did you say that for? ... I blow him out about you ... and then you come along with your lousy leer and your gloomy jesuit jibes ... Why don't you play them as I do?" (and then he adds, to appease Stephen, "To hell with them all. Let us get out of the kip"; *U* 1.496–507.)

Later, in "Proteus," Stephen will recall that "The cold domed room of the tower waits" – a formulation that pictures his own home as a prison (like the Tower of London) – inhabited by "the panthersahib and his pointer" (*U* 3.271–78). Here Stephen is representing Haines (with his gun, raving about a black panther) as a white British colonial hunter, a sahib with his trusty native guide or hunting dog (his "pointer," Mulligan), tracking panthers or elephants in the jungle. Stephen's metaphor melds the ethnographic encounter with a safari, the Great White Hunter in search of the elusive Great Irish Folktale: in either case, the result will be colonial exploitation and profit (whether in the form of local color, museum exhibits, animal skins, ivory, rubber, and the like) in which the object of exploitation is the racialized colonial native, whether Irish, Indian, African, Jewish, or "black panther."

Earlier in the morning Haines had asked who had the key, and Mulligan had answered that Stephen had it. At this point, in line 528 of "Telemachus," Stephen now takes out his ashplant – a traditional Celtic kingmaker and weapon (Gifford, *"Ulysses" Annotated*, 22). But both his key and his sword/ashplant are but hollow symbols of a Celtic home rule, for Stephen is the usurped Telemachus at Ithaca and the usurped Prince Hamlet at Elsinore, living in a domed tower/ prison. When Haines now asks if they pay rent for the tower, Mulligan answers that they pay "Twelve quid" and Stephen adds "To the secretary of state for war" – for the tower is owned by the Royal War Office. After all, Buck Mulligan reminds us, the towers were built by "Billy Pitt ... when the French were on the sea" (*U* 1.539–44): that is to say (in quoting a late-eighteenth-century Irish ballad; Gifford, *"Ulysses" Annotated*, 23), they were defenses erected by William Pitt against the French, whose navy between 1796 and 1798 made several attempts to provide military support to the Irish revolutionaries. As such, the Martello towers are appropriate symbols of the rule of Britannia on the imperial waves; it is one more "kip" in which the Irish have to pay rent on what should in fact belong to them. Haines – as "The seas' ruler" – represents, to Stephen, Britannia ruling the waves, with Mulligan as his cohort and collaborator: "He wants that key. It is mine. I paid the rent" (*U* 1.630–31). In fact, this is the exact dilemma of agrarian Ireland: having to pay exorbitant rents to British landlords just to live on one's own land. Even more ironically, Stephen pays money to be allowed to live on a military structure constructed for the express purpose of keeping Irishmen like himself in continued thrall to the British (by repulsing foreign aid to Irish liberation); he has to fund his own servitude.

No wonder that Stephen refuses to agree with Haines's comment that "You are your own master," pointing out instead that "I am a servant of two masters, an English and an Italian ... The imperial British state ... and the holy Roman catholic and apostolic church"

(*U* 1.636–44). Later, in the parodies of "Oxen of the Sun," Stephen again bitterly complains (to an invoked "Erin") that he is: "the slave of servants ... forget me not, O Milesian. Why has thou done this abomination before me that thou didst spurn me for a merchant of jalaps?" (*U* 14.371–73) Haines's response to Stephen is a classic evasion: " – I can quite understand that ... An Irishman must think like that, I daresay. We feel in England that we have treated you rather unfairly. It seems history is to blame" (*U* 1.647–49). Haines's ability to blame "history" but not himself absolves his own repressed "agenbite" of conscience by occluding any consciousness of his own role in exploiting the islanders, of the parallel between his father's (the "merchant of jalaps") exploitation of the Zulus for personal profit (for that is but "history") and his own presence and activities in Ireland. Haines's logic is an exact depiction in microcosm of the reasoning of English (and other Western) liberals, who can deplore colonial injustice even as they continue to reap the benefits (economic and cultural) of that colonial injustice and of its continuing economic/ cultural imperialism (even in postcolonial economies today). The "history" which is to blame, unfortunately, cannot so conveniently be relegated by the colonials themselves to the "past" – for to them it is a continuing reality with very real and continuing consequences.

Later in the morning, on the beach in "Proteus," Stephen will encounter a dog; in spite of Stephen's fear of the dog, he reminds himself to "Respect his liberty. You will not be master of others or their slave" (*U* 3.295–96) – for the beach makes him conscious of Irish "history" as a continuing series of foreign invasions and master–slave relationships. Thus, he thinks of the "galleys of the Lochlanns" (Norsemen) which ran here on the beach, "in quest [like "panthersahib" Haines] of prey, their bloodbeaked prows riding low" and of the "Dane vikings, torc of tomahawks aglitter on their breasts when Malachi wore the collar of gold." Stephen thus recalls both the long history of invasion and conquest in Ireland, and the equally long history of patriotic Irish resistance to foreign domination (Malachi, High King of Ireland, struggled to repulse the Scandinavian invaders in the tenth and eleventh centuries): "The Bruce's brother, Thomas Fitzgerald, ... Perkin Warbeck, ... Lambert Simnel" (*U* 3.295–316) – all examples of pro-Irish conspirators against the English crown (see Gifford, *"Ulysses" Annotated*, 59–60) in the annals of that "history" of English–Irish relationships which Haines would wash his hands of and would relegate to the past ("seems history is to blame").

Near the end of the episode, Haines's seemingly broad-minded interest in Irish culture is finally exposed altogether as self-centered ethnocentrism by his defensive, xenophobic racism: "Of course I'm a Britisher ... and I feel as one. I don't want to see my country fall into the hands of German jews either. That's our national problem, I'm afraid, just now" (*U* 1.666–68).[7] In the context of an episode about cultural imperialism, culture and anarchy, Hellenism and Hebraism – Haines's attitudes encapsulate the Anglo-Saxonist racism of the nineteenth century as discussed in chapter 2 of this study: within a binary polarity of apes and angels, of Anglo-Saxons and Celts, of Greeks and Jews, Stephen is quite aware of what side of the English Pale he himself falls on. When, at the end of the episode, Stephen sees Haines smiling at him, "smiling at wild Irish" – at that comfortable stereotype of the wild and primitive Irish the English race needs to believe in – Stephen at least knows to beware of the "Horn of a bull, hoof of a horse, smile of a Saxon" (*U* 1.730–2). He trusts Haines no more than he does the wooden-horse-play of equine, oak-haired Mulligan, the "Usurper" (*U* 1.743). When Mulligan now demands the key (and twopence) from Stephen, Stephen surrenders the key with the awareness that he has after all already lost the power it stands for; for he knows quite well that he has already been displaced, that – like Ireland herself – he has no rule in his own home or tower: "I will not sleep here tonight. Home also I cannot go" (*U* 1.739–40). The young man who declared his *non serviam* at the end of *A Portrait* has not yet found his freedom from servitude and usurpation. As with so many Irish émigrés and with Joyce himself, he must seek it elsewhere – somewhere, or some site, beyond discursive constructions of cultural essence and colonial stereotypes.

The school kip

If "Telemachus" could be imagined as an ethnographic encounter, the "Nestor" episode can perhaps be conceived of as a study in what Gramsci calls "cultural hegemony" – for it is in cultural institutions such as the school where Stephen works that the real processes of colonial hegemony operate, at the level of cultural formation in which the Arnoldian discourse gets inculcated into the youngsters of an aspiring shoneen class, so that – in the Gramscian elaborations of "hegemony"[8] – the values and hierarchies of the conquerors will be adopted voluntarily and consensually, without the need for imposed force.

12. "Doonesbury," August 23, 1992 (in *Los Angeles Times*). Comic strip by Garry B. Trudeau. DOONESBURY copyright 1992 G. B. Trudeau. Reprinted with permission of UNIVERSAL PRESS SYNDICATE. All rights reserved.

The school is situated in the wealthy Dublin suburb of Dalkey, where an aspiring native class is being inculcated into the ways of the English ruling class: "Welloff people," Stephen thinks of a student's family, "proud that their eldest son was in the navy" (presumably in military service for the British Empire); the boys themselves pay Stephen little heed, for they are "aware of my lack of rule and of the fees their papas pay" (*U* 2.25–30). Stephen himself is paid quite well for his services, in spite of his lack of interest; no wonder Mulligan calls it "the school kip." There is a clear parallel between Stephen's situations in the tower and at the school, for in each case Stephen is willing to sell his wits to a member of the ruling class (Haines, Deasy): he plans to save his witty comment in the classroom (about Kingstown pier as a "disappointed bridge") to entertain Haines with tonight – "For Haines's chapbook ... a jester at the court of his master, indulged and disesteemed, winning a clement master's praise" (*U* 2.43–44). There is little difference between the tower kip and the school kip.

Later that morning, on the beach in "Proteus," Stephen thinks of how families such as his own or his aunt Sara's are similarly taught, like his students' families, to aspire to a gentrified status associated with hegemonic notions of Culture, class, and superiority: "Houses of decay, mine, his and all. You told the Clongowes gentry you had an uncle a judge and an uncle a general in the army. Come out of them, Stephen. Beauty is not there" (*U* 3.105–7). As Stuart Hall puts it (in discussing Gramscian hegemony), "within the [hegemonic] 'bloc' will be strata of the subaltern and dominated classes, who have been won over by specific concessions and compromises and who form part of the social constellation but in a subordinate role" ("Gramsci's Relevance," 15). Stephen now realizes that his childhood pretensions to ruling-class gentry and Culture are hollow ("Beauty is not there"); that they are manifestations of a hegemonic training of cultural Desire based on one's own lack, a cultural aspiration that makes one want to remold oneself in the conqueror's image (as transmitted through cultural processes such as the Arnoldian educational agenda); and that schools like Clongowes or the school in Dalkey participate in the conqueror's hegemonic cultural agenda, no less so than the National Schools which Bloom thinks about (e.g., *U* 4.136) and which "were dominated by an English Protestant point of view and were regarded by the Irish as part of an English plot to control Ireland religiously and socially as well as politically" (Gifford, *"Ulysses" Annotated*, 73). In Gramsci's words, the state's activities are also "educative and formative," actively raising "the great mass of the population to a particular cultural and moral level" through the "educative functions of such critical institutions as the school" (*Prison Notebooks*, 263; Hall, "Gramsci's Relevance," 19); this is, as Hall points out, "the point from which hegemony over society as a whole is ultimately exercised" so as to obtain "the active consent of those over whom it rules" (18–19).

The schoolboys' specific agenda for the morning is suggestive and typical, for this is not a "hedge school" but a hegemonic school: first Greco-Roman history (about Pyrrhus and Julius Caesar), the canonized version of history, what in "The Encounter" Father Butler had insisted young boys should read (" – What is this rubbish? ... *The Apache Chief!* Is this what you read instead of studying your Roman History?" in *D* 20); followed by Milton's "Lycidas," English poetry in the grand Virgilian style by the most canonical and Anglo-Protestant (and virulently anti-Catholic) of English poets; and then the English game of field hockey, just as at Clongowes they played the English game of cricket (instead of the Irish sport of hurling, popularly associated with the Irish Revival). While Stephen is aware that "History is a nightmare from which I am trying to awake" (*U* 2.377) no less for his students than for him – "for them too history was a tale like any other too often heard, their land a pawnshop" (*U* 2.43–47) – nevertheless Stephen is himself engaged in training the boys to accept the hegemonic perspectives and English versions of Western history. It comes as hardly a surprise to learn that the school, playing English sports and teaching English notions of history, is run by an Orangeman; "Nestor" reveals how hegemonic "consent" is obtained through cultural institutions and discursive processes.

As Stephen is being paid by Deasy, his eyes take in all the signs of imperial power and money in Deasy's office. Being paid in "sovereigns" and "crowns," Stephen again reflects on their sovereignty, for they are "symbols too of beauty and of power ... symbols soiled by greed and misery" (*U* 2.226–28). Those that have the sovereigns also tend to have the sovereignty; Deasy is perhaps correct in observing that "Money is power." But when Deasy urges him to buy a change purse ("Put but money in thy purse"), Stephen notes wryly that the line is Iago's; when Deasy asks "what was the proudest word you will ever hear from an Englishman's mouth?" Stephen, seeing in Deasy (as he had seen in Haines) "The seas' ruler", guesses "That on his empire ... the sun never sets" (*U* 2.243–48). Deasy's insistence that the Englishman's proudest boast is actually "*I paid my way"*, however, is ironically undercut by his previous claim that "Money is power": for what Deasy does not understand (as Stephen and Mulligan do) is that, since money is power, the Englishman can claim to pay his way only because he has exploited others so as to control (and thus have) both money and power. Appropriately, "I paid my way" is the motto of Ulster (Gifford, *"Ulysses" Annotated*, 206). Equally appropriately, Stephen notices over Deasy's mantelpiece the "princely presence" of "Albert Edward, prince of Wales" (King Edward VII by 1904) and "Framed around the walls images of vanished horses stood in homage" (*U* 2.266–67, 299–303); these images of royalty and of royal horses (Lord Hastings's Repulse, the Duke of Westminster's Shotover, and so on) serve not only to remind us that Edward VII was a great fancier of horses, but also that horses were figures for imperial power (see chapter 9 of this study) – a power and status flatly denied Irish Catholics, since the Penal Laws forbade any Irish Catholic to own a horse valued above five pounds.

As Deasy begins to rant about his own patriot roots in the Orange lodges ("You fenians forget some things"; Stephen is hardly a fenian), Stephen's own mental commentary provides an ironic counterpoint to Deasy's claim to liberality and tolerance, tracing a capsule history of Orange tyranny and exploitation over Irish Catholics. First Stephen recalls the Orange toast to King Billy: "Glorious, pious and immortal memory" (*U* 2.273) – "To the glorious, pious and immortal memory of the Great and Good King William III, who saved us from popery, slavery, arbitrary power, brass money and wooden shoes" (Gifford, *"Ulysses" Annotated*, 36). He then thinks of the history of the Orange lodges: the "lodge of Diamond," the "planters' covenant," the "black north," and the "true blue bible" are all examples of how the Orange lodges abused or massacred Irish Catholics. "Croppies lie down" ("croppy boys" were peasant Catholic rebels) is the refrain of a number of anti-Catholic, Orange songs (like the Orange slogan Stephen recalls moments later, *"For Ulster will fight / And Ulster will be right"* in *U* 2.397–98). When at this point Deasy insists that "I have rebel blood in me too," claiming descent from Irish patriot Sir John Blackwood and asserting that "We are all Irish, all kings' sons" – Stephen's ironic comment is "Alas." Silently, he thinks instead of *"The rocky road to Dublin,"* a song about an Irish Catholic boy from Connacht who goes to Liverpool and is abused by the English (*U* 2.273–85).

As with Haines in "Telemachus," Deasy's pretensions to broad-

166

mindedness and tolerance are finally exploded by his own anti-Semitic racism, as his Anglo-Saxonist ethnophobia allies him with Haines: "Mark my words, Mr Dedalus ... England is in the hands of the jews ... And they are the signs of a nation's decay ... As sure as we are standing here the jew merchants are already at their work of destruction" (*U* 2.346–50). Stephen finally speaks up openly to reject the essentialist stereotype: " – A merchant is one who buys cheap and sells dear, jew or gentile, is he not?" But Deasy's response is one which insists on stamping a monologic essence on Jewishness, and one that echoes the ethnophobic anti-Semitism of influential English racial theorists of the nineteenth century, such as Robert Knox, MD, author of *The Races of Men*[9]: "They sinned against the light ... And you can see the darkness in their eyes. And that is why they are wanderers on the earth to this day" (*U* 2.361–63). At this point, Deasy further compounds his racism with misogyny, blaming the world's ills on women – from Eve to Helen of Troy to Kitty O'Shea (*U* 2.390–5). His parting shot – that "Ireland, they say, has the honour of being the only country which never persecuted the jews ... Because she never let them in" (*U* 2.437–38) – is by this point a delicious irony, for in a chapter about history and history lessons at an establishment school, it is the schoolmaster himself who keeps getting his history all wrong. After all, we are about to meet an Irish Jew at 7 Eccles Street.

Stephen, walking away, notices that on Deasy's shoulders "through the checkerwork of leaves the sun flung spangles, dancing coins" (*U* 2.448–49). This striking description (of sunlight as coins) concluding the episode serves subtly to remind us of the relationship between the money-minded Deasy, coins, sovereigns, money, power, sun, light (sweetness and light; sinning against the light) – and that empire on which the sun never sets.

A little while later, in "Proteus," Stephen finds himself thinking of "the wild goose, Kevin Egan of Paris" (*U* 3.164). Kevin Egan is Joyce's portrait of Joseph Casey, a Fenian who was imprisoned for his active involvement in Fenian violence (see Gifford, *"Ulysses" Annotated*, 52). Stephen recalls Egan's conversations with him "in the bar MacMahon" (named after a French descendant of the Wild Geese) as Egan "roll[ed] gunpowder cigarettes," nostalgically speaking

Of Ireland, the Dalcassians, of hopes, conspiracies, of Arthur Griffith now, AE ... queen Victoria? Old hag with the yellow teeth ... Maud

Gonne, beautiful woman, *la Patrie* ... How the head centre got away, authentic version. Got up as a young bride, man, veil, orangeblossoms ... Of lost leaders, the betrayed, wild escapes.

(*U* 3.226–44)

(The Dalcassians were tribal troops of the medieval Irish kings of Munster; an apocryphal story had it that James Stephens, Head Centre of the Fenian Society, had managed his escape from prison by disguising himself as a bride.)

Stephen, intent on avoiding the binary dialectic/trap of the Fenian-Nationalist response to English imperialism, is aware that Egan – like his schoolfellows in chapter v of *A Portrait* – is trying to recruit him to his militant cause by hailing him as a fellow Irish patriot: "To yoke me as his yokefellow, our crimes our common cause. You're your father's son. I know the voice" (*U* 3.229–30). As Egan sings *"The boys of Kilkenny are stout roaring blades,"* Stephen images Egan's interpellation of Stephen to his cause in terms of a well-known patriotic Irish song, "The Wearing of the Green" ("They're hanging men and women there for the wearing of the green"): "He [Egan] takes me, Napper Tandy, by the hand ... Weak wasting hand on mine" (*U* 3.257–63). James Napper Tandy was an Irish revolutionary who was instrumental in arranging the French attempt to support the Irish revolution in the 1790s – the very revolt against which the Martello towers were built as defences.

Stephen thinks about the pathos of Egan remembering Ireland: "In gay Paree he hides, Egan of Paris, unsought by any save by me ... They have forgotten Kevin Egan, not he them. Remembering thee, O Sion" (*U* 3.249–64). Stephen's use of the well-known phrase equates Zion with Ireland, associating once again the plight of Irish exiles and wild geese with that of the Jews in Babylonian exile: "By the rivers of Babylon, there we sat down, yea, we wept, when we remembered Zion" (Psalm 137). The reference also recalls the opening words this morning at the Martello Tower, first spoken by the Jews in Babylonian exile: *Introibo ad altare dei* (Psalm 43). In the context of Arnoldian Hellenism (versus Hebraism) and of English racism (embodied in Haines and Deasy) directed against both the Jews and the Irish, Stephen's mind picks up the racialized equation between Irishness and Jewishness as the persecuted Other; it is fitting that, having thought moments earlier of the "fleshpots of Egypt" (*U* 3.177–78; from Exodus 16:2–3), Stephen now notices "the red Egyptians" (i.e., Gypsies) on the beach (*U* 3.370). The moment triggers a memory of a dream he had the previous night:

After he woke me last night same dream or was it? Wait. Open hallway.
Street of harlots. Remember. Haroun al Raschid. I am almosting it. That
man led me, spoke. I was not afraid. The melon he had he held against
my face. Smiled: creamfruit smell. That was the rule, said. In. Come. Red
carpet spread. You will see who.

(U 3.365-69)

This lush dream is not the nightmare of a history of dispossession
and diaspora, nor Haines's nightmare of the black panther, but an
Orientalized and popularly disseminated vision of desire and luxury
in the fabled East of the Caliph of Baghdad (Haroun al Raschid), a
dream of comfort and freedom and home rule in a place where one is
wanted and welcome ("That was the rule, said. In. Come. Red carpet
spread"). As a wish-fulfillment fantasy – of at once another country
and a return from exile; at once exotic otherness as well as homecoming and home rule – this dream serves equally well for the
dispossessed Irish as for the dispossessed Jew. We are ready now for
Leopold Bloom.

Seeing ourselves: Orientals, Negroes, and Jews

Whereas Haines is able conveniently to compartmentalize history as
something which can be blamed on and consigned to the past, for
Stephen and his fellow Irishmen imperial history is very much an
oppressive nightmare of the present from which it is hard to awake –
if for no other reason than that its oppressive presence and
hegemonic, discursive terminology is written all over the face of
Ireland and of its cultural constructions, and thus forms the hour-by-
hour subtext and context of all their thoughts and experiences. For
example, in "Hades" the funeral cortege first passes the statue of
William Smith O'Brien, a patriotic hero of the rebellion of 1848, and
Bloom notices: "Someone has laid a bunch of flowers there ... Must
be his deathday" (U 6.226–27); Bloom has guessed correctly, since
O'Brien died on June 16, 1864 (Gifford, *"Ulysses" Annotated*, 109). Not
only is it the anniversary of a national hero's death, but the funeral
cortege route – like a ramble through the streets of Dublin or through
any episode of *Ulysses* – is an object lesson in the omnipresent history
of imperial domination and nationalist insurrection: having passed
the O'Brien statue on the anniversary of his death, the mourners then
pass "the hugecloaked Liberator's form" (U 6.249), Daniel O'Connell's statue; then "Nelson's pillar" (U 6.293), a hated English
imperial symbol which, like King Billy's statue on College Green, has

since been destroyed by Irish dissidents; then the "Foundation stone for Parnell" (*U* 6.320: now the completed Parnell Memorial in Parnell Square); later in the cemetery they pass "The O'Connell circle" (*U* 6.641) where the Liberator was originally buried; then "the chief's grave" where Parnell is buried (*U* 6.919), though some believe the popular rumor that he is "not in the grave at all" but alive and living in South Africa (*U* 6.919–23, Gifford, *"Ulysses" Annotated*, 123; the rumor was fueled by Irish sympathy for South Africa's resistance to English colonization); and finally the spot where some think "Robert Emmet was buried here by torchlight, wasn't he?" (*U* 6.978). In fact, the cultural and linguistic constructions of daily life are inextricably (and often unconsciously) enmeshed with those of Empire (much as in New England names like "Colonial Motor Inn" are typical and even nostalgically marketable, without one's conscious awareness of the unacknowledged implications being transmitted): everything in Dublin from the "the royal canal" (*U* 6.438) to "Brian Boroimhe house" (*U* 6.453; a pub) to the description in "Lestrygonians" of "the Empire ... Where Pat Kinsella had his Harp theatre before Whitbred ran the Queen's" (*U* 8.599–601) – the Empire was a pub; the Harp theatre was a music hall named after the traditional symbol of Ireland (a key musical instrument in the Celtic cultural revival), as well as a slang term for "Irish-Catholic"; the Queen's Royal Theatre was a house on Great Brunswick Street.

Ulysses presents a detailed and symptomatic portrayal of how cultural hegemony shapes the discourse and fabric (and fashions) of everyday life: for example, Bloom imagines that if Rudy were alive today he would be "Walking beside Molly in an Eton suit" (*U* 6.76). The European construction of Orientalism is another case in point, manifest in the popular culture's images of the Orient, such as the song which Bloom recalls Martin Cunningham's drunk wife singing (*U* 6.355), "The Jewel of Asia," from the very popular musical *The Geisha*; later, in "Circe," Bloom fantasizes Mrs. Cunningham dressed in "merry widow hat and kimono gown" as she "glides sidling and bowing, twirling japanesily" and singing "And they call me the jewel of Asia!" (*U* 15.3857–61); even later, in the wee hours Molly imagines that "theyre just getting up in China now combing out their pigtails for the day" (*U* 18.1540–41). Joyce repeatedly demonstrates how much the Orientalized constructions of Other peoples are a hegemonic discourse created by colonialism but propagated by popular culture, and thus a pervasive and unavoidable discursive mind-set absorbed (and recycled) by the members of the culture.

A clear illustration of this is the universal and unchallenged use of derogatory, stereotypical constructions of negritude in the popular references of the day. Gerty MacDowell, the novel's most salient receptacle and devotee of popular culture, exemplifies the cultural ingrained-ness of such received racist discourse, as her fashion-conscious mind notices such things as "a hat of wideleaved nigger straw" or "Madcap Ciss with her golliwog curls" (*U* 13.156, 270). While a golliwog was a black doll of grotesque features and fuzzy hair (with implicitly racist implications), the racism of Gerty's received terminology is not Gerty's so much as that of an entire culture. Bloom likewise thinks of Cissy as "the dark one with the mop head and the nigger mouth" (*U* 13.897–98); the insidiousness of racist discourse is that it is inherited by otherwise perfectly well-meaning people who absorb the cultural stereotypes and perpetuate them unconsciously. Similarly, in "Penelope" Molly thinks of one of Mina Purefoy's kids looking "something like a nigger with a shock of hair on it" and then repeats a popular Dublin ditty, "Jesusjack the child is a black" (*U* 18.162–63; Gifford, *"Ulysses" Annotated*, 611).

It is thus perhaps unavoidable, in a novel of interior monologues, that the very fabric of Dubliners' thoughts about cultural otherness and difference are constructions of the Orientalized and essentialist discourse of the culture. As Edward Said has argued about the encompassing influence of the Orientalist discourse, "every European, in what he could say about the Orient, was consequently a racist, an imperialist, and almost totally ethnocentric" (*Orientalism*, 204). Thus, Bloom's images of the Orient (mostly the Near East) can be discursively traced to popular sources such as the images of the Caliph of Baghdad (Haroun al Raschid) in the *Arabian Nights*, or to Sinbad the Sailor and Turko the Terrible in the popular pantos (music hall pantomimes) of the day, or to the sentimentalized images of the East in Thomas Moore's popular epic *Lalla Rookh, an Oriental Romance* which Bloom quotes (e.g., "the dear gazelle" and "I never loved a dear gazelle" in *U* 15.435, 15.1323); Moore's work could only continue to recycle previously constructed stereotypes – since he wrote it without any direct, personal experience of the Orient. Bloom's fantasies of "Agendath Netaim" as a land of "eucalyptus trees" and "Orange-groves and immense melonfields" (*U* 4.154–55), as "rich fruits spicy from Jaffa. Agendath Netaim. Wealth of the world" and "Perfume of embraces" (*U* 8.635–39), is similarly constructed along the received stereotypes of a lush, exotic Orient symbolized by lush, exotic fruit. In recent years, several Joycean commentators have done excellent cultural studies excavating the Orientalist sources and popular cultural images in *Ulysses* (I have in mind particularly Cheryl Herr, Brandon Kershner, Carol Shloss, and Mary Power, among others), and it is not my intention to do so in any detail here except insofar as it propels the arguments I am unfolding.

The dream of a luxurious and hospitable "street of harlots" that Stephen experienced the previous night depends on the received Orientalism which Edward Said has so compelllingly analyzed: "Street of harlots. Remember. Haroun al Raschid ... The melon he had he held against my face. Smiled: creamfruit smell ... In. Come. Red carpet spread" (*U* 3.365–69), and again later "Last night I flew. Easily flew. Men wondered. Street of harlots after. A creamfruit melon he held to me. In. You will see" (*U* 9.1207–9); and in "Circe": "Mark me. I dreamt of a watermelon ... It was here. Street of harlots. In Serpentine avenue Beelzebub showed me her, a fubsy widow. Where's the red carpet spread ... No, I flew. My foes beneath me" (*U* 15.3922–35). This is the Araby of untold luxury transmitted intact from the early pages of *Dubliners*, the fantasy of harems and seraglios and veiled houris in exotic slippers and harem pants, with their suggestively lush, ripe "fruit" (like Molly's own "melons"). It is, of course, significant that Bloom has just had much the same dream: "Come in, all is prepared. I dreamt" (*U* 13.878); "Dreamt last night? Wait. Something confused. She had red slippers on. Turkish. Wore the breeches" (*U* 13.1240–41); "having dreamed tonight a strange fancy of his dame Mrs Moll with red slippers on in a pair of Turkey trunks" (*U* 14.509); and then most fully in a fantasy in "Circe," where Molly appears:

a handsome woman in Turkish costume stands before him. Opulent curves fill out her scarlet trousers and jacket, slashed with gold. A wide yellow cummerbund girdles her. A white yashmak, violet in the night, covers her face, leaving free only her large dark eyes and raven hair ... A coin gleams on her forehead. On her feet are jewelled toerings. Her ankles are linked by a slender fetterchain. Beside her a camel, hooded with a turreting turban, waits. A silk ladder of innumerable rungs climbs to his bobbing howdah. He ambles near with disgruntled hindquarters. Fiercely she slaps his haunch, her godcurb wristbangles angriling, scolding him in Moorish.

(*U* 15.298–317)

The fact that Stephen's and Bloom's shared dream actually corresponds to what Molly herself desires and fantasizes – "Id have to get a nice pair of red slippers like those Turks with the fez used to sell" (*U* 18.1494–95; she already owns "a pair of outsize ladies' drawers of

India mull"; *U* 17.2094) – suggests not only the coincidence of the three characters' fantasies, but the fact that this Orientalized discourse is not an individual dream but, as Said has shown, a luxurious vision of the East that formed the shared fantasy of an entire Western culture, "Europe's collective daydream of the Orient" (*Orientalism*, 52, quoting V. G. Kiernan).

Later, Bella Cohen's brothel will itself be racialized into an Oriental harem, with the whores/houris becoming the Daughters of Erin/Jerusalem (Bloom addresses them as such: "Weep not for me, O ye daughters of Erin" (*U* 15.1936). Thus, when Bloom quotes from Moore's Oriental epic *Lalla Rookh* ("I never loved a dear gazelle . . . "), Zoe responds with "*Schorach ani wenowach, benoith Hierushaloium*" – lines from the sensual, racialized text of the Song of Solomon: "I am black, but comely, O ye daughters of Jerusalem" (*U* 15.1333–34; Gifford, *"Ulysses" Annotated*, 470); Bloom addresses her with: "More, houri, more" (*U* 15.1989). Later, Florry and Zoe are Africanized as "*Florryzoe jujuby women*" (*U* 15.4123; Doyle, "Races and Chains," 13). The whole encounter at Bella Cohen's is a parody of the *luxe et volupté* contained in the discourse of the Orient – bazaars, harems, voluptuous houris in Arabian nights – dreamt of by the boy in "Araby" and by an entire European culture.

Bloom understands that this Orientalist luxury has to do with a fascination for the foreign and exotic Other; we find him considering what it was about him that attracted Molly: "Why me? Because you were so foreign from the others" (*U* 13.1209–10). Bloom's appearance as a seemingly dark foreigner (which can thus be exoticized as a racial Other) is also what Gerty MacDowell finds attractive about him: "She could see at once by his dark eyes and his pale intellectual face that he was a foreigner" (*U* 13.415–16); her response to him is in ironic contrast to the response to the "foreign" Other by her own grandfather, the xenophobic "Citizen." Bloom understands the phenomenon of the exotic Other as an attractive fantasy:

> She [Molly] often said she'd like to visit [Nighttown]. Slumming. The exotic, you see. Negro servants in livery too if she had money. Othello black brute. Eugene Stratton. Even the bones and cornerman at the Livermore christies. Bohee brothers. Sweep for that matter.
>
> (*U* 15.408–11)

Bloom is quite right about Molly's taste for the exotic, as Molly herself admits in (thinking about men): "theyre all made the one way only a black mans Id like to try" (*U* 18.483–84). But Molly herself –

being the inherited Spanish/Moorish-Irish product of a poly-cultural Gibraltar that has left her (as she describes it) a mixed-up "harum-scarum" (*U* 18.1470) – also realizes that Bloom may have been likewise attracted to her because she also seems an exotic Other: "I suppose on account of my being jewess looking after my mother" (*U* 18.1184–85).

In his reasoning about "The exotic" in the passage quoted above, Bloom understands that the attraction is for a perceived exoticism – and his mind naturally wanders to the received, popular images of such exotic "negritude": Othello as a "black brute" (almost always played by a white actor in blackface); Eugene Stratton (a well-known blackface impersonator playing in Dublin that very night); the Livermore Brothers World Renowned Court Minstrels (they played Dublin in 1894), who were "christy minstrels" in blackface and whose show included blackface "cornermen" armed with "bones" (see Gifford, *"Ulysses" Annotated*, 458); and the Bohee brothers, another pair of blackface "christies" who had played Dublin. Bloom's Circean fantasy now conjures up a typical scene from one of these minstrel shows: *"Tom and Sam Bohee, coloured coons in white duck suits, scarlet socks, upstarched Sambo chokers and large scarlet asters in their buttonholes ... Flashing white kaffir eyes ... with smackfatclacking nigger lips"* playing their banjos and singing "There's someone in the house with Dina" (*U* 15.412–18). Although this is one of Bloom's fantasies in "Circe," it is also a quite accurate depiction of what minstrel shows like the Livermore Brothers or the Bohee Brothers were in fact like, with their exaggerated and stylized representations of "negro" stereotypes; "white kaffir eyes" refers to G. H. Chirgwin, another music-hall entertainer who "performed in blackface with large white diamonds painted around his eyes, billing himself as the White-Eyed Kaffir" (Gifford, *"Ulysses" Annotated*, 366). In understanding the attraction of the images of the "exotic" as portrayed in "Negro" blackface (like the white-eyed kaffir), Bloom understands that the "coon" is a blackface parody of negritude. Even more significantly, Bloom (throughout *Ulysses*) does not make a distinction in his thoughts between black and blackface: after all, since the presentation of blackness in Ireland and England was a purely cultural construct feeding cultural desires for exoticism, the reified image of negritude (i.e., the blackface music-hall stereotype) becomes the dominant (perhaps even exclusive) one. No distinction is (or can be) made between real blacks (since these were almost never experienced by Irish people) and blackface "negroes" by a culture in which the only available experience of "blackness" is the essentialized otherness of a stereotyped construction (as opposed to the Parisian culture Joyce was writing in, in which he *was* brought into familiar contact with black people[10]). Thus, this becomes an individual's "authentic" knowledge and experience of blackness.

As the above passage also suggests, Bloom is a receptive repository of these popular constructions of otherness: his mind is saturated with images and phrases like "Paradise and the peri" (*U* 5.132–33), the title of an interpolated poem in Moore's *Lalla Rookh* (a peri was a sort of genie in Persian myths); or like "Mohammed cut a piece out of his mantle not to wake [the cat]" (*U* 5.235, a traditional Islamic tale). Bloom's mind is an open receptacle of cultural constructs, a dialogic site for the contact of a variety of Orientalized representations – which he is not above exploiting in his realization that Martha Clifford may also be attracted to his "foreign" exoticness: "Martha, Mary. I saw that picture somewhere ... Tell about places you have been, strange customs. The other one, jar on her head, was getting the supper: fruit, olives, lovely cool water out of a well ... Tell her: more and more: all" (*U* 5.289–99).

The hegemonic power of a dominant ideology is such that it imbues the entire culture with, in this case, an Orientalized discourse of otherness – so that, inevitably, the very terms by which an individual in the culture thinks are inescapably tainted by such constructions: again (in Said's words), "every European, in what he could say about the Orient, was consequently a racist, an imperialist, and almost totally ethnocentric." This is inevitably true of Leopold Bloom as of every Irish person of the time (including, of course, James Joyce). What is interesting and distinctive about Bloom, however (and thus also about Joyce in choosing to depict Bloom thus), is his self-conscious and unceasing skepticism and questioning of such constructed images, repeatedly both absorbing and problematizing the propagated discourse.

For example, Bloom's first image during the day of the East is pure Orientalism and pop culture:

Somewhere in the east ... Walk along a strand, strange land, come to a city gate ... Wander through awned streets. Turbaned faces going by. Dark caves of carpet shops, big man, Turko the terrible, seated cross-legged, smoking a coiled pipe. Cries of sellers in the streets ... The shadows of the mosques among the pillars ... A girl playing one of those instruments what do you call them: dulcimers.

(*U* 4.84–98)

But Bloom immediately also recognizes the process of imaginary stereotyping involved in such images: "Probably not a bit like it really. Kind of stuff you read: in the track of the sun" (*U* 4.99–100). Bloom both participates in and sees through (and rejects: "not a bit like it really") the Orientalized discourse; it *is*, in fact, the kind of stuff you read, since *In the Track of the Sun: Diary of a Globe Trotter* (London, 1893), a volume Bloom has at home in 7 Eccles Street (*U* 17.1395–96), was a book (in the popular travel-journal genre) concentrating on the Orient and the near East; its title page features an Oriental girl playing stringed instruments (Gifford, *"Ulysses" Annotated*, 72).

Moments later, Bloom thinks of the Near East and "Agendath Netaim" in terms of images of ripe fruitfulness and "Orangegroves and immense melonfields." Once again, he stops himself with an awareness that the popular image is "not like that" but is perhaps a discursive fantasy, as he remembers the Dead Sea: "No, not like that. A barren land, bare waste. Vulcanic lake ... A dead sea in a dead land, grey and old" (*U* 4.219–23). A bit later in "Lotus-Eaters," Bloom again indulges himself in thoughts of: "The far east. Lovely spot it must be: the garden of the world, big lazy leaves to float about on, cactuses, flowery meads, snaky lianas they call them ... Those Cinghalese lobbing about the sun in the *dolce far niente*." But once again, as soon as he conjures up the popularized image, Bloom is led to question it – "Wonder is it like that" (*U* 5.29–32) – always skeptical and sensitive to the possibilities of essentialist typing. As with *In the Track of the Sun*, he repeatedly recalls that his images derive from cultural constructions, the kind of stuff you read in books or magazines: "Where was the chap I saw in that picture somewhere? Ah yes, in the dead sea floating on his back, reading a book with a parasol open" (*U* 5.37–38). It *is* inevitable that Bloom is both a consumer and a product/propagator of the dominant (and racist) cultural discourse about otherness; but – perhaps because he is himself repeatedly being typed by his fellow Irish as just such a reified Other – he is repeatedly skeptical of such images and sensitive to the cultural processes by which they are erected.

Bloom, we discover, has an intense fascination with and awareness of the viewpoint of the other, of cultural difference – as evidenced in his interest in the customs of other peoples. For example, he imagines a widow becoming *suttee*, the Hindu custom of widow suicide (following the husband's death): "There's the widow ... *From the suttee pyre the flame of gum camphire ascends*" (*U* 15.3231–32); earlier at the cemetery, he had thought of widows following their husbands to the grave: "For Hindu widows only" (*U* 6.548). Unlike most Westerners, Bloom is aware of the custom but does not condemn it as barbaric or heathen (whereas the British government had passed a law outlawing *suttee* in its Indian colony), simply accepting it as foreign ("For Hindu widows only").[11] Or he thinks about Jewish burial customs such as "a mother and deadborn child ever buried in the one coffin" (*U* 6.819–20); or about the Eastern preference for cremation which the Catholic "Priests [are] dead against" (*U* 6.984); or about the habit of the "Chinese eating eggs fifty years old, blue and green again" (*U* 8.869; a real delicacy in traditional Chinese cuisine). Not only does Bloom repeatedly show an interest in foreign customs and cultural difference, but he seems always to accept them without having to label or type them as barbaric, perverse, or unacceptable – in stark contrast to the way we repeatedly see his xenophobic fellow Irishmen, fearing foreignness, label him with the stigmatized marks of an absolute difference. Bloom is able to hold simultaneous perspectives, to imagine being other and thus to transcend the monologic narrowness of a single, cycloptic perspective: as he reasons in "Hades" (thinking about burials and burial customs), "If we were all suddenly somebody else!" (*U* 6.836) This is a multivalent perspective (and imaginative courage) in which many of his fellow Irishmen (such as those he will encounter later in "Cyclops") are lacking.

For example, in "Sirens" Bloom thinks about the Shah of Persia (who had visited England twice during the Victorian period and who had caught the popular fancy; Gifford, *"Ulysses" Annotated,* 307) going to the music hall: "Shah of Persia liked that best ... Wiped his nose in curtain too. Custom his country perhaps" (*U* 11.1050–52). Bloom is willing to accept what might appear to a European to be barbaric behavior as something potentially acceptable, even expected, in a different culture. A few moments later, Bloom needs to fart: "I must really. Fff. Now if I did that at a banquet. Just a question of custom shah of Persia" (*U* 11.1247–48). Once again, Bloom is willing to consider cultural relativism and difference – for, in fact, you *are* expected to belch (if not to fart) at a Persian feast as a sign that you have been pleased by the repast; otherwise your Persian host might take offense. It is, as Bloom says, "Just a question of custom."

What Bloom is thus also able to do, or at least to visualize, is to – in his (and Robert Burns's) oft-quoted line – "See ourselves as others see us" (*U* 13.1058). The issue of negritude (in *Ulysses*) provides an interesting case study concerning the ability to visualize blackness in terms which transcend either "niggerlips" music-hall stereotypes or the "white man's burden." When the funeral carriage passes the Queen's Theatre in "Hades," Bloom notices the theatre advertisements and thinks of "Eugene Stratton, Mrs Bandmann Palmer" (*U* 6.184–85), both of whom were in fact performing that night in Dublin. Stratton was "an American who became a music-hall star as a Negro impersonator ... His routine involved 'coon songs' with whistled refrains and soft-shoe dancing" (Gifford, *"Ulysses" Annotated*, 108). As a result of the theatre posters throughout Dublin this day announcing Stratton's performance, *Ulysses* provides us with several different Dubliners' perspectives on Stratton's "black" image.

At the end of "Wandering Rocks," we follow the route of the viceregal cavalcade carrying the viceroy and his cortege, the embodiment of English imperial rule; when it passes the shoneen Trinity College, a military band welcomes the royal presence and plays (appropriately) *"My girl's a Yorkshire girl"* (*U* 10.1242). But then, "At the Royal Canal bridge, from his hoarding, Mr Eugene Stratton, his blub lips agrin, bade all comers welcome to Pembroke township" (*U* 10.1273). The juxtaposition of the poster of blackface Stratton and the cavalcade crossing the Royal Canal into Pembroke township is deeply ironic – for the response of real Africans to English invasion and colonization was hardly "blub lips agrin." The latter, rather, is a European fantasy about colonized races (such as Africa or India) being deeply grateful to be conquered and ruled by the civilized white empire who brought them light – as suggested in "Cyclops" during the parodic description of the Queen's image on a penny coin:

the image of a queen of regal port, scion of the house of Brunswick, Victoria her name, Her Most Excellent Majesty, by grace of God of the United Kingdom of Great Britain and Ireland and of the British dominions beyond the sea, queen, defender of the faith, Empress of India, even she, who bore rule, a victress over many peoples, the wellbeloved, for they knew and loved her from the rising of the sun to the going down thereof, the pale, the dark, the ruddy, and the ethiop.

(*U* 12.293–99)

Contrary to the popular image propagated at home in England, the Empress Victoria was hardly "wellbeloved" among the other races in her far-flung empire on which the sun never sets: "the dark, the ruddy, and the ethiop" may suggest the Indian, the Irish, and the African in a solidarity of colonized servitude to the "pale" faces.

In the same episode ("Wandering Rocks"), Father Conmee sees the poster of Eugene Stratton: "From the hoardings Mr Eugene Stratton grimaced with thick niggerlips at Father Conmee." Conmee's reaction is that of the White Man's Burden and its civilizing mission in Africa:

> Father Conmee thought of the souls of black and brown and yellow men and of his sermon on saint Peter Claver S. J. and the African mission and of the propagation of the faith and of the millions of black and brown and yellow souls that had not received the baptism of water when their last hour came like a thief in the night. That book by the Belgian jesuit, *Le Nombre des Elus*, seemed to Father Conmee a reasonable plea. Those were millions of human souls created by God in His Own likeness to whom the faith had not (D. V.) been brought. But they were God's souls, created by God. It seeemed to Father Conmee a pity that they should all be lost, a waste.
>
> (*U* 10.141–52)

Conmee is only able to view the white Christian's perspective as a "reasonable" one, for the missionaries and the whites are "saving" those heathen, unbaptised black souls from eternal damnation; he is unable to conceive the possibility that the natives might resent the incursion as hardly a favor – but rather as an insult to their own religious beliefs, not to speak of their sovereignty.

In stark contrast, Leopold Bloom thinks of the same sermon by Conmee about the same Belgian missionary in very different terms from those of the White Man's Burden:

> Same notice on the door. Sermon by the very reverend John Conmee S. J. on saint Peter Claver S. J. and the African Mission. Prayers for the conversion ... The protestants are the same. Convert Dr William J. Walsh D. D. to the true religion. Save China's millions. Wonder how they explain it to the heathen Chinee. Prefer an ounce of opium. Celestials. Rank heresy for them. Buddha their god lying on his side in the museum ... He's not going out in bluey specs with the sweat rolling off him to baptise blacks, is he?
>
> (*U* 5.322–34)

Bloom problematizes the concept of "the true religion" by trying to see ourselves as others see us, by imagining the response of the Other(s): how do you explain it to the "heathen" Chinese who may choose opium rather than Mass as their own preferred opiate of the masses; and for whom it is Christianity that may seem a "rank heresy," since it's "Buddha [who is] their god"? (Later in *U* 6.982–83 he remembers that he read "in that *Voyages in China* that the Chinese say a white man smells like a corpse.") Bloom's ability to step outside the entrenched monologism of his culture allows him at least to *imagine* the Other's perspective – here, the Chinese or Africans who may not wish to be converted.

Joyce's Dubliners, themselves having suffered religious persecution at the hands of the Protestant English, can be quite conscious at one level of the perspective of the "heathen" Other: as the Citizen puts it, "What about sanctimonious Cromwell and his ironsides that put the women and children of Drogheda to the sword with the bible text *God is love* pasted round the mouth of his cannon? The bible! Did you read that skit in the *United Irishman* today about that Zulu chief that's visiting England?" (*U* 12.1506–10). He then reads from the paper an anti-English skit supposedly penned by Arthur Griffith (in one of his pseudonyms), in which a Zulu chief drinks *Black and White* whiskey with his English oppressors and then praises and admires both the Bible and Queen Victoria (*U* 12.1514–33). The skit was, of course, meant in its satire to voice a parallel Irish resentment against the colonial exploitation by the British Empire.[12] The men in the bar then go on to discuss the report in the papers by "an Irishman" named "Casement" about Belgian exploitation in the Congo, "Raping the women and girls and flogging the natives on the belly to squeeze all the red rubber they can out of them"; as J. J. O'Molloy comments about the English, "if they're any worse than those Belgians in the Congo Free State they must be bad" (*U* 12.1542–47). This is the same Roger Casement who in 1916 would be hanged for treason as a Sinn Feiner; Joyce had one of his books in his Trieste library. As Gifford points out: "In February 1904, while serving as a consul in the Congo, Casement filed a report on the forced labor in rubber plantations and other cruelties to natives under the Belgian administration there. The report was published" (*"Ulysses" Annotated*, 366); it is this report, and the consequent public outcry, to which the men are referring. So on the one hand the Irishmen with their nationalistic fervor are able to view themselves in solidarity with Zulu and Congolese blacks under similar colonial servitude to European powers; on the other hand, the sharp irony is that, under the binary trap of a mirrored system of racist hierarchies and ethnocentrisms, these same Dubliners nevertheless can slur Bloom with derogatory racist remarks, just as Griffith could approve of black slavery. The ability to imagine otherness here is a very limited imagining.

Thus, the Citizen immediately (just having bemoaned the English and Belgian treatments of blacks) now goes on to cast a black racial slur in Bloom's direction, calling him a "whiteeyed kaffir ... that never backed a horse in anger in his life," to which Hynes adds that "He's a bloody dark horse himself" (*U* 12.1552–58). Both depictions of Bloom – as the blackface "whiteeyed kaffir" (a phrase from a Kipling poem about the Boer War[13]) and as a "dark horse" – serve to ally Bloom with the dark throwaways of the world, such as the Zulus under English rule or the natives in the Belgian Congo whom Casement wrote about. Earlier, John Henry Menton had similarly referred to Bloom as a "coon": "what did she [Molly] marry a coon like that for?" (*U* 6.704–5). Interestingly, the word "coon" is at once a derogatory slang term for both black and for Jew: for the Irishmen are racializing Bloom simultaneously as both Jew and as black – a racialization, ironically, of which the Irish themselves had long been subjected to by the English. At the end of "Cyclops," as Martin Cunningham and Jack Power try to whisk Bloom away from the confrontation with the Citizen, one of the bystanders starts singing *"If the man in the moon was a jew, jew, jew"* – again equating Bloom the Jew with blackness and with the dark horse, since the reference is to a popular American song at the time, "If the Man in the Moon were a Coon, Coon, Coon" (Gifford, *"Ulysses" Annotated*, 378). Once again, the Dubliners are doing to Bloom (racializing him as a black in derogatory terms) precisely what the English had done to them: the dreadful irony of such a blind and mirrored binarity of nationalistic ethnocentrisms is precisely Joyce's point.

Bloom's own musings about Africans stand in stark contrast. Earlier, in Davy Byrne's, Bloom, having been disgusted by the men eating at Burton's, now thinks about what to eat for lunch – and about vegetarianism, eating meat, cannibals, and race:

Sandwich? Ham and his descendants musterred and bred there. Potted meats ... Dignam's potted meat. Cannibals would with lemon and rice. White missionary too salty. Like pickled pork. Expect the chief consumes the parts of honour. Ought to be tough from exercise. His wives in a row to watch the effect. *There was a right royal old nigger. Who ate the something the somethings of the reverend Mr MacTrigger ... His five hundred wives. Had the time of their lives ... It grew bigger and bigger and bigger*

(*U* 8.741–83).

While it is clear that Bloom is having some fun, first with a gastronomic joke about sandwiches (Ham, "bred," and "musterred") and then with an obscene (not to speak of racist) limerick, at the same time Bloom is also again trying (even if in humor) to see things from the cannibal/Other's perspective, to see oneself as the Other would: "White missionary too salty," and so on. Joyce, however, has yet another purpose – for Bloom's pun on ham sandwiches involves Ham, one of Noah's sons, who saw his father drunk and naked, and was then cursed and banished by Noah, condemned to be "a servant of servants ... unto his brethren" (Genesis 9:22–27); Ham reputedly then became the father of the Negroid races, "the sons of Ham." Thus, the reference to "Ham and his descendants" who "musterred and bred" significantly allies black races with Stephen Dedalus and with the Irish colonial condition ("a server of a servant"), reinforcing the racialization and solidarity (in non-pejorative fashion) between the Irish and blacks as marginalized others. Like Ham's descendants (such as, presumably, African "cannibals"), the Irish too might not find foreign incursions and influences (such as white missionaries) much to their taste. While Bloom's little jokes may seem taste*less* or unconsciously offensive as humor, he is again trying to "see ourselves as others see us" – while Joyce is underscoring the perspective of the black other (cannibal/Caliban) here as allied to that of the Irish condition of servitude, within a positive, racialized solidarity of the downtrodden others – Irish, Black, and Jew.

Bloom's ability to view the white man from the perspective of the other allows him to have broad religious tolerance; as he said about the missionary missions to the "heathen Chinee," Christianity might seem "rank heresy" in the eyes of the latter. On witnessing the Catholic Holy Communion, Bloom ponders the phenomenon of the Eucharist from several viewpoints: it's a "Rum idea: eating bits of a corpse" and perhaps that's "Why the cannibals cotton to it"; it's "Something like those [Jewish] mazzoth: it's that sort of bread unleavened shewbread"; it's a placebo: "Look at them. Now I bet it makes them feel happy ... Lourdes cure, waters of oblivion, and the Knock apparition, statues bleeding." But his tolerant conclusion, finally, is quite non-judgmental: "Thing is if you really believe in it" (*U* 5.358–66); if it works for you, it's fine. Similarly, he now regrets his youthful intolerance of his father's Judaism, since he now understands the cultural relativism involved in all religions: "How did [his father's Jewish] beliefs and practices now appear to him? / Not more rational than they had then appeared, not less rational than other beliefs and practices now appeared" (*U* 17.1902–4). One comical result of such broad-mindedness is that Bloom, a Jew, has been baptised three times (as both Protestant and Catholic; *U* 17.540): he is almost a walking parody of ecumenical tolerance and cultural pluralism. Bloom's ability to accept all visions and "truths" as cultural differences that do not have to be seen as competitive and mutually (even militantly, violently) exclusive, calls to mind Kublai Khan's comments to Marco Polo (an attitude towards different religions which many Chinese still hold):

There are four great Prophets who are reverenced and worshipped by the different classes of mankind. The Christians regard Jesus Christ as their divinity; the Saracens, Mahomet; the Jews, Moses; and the idolaters, Sogomombar-kan, the most eminent among their idols. I do honour and show respect to all the four, and invoke to my aid *whichever amongst them is in truth supreme in heaven*.

(quoted in Anderson, *Imagined Communities*, 16)

Bloom's ability to "see ourselves as others see us" extends not only to the viewpoints of others different from oneself, but even to an ability and willingness to imagine viewpoints detrimental or derogatory to oneself. For example, he is able to imagine how someone like Sir Frederick Falkiner (whom he observes), a fashionable member of "the bluecoat school" – that is, those with "an education befitting a member of the Protestant Anglo-Irish Establishment" (Gifford, *"Ulysses" Annotated*, 187) – might make fun of him: "I suppose he'd turn up his nose at that stuff [the glass of burgundy] I drank. Vintage wine for them, the year marked on a dusty bottle" (*U* 8.1154–55). When he later remembers those newsboys who had aped his walk behind his back in "Aeolus," Bloom can comment sanguinely: "Still you learn something. See ourselves as others see us." (However, there *are* cultural and gendered limits to Bloom's unflappable tolerance, as he adds: "So long as women don't mock what matter?"; *U* 13.1056–59). Bloom can even hilariously imagine the perspective of pigeons preparing to dive bomb him (the fellow in black): "Their little frolic after meals. Who will we do it on? I pick the fellow in black. Here goes. Here's good luck. Must be thrilling from the air" (*U* 8.402–3). Finally, later (in "Nausicaa") when Bloom recalls his heated argument with the Citizen, who after all had just repeatedly mocked and insulted him – "Then that bawler in Barney Kiernan's. Got my own back there. Drunken ranters what I said about his God made him wince ... Ought to go home and laugh at themselves ... Look at it the other way round" – even in this case, Bloom is willing to look at it kindly from the perspective of his enemy, the Citizen himself: "Perhaps not to hurt he meant" (*U* 13.1215–20). I find this last line very moving, because it suggests a catholic willingness on Bloom's part always to risk stepping beyond the boundaries of one's personal ego (and national ego, since "Nations have their ego, just like individuals") to try to understand the perspective of others, even of one's detractors and enemies. For "seeing ourselves" is an act of sympathetic imagination that requires more than one eye and one narrow (personal or national) viewpoint, requires multiple vision and multivalent perspectives – precisely what the monologic vision of a one-eyed Cyclops (whose nationalistic motto *Sinn Fein* suggests, by contrast, the limited, tunnel-visioned perspective of "Ourselves alone") is unable to do, an inability "to go home and laugh at themselves" and "Look at it the other way round."

7.

Imagining nations

Whose nation?: "Aeolus"

All day long on June 16, 1904, Leopold Bloom finds himself repeatedly stereotyped and essentialized by his fellow male Dubliners as a foreigner and a "dirty Jew," enduring racial slurs and anti-Semitic comments – such as "Ikey Moses Bloom," "the sheeny," "the jewman," "that coon," "a bit off the top," and so on – in spite of the fact that he too was born and raised in Ireland. In fact, Bloom is – as we have seen – as much a product of the dominant cultural discourse as they are, having also (and inevitably) absorbed the culture's Orientalist discourse and racist terminology. For example, he, too, is capable of participating in Jewish stereotyping, as when he praises a smart idea as an "Ikey touch that" (*U* 4.103); or when he is willing to join the other men in the funeral carriage in joking about Reuben J. Dodd's "Jewish" stinginess, as he tells the story about Dodd's son being rescued from drowning ("Isn't it awfully good?" Bloom says; *U* 6.290). Similarly, his cultural aspirations are not that dissimilar from Buck Mulligan's Hellenist agenda, fueled as they both are by a hegemonic hierarchy and Arnoldian discourse that ranks Greek culture as the pinnacle of civilized, enlightened "high culture." Like Mulligan, Bloom affects the Greek: " – Metempsychosis ... It's Greek: from the Greek. That means the transmigration of souls." Molly, however, sees through, and shatters, such hegemonic pretentiousness: " – O, rocks! ... Tell us in plain words." (*U* 4.341–43). Later, Bloom struggles with the meaning and Greek etymology of "parallax": "I never exactly understood ... Par it's Greek: parallel, parallax. Met him pike hoses she called it till I told her about the transmigration. O rocks!" – but he is willing to concede her point about the cultural and

185

intellectual affectation, based as it is on a privileging of Greco-Latinate polysyllabics: "She's right after all. Only big words for ordinary things on account of the sound" (*U* 8.110–15). Joyce, of course, does in *Ulysses* "Hellenise" Ireland – as well as "Hebraicize" it – by turning it into, simultaneously, the Odyssey and the Middle East, making the racialized equation between Greek, Jew, and Irish.

An episode about rhetoric, "Aeolus" is in a sense a dialogic and rhetorical discussion about Nation (and its corollaries, nationality and nationalism), setting up the issues that will erupt later in the "Cyclops" episode. Under the headline of "ERIN, GREEN GEM OF THE SILVER SEA," the men in the newspaper office make fun of Dan Dawson's excessive rhetoric about the Irish countryside: "How that for high?" Ned Lambert asks (*U* 7.248–49). While they may make fun of the fulsome bombast, Dawson's rhetoric is in fact not unlike the linguistic excesses of the Celtic Revival which Joyce will parody in the "Cyclops" episode:

– As 'twere, in the peerless panorama of Ireland's portfolio, unmatched, despite their wellpraised prototypes in the vaunted prize regions, for very beauty, of bosky grove and undulating plain and luscious pastureland of vernal green, steeped in the transcendent translucent glow of our mild mysterious Irish twilight ...

(*U* 7.320–24)

Simon Dedalus's sarcastic response – "And Xenophon looked upon Marathon ... and Marathon looked on the sea" (*U* 7.254–55) – alludes not only to the Greek Xenophon, one of the leaders of the Ten Thousand who looked on the sea in victory and cried "Thalatta! Thalatta!" (thus recalling Mulligan's Hellenist agenda in *U* 1.80), but should also invoke the concept of "xenophobia" (*Webster's*: "Fear and hatred of strangers and foreigners") as the source of ethnocentric and racial prejudice, for the fear and hatred of strangers is very much an issue in this episode. When Bloom asks what it is they are all laughing about, Professor MacHugh names Dawson's speech, "*Our lovely land*"; "– Whose land? Mr Bloom said simply. / – Most pertinent question, the professor said" (*U* 7.271–73). It is a most pertinent question indeed.

For the relationship between race and nationhood is very much the subtext of the "Aeolus" episode, just as it will later become the overt text of the "Cyclops" episode. In the newspaper office, Bloom discusses a possible ad for the paper with the print foreman, Joseph Patrick Nannetti, an actual Irish-Italian printer and politician who in 1904 was the member of Parliament for Dublin's College Green

Division. Bloom thinks: "Strange he never saw his real country. Ireland my country. Member for College green ... Cuprani too, printer. More Irish than the Irish" (*U* 7.87–100). Here, Bloom (who was born in Ireland as was Nannetti) lapses into the binary trap himself: aware that his own country is Ireland in spite of the fact that the other men may see him as an untrustworthy foreigner, Bloom himself makes the same essentialist mistake here by assuming that Nannetti's "real country" is Italy and not Ireland. Ironically, Nannetti will that very afternoon prove how "Irish" he is by (as we learn in "Cyclops") traveling to London so as to ask questions in Parliament about the prohibition against playing Irish games – such as hurling – in Phoenix Park at the same time that English games such as polo were being allowed. Not only did Nannetti do just that in real life (on June 17, 1904), but both Joyce and his Irish readers in 1922 would be aware that in 1906 Nannetti would be elected Lord Mayor of Dublin – a reminder Joyce had similarly brought up in "Ireland, Island of Saints and Sages" when he had likewise argued the absurdity of proclaiming any threads of racial purity within the motley fabric of Irish society (*CW* 163).

The piece Bloom is working on is the "HOUSE OF KEY(E)S" advertisement for Alexander Keyes, tea, wine and spirit merchant. As Bloom explains to Nannetti: "The idea ... is the house of keys. You know, councillor, the Manx parliament. Innuendo of home rule. Tourists, you know, from the isle of Man" (*U* 7.141–45). The ad puns on the House of Keys, the name of the Manx parliament, with its "innuendo of home rule." The irony is that neither Bloom nor Nannetti nor Stephen are accorded any sovereignty in their own homes or nation: both Bloom and Stephen are missing the literal keys to their homes, 7 Eccles and the Martello Tower – as well as the figurative keys of rule in their own usurped abodes; both of them feel marginalized by their own countrymen. Similarly, Ireland herself is lacking in Home Rule – in contrast to its tiny neighbor, the Isle of Man. Here, Joyce is setting up an analogy linking both Bloom's domestic dilemma and Stephen's living situation with Ireland's lack of autonomy (in contrast to the Isle of Man); it is, of course, as the episode goes on to elaborate, also the dilemma of the Jewish race. Ireland, the Jews, Bloom and Stephen are all in the same figurative space and condition of homeless usurpation.

Nationalism, and the struggle for Irish autonomy from English usurpation, form very much the underlying fabric of the language in the newspaper office. For example, MacHugh teases Myles Crawford

187

about being "the sham squire himself!" (*U* 7.348), a reference to the infamous turncoat informer, Francis Higgins, who in 1798 accepted a bribe for revealing Lord Edward Fitzgerald's whereabouts to Major Sirr. Then, under the headline "MEMORABLE BATTLES RECALLED" we find Crawford responding in irony: " – North Cork militia! ... We won every time!" (*U* 7.358–60); the North Cork Militia, loyal to the Crown in the Rebellion of 1798, "enjoyed the dubious distinction of having disgraced itself ... in every action it was involved in" (Gifford, "*Ulysses*" *Annotated*, 135). The section which follows is headlined "O, HARP EOLIAN!" (*U* 7.370), referring not only to MacHugh's dental floss but also to the national symbol of Ireland (and slang term for Irish Catholic). A page later we find the newsboys in the hallway singing " – *We are the boys of Wexford / Who fought with heart and hand*" (*U* 7.427–28), lines from "The Boys of Wexford," a ballad celebrating the total defeat in 1798 of the North Cork Militia by the Boys of Wexford. A few pages later, when Stephen and O'Madden Burke enter, they are asked: "You look like communards ... Like fellows who had blown up the Bastile ... Or was it you shot the lord lieutenant of Finland between you? You look as though you had done the deed, General Bobrikoff"; Stephen responds that " – We were only thinking about it" (*U* 7.599–603). The reference is a very topical one: earler that same morning, June 16, 1904, Finnish insurrectionists had assassinated General Nikolai Ivanovitch Bobrikoff, the Russian Goveral-General of Finland; the news had just reached Dublin, where the Irish could not help but see the parallel with their own attempts at colonial insurrection against a hated imperial power. The men in the news-room then go on to discuss Ignatius Gallaher's reporting of the trial of the Invincibles for the Phoenix Park Murders, the Irish version in 1882 of the assassination of the Russian General. Throughout the episode, Irish Nationalism and colonial history are the threads woven into the very fabric of the language of "Aeolus."[1]

When Crawford sings to MacHugh two lines from "The Rose of Castile" – "'*Twas rank and fame that tempted thee, / 'Twas empire charmed thy heart*" (*U* 7.471–72), the discussion in the room begins to focus around the issue of selling out to the temptations of the dominant powers of empire. (Ironically, Crawford is himself about to tempt Stephen to sell out his artistic talents to the hegemonic institution of the press.) In response, MacHugh discusses the "*Imperium romanum*":

... We think of Rome, imperial, imperious, imperative ... What was their civilisation? Vast, I allow: but vile. *Cloacae*: sewers. The jews in the wilderness and on the mountaintop said: *It is meet to be here. Let us build an altar to Jehovah.* The Roman, like the Englishman who follows in his footsteps, brought to every new shore on which he set his foot ... only his cloacal obsession. He gazed about him in his toga and he said: *It is meet to be here. Let us construct a watercloset* ... And Pontius Pilate is [their] prophet.

(U 7.489–501)

In drawing a direct parallel between the Roman Empire ruling the Jews (and killing Jesus) and the British Empire ruling Ireland, MacHugh is again suggesting a favorite Irish analogy between Irish servitude to England and the Israelites under an imperial yoke.

MacHugh's logic also follows the Celticist "binarist" urge to turn the tables and, in mirror fashion, simply re-label (within a static hierarchy of labels) the imperial aggressor as the primitive philistine, obsessed only with waterclosets, and name oneself instead into the privileged position of arbiter in matters of the spirit: "I teach the blatant Latin language. I speak the tongue of a race [the English] the acme of whose mentality is the maxim: time is money. Material domination. *Domine!* Lord! Where is the spirituality? ... A sofa in a westend club" (*U* 7.555–58). He goes on, like Mulligan, to wax about "The Greek!" as "The radiance of the intellect": "The closetmaker and the cloacamaker will never be lords of our spirit. We are liege subjects of the catholic chivalry of Europe that foundered at Trafalgar and of the empire of the spirit, not an *imperium*" (*U* 7.562–67). But MacHugh's eloquence is undercut by his implied admission of selling out and of servitude to the empire, a professor teaching the blatant Latin language of the supposedly barbaric imperia which he mocks – a server of a servant.

Nationalism, servitude, and the lure of co-option by the empire now invoke John F. Taylor's famous speech at the college historical society, in which (as the story goes) Taylor dragged himself from his sickbed to speak in extemporaneous response to Mr Justice Fitzgibbon's paper "advocating the revival of the Irish tongue" (*U* 7.795–96): it was, in other words, a Nationalist debate on the more purist positions in the Celticist agenda, focusing around Douglas Hyde's movement to de-Anglicize the Irish tongue. Once again, the favored analogy is between the Jews (under Pharaoh) and the Irish; MacHugh quotes Taylor's speech, imagining the words of the Egyptian high priest speaking to a youthful Moses:

– *Why will you jews not accept our culture, our religion and our language? You are a tribe of nomad herdsmen: we are a mighty people. You have no cities*

*nor no wealth: our cities are hives of humanity and our galleys, trireme and
quadrireme, laden with all manner merchandise furrow the waters of the known
globe. You have but emerged from primitive conditions: we have a literature, a
priesthood, an agelong history and a polity.*

The parallels are quite precise, since the Irish also differed from the
English in culture, religion, and (at one time) language; since Ireland
was rural and poor ("no cities nor no wealth"); since England was
"the seas' ruler" while under English servitude the Irish ports lay
fallow and unused; and since, in their poverty, the Irish Catholics had
been essentialized as "primitives" without a culture of their own.

*– You pray to a local and obscure idol: our temples, majestic and mysterious,
are the abodes of Isis and Osiris, of Horus and Ammon Ra. Yours serfdom, awe
and humbleness: ours thunder and the seas. Israel is weak and few are her
children: Egypt is an host and terrible are her arms. Vagrants and daylabourers
are you called: the world trembles at our name.*

This is the dominant discourse of hegemonic power, tempting the
subservient with the lure of joining the side of the conqueror. Taylor
concludes the speech with his own stirring response to that lure:

*– But, ladies and gentlemen, had the youthful Moses listened to and accepted
that view of life, had he bowed his head and bowed his will and bowed his spirit
before that arrogant admonition he would never have brought the chosen people
out of their house of bondage, nor followed the pillar of the cloud by day. He
would never have spoken with the Eternal amid lightnings on Sinai's
mountaintop nor ever have come down with the light of inspiration shining in
his countenance and bearing in his arms the tables of the law, graven in the
language of the outlaw.*

(U 7.845–70)

Taylor's speech is a piece of rhetoric which (unlike Dawson's)
genuinely moves all the men in the room; it moved Joyce, too, who
knew it by heart and recorded (on phonodisc) this passage for
posterity. Taylor's is an eloquent and persuasive argument about
maintaining Irish cultural and national integrity and pride, as the
Israelites had done under Moses, invoking in the analogy a solidarity
of the oppressed and the enslaved. In this way, the Irish men can –
like Joyce himself – appropriate the racialization (used against them
by the British) of Irish racial otherness by invoking a racialized
analogy in a *potentially* positive, empowering (rather than debilitating) manner – by using the model of the Israelites resisting
Egyptian tyranny.

But Joyce's very dramatic irony is clearly that, even so, these
Irishmen can appropriate this notion of an Irish/Jewish analogy with

conviction only insofar as it serves their own narrow purposes, which are those of an ethnocentric and nationalistic hierarchy mirroring that of their oppressors, a binary trap in which they wish simply to replace the English conquerors with themselves in the privileged position – for, even as they repeatedly invoke the Judaic/ Irish analogy, they continue to mistreat and derogate the actual Jewish "other" in their midst with the same old pejorative, ethnocentric and xenophobic categories of racial impurity and absolute difference. Whereas the empowering analogy *should* allow the possibility of mutual learning from the experience of a shared servitude among different peoples, instead the Nationalist agenda erases that experience from the national consciousness only to replace it with another masculist imperium that would again occlude or write out ethnic and cultural difference. The internal contradiction is trenchant – and so the John F. Taylor passage operates at various, clashing levels of ideological (and rhetorical) power, meaning, and irony.

"What is a Nation?": Nationalism, Ireland, and "Cyclops"

What does it mean to be Irish? Who qualifies as "Irish?" What *is* Ireland? What is a nation? These are crucial questions which Bloom's mental observations about himself and the "Italian" Nannetti ("Ireland my country") invoke; they form a key subtext of *Ulysses*, especially in the "Aeolus" and "Cyclops" episodes, evoking the controversy then raging in Ireland regarding who could qualify as being "truly" Irish. This was an issue frequently discussed in Arthur Griffith's *United Irishman*, articulating the Celticist debate in the Nationalist revival – in which the racial purists argued that "only Gaels" were truly Irish, as opposed to the more liberal viewpoint that any "Irish-born man" should be considered Irish. As Gifford (130) points out: "It is interesting that the purist position would deny the distinction 'Irish' to many outstanding Irish-born people, including Swift, Sheridan, and Burke, Grattan and the members of his Parliament, Wolfe Tone and most of the United Irishmen, Parnell, Yeats and Synge, the Irish-born Italian Nannetti, and of course, the Irish-born Bloom." Joyce found such arguments for racial purity ridiculous; he had written to Stannie from Trieste that he would consider himself a Nationalist if it weren't for the Celticist insistence on the Irish language (Gaelic) – and if Griffith's newspaper weren't, in Joyce's words, "educating the people of Ireland on the old pap of racial hatred" (*Letters* II, 187).

In the "Cyclops" episode's debate between Bloom and the Citizen, Bloom is asked to define what a nation is ("do you know what a nation means?" in *U* 12.1419), echoing the famous question (and essay), "*Qu'est-ce qu'une nation?*" by Ernest Renan (whose work Joyce was familiar with and whose birthplace he visited; Ellmann, *JJII*, 567). With that debate (in "Cyclops") in mind, I would like first to contextualize my reading of that episode (and of *Ulysses* in general) by briefly discussing the concept of Nation within some recent ideological studies on nationalism. The existence of one's "nation" as a natural trait that we are born into – like one's epoch, sex, "race," or gender – is for most of us an unquestioned fact so taken for granted that we seldom if ever wonder what it is that we may mean by our "nation" (though the recent breakdown of Eastern Europe into ethnic warfares and new nationalisms has focused renewed attention on that elusive concept of "nation").

In his provocative study *Imagined Communities: Reflections on the Origin and Spread of Nationalism*, Benedict Anderson suggests that "nation-ness is the most universally legitimate value in the political life of our time" (3), able to "command such profound emotional legitimacy," in spite of the fact that "nation-ness, as well as nationalism, are cultural artefacts" which have emerged only in relatively recent history, products of discursive and ideological formations (3–4) – and in spite of the fact that, to cite Hugh Seton-Watson, "no 'scientific definition' of the nation can be devised; yet the phenomenon has existed and exists" (Anderson, 3). In view of this phenomenon, I would like to invoke Anderson's important and thought-provoking formulation of "nation" in terms of the concept of an "imagined community." Anderson begins:

In an anthropological spirit, then, I propose the following definition of the nation: it is an imagined political community – and imagined as both inherently limited and sovereign.

It is *imagined* because the members of even the smallest nation will never know most of their fellow-members, meet them, or even hear of them, yet in the minds of each lives the image of their communion ... In fact, all communities larger than primordial villages of face-to-face contact (and perhaps even these) are imagined. Communities are to be distinguished, not by their falsity/genuineness, but by the style in which they are imagined.

(6)

While a lot of Joyce's Dubliners do in fact seem to know each other (but they certainly know no more than a very small slice of the heterogeneity and variety of the entire country), nevertheless they are capable of imagining an Irish nation as a cohesive community of Celtic racial origins and Irish national character – in spite of the palpable, material reality and presence within their midst of variants such as Leopold Bloom, Reuben J. Dodd, Joseph Nannetti, W. B. Yeats, and Charles Stewart Parnell. Anderson continues:

> The nation is imagined as *limited* because even the largest of them ... has finite, if elastic, boundaries, beyond which lie other nations. No nation imagines itself coterminous with mankind. The most messianic nationalists do not dream of a day when all the members of the human race will join their nation in the way it was possible, in certain epochs, for say, Christians to dream of a wholly Christian planet.

Although the entire community of a nation necessarily encompasses a great spectrum of heterogeneous characters and difference, yet nations imagine themselves as somehow inherently (and essentially) different from each other, and therefore rivals and competitors. As Anderson notes, even messianic nationalists don't dream of all members of the human race becoming one nation; but messianic Leopold Bloom, the utopian prophet of the New Bloomusalem, will, in his fantasies in "Circe" – as does, to a more limited degree, James Joyce, who, I would argue, does at least posit the desirability of a more culturally inclusive alternative to the limits of Irish Nationalism.

> It is imagined as *sovereign* because the concept was born in an age in which Englightenment and Revolution were destroying the legitimacy of the divinely-ordained, hierarchical dynastic realm ... nations dream of being free ... The gage and emblem of this freedom is the sovereign state.

I will have more to say on this idea (a truly imagined one) of Ireland as a "sovereign" state later, and would like to bracket this till our reading of "Cyclops."

> Finally, it is imagined as a *community*, because, regardless of the actual inequality and exploitation that may prevail in each, the nation is always conceived as a deep, horizontal comradeship. Ultimately it is this fraternity that makes it possible, over the past two centuries, for so many millions of people, not so much to kill, as willingly to die for such limited imaginings.

(Anderson, *Imagined Communities*, 7)

Which is to say that the imagined horizontal community allows for imaginary constructs – such as "national character" or national identity and values – to be reified, which in turn makes it possible for patriotic sentiments and identifications to attach themselves to such reified constructs, to such an extent that people are willing to go to war or to die for these imaginary inventions.

In such a perspective, the idea of "nation" leads to the discursive reification of a rather arbitrary and homogeneous "national character" imposed upon a necessarily very heterogeneous collection of different people(s) over a wide expanse of territory, a notion that thus – in the process which Anderson calls "imagining the nation" and which Homi Bhabha calls "writing the nation" – writes out (erases) difference and the realities of a pluralistic and culturally diverse "contact zone" (to use Mary Pratt's term), so as to establish an essentialized (but largely imaginary) "national character." The nation is thus imagined as "a solid community moving steadily down (or up) history"; as Anderson points out, "An American will never meet, or even know the names of more than a handful of his 240,000,000-odd fellow-Americans. He has no idea of what they are up to at any one time. But he has complete confidence in their steady, anonymous, simultaneous activity" (26). As a result, the nation becomes a totalized version of the universal-particular,[2] an attempt to universalize individual difference, to homogenize heterogeneity: nation-formation leads to the imagined/imaginary collectivity which results in essentialism – so that "Finally, the imagined community . . . thinks of the representative body, not the personal life" (*Imagined Communities*, 32).

This totality is, as Homi Bhabha points out in his collection *Nation and Narration*, "an idea whose cultural compulsion lies in the impossible unity of the nation as a symbolic force" (1), based on the imagined premise of "the many as one": "We may begin by questioning that progressive metaphor of modern social cohesion – *the many as one* – shared by organic theories of the holism of culture and community, and by theorists who treat gender, class, or race as radically 'expressive' social totalities" (294).

Such a totalizing movement was very much behind the Irish Nationalist construction of an Irish/Celtic national character, as Seamus Deane has argued in his essay on "National Character and National Audience: Races, Crowds, and Readers." Deane points out:

In almost all the literature of nineteenth century Ireland, national character and the appeal of its various embodiments to a new national audience, is a constant refrain. Maria Edgeworth, Lady Morgan, Thomas Moore, Gerald Griffin, the Banim brothers, Mrs. Hall, William Carleton,

Father Prout, William Maginn, Somerville and Ross, the Young Ire-
landers, Standish O'Grady, the young Yeats, and Shaw ... all give it
prominence.

("National," 40–41)

Deane shows how the leading nineteenth-century Irish authors – up
to and including Yeats, Shaw, Synge, and Douglas Hyde (in trying,
as Yeats put it, "To write for my own race") – tried repeatedly to
imagine (both for their subject matter and as their ideal audience)
"imagined communities" which they defined as the Irish nation and
race, with all the desired "national character" and radical uniqueness
which each one fantasized (and endowed their writing with).

This is very much part of the process that Bhabha calls "writing
the nation":

> The scraps, patches, and rags of daily life must be repeatedly turned into
> the signs of a national culture, while the very act of the narrative
> performance interpellates a growing circle of national subjects ... It is
> through this process of splitting that the conceptual ambivalence of
> modern society becomes the site of *writing the nation*.
>
> ("DissemiNation," 297)

In such a process, the ambivalence involves a discursive occlusion (in
both the present and past history) of the internal cultural differences
which exist within any large and heterogeneous contact zone: "The
barred Nation *It/Self*, alienated from its eternal self-generation,
becomes a liminal form of social representation, a space that is
internally marked by cultural difference and the heterogeneous
histories of contending peoples, antagonistic authorities, and tense
cultural locations" (Bhabha, "DissemiNation," 299). The result is
essentialized national stereotypes (of both the national Self and of its
Others), constantly driven by a nostalgia for pure origins in an
"attempt to hark back to a 'true' national past, which is often
represented in the reified forms of realism and stereotype" (Bhabha,
"DissemiNation," 303).

As a result, we have the popular investments in an imagined and
essentialized national identity; as Anderson points out, "each
communicant" in such a national community assumes that his daily
experience is more or less typical of those of "thousands (or
millions) of others of whose existence he is confident, yet of whose
identity he has not the slightest notion," for he/she has been
"continually reassured that the imagined world is visibly rooted in
everyday life, creating that remarkable confidence of community
which is the hallmark of modern nations" (*Imagined Communities*,

35–36). Anderson's observations about "imagined communities" (like most important discoveries) seem almost obvious once they are pointed out. Yet the point is brilliant and important – and reflects an experiential reality we have each discovered in getting to know other people: for the fact is that I, for example – as a Chinese male who grew up in various countries overseas but who am now a naturalized American – have perhaps much more in common with, say, certain individual Canadian women, or individual Dutch nationals, or individual black Americans, or individual gay males – than with most other heterosexual Chinese-American males. Any large and heterogeneous group with whose individual membership one cannot be personally familiar, but which is nonetheless characterized or shaped in terms of presumed shared traits, is, finally, an essentialized and imagined/imaginary community.

Nevertheless, so strong is this neo-religious impulse towards nation-ness, that the nations to which these "imagined communities" give political expression are then conceived so as to "always loom out of an immemorial past, and, still more important, glide into a limitless future. It is the magic of nationalism to turn chance into destiny" (Anderson, *Imagined Communities*, 11–12). Like Jay Gatsby (and like the imagined American "national character" he represents), nations – once born – tend to create an immemorial past for themselves, as if they had always been there, and a limitless future whose destiny has always been written; as Bhabha puts it, "Nations ... lose their origins in the myths of time and only fully realize their horizons in the mind's eye" (*Nation*, 1).

The sentimental vocabulary for patriotic love-of-one's-nation suggests to what extent "nation" becomes internalized as a natural and unquestioned condition of essence and destiny, often "either in the vocabulary of kinship (motherland, *Vaterland, patria*) or that of home (*heimat* or *tanah air*)" – for both idioms "denote something to which one is naturally tied" and "In this way, nation-ness is assimilated to skin-colour, gender, parentage and birth-era – all those things one cannot help ... To put it another way, precisely because such ties are not chosen, they have about them a halo of disinterestedness" (Anderson, 143). This halo of "natural" inevitability surrounding one's nation-ness is patently ludicrous to any marginal or diasporic peoples, or to anyone living by choice in a "contact zone," for they have not been granted such an aura – people (like myself) who, whether by choice or circumstance, do not assume that "Chinese" (or whatever) is a nationality by destiny, but instead might opt to become American, Brazilian, Swazi, or whatever. Joyce's Bloom, by contrast, is in the unenviable position of being unable to *choose* (or even to wish) to become Irish, since he was born in Ireland and already *is* Irish; yet he is, nonetheless, unceasingly typed as a foreigner always belonging somewhere else, essentialized within another static, reified "natural" state (Jewish heritage) that he didn't choose either. The absurdity of such presumed inevitability is mocked by the very fact that almost every nation has an institutional process by which foreigners *can* become nationals: but even the term we use for that process – "naturalization" ("wonderful word!" as Anderson [145] notes) – is an attempt linguistically to deceive ourselves into imagining the acquired identity as something eternal and natural.

The effect of such an imagined national character and community is, in Anderson's term, "unisonance": "Singing the Marseillaise, Waltzing Matilda, and Indonesia Raya provide occasions for unisonality, for the echoed physical realization of the imagined community" – when, perhaps, in truth "Nothing connects us all but imagined sound" (*Imagined Communities*, 145). The composite reality of, say, "France," in the full range of its internal cultural/ethnic/individual heterogeneity and difference, may not be very much different from the corresponding heterogeneous ranges and realities of any (not purely tribal) nation – whether Indonesia, Algeria, Australia, the United States, Canada, and so on. It is the tragedy of a unisonant, monologic perspective that it is blind to the pluralism, heterogeneity, and multivalence of perspectives available – even within one's own nation. It is for this reason that Joyce's representation of nationalistic xenophobia and chauvinistic myopia through the trope of the one-eyed Cyclops is such a brilliantly effective and resonant choice.

The "Cyclops" episode of *Ulysses* presents and explores many of the above issues and ideas about Nation. Throughout the episode, the increasingly drunken men at Barney Kiernan's pub repeatedly slander Bloom with racial slurs on his Jewishness – "A bit off the top" (*U* 12.20), "the little jewy" (*U* 12.31), "the prudent member" (*U* 12.211), "those jewies does have sort of a queer odour" (*U* 12.452–53), "old shylock" (*U* 12.765), "the bottlenosed fraternity" (*U* 12.1086), and so on. At the same time, such slurs, ironically, are often immediately followed by unconscious references such as "How are the mighty fallen!" taken from the Jewish Old Testament or, more consciously, repeated comparisons of the situation of the Irish to that of the exiled Israelites under Pharoah (as already manifest in "Aeolus"), such as the following description of Irish heritage in terms of Judaic tribes: "the high sinhedrim of the twelve tribes of Iar, for every tribe one man, of the tribe of Patrick and of the tribe of Hugh and ... " (*U* 12.1125) – for Iar was one of the three sons of Mileadh and the legendary Milesian ancestor of the Irish clans, of "Iar-land" (Gifford, *"Ulysses" Annotated*, 347). The men in the pub, however, are blind to the self-contradicting irony inherent in such anti-Semitism – for they have the limited, monologic, cycloptic vision of an ethnocentric and xenophobic nationalism. This is true of the various men drinking in the pub – but especially of the Citizen, based on Michael Cusack (1847–1907), the founder of the Gaelic Athletic Association, that "notably contentious" association "dedicated to the revival of Irish sports such as hurling, Gaelic football, and handball" (Gifford, *"Ulysses" Annotated*, 316). Cusack, who referred to himself as "Citizen Cusack," was notoriously contentious himself, greeting people thus: "I'm Citizen Cusack from the Parish of Carron in the Barony of Burre in the County of Clare, you Protestant dog!" (Ellmann, *JJII*, 61) As the episode opens, its curmudgeonly narrator notices the Citizen in the bar: "There he is ... working for the cause" (*U* 12.123–24); ironically, the only cause the Citizen seems to be working for the entire episode is cadging free drinks, while it is Bloom who is actively engaged in a humanitiarian activity at the moment (meeting Cunningham and Power to set up a charity for the Dignam family).

Right away the episode's narrator mockingly describes the Citizen as "Doing the rapparee and Rory of the hill" (*U* 12.134) – "rapparees" (Irish for robbers or outlaws) were originally Catholic landlords displaced by Cromwell who turned to blackmailing and plundering the Cromwellian Protestants who had taken over their lands; they were idealized in the nineteenth century by Charles Gavan Duffy in "The Irish Rapparees: a Peasant Ballad" praising their retributive violence in response to the Cromwellers. "Rory of the hill" was the signature "adopted in about 1880 by letter writers who threatened landlords and others in the agitation for land reform"; it was also the title of a nineteenth-century poem by Charles Joseph Kickham sentimentally avowing that "dear Ireland's strength / Her honest strength – is still / The rough-and-ready roving boys, / Like Rory of the Hill" (Gifford, *"Ulysses" Annotated*, 320). Thus, from the start of "Cyclops," Joyce illustrates how the Citizen's prototypically macho qualities of physical strength and retributive violence ("rough-and-ready roving boys") get sentimentalized and idealized into national legendry, the very stuff Joyce is parodying in the episode.

Throughout the episode, Joyce satirizes – through the parodic sections of the narration – the xenophobic ideologies of radical Celticists such as Michael Cusack. These parodies repeatedly take on the forms of the nineteenth-century Irish nationalist literature which had sentimentalized stereotypes of a "national character" (as Deane points out), usually bathed in a nostalgia for origins – "that attempt to hark back to a 'true' national past" (Bhabha, 303) through what David Lloyd calls "the recurrent reproduction of Celtic material as a thematica of identity" ("Writing," 85).³ In his 1903 essay "The Soul of Ireland," a review of Lady Gregory's *Poets and Dreamers*, Joyce had already derided such attempts to sentimentalize an Irish essence from the misty dreams of the distant past (rather than by creating a vital, new national literature), describing her book (which also included translations of some West Irish ballads and some of Hyde's poems) as explorations "in a land almost fabulous in its sorrow and senility" (*CW* 103); this is the review Mulligan refers to in the Library when he tells Stephen: "Longworth is awfully sick ... after what you wrote about that old hake Gregory ... She gets you a job on the paper and then you go and slate her drivel to Jaysus. Couldn't you do the Yeats touch?" (*U* 9.1158–61).

Here, in "Cyclops," Joyce composes within the episode's narration a number of extended and hilarious send-ups of sentimentalized, nostalgia-laden, heroic Irish literature and legendry in the Celtic-revival mode, taking off everyone from James Clarence Mangan to Hyde's *Lovesongs from Connacht* ("Those delightful lovesongs with which the writer who conceals his identity under the graceful pseudonym of the Little Sweet Branch"; *U* 12.723–25) to Dan Dawson: "In Insifail the fair there lies a land ... a pleasant land it is in sooth of murmuring waters, fishful streams where sport the gurnard, the plaice, the roach, the halibut" (*U* 12.69–73) and so on. These parodies are appropriately endowed with that narrow vision of the binary trap, imposing reified oppositions of Celtic purity and English depravity as poles of absolute difference. Hyde, the leader in the radical movement to de-Anglicise Ireland and return it to the Gaelic language, had posited in his *A Literary History of Ireland from the Earliest Times to the Present Day* (1899) an "Irish-speaking population ... who ... have a remarkable command of language and a large store of traditional literature learned by heart" in contrast to the "anglicized products of the National Schools" to whom "poetry is an unknown term" and among whom "there exists little or no trace of traditional Irish feelings"; as Deane summarizes Hyde's position on "culture": "The Irish had it, the English and the Anglicized had not" ("National," 40, 42) – a simplistic and mirrored reversal of the Anglo-Saxonist prejudice towards the barbarian Celt. Thus, for example, one of the best-known "Cyclops" parodies – obviously suggesting that the Irish are the greatest race on earth and are responsible for all the world's great achievements – lists in its catalogue of "the tribal images of many Irish heroes and heroines of antiquity" (*U* 12.175) such "Celtic" greats as Dante Alighieri, Christopher Columbus, Saint Brendan (whom some Celtic enthusiasts argued had discovered America in the sixth century AD), Muhammad, "Brian Confucius," "Patrick W. Shakespeare," and so on.[4] Earlier, in the Library, Eglinton had referred to Judge Barton "searching for clues" that Hamlet ("Has no-one made him out to be an Irishman?") or Shakespeare was Irish (*U* 9.510–21); Sir Dunbar Plunket Barton did indeed eventually publish his *Links Between Ireland and Shakespeare*, including suggestions that there was some "Celt in Shakespeare" (Gifford, *"Ulysses" Annotated*, 225). The patent absurdity of such claims is further exposed by the "Cyclops" narrator also throwing into this catalogue equally ridiculous possibilities such as "Francy Higgins" (the "Sham Squire"), "the first Prince of Wales," and "Arthur Wellesley" (Duke of Wellington) – all of whom were (ideologically) on the English side of the dualism. (Like Higgins, the latter *was* Irish, but "the Dublin-born duke was not the soul of popularity in his native country, since as prime minister [1828–30], he symbolized rigorous English militarism and a conservative resistance to reform" [Gifford, *"Ulysses" Annotated*, 325]; see also chapter 10 of this study, "The general and the sepoy," on Wellington.)

Perhaps the most hilarious and effective of these parodies is the extended account of Robert Emmet's hanging in *U* 12.524–678, an exploration into the dynamics of patriotic martyrdom. Anderson, in analyzing the nature and the strength of patriotic fervor for the imaginary constructions of "nation," has wondered "why people are ready to die for these inventions" (*Imagined Communities*, 141). An episode earlier, Bloom had listened to Ben Dollard in the Ormond singing "The Croppy Boy" and had thought about the lines from this song of national heroes and martyrs: "All gone. All fallen. At the siege of Ross his father, at Gorey all his brothers fell. To Wexford, we

are the boys of Wexford, he would. Last of his name and race ...
Ireland comes now. My country above the king" (*U* 11.1063–72).
When he emerges into the street, Bloom sees "Robert Emmet's last
words" in a shop window (and farts). Now, in "Cyclops," we have a
dramatization of Emmet's final moments.

The narrator in the pub tells us that at this point "they started
talking about capital punishment and of course Bloom comes out with
the why and the wherefore" (*U* 12.450–51), arguing against capital
punishment. The discussion then turns to hanging, and to the hanging
of the Invincibles, and then to violent revolution: "So of course the
citizen was only waiting for the wink of the word and he starts gassing
out of him about the invincibles and the old guard and the men of
sixtyseven" (*U* 12.479–81). The Citizen can only answer Bloom's
reasoned arguments by resorting to cant and slogans: " – *Sinn Fein!* ...
sinn fein amhain! The friends we love are by our side and the foes we
hate before us" (*U* 12.523–24). This latter sentence is a startlingly stark
and clear statement of binary opposition and essentializing; of the
need to demarcate the Self and the Other as polar enemies marked by
absolute difference; of limited, one-eyed vision. Ironically, the sentence (although it corresponds to "Ourselves, ourselves alone") is not
Cusack's but a quotation from a sentimental Thomas Moore song in
the *Irish Melodies* – which goes to show to what extent the Irish
Nationalist logic of a binary opposition had been already systemically
internalized into the popular cultural discourse.

Soon, the Citizen and Bloom are "having an argument about the
point, the brothers Sheares and Wolfe Tone beyond on Arbour Hill
and Robert Emmet and die for our country, the Tommy Moore touch
about Sara Curran and she's far from the land" (*U* 12.498–501).
These specific references are instructive in terms of the nature of the
myth-making of Irish nationalism: in the Rebellion of 1798, the
Sheares brothers were both members of the United Irishmen who
were betrayed by an informer; according to the sentimentally
popular version of the story, they supposedly went hand in hand to
their execution (though there is no evidence for this version). Sara
Curran was secretly engaged to Robert Emmet, who – according to a
popular but equally apocryphal legend – was captured when he
went to bid her good-bye before fleeing the country; a *very*
sentimentalized version of her story was then told by Thomas Moore
in his *Irish Melodies* ("the Tommy Moore touch"), in a poem titled
"She Is Far From the Land" (Gifford, *"Ulysses" Annotated*, 332–33).
Emmet, of course, was hanged and beheaded (after a farcical and

doomed attempt at capturing Dublin Castle), in a "brutally botched public execution" (Gifford, *"Ulysses" Annotated* 124) after speaking his famous last words ("When my country takes her place among the nations of the earth then and not till then, let my epitaph be written. I have done") – and, as a result of this hopeless farce, has since been somehow incredibly raised to the highest mythological pantheon of legendary Irish heroes.[5]

Joyce's parody narrates the Emmet hanging in the stylized language of a newspaper socialite report in the society pages. The result is absurd and outrageous: but the effectiveness of the humor is also Joyce's comment on the nationalist tendency to nostalgize and sentimentalize (as do the society columns) what are basically terrible things: death, martyrdom, capital punishment. Thus, the hanging (like a celebrity wedding) becomes an over-hyped gala event, a socialite occasion attended by all sides – for among those present are the "viceregal houseparty which included many wellknown ladies" as well as the "Friends of the Emerald Isle," not to speak of high dignitaries from all over the world (such as "Ali Baba Backsheesh Rahat Lokum Effendi"). Like the sentimentalizing clichés of the society pages (shaping minds like Gerty MacDowell's), the narrative describes "An animated altercation" which ensued and in which "blows were freely exchanged," after which however order was "promptly restored" and "general harmony reigned supreme," at which point the hangman Rumbold "stepped on to the scaffold in faultless morning dress and wearing his favourite flower, the *Gladiolus Cruentus*" while "on a handsome mahogany table near him were neatly arranged the quartering knife, the various finely tempered disembowelling appliances," and so on. This is wonderfully funny stuff:

The *nec* and *non plus ultra* of emotion were reached when the blushing bride elect burst her way through the serried ranks of the bystanders and flung herself upon the muscular bosom of him who was about to be launched into eternity for her sake. The hero folded her willowy form in a loving embrace murmuring fondly *Sheila, my own.*

– this *is* the collective mind of Gerty MacDowell speaking.

It is interesting to note that Joyce's Emmet here calls his "blushing bride elect" Sheila: since Sheila-ni-Gara was an allegorical name for Ireland, Emmet here is allegorically engaged to Ireland (as his bride). He now goes to his death in heroically sentimentalized fashion, "with a song on his lips as if he were but going to a hurling match in

Clonturk park." At this moment "A most romantic incident occurred when a handsome young Oxford graduate ... stepped forward and, presenting his visiting card, bankbook and genealogical tree, solicited the hand of the hapless young lady, requesting her to name the day, and was accepted on the spot." While this melodramatic absurdity fits in with the sentimentally romanticized drivel of the passage, it is also Joyce's ironic comment on Irish betrayal – on a history of Ireland herself (Sheila-ni-Gara) selling out to England and allegorically betraying her Irish lover (just as Emmet, the Sheares, Fitzgerald, Parnell, and others had been betrayed by Irish informers and turncoats) even as he is about to be hanged. The Oxonian pretender, with his bankbook and his genealogical tree, evokes "the oxy chap" Haines and the English hegemonic ability to tempt the shoneen mentality with the dual attractions of material success and cultural/ social pretensions.

As a result of this happy and unexpected connubial development, we are told (as the parodic passage comes to an end) that "Every lady in the audience was presented with a tasteful souvenir of the occasion in the shape of a skull and crossbones brooch" and

even the stern provostmarshal, lieutenantcolonel Tomkin-Maxwell ffrenchmullan Tomlinson, who presided on the sad occasion, he who had blown a considerable number of sepoys from the cannonmouth without flinching, could not now restrain his natural emotion ... and was overheard ... to murmur to himself in a faltering undertone:
– God blimey if she aint a clinker, that there bleeding tart. Blimey it makes me kind of bleeding cry ...

The parody is both hilariously and poignantly effective precisely because it exposes the sort of rose-tinted nationalistic sentimentality that can (on the Irish side) canonize a pointless and farcical martyrdom into the pantheon of sacred national symbols, or (on the mirrored English side) sentimentalize "our boys" (such as lieutenant-colonel Tomlinson) "over there" in the Indian colonies as strong silent types hiding a soft heart beneath their courageous and stoic exterior – and thus gloss over or ignore brutal outrages and realities such as the "considerable number of sepoys" they had blown "from the cannonmouth without flinching," an actual British practice during the bloody Sepoy Rebellion of 1857.[6] For Bloom as for Joyce, the pointless spilling of blood was tragic but not either noble nor heroic: the Emmet parody in "Cyclops" helps to demythologize the sentimentalizing, mythmaking process by which – as Anderson puts it in describing the imagined community/comradeship of Nation –

"this [imagined] fraternity ... makes it possible ... for so many millions of people, not so much to kill, as willingly to die for such limited imaginings" (7).

At this point, while Bloom is trying to argue the need (so well illustrated in this episode itself) for more temperance in an Ireland held hostage to "drink, the curse of Ireland" (*U* 12.684) – the Citizen brings up instead the issue of the Irish language, the movement spurred by Hyde for a "return" to the "purity" of the Gaelic language and the de-Anglicization of Ireland: "So then the citizen begins talking about the Irish language and the corporation meeting and all that and the shoneens that can't speak their own language" (*U* 12.679–81); as we had learned earlier in "Wandering Rocks," at City Hall the "Corporation" was in fact (on June 16, 1904) debating that very issue about "their damned Irish language" (*U* 10.1010).[7] As Anderson (*Imagined Communities*, 154) points out, the arena of language often takes on a central role in the "imagining" of nation and national identity as a community homogeneously shaped by a shared (and stridently defended) vernacular-as-destiny:

What the eye is to the lover – that particular, ordinary eye he or she is born with – language – whatever language history has made his or her mother-tongue – is to the patriot. Through that language, encountered at mother's knee and parted with only at the grave, pasts are restored, fellowships are imagined, and futures dreamed.

But, while the issue of a return to Gaelic as the national language was obviously a central item in the cultural agenda of the Gaelic Revival, the disputed cultural space in "Cyclops" is not so much language or even literature but sports. The debate about sports in "Cyclops" affords a paradigmatic case study (and microcosm) of the Celticist agenda and dynamics. This is hardly inappropriate or coincidental here, for after all Michael Cusack was the head and founder of the Gaelic Athletic League. As Joe Hynes says about the Citizen: " – There's the man ... that made the Gaelic sports revival. There he is sitting there ... The champion of all Ireland at putting the sixteen pound shot" (*U* 12.880–82). Not only devoted to reviving Irish sports like hurling, Gaelic football, and handball, Cusack's Gaelic Athletic Association was also militantly engaged in " 'banning' as un-Irish those who participated in or watched such 'English' games as association football (soccer), rugby, field hockey, and polo" (Gifford, *"Ulysses" Annotated*, 316). Sports had thus become a serious issue in the Nationalist and anti-English agenda (in

A Portrait, 202, Stephen had derided Davin about this "rebellion with hurleysticks"), having been politicized from the realm of athletic activity into a binary-polar politics in which particular games were now being labeled as either Irish, or as English and thus un-Irish. We have already seen how schools in the hegemonic cultural system played "English" sports like cricket (Clongowes) and field hockey (Deasy's school in Dalkey). Earlier in the day Bloom had thought about the "banning" of cricket: "They can't play it here ... Still Captain Culler broke a window in the Kildare street club with a slog to square leg" (*U* 5.559–61). The Kildare Street Club was the most fashionable and expensive shoneen club in Ireland, whose "membership was dominated by wealthy Irish landlords well known for their pro-English sentiments" and "reputedly the only place in Dublin where one could get decent caviar" (Gifford, *"Ulysses" Annotated*, 99) – and obviously a place where one would still play cricket. And Stephen had thought of Lord Tennyson as "Lawn Tennyson, gentleman poet" (9.648) – blending two emblems of the genteel English establishment, lawn tennis and the Poet Laureate; recall, too, that the "Oxy chap" Haines is wearing a tennis shirt today.

Now, in "Cyclops," Joe Hynes reports that "Field and Nannetti are going over tonight to London to ask about [foot and mouth disease] on the floor of the house of commons" and that "the league [the Gaelic League] told [Nannetti] to ask a question tomorrow about the commissioner of police forbidding Irish games in the park ... The *Sluagh na h-Eireann*" (*U* 12.850–59). The "Sluagh na h-Eireann," or "Army of Ireland," was a patriotic organization that, on June 16, 1904, did in fact complain to Parliament (through Nannetti) that it was not being allowed by the police commissioners to play Irish games in Phoenix Park; "the complaint noted that polo (presumably an English and foreign sport) was allowed" (Gifford, *"Ulysses" Annotated*, 341).

What immediately follows in the episode is a parody of parliamentary debate (between MPs with names like "Mr Cowe Conacre" and "Mr Allfours") about the slaughtering of cattle (Bloom had just been arguing for "Humane methods because the poor animals suffer and experts say and the best known remedy that doesn't cause pain to the animal"; *U* 12.843–44) and also about sports: "Have similar orders been issued for the slaughter of human animals who dare to play Irish games in the Phoenix park?" (*U* 12.869–71). The parliamentary debate mirrors that in the pub, which now also moves to the subject of games: "So off they started about Irish sports and shoneen games the like of lawn tennis and about hurley and putting the stone and racy of the soil and building up a nation once again and all to that" (*U* 12.889–91). By 1904 the Celticist arguments for racial purity, and for a culture and a literature that is "racy of the soil" and would help in "building up a nation once again," had moved beyond the realms of Irish language and the Irish literary revival even into the now racialized and nationalized arena of popular sports. So we get a somewhat Celticized parodic version of the above narration: "A most interesting discussion took place in the ancient hall of *Brian o'Ciarnain*'s [Barney Kiernan's] in *Sraid na Bretaine Bheag* [in, ironically, Little Britain Street], under the auspices of *Sluagh na h-Eireann*, on the revival of ancient Gaelic sports and the importance of physical culture ... for the development of the race" (*U* 12.897–901). Hynes makes an "eloquent appeal for the resuscitation of the ancient Gaelic sports and pastimes, practised morning and evening by Finn MacCool, as calculated to revive the best traditions of manly strength and prowess handed down to us from ancient ages" (*U* 12.908–12). The men then join in singing "the immortal Thomas Osborne Davis's evergreen verses (happily too familiar to need recalling here) *A Nation Once Again*" (*U* 12.916–17); "A Nation Once Again" was a song by Davis, an Irish poet and patriot whose poems had been praised by Charles Gavan Duffy as "evergreen" (Gifford, *"Ulysses" Annotated*, 342; in the West of Ireland, many pubs still mark closing time by having everyone join in a communal singing of "A Nation Once Again," long the unofficial anthem of the IRA).[8]

By labeling particular games as "racy of the soil" and "Irish," and by "banning" particular others as un-Irish or shoneen or English, this "banning" practice of the Gaelic revival was again falling into the binary trap, not only by being unable to break free of an Irish–English dialectic, but also by maintaining a static hierarchy of labels and valuations, even about sports – much as arguments for Celtic racial purity still maintained a vertical hierarchy of pejorative labels (degrees of racial impurity, such as Chinese or Hottentot) which still mirrored the imposed and inherited system of the Anglo-Saxonist racist oppression. Bloom refuses to value individual sports along polarized lines of national politics, but rather is able to break out of the Irish–English binary structures by arguing for particular sports according to their individual and humanitarian use-value: for example, "if a fellow had a rower's heart violent exercise was bad"

(*U* 12.892–93). When the men now start discussing boxing – "Talking about violent exercise . . . were you at that Keogh–Bennett match?" at which Boylan had "made a cool hundred quid over" (*U* 12.939–43) – Bloom argues instead for a less brutal game like tennis: "What I meant about tennis, for example, is the agility and training of the eye." As opposed to masculist violence and retributive brutality (represented here by pugilism, Fenianism [which Joyce had called "a desperate and bloody doctrine" (CW 191)], Blazes Boylan, and the Citizen), Bloom counters the general enthusiasm for boxing with other physical considerations: "And Bloom cuts in again about lawn tennis and the circulation of the blood" (*U* 12.940–52). Stephen had in the school that morning shown his awareness of how games of violent and aggressive competition, such as the boys' hockey game going on outside, were – like the playing fields of Eton – training grounds for a male ideology and tradition of blood and warfare: "Again: a goal . . . their battling bodies in a medley, the joust of life . . . Jousts. Time shocked rebounds, shock by shock. Jousts, slush and uproar of battles, the frozen deathspew of the slain, a shout of spearspikes baited with men's bloodied guts" (*U* 2.314–18). Bloom – who also wonders about "children playing battle. Whole earnest. How can people aim guns at each other" (*U* 13.1192–93) – like Stephen and like Joyce, deplores violent sports, such as boxing, that just breed more violence and brutality.

The Bennett–Keogh fight – between an English soldier (Sergeant-major Bennett) and an Irish "pucker" (Keogh) – is an emblematic representation of those very dynamics involved in a closed, binary, polarized England–Ireland dialectic, with its resultant and systemic violence, a microcosm of warfare:

The soldier got to business, leading off with a powerful left jab to which the Irish gladiator retaliated by shooting out a stiff one flush to the point of Bennett's jaw. The redcoat ducked but the Dubliner lifted him with a left hook, the body punch being a fine one. The men came to handgrips . . . It was a fight to a finish and the best man for it.

This is the masculist, binary, imperialist logic in an emblematic moment – a closed system of mirrored hatred and violence, a duel of dual and mirrored images.

But the men in the pub have limited vision and only see the binary poles, see everything in stark categories of black and white, English or Irish – thus, they accuse Breen (and presumably Bloom) of being a "half and half," "A fellow that's neither fish nor flesh" (*U* 12.1055–57);

a bit later, they will label Bloom as a "mixed middling" ("Do you call that a man?" they ask, in *U* 12.1654–58), for Bloom doesn't fit into the static categories of maleness and masculinity which they can understand. Sports becomes just one more arena in which the homogenization of individual and cultural differences and preferences takes place, resulting in an oppressive hierarchy of fixed, essentialized labels.

The debate in the pub begins itself to resemble a boxing match, as the Citizen becomes more and more aggressive and tries to provoke Bloom into a good hard fight to the finish – which Bloom declines, continuing to voice reasoned arguments. The Citizen, however, rains a series of low blows – as he accuses Bloom first of "Swindling the peasants ... and the poor of Ireland. We want no more strangers in our house" (*U* 12.1150–51). Again, he sets up the binary oppositions of xenophobia (fear of strangers): strangers/foreigners, versus our house; "them" versus "us." "Strangers in our house" was a term used to refer to the British, for Yeats's Cathleen complained about "Too many strangers in the house ... My land was taken from me ... My four beautiful green fields" (the four provinces) – lines Stephen had also referred to earlier ("Gaptoothed Kathleen, her four beautiful green fields, the stranger in her house" in *U* 9.36–37). Thus, the Citizen's one-eyed logic is unable to distinguish the English invaders from Bloom, an Irishman born in Ireland. Even more ironic is the fact that they themselves are *all* foreigners, having been descended from Celts, Danes, Saxons, and others who each in their turn had once been "strangers in our house." The Citizen continues: " – The strangers ... Our own fault. We let them in. We brought them in. The adulteress and her paramour brought the Saxon robbers here ... A dishonoured wife, ... that's what's the cause of all our misfortunes" (*U* 12.1156–65). This is exactly the same logic as that of the Ulsterman Deasy's attack on women earlier (*U* 2.389–97), in its combination of racism, xenophobia, and misogyny – for all three of these (racism, xenophobia, misogyny) are binary, totalizing structures which mirror each other, whether espoused by Celticist radical (Cusack) or pro-English Ulsterman (Deasy). All of these binary structures get focused in the person of the Citizen and his ideology – and Bloom, like Joyce, refuses to be sucked into their trap.

When John Wyse Nolan walks in, the Citizen asks him about another binary issue, the language question being debated that afternoon in City Hall: "What did those tinkers in the city hall at their caucus meeting decide about the Irish language?" (*U* 12.1181–82)

The Citizen's own opinion is predictable – "To hell with the bloody brutal Sassenachs and their *patois*" – engaging in precisely the binary logic of Celticist racial venom, accusing England (and its culture) of exactly what Anglo-Saxonist racism had previously stigmatized as "Irish": "No music and no art and no literature worthy of the name. Any civilisation they have they stole from us. Tonguetied sons of bastards' ghosts ... *Conspuez les anglais!*" ("*Perfide Albion!*" adds Lenehan; *U* 12.1191–201). Bloom and J. J. O'Molloy, on the other hand, are willing to try to see more than one side to an issue: "So J. J. puts in a word ... about one story was good till you heard another and blinking facts and the Nelson policy [recall that Nelson, too, like Cyclops, had only one good eye], putting your blind eye to the telescope and drawing up a bill of attainder to impeach a nation, and Bloom trying to back him up moderation and botheration and their colonies and their civilization" (*U* 12.1192–96: Sinn Fein had earlier tried to draw up a bill to "impeach" England in the court of "world opinion"; Gifford, "*Ulysses*" *Annotated*, 349). The Citizen's response is to drink some more: "then lifted he in his rude great brawny strengthy hands the medher of dark strong foamy ale and, uttering his tribal slogan *Lamb Dearg Abu* ['Red Hand to Victory,' both the heraldic symbol of Ulster and the O'Neills, and the label of the Allsop's bottled ale he is drinking], he drank to the undoing of his foes" (*U* 12.1210–14).

At this moment the results of the Gold Cup race are announced in the bar, introducing the issues of favorites and dark horses, Sceptres and Throwaways. The phallic "sceptre" of imperial and patriarchal rule is represented in the pub by the male-centrist, one-eyed, racist intolerance of the Citizen's rabid Celticist logic, which mirrors that of the same British imperialism he so hates. As Bloom now points out: "Some people ... can see the mote in others' eyes but they can't see the beam in their own" (*U* 12.1237–38) – as the Citizen launches into an extended encomium about the unsurpassed greatness of Ireland (*U* 12.1240–58). Appropriately, the men now turn their attention to a newspaper with a "Picture of a butting match, trying to crack their bloody skulls, one chap going for the other with his head down like a bull at the gate" – much like the Bennett–Keogh boxing match and the macho logic of the Citizen's anti-English venom. The newspaper also features a second picture: "*Black Beast Burned in Omaha, Ga.* A lot of Deadwood Dicks in slouch hats and they firing at a Sambo strung up in a tree with his tongue out and a bonfire under him" (*U* 12.1321–28). This second image (in the "Cyclops" narrator's racist language) of a black man being lynched in America is equally appropriate within a Joycean panoply of binary systems of masculist "imperialism," brutality ("the brutish empire"), racism, and retributive justice ("lynching," a term associated in Ireland with "the Galway Lynches," was evoked a few lines earlier in *U* 12.1304) – for it is a depiction of the literally black-and-white dynamics ("Sambos" and "Deadwood Dicks") within the black-and-white monologic (monochrome) vision of racism. (This was an actual lynching incident reported in the international papers.[9])

"That's your glorious British navy," continues the Citizen as he now discusses naval discipline, "that bosses the earth ... That's the great empire they boast about of drudges and whipped serfs ... And the tragedy of it ... [is] they believe it. The unfortunate yahoos believe it" (*U* 12.1346–53). The Citizen merely illustrates Bloom's point about the mote in one's eye: he sees through the pretense of British greatness, but he cannot see himself as others see him; he names *them* as "yahoos," employing the same mirrored logic of primitivizing racism which they had used to essentialize him as an Irish Caliban. Bloom understands the vicious cycles of such mirrored violence. Earlier he had thought about the Old Testament Exodus and dispossession of the Jews:

Poor papa with his hagadah book, reading backwards with his finger to me. Pessach. Next year in Jerusalem. Dear, O dear! All that long business about that brought us out of the land of Egypt and into the house of bondage *alleluia. Shema Israel Adonai Elohenu* ... Then the twelve brothers, Jacob's sons. And then the lamb and the cat and the dog and the stick and the water and the butcher. And then the angel of death kills the butcher and he kills the ox and the dog kills the cat ... Justice it means but it's everybody eating everyone else.

(*U* 7.206–14)

In thinking about the *Haggadah*, Passover (Pessach), "next year in Jerusalem" and the "lamb," Bloom is referring to traditional Judaic interpretations of the Passover story, in which the "kid" or lamb, signifying the people of Israel, will eventually emerge from a history of successive empires destroying and swallowing one another (Egypt, Assyria, Babylon, Persia, and so on): "The killing of the Angel of Death marks the day when the kingdom of the Almighty will be established on earth" (Abraham Regelson, *The Haggadah of Passover*, 63; see Gifford, *"Ulysses" Annotated*, 133). But Bloom is aware that such a scheme of just retribution is a binary system of re-establishing (in Derrida's phrase) the "Empire of the Selfsame"

(Young, *White Mythologies*, 3) all over again: "Justice it means but it's everybody eating everyone else." As Bloom now asks the Citizen: "But, says Bloom, isn't discipline the same everywhere. I mean wouldn't it be the same here if you put force against force?" (*U* 12.1361–62)[10]

The Citizen responds with blind and vengeful machismo:

– We'll put force against force ... We have our greater Ireland beyond the sea [America] ... the *Times* rubbed its hands and told the white-livered Saxons there would soon be as few Irish in Ireland as redskins in America ... Ay, they drove out the peasants in hordes. Twenty thousand of them died in the coffinships. But those that came to the land of the free remember the land of bondage. And they will come again and with a vengeance, no cravens, the sons of Granuaaile, the champions of Kathleen ni Houlihan.

(*U* 12.1365–75)

The irony again lies in his invoking the racialized metaphors of the Irish as Israelites (remembering the land/house of bondage) and as "redskins," at the same time as he is slurring the Jew in his midst as a "coon" and racial Other. But Bloom sticks to his reasoned argument that force engenders force, that violent persecution creates hatred among nations which results in new cycles of retributive violence and persecution:

– Persecution, says he, all the history of the world is full of it. Perpetuating national hatred among nations.
– But do you know what a nation means? says John Wyse.
– Yes, says Bloom ... A nation is the same people living in the same place ... Or also in different places.
– What is your nation if I may ask? says the citizen.
– Ireland, says Bloom. I was born here. Ireland.

(*U* 12.1417–31)

This is an important passage about the difficult issue we have been exploring, "what is a nation?" As we have seen, nations tend to construct themselves as imagined communities with a national essence, character, and identity, resulting in a value-laden hierarchy that writes out or homogenizes non-conforming "others." Bloom, as one of those "others" which Celticist nationalism would write out (even though, as he points out, he was born Irish), responds simply that "A nation is the same people living in the same place" – or, in some cases, "in different places." While his flustered answer is one the men make fun of, it is nonetheless significant (and powerful) in its tolerant breadth: by defining a nation simply as a people generally within a geographical location, Bloom's answer refuses either to hierarchize or to "imagine" an essentialized community, but rather allows for personal or ethnic difference and heterogeneity without denying the status of "citizens" or "nationals" to anyone within the community.

Speaking himself into boldness, Bloom points out that the Irish aren't the only people being persecuted:

– And I belong to a race too, says Bloom, that is hated and persecuted. Also now. This very moment. This very instant ... Taking what belongs to us by right. At this very moment, says he, putting up his fist, sold by auction in Morocco like slaves or cattle.
– Are you taking about the new Jerusalem? says the citizen.
– I'm talking about injustice, says Bloom.

(*U* 12.1467–74)

Although it sounds like Bloom is merely waxing melodramatic here, he is actually right on two counts: first, he is of course being hated and persecuted by the Citizen and his cohorts at "this very moment"; but also, Bloom is aware that in 1904 Jews were in fact still being bought and sold by the Moslem majority of Morocco to perform so-called "compulsory service," a practice of slavery not abolished till 1907 (Gifford, *"Ulysses" Annotated*, 364); in fact there had been some massacres of Jews in Morocco recently reported in the international newspapers.[11]

Having argued for non-violence, Bloom has restrained himself thus far from the Citizen's blatant provocations. Now, Nolan tells him: " – Right, says John Wyse. Stand up to it then with force like men." But if that is what it means to be manly ("like men"), Bloom rejects it:

– But it's no use, says he. Force, hatred, history, all that. That's not life for men and women, insult and hatred. And everybody knows that it's the very opposite of that that is really life ... Love ... I mean the opposite of hatred. I must go now.

(*U* 12.1476–85)

And off he runs in search of Martin Cunningham, while the Citizen mocks him: " – A new apostle to the gentiles ... Universal love ... Beggar my neighbour is his motto" (*U* 12.1489–91). But, in spite of the narrator's hilarious parody of "universal love" ("Love loves to love love" and so on), Bloom's action speaks louder than their mockery – for he is in fact off on an errand of *caritas* ("love," "the opposite of hatred") to help the Dignam family, proving himself a much better citizen than the "Citizen" and his drunken fellows "stand[ing] up to it ... like men" – at the bar.

While Bloom is out looking for Cunningham, the men in the pub – thinking Bloom has gone to cash in his "shekels" on Throwaway but being too cheap to stand them drinks – continue slandering him: "Ireland my nation says he ... never be up those bloody ... Jerusalem ... cuckoos"; "Defrauding widows and orphans"; and so on (*U* 12.1570–72, 1622). John Wyse Nolan tries to defend Bloom, "saying it was Bloom gave the ideas for Sinn Fein to Griffith to put in his paper all kinds of jerrymandering, packed juries and swindling the taxes off of the government and appointing consuls all over the world to walk about selling Irish industries" – a claim Martin Cunningham, who works in Dublin Castle, corroborates as he now joins the group: "it was he drew up all the plans according to the Hungarian system. We know that in the castle" (*U* 12.1574–77, 1635–37). They believe this about Bloom because of his Hungarian background: the Hungarian resistance to Austrian imperial domination had followed tactics similar to those now advocated by Griffith, who was also "rumored to have a Jewish adviser-ghostwriter" (Gifford, *"Ulysses" Annotated*, 366). As Nolan points out: " – And after all, ... why can't a jew love his country like the next fellow?" (*U* 12.1628–29)

Whereas it is quite unlikely that Bloom (even in fiction) was the man behind Arthur Griffith's ideas, Nolan is correct at least to claim that Bloom is a Jew who loves his country – and, in spite of the attacks on him as a "foreigner," quite a conscientious patriot in his own ways. Bloom is, as we shall later learn, a big fan and advocate of Arthur Griffith's ideas. Indeed, in his youth (Molly recalls and derides his "socialist" ideas in "Penelope"), Bloom apparently had radical sympathies and was involved in anti-English activism. In "Lestrygonians" he thinks of "The patriot's banquet. Eating orangepeels in the park" (*U* 8.516–17), a gesture employed by Nationalists at patriotic assemblies in Phoenix Park so as to irritate Orangemen (Gifford, *"Ulysses" Annotated*, 172–73); he thinks of James Stephens, Garibaldi, Parnell, Griffith, and Irish Nationalist debates, such as "That the language question should take precedence of the economic question" (we will later learn that Bloom favors the reverse); and he recalls the time he was involved in a protest against Joseph Chamberlain at Trinity, almost getting beaten up in the process by mounted policemen: "That horsepoliceman the day Joe Chamberlain was given his degree in Trinity he got a run for his money ... His horse's hoofs clattering after us down Abbey street. Lucky I had the presence of mind to dive into Manning's or I was souped" (*U* 8.423–26). Chamberlain, a foe of Home Rule and an aggressive imperialist associated with the English policies in the Boer War, was understandably hated in Ireland. On December 18, 1899 he came to Dublin to receive an honorary degree at Trinity College; O'Leary, Maud Gonne, and other radicals organized a pro-Boer demonstration which resulted in the clashes with the police which Bloom recalls (Gifford, *"Ulysses" Annotated*, 168). We will encounter considerably more evidence of Bloom's patriotic sentiments and activities in later episodes.

But the Citizen's polarized system of absolute differences cannot accommodate for a Bloom or a Jew who is an Irish patriot; he continues mocking Bloom ("the new Messiah for Ireland!"; *U* 12.1642) in his xenophobic obsession with racial purity: " – Saint Patrick would want to land again at Ballykinlar and convert us, ... after allowing things like that to contaminate our shores" (*U* 12.1671–72). When Bloom returns to find Cunningham at last, the Citizen now lashes out at him so viciously that Bloom can no longer restrain himself: as Cunningham and Power drag him away from the Citizen's violence (while the bystanders again racialize him as a "coon" by singing *"If the man in the moon was a jew, jew, jew"* – echoing a popular American tune of the time, "If the man in the moon were a coon, coon, coon"; Gifford, *"Ulysses" Annotated*, 378), Bloom retorts proudly in defence of his Judaic heritage: " – Mendelssohn was a jew and Karl Marx and Mercadante and Spinoza. And the Saviour was a jew and his father was a jew. Your God ... Christ was a jew like me." Typically, Bloom gets it only approximately right – for Mercadante was not a Jew and, as Cunningham reminds him, the Saviour "had no father"; but Bloom's basic point is quite correct and eloquently driven home. This is too much for the Citizen – but, ironically, even his very words of emotive anger unconsciously prove Bloom's point, for in responding to the perceived insult to his god (Christ) he takes His name in vain, swearing (by Jesus) that he will do to Bloom ("crucify") precisely what the Jews did to the Christ he holds so sacred: " – By Jesus, says he, I'll brain that bloody jewman for using the holy name. By Jesus, I'll crucify him so I will" (*U* 12.1801–12). It is a wonderfully concise illustration of the cycloptic myopia of polarized binarities.

Meantime, as the "new Messiah" and "apostle to the gentiles," Bloom (in narrative parody) ascends to heaven like Elijah, only to return later in "Circe" as the Messiah of the New Bloomusalem and the Nova Hibernia of the future. Significantly, the fantasized New Bloomusalem is a tolerant nation whose characteristics are pluralistically inclusive rather than exclusive: "Union of all, jew, moslem and gentile ... universal brotherhood ... Mixed races and mixed marriage" (*U* 15.1686–99).

We have been exploring the arguments in "Cyclops" within the discourse of Nation. As Anderson pointed out, nations tend to construct themselves as imagined communities with a cohesive national character, sovereignties retrospectively endowed with a revisionist history of antiquity and racial purity: for they "always loom out of an immemorial past, and, still more important, glide into a limitless future. It is the magic of nationalism to turn chance into destiny" (*Imagined Communities*, 11–12). Thus, the favorite metaphor of emerging nations "discovering" their forgotten but ancient past (consider the Celtic "Revival") – as Anderson points out in his resonant discussion of Renan's use of "memory" and "forgetting" within the dynamics of a national consciousness – is "sleep" (or "remembering"/reviving what had been forgotten): "[No other metaphor] seemed better than 'sleep,' for it permitted those intelligentsias and bourgeoisies who were becoming conscious of themselves as Czechs, Hungarians, or Finns [or Celts] to figure their study of Czech, Magyar, or Finnish languages, folklores, and musics as 'rediscovering' something deep-down always [already] known" (196). As a result, this "destiny" of one's nationality acquires a quasireligiosity about it that seems natural, eternal, and even worth dying for: "Dying for one's country ... assumes a moral grandeur which dying for the Labour Party, the American Medical Association, or perhaps even Amnesty International can not rival, for these are all bodies one can join or leave at easy will" (Anderson, *Imagined Communities*, 144). Just as ethnocentric nationalism endows the Self with a somehow unchanging racial purity and essence (in spite of centuries of invasion and intermarriage), so it endows the other with a static stigma of racial Otherness: a Jew is a "Jew" (with all the attendant stereotypes) no matter where he is born (even Ireland); one drop of African blood makes you a "black"; and so on. Race and nation-ness acquire the essentialized aura of destiny.

At this point I would like to return to the part of Anderson's definition of a nation that we had earlier bracketed: "it is imagined as *sovereign*" (*Imagined Communities*, 7). If the sovereignty of Ireland seems like immemorial destiny and nature, as Celticists like the Citizen argued, it is indeed a very strange sort of sovereignty and of destiny. In waxing nostalgic about recovering the "sovereignty" of

"Ireland" as a "nation" – *A Nation Once Again*, as in the patriotic song by Thomas Osborne Davis sung by the men in "Cyclops," with its refrain "And Ireland, long a province, be / A nation once again!" – we might do well to reflect on what that means, on the inherent contradiction in such a desire for a return to being a "nation" called Ireland. For the fact is that (at least before 1922) there never has been such a thing;[12] "Ireland" as such has *never* been a nation! Unlike, say, the condition of France under German occupation during the Second World War (dreaming of a return to national sovereignty), this patriotic Irish dream of a return to Irish national sovereignty which so many of the Irish had and have been willing to die for – while arguably a worthy cause – is a purely imagined construct introduced into the retrospectively revisionist "memory" of the culture's historical consciousness. When was Ireland ever *not* either a colony of some foreign power or other, or else a loose collection of rival and warring tribes or kingdoms? From the prehistoric islanders to the times of the Celtic migrations or the Belgae/Fir-Bolgs (each group itself steeped in internecine tribal warfare) to the resultant "Gaels" (a term denoting the peoples of the island, never a nation) to the Viking and Danish invaders to the many small warring kingdom-states (occasionally joining under a High King to fight the Danes) to the Norman invasions and then the Saxons: when was the island ever a *sovereign* state, "Ireland"? And so what can one mean in arguing so passionately and "patriotically" (imagining *patria*) for the solidarity and integrity of Ireland and of its "national" purity (within the logic even of "ethnic cleansing")? Even to the point of denying some of its own native citizens (like Bloom or Parnell) the mythical status of true "Irishness" – when such a citizenship or thing has never existed? In invoking Irish racial purity by invoking Celtic, Gaelic, or Milesian roots, racial purists necessarily occlude the fact that the Milesians and Gaels and Celts were themselves engaged in internecine tribal warfare, none holding a cohesive sovereignty over the island – and certainly none of them thought of themselves as "Irish"! The terms "Irish" and "Ireland" as *national* signifiers are purely retrospective constructs imposed upon an earlier (and unsuspecting) history by "imagining" for the island a historically-continuous community with a homogenous national character, whereas such a sovereign community has never existed in history. But history rewrites itself as one long "Irish" tradition (with mists of inevitability) – in which the differences between Milesians,

Gaels, Celts and even Danes and Spaniards get written out; in which the Anglo-Irish get bracketed; in which Jews get written out altogether (in spite of their material presence in one's midst); and in which the purity of an Irish "race" is proclaimed in spite of the fact that there never was such a thing as an Irish "nation" and in spite of the many racial/ethnic interminglings of the extended, pluralistic contact zone known as "Ireland."

Joyce, who had decried what he called "the old pap of racial hatred" on which such militant Irish Nationalism was founded, had – in his 1907 essay in Trieste on "Ireland, Island of Saints and Sages" – rejected wholesale the Celticist argument for racial purity and national characteristics, which he found to be as specious as the English stereotyping of the Irish character as apes and Calibans, reminding us that "the Celtic race" was "compounded of the old Celtic stock and the Scandinavian, Anglo-Saxon and Norman races ... with the various elements mingling and renewing the ancient body." The Irish, Joyce argued, are in fact a very mixed people – "Do we not see that in Ireland the Danes, the Firbolgs, the Milesians from Spain, the Norman invaders, and the Anglo-Saxon settlers have united to form a new entity?" (*CW* 161–62; the present mayor of Dublin, Mr. Nannetti, he informs his Triestine audience, is Italian). Joyce's representation of the Irish, cogently articulated in a significant passage, is very much a vision of a complex mix of racial and cultural strains operating within a fluid "contact zone":

Our civilization is a vast fabric, in which the most diverse elements are mingled, in which nordic aggressiveness and Roman law, the new bourgeois conventions and the remnants of a Syriac religion [Christianity] are reconciled. In such a fabric, it is useless to look for a thread that may have remained pure and virgin without having undergone the influence of a neighbouring thread. What race, or what language ... can boast of being pure today? And no race has less right to utter such a boast than the race now living in Ireland.

(*CW* 165–66)

Joyce – in first noting the absurdities of such Nationalist imaginings in his 1907 essay and then in displaying them so fully and symptomatically in *Ulysses* – did not (unlike Renanesque national consciousness) "forget to remember" the actual racial heterogeneities that were occluded by the imagined "Irishness." While Joyce's writings, both fiction and non-fiction, are often arguably "nationalist" in intention[13] – and certainly do not deny the vital importance and necessity of nationalism and nationalist feeling in mobilizing resistance to English oppression – *Ulysses* repeatedly reminds us that it is very important to be self-consciously vigilant about the *forms* such "national consciousness" (to use Fanon's phrase) takes, within the range of possible nationalisms in the plural: for one must be aware of the pitfalls and limits of certain very alluring but limited nationalist visions – or else one is doomed to failure by reproducing the same binary hierarchies inherited from one's oppressors.[14]

8.

Imagining futures: nations, narratives, selves

The new Bloomusalem in the Nova Hibernia of the future

In the "Cyclops" episode, the Citizen had mocked Bloom as a "new Messiah for Ireland" and a "new apostle to the gentiles" (*U* 12.1642, 1489). The fantasies of "Circe" now allow Bloom the psychological (and therapeutical) space by which to counter and refute all the Citizen's innuendos and accusations, for in "Circe" Bloom does imagine himself as just such a Messiah, come to institute the New Bloomusalem according to his own ideals and in direct opposition to the Citizen's agenda. Although the fantasy – like all such passages in "Circe" – contains elements that are highly fantastic, parodic, contradictory, or just plain absurd, yet there is woven throughout the passage a certain coherence consistent with Bloom's brand of utopian vision, combining humanitarian concerns, socialistic agenda, impractical imagination, and practical reform within a redefinition of Irish nationhood. For "Circe" allows Bloom to play out in unrestricted imagination his ultimate utopian fantasies as an Irish Messiah and reformer.

This fantasy begins when Bloom is cheered as the "Lord mayor of Dublin!" (*U* 15.1363), and he responds with the practical solution to Dublin's traffic problem he had advocated earlier (*U* 6.400–2) in the funeral carriage: "better run a tramline, I say, from the cattlemarket to the river. That's the music of the future. That's my programme" (*U* 15.1367–69). Now he launches into a speech outlining his agenda of reform; his speech is a mock-socialistic, neo-Marxist attack on the Orange (the "Dutchmen") ascendancy and the English nobility as a wealthy and lazy elite spending their time hunting and gambling while the Irish poor starve in "prostituted" servitude:

(*impassionedly*) These flying Dutchmen or lying Dutchmen as they recline in their upholstered poop, casting dice, what reck they? Machines is their cry ... manufactured monsters for mutual murder, hideous hobgoblins produced by a horde of capitalistic lusts upon our prostituted labour. The poor man starves while they are grassing their royal mountain stags or shooting peasants and phartridges in their purblind pomp of pelf and power. But their reign is rover for rever and ever and ev ...

(*U* 15.1390–97)

This speech elicits the applause of a large crowd of people bearing streamers reading "*Cead Mile Failte*" (Gaelic: a hundred thousand welcomes; still the slogan of the Irish Tourist Bureau) and "*Mah Ttob Melek Israel*" (Hebrew: "How goodly are [thy tents] King of Israel") – again equating the Celts and the Jews, for in Bloom's vision of an Irish nation they would both be welcome ("a hundred thousand welcomes") under his tents as King of Israel/Ireland. Thus, the procession of supporters which cheers him on is seen to include a broad representation of Irish people from all religions and walks of life ("newspaper canvassers," "chimneysweepers," "Italian ware-housemen," and so on). Someone yells out: "That's the famous Bloom now, the world's greatest reformer. Hats off!" (*U* 15.1459); Parnell's brother (John Howard Parnell) proclaims him to be "Illustrious Bloom! Successor to my famous brother!" Bloom thanks them "for this right royal welcome to green Erin, the promised land of our common ancestors" – again underlining the common link between Irish and Jew, seeking their "promised land" in which all are welcome and can live in tolerant harmony, and in which a Jew can also be Irish (to prove the point "*He shows all that he is wearing green socks*"; *U* 15.1513–21). His patriotism (which had been questioned in "Cyclops") is now affirmed, with John Wyse Nolan (who had also defended him in "Cyclops") praising him as "the man that got away James Stephens"; in this world of heterogeneous harmony, even "A BLUECOAT SCHOOLBOY" yells out "Bravo!" (*U* 15.1534–36; the Bluecoat School was a fashionable Anglo-Irish Protestant school and a term that came to represent the values of the Protestant Ascendancy). Bloom, as Messiah to the promised land of Erin, proclaims the new nation (in appropriately Biblical language):

My beloved subjects, a new era is about to dawn. I, Bloom, tell you verily it is even now at hand. Yea, on the word of a Bloom, ye shall ere long enter into the golden city which is to be, the new Bloomusalem in the Nova Hibernia of the future.

(*U* 15.1542–55)

Asked by the crowd "When will we have our own house of keys?",
Bloom spells out his reform agenda for the Nova Hibernia[1] as a
Home Rule without hierarchy and without labels of difference:

I stand for the reform of municipal morals and the plain ten command-
ments. New worlds for old. Union of all, jew, moslem and gentile. Three
acres and a cow for all children of nature. Saloon motor hearses.
Compulsory manual labour for all. All parks open to the public day and
night. Electric dishscrubbers. Tuberculosis, lunacy, war and mendicancy
must now cease. General amnesty, weekly carnival with masked licence,
bonuses for all, esperanto the universal language with universal brotherhood. No more patriotism of barspongers and dropsical impostors. Free
money, free rent, free love and a free lay church in a free lay state ...
Mixed races and mixed marriage.

(U 15.1683–99)

This is Bloom's reform manifesto, some parts of which seem
clearly ludicrous in their mix of utopian idealism and mundane or
inane specificities. And yet, under close review, even these latter
contain appropriate and suggestive ideological significances based
on Bloom's thoughts and experiences during the day. "Three acres
and a cow for all" sounds like a fanciful Joycean absurdity – but in
fact "Three acres and a cow" was a phrase that became "the rallying
cry for Irish land reform" after its use by Jesse Collings in "a
successful effort to force a measure of land reform on Lord
Salisbury's conservative and reluctant government in 1886" (Gifford,
"Ulysses" Annotated, 479). In other words, Bloom is advocating an
equitable land reform program that redistributes Irish territory to the
Irish; later we will learn that Bloom was an avid supporter of
Davitt's Land League activism. "Saloon motor hearses" refers to
Bloom's earlier suggestion (in "Hades") for motorized funeral
carriages or for funeral trains as both more efficient and more
humane (*U* 6.405–7). "Compulsory manual labour for all" suggests,
by the logic of inversion, a shared redistribution of labour along
socialist lines, rather than a capitalistic demarcation between labor
and capital as social classes; more specifically, it speaks to Bloom's
very recent condemnation (in "Cyclops") of human slavery in places
like Morocco, where Jews were being bought and sold to do that
society's servile, dirty work under the euphemistic title of "compulsory service." "Electric dishscrubbers" is typical of Bloom's practical
ideas with humanitarian consequences, especially his thoughts
during this day about the hard life of women in Irish society (no
public toilets; difficult and frequent childbirths; and so on). Idealistic

Bloom also wishes for a world without sickness ("tuberculosis"), "lunacy" (such as what poor Josie Breen endures in her husband), poverty ("mendicancy"), and – perhaps most importantly – "war" (the central topic of his argument with the Citizen about force and violence). The Citizen's arguments for retributive violence are countered here by "General amnesty" and a policy of forgiveness. The language issue (Gaelic versus English) is also present in Bloom's advocacy of "esperanto the universal language," an attempt to step beyond a closed and binary Irish–English dialectic to a broader internationalist perspective; Esperanto (meaning "hopeful") was a popular hope among international idealists in Joyce's day. Even the sports issue (Irish versus English games in Phoenix Park) is indirectly hinted at here in Bloom's advocacy of parks being open to everyone without stated restrictions (reflective of his inclusive definition of a "nation"): "All parks open to the public day and night." Bloom also calls for a more honest and true patriotism (such as Bloom's quiet, unboastful sort – as we will later see confirmed in "Eumaeus" and "Ithaca"), rather than that of drunken "impostors" like the so-called "Citizen": "No more patriotism of barspongers and dropsical impostors."

Interspersed with these suggestive if somewhat comic details are clearer, larger statements of Bloom's utopian vision of the Nova Hibernia as an inter-heterogeneous contact zone eschewing absolute hierarchies and homogenization of difference, in accordance with his earlier definition of "nation" ("the same people living in the same place"): "Union of all" of whatever religious persuasion ("jew, moslem and gentile"). Bloom advocates a tolerant society of "universal language with universal brotherhood," not fractured by binary and exclusive allegiances (such as to language), a contact zone willing to acknowledge and accept its own ethnic/racial heterogeneities: "Mixed races and mixed marriage." As we see, then, the above manifesto for a New Bloomusalem is typically Bloom in its happy mixing of the idealistic and the mundane (the sacred and the profane) – but we have also grown to recognize its basic elements and tenets (as well as its "sacred/profane" mix) as Joyce's. Even in the "real world," one demanding pragmatics rather than idealistic fantasy, one could have a lot worse political agendas to believe in.

In "Penelope," Molly tells us of Bloom's stated opinion that Christ the carpenter, the advocate of "love thy neighbour," was a revolutionary and "the first socialist" (*U* 18.175–78). Bloom's own reform platform of "universal love" is, similarly, much too radical for his compatriots, and – like Christ – he ends up in "Circe" being persecuted and crucified, a new martyr/Messiah. And so at this point he gets scapegoated by the angry mob: "Stage Irishman!"; "Caliban!"; "Lynch him! Roast him! He's as bad as Parnell was. Mr Fox!" (*U* 15.1729–62) When in doubt, persecute Bloom: the accusations are resonant, for Bloom (who was a bit earlier accused of being "of Mongolian extraction" [*U* 15.954]) is now being persecuted and martyred as a racialized combination of Jew, stage Irishman, Caliban, a black man being lynched, the national martyr Parnell (an Anglo-Irishman, whose pseudonym was "Mr. Fox"), and the helpless fox hunted down as sport by the aristocratic establishment (as Oscar Wilde – who called fox-hunting "the unspeakable in pursuit of the uneatable," a quip often quoted by Joyce – had been by respectable Victorian England). Asked if he is "the Messiah ben Joseph or ben David," Bloom answers (like Christ to Pilate): "You have said it" (*U* 15.1834–36); we are now told in Biblical prose that he is dying for our sins: "And he shall carry the sins of the people to Azazel, the spirit which is in the wilderness, and to Lilith, the nighthag. And they shall stone him and defile him, yea, all from Agendath Netaim and from Mizraim, the land of Ham" (*U* 15.1898–901). Mizraim, or the land of Ham (i.e., Egypt), is identified in the Old Testament as the tribal homeland of the black race, the "sons of Ham" (Genesis 10:6); as messianic martyr, Bloom accepts his racialized status as Orientalized Jew, Irishman, black – as martyr for Everyman. Pronouncing that "Jewgreek is greekjew" (*U* 12.1097–98), Bloom is now turned into the second coming of Elijah in the New Bloomusalem, as "THE GRAMOPHONE" begins to play "The Holy City" ("Jerusalem! / Open your gates and sing / Hosanna") and a bursting rocket becomes a falling star *"proclaiming the consummation of all things and second coming of Elijah"* (*U* 15.2170–76).

In the fantasy pages when Messiah Bloom does finally seem to be killed in martyrdom, he is dressed in a priest's liturgical garment ("marked I. H. S." – which for Bloom had meant "I have suffered" [*U* 5.373]) and says ("amid phoenix flames"): "Weep not for me, O daughters of Erin" (*U* 15.1935–36) – again making the equation between Erin and Jerusalem (Luke 23:27: "Daughters of Jerusalem, weep not for me"); when he dies, his widow throws herself on a Hindu "suttee pyre" while "THE CIRCUMCISED" and Bloom's Jewish friends weep for him in Hebrew (*U* 15.3220–36). "COUNCILLOR NANNETTI" (who would in actuality, like Bloom in fantasy, become Lord Mayor) shows up to speak Robert Emmet's lines at the moment of patriotic martyrdom: "When my country takes her place among the nations of the earth, then, and not till then, let my epitaph be written. I have ... " (*U* 12.3385–88). In short, Bloom as national martyr and Messiah is willing to take on (as Everyman) all heterogeous identities – Jew, Moslem, gentile, Hindu, black, Irishman, Englishman, and so on – in a revolutionary statement of "universal brotherhood" and tolerance within a "Nova Hibernia" that would accept Jews like himself or Italians like Nannetti or Anglo-Irish like Parnell within its national sovereignty. Now *that* is an idea to die for.

Stephen Dedalus and the "Brutish Empire": "Circe"

Woven into the very texture and fabric of the pages of *Ulysses* are the discourses and issues of British imperialism and of colonial resistance to the Empire – in quite culturally specific and topical detail (whether about Ireland, Africa, India, and so on). These are precise and historicized building blocks from which the text (like the city of Dublin itself) is constructed. In "Wandering Rocks," for example, Ned Lambert points out that "We are standing in the historic council chamber of saint Mary's abbey where Silken Thomas proclaimed himself a rebel in 1534," renouncing his allegiance to Henry VIII (*U* 10.406–9). O'Molloy and Lambert then discuss the Gunpowder Plot, a conspiracy among English Catholics in 1605 to destroy Parliament (Stephen refers to this also in the library), and the Irish Earl of Kildare who had set fire to Cashel Cathedral in his resistance to Henry VII (*U* 10.442–49). The specific details and issues of colonial history are omnipresent in the book.

A few pages later in this same episode, we have a vignette involving Tom Kernan, who, as we had learned in *Dubliners* ("Grace"), is Anglo-Irish Protestant. He thinks of "Some Kildare street club toff" (*U* 10.745; the Kildare Street Club was Dublin's most exclusive and fashionable Anglo-Irish men's club), then walks by the place where "Down there Emmet was hanged, drawn and quartered. Greasy black rope. Dogs licking the blood off the street when the lord lieutenant's wife drove by in her noddy" (*U* 10.764–66). The thought leads Kernan to think of the

Times of the troubles ... Somewhere here lord Edward Fitzgerald escaped from major Sirr. Stables behind Moira house ... That ruffian, that sham squire, with his violet gloves gave him away. Course they were on the wrong side. They rose in dark and evil days. Fine poem that is: Ingram. They were gentlemen. Ben Dollard does sing that ballad touchingly. Masterly rendition. *At the siege of Ross did my father fall.*

(*U* 10.781–93)

In the following episode ("Sirens"), Bloom will hear Dollard's masterly rendition of "The Croppy Boy," a ballad of a peasant martyr in the rebellion of 1798 (the "Times of the troubles"); "They rose in dark and evil days" is a line from "The Memory of the Dead" by John Kells Ingram, a patriotic poem about the rebellion of 1798. Lord Edward Fitzgerald, the United Irishmen leader who was the mastermind of the rebellion, was betrayed for a thousand pound reward by the "sham squire" (Francis Higgins) to Henry Charles Sirr. Major Sirr, town mayor of Dublin (and like Corley son of a policeman), "was notorious for his ruthless use of informers and for the brutality of the police he led" (Gifford, *"Ulysses" Annotated*, 275); informed of Fitzgerald's whereabouts, he set a trap and captured Fitzgerald, in the process of which the latter suffered mortal wounds. (Moira House is where Fitzgerald's wife hid, and where they would meet in secret while he was in hiding.) Kernan's perspective is an interesting one here, because he is of course a West Briton: his Anglo-Irish view of the rebellion is necessarily an ambivalent one, balancing the elements of the rebels' tragic heroism with the hegemonic reminder that "Course they were on the wrong side" but with the exonerating rationalization that "They were gentlemen"; the latter was a typical West Briton phrase used to excuse genteel Anglo-Irish Protestant revolutionaries (including Fitzgerald, Tone, Emmet, Parnell, Yeats) from the Orange hatred directed at Irish peasants such as the croppies (Gifford, *"Ulysses" Annotated*, 275). Appropriately, at this moment the viceregal "cavalcade in easy trot along Pembroke quay passed" and Kernan, a bit too late, is unhappy to have missed the opportunity to view the distinguished representatives of the Crown: "His Excellency! Too bad! Just missed that by a hair. Damn it! What a pity!" (*U* 10.794–98)

Presented in ironic counterpoint (in this same episode) is one deplorable result of being on the "right side": the one-legged sailor. A victim of British military recruitment efforts, "A onelegged sailor crutched himself round MacConnell's corner," growling " – *For England … home and beauty*" (*U* 10.228–36). The line is from "The Death of Nelson," a song whose refrain (already invoked by Mulligan in "Telemachus") includes: "England expects that every man / This day will do his duty ... For England, home and beauty, / For England, home and beauty." It is ironic that a few minutes later "The onelegged sailor growled at the area of 14 Nelson street: – *England expects* ... " (*U* 10.1063–64; Nelson Street is off Eccles Street), for the refrain's first line ("England expects ...") was a famous statement by Admiral Nelson, great defender of the Empire: the effect of a one-legged sailor singing this song is terribly ironic – for the duty to "England, home and beauty" comes at the cost of one's leg, even when England is *not* even your own "home" and country (but its oppressor).

Unlike Kernan's West Briton hegemonic outlook or the one-legged sailor's dogged loyalty to the Crown, Stephen and Bloom each, during the day, quietly (unlike the vocal Citizen and their fellow Dubliners) express in their minds their respective resentments of the English imperial presence. Stephen's colonial resentments of the nightmare of Irish history have been focused today, as we have seen, in two concrete embodiments, Haines and Deasy, the usurping representatives of the "seas' empire" ruling the waves of Stephen's life. And he is about to find himself in an incident with two British redcoats in "Circe." Bloom resents both the British soldiers and their hand-in-hand collaborators, the police: "a lot of those policemen, whom [Bloom] cordially disliked, were admittedly unscrupulous in the service of the Crown" (*U* 16.76–77). Bloom's opinion (from "Eumaeus") of the police, like that of Stephen's, seems also to be that of Joyce's, who repeatedly depicted the police as brutes in collusion with the Castle, starting with *Dubliners* and its allusions to Major Sirr and the brutality of his police force, especially in "Two Gallants" (and the corresponding argument by Giuglemo Ferrero) in the person of Corley, the policeman's son with a military gait and a brutish nature; no sooner does Bloom voice his opinion of the police to Stephen in "Eumaeus" than, appropriately, Corley himself shows up to ask Stephen for a loan: "Lord John Corley some called him ... He was the eldest son of inspector Corley of the G division" (*U* 16.130–33). As Gifford notes, "A common Irish criticism of the Dublin Metropolitan Police" was that they were "all too readily associated with the English Establishment." This was especially true of the powerful Royal Irish Constabulary in Dublin Castle, for whom the aptly named Jack Power works; Gladstone himself had called the R. I. C. a "semi-military police," since it was armed and assigned with the charge of suppressing political dissension against the Crown ("*Ulysses*" *Annotated*, 536, 104).

Recall that Bloom himself has, from personal experience, reason to fear the imperial power of the police, for he had in younger days nearly been beaten and arrested in a charge by mounted policemen when he was present at a pro-Boer demonstration against the English imperialist Joseph Chamberlain (*U* 8.420). Bloom's opinion of actual English soldiers, the ubiquitous redcoat presence in Dublin, is not much higher. Thinking of the "royal Dublin fusiliers" (Molly's father's regiment) and "Redcoats," Bloom recalls: "Maud Gonne's letter about taking them off O'Connell street at night: disgrace to our Irish capital. Griffith's paper is on the same tack now: an army rotten with venereal disease: overseas or halfseasover empire" (*U* 5.68–73). Bloom is recalling how during the Boer War the British army, so as to encourage recruitment, allowed redcoats to spend the night in the city rather than in barracks, resulting in their prowling the streets for female companionship; Maud Gonne mounted a campaign against Irish enlistment and distributed a pamphlet "on the shame of Irish girls consorting with the soldiers of the enemy" (*A Servant of the Queen* [London, 1938], 292; see Gifford, *"Ulysses" Annotated*, 86). Many Dubliners – such as the Citizen (talking about the "syphilisation" of the English in *U* 12.1197) and Molly ("I suppose the half of those sailors are rotten again with disease" in *U* 18.1425–26) – felt, along with Griffith in his *United Irishman*, that the British army was thus polluting the nation with venereal disease and with intoxicated ("halfseasover") brutishness. "Circe" will culminate with an example of the latter, in the persons of Privates Carr and Compton.

Of course it is the colonial history of brutal killing and suppression that the Dubliners most resent about the presence of the redcoats in their midst – from Cromwell's massacre at Drogheda to the hundreds of sepoys shot from cannons in India. In 1904, Irish resentment of English imperial policies still strongly revolved around the very recent (1899–1902) Boer War which England had conducted in South Africa. Whereas entrepreneurs like Haines's father (selling "jalap to the Zulus") and Boylan's father (selling "the same horses twice over to the government to fight the Boers"; *U* 12.997–99) might take advantage of colonial opportunities in Africa, many Irish people, in solidarity with resistance to English colonialism, were vehemently against the Boer War. In his discussion of Hamlet at the library, Stephen calls Hamlet "The absentminded beggar ... Khaki Hamlets don't hesitate to shoot. The bloodboltered shambles in act five is a forecast of the concentration camp sung by Mr Swinburne" (*U* 9.133–35). The pacifist Stephen is speaking both about the violence in *Hamlet* and that in the Boer War, for "The Absentminded Beggar" was a propaganda poem by Rudyard Kipling, set to music by Sir Arthur Sullivan; it was written to raise funds ("The Absent Minded Beggar Fund") for the troops in the Boer War ("Will you kindly drop a shilling in my little tambourine / For a gentleman in khaki ordered South?"; Gifford, *"Ulysses" Annotated*, 201). Stephen's comments combine the bitter Irish opposition to the war (and its "Khaki Hamlets") with the Irish resentment of imperial (and police) oppression at home, for

The slogan "Don't hesitate to shoot" became a rallying cry for Irish anger at the English policy of coercion in the 1880s. According to Irish anecdotal history, the command was first used by a Capt. "Pasha" Plunkett, who was in charge of a police barracks at Mitchelstown, County Cork, during a riot in 1887 [three men were killed] ... The thrust of Stephen's remark is that the wholesale killing in modern warfare is not unlike the wholesale killing in *Hamlet*.

("Ulysses" Annotated, 202).

The "concentration camp sung by Mr Swinburne" refers to those set up in South Africa by Lord Kitchener for holding Boer civilians, often women and children. The inhumanity and cruelty of the camps resulted in widespread controversy, even in England, where Swinburne's sonnet "On the Death of Colonel Benson" – a jingoistic piece defending the camps and insensitively describing the Boer women and children as "whelps and dams of murderous foes" – was attacked as "unthinking" and "excessive." Thus, hidden and woven into his remarks on the bloody killing in Shakespeare's *Hamlet* are pacifist Stephen's opinions about the brutal killing in Africa and in Ireland by Shakespeare's countrymen. In the parody of parliamentary debate in "Cyclops," an opposition MP asks: "Has the right honourable gentleman's famous Mitchelstown telegram inspired the policy of gentlemen on the Treasury bench?" while another adds ironically "Don't hesitate to shoot" (*U* 12.873–77) – for "So solid was Conservative sentiment for coercion in Parliament that Balfour, then chief secretary for Ireland, could answer angry opposition questions merely by quoting the cursory police report (a telegram). Gladstone subsequently used the slogan 'Remember Mitchelstown' to rally the opposition" (Gifford, *"Ulysses" Annotated*, 341–42).

A few pages later Stephen argues that Shakespeare was a miserly merchant and an imperialistic jingoist (*U* 9.753–57):

... The lost armada is his jeer in *Love's Labour Lost*. His peasants, the histories, sail fullbellied on a tide of Mafeking enthusiasm. Warwickshire jesuits are tried and we have a porter's theory of equivocation. The *Sea Venture* comes home from Bermudas and the play Renan admired is written with Patsy Caliban, our American cousin.

Once again, Stephen's ostensible comments about Shakespeare veil his underlying political resentment of English imperial policy, for Mafeking was one of the English high points during the Boer War: the Boer defeat at Mafeking led to jubilantly extravagant displays of enthusiasm in England for the Empire and its expansionist policies (thus "Mafeking enthusiasm"); similarly, after the defeat of the Spanish Armada, England (under Elizabeth I) basked in unabashedly enthusiastic nationalism. Irish Catholic Stephen now recalls the Catholic Gunpowder Plot (in Elizabethan England) by Warwickshire Jesuits to blow up Parliament; and Shakespeare's "The Tempest" (admired by Ernest Renan), featuring Caliban, the racialized primitive brute whom Victorian England had stereotyped as the Irish Catholic essence (thus "Patsy Caliban, our American cousin"). In these veiled comments we again find a Stephen quietly seething at the English attitudes toward and treatments of its colonies.

Later, in one of the fantasies in "Circe," Bloom finds himself on trial for various imaginary accusations. In an attempt to defend himself ("Gentlemen of the jury, let me explain"), he concocts an outrageous tissue of lies, including:

... My wife, I am the daughter of a most distinguished commander, a gallant upstanding gentleman, what do you call him, Majorgeneral Brian Tweedy, one of Britain's fighting men who helped to win our battles. Got his majority for the heroic defence of Rorke's Drift ...

The royal Dublins, boys, the salt of the earth, known the world over. I think I see some old comrades in arms up there among you. The R.D.F., with our own Metropolitan police, guardians of our homes, the pluckiest lads and the finest body of men, as physique, in the service of our sovereign ...

I'm as staunch a Britisher as you are, sir. I fought with the colours for king and country in the absentminded war under general Gough in the park and was disabled at Spion Kop and Bloemfontein, was mentioned in dispatches. I did all a white man could.

(*U* 15.775–97)

Rorke's Drift was a battle (on which the film *Zulu* was based) in the Zulu War between the British and the Zulus; Spion Kop and Bloemfontein were sites of battles in the Boer War ("the absentminded war"). Since we know that Bloom did not fight in the Boer War and is not fond of either the redcoats or the Metropolitan Police, these are clearly lies outrageously manufactured in a fantasy of legal self-defense; at this very moment "A VOICE" yells out: "Turncoat! Up the Boers! Who booed Joe Chamberlain?" In stark contrast to the obvious lies immediately preceding, this accusation stands out as a verifiable truth – for we have already learned that a younger Bloom had in fact "booed Joe Chamberlain" (and had been harassed by the Metropolitan police) during a pro-Boer demonstration against Chamberlain when the latter, a shaper of English Boer policy, had come to Dublin in December 1899 (*U* 8.420–36).

The confrontation in "Circe" between Stephen and the soldiers provides an instructive case study, both of Stephen's attitudes and of the dynamics inherent in the presence of colonial troops in Ireland. As the episode opens, Private Carr and Private Compton are described as "redcoats" dressed in symbolically colored "*tunics bloodbright*" (*U* 15.61–63). They meet up with a drunken Irish "NAVVY," who challenges "*the two redcoats*" with "Come on, you British army!", then staggers off shouting "We are the boys. Of Wexford" (*U* 15.613–22). At this point, the soldiers' conversation reveals that they are serving under Sergeantmajor Bennett – the same English Sergeant Bennett who had fought the Irish boxer Keogh in that emblematic boxing match between English and Irish that the men had discussed at Barney Kiernan's. Another version of this political duel will now take place at the end of "Circe," when Redcoat Carr will punch out Irish Stephen, in another symbolic demonstration of boxing as a masculist sport replicating the binary dynamics of war – with the difference that Stephen, like Joyce (and like Bloom with the Citizen), refuses to partake in this pointless binary struggle of violent bellicosity.[2]

Stephen, having run out of Bella Cohen's, encounters the two redcoats; eager for a brawl, they accuse Stephen of having insulted Cissy Caffrey. A drunken Stephen responds by reminding them that they are (to quote Yeats's Cathleen) "Strangers in the house": "You are my guests. Uninvited. By virtue of the fifth of George and seventh of Edward. History to blame" (*U* 15.4370–71). "LORD TENNYSON" materializes as "gentleman poet in Union Jack blazer and cricket flannels" saying "Theirs not to reason why" (*U* 15.4397): as Poet Laureate and renowned pillar of the English aristocracy (symbolically dressed here in cricket wear), Tennyson had derided the Celtic race in "In Memoriam" and elsewhere (see chapter 2 of this study) and had written imperialist jingles (such as "The Charge of the Light Brigade," about Balaclava, including the famous lines "Theirs is not to reason why, / Theirs is but to do or die"). Stephen, unlike the soldiers ("Say, how would it be, governor, if I was to bash in your jaw?"), is much more interested in "reasoning why" than in doing or dying: "The bold soldier boy ... Noble art of selfpretence. Personally, I detest action" (*U* 15.4413–14); as with Bloom's attitudes on violent sports like boxing, Stephen demythologizes the euphemistically noble art of self-defence (pugilism) as mere machismo and braggadocio, "Noble art of selfpretence." But Private Carr is urged on, at this point, by "DOLLY GRAY," waving her handkerchief from the balcony: "Cook's son, goodbye. Safe home to Dolly. Dream of the girl you left behind and she will dream of you" (*U* 15.4417–20). This is an illustration (like the American penchant for yellow ribbons during the recent Gulf War) of the way patriotic sentimentalism manages (via the popular culture of song and slogan) to condone the atrocities of war, for the "Cook's son" is a phrase from Kipling's "The Absent-Minded Beggar" referring to a typical Tommy off to fight in the Boer War; and "Good-bye, Dolly Gray" was another popular Boer War song, in which Dolly Gray is the girl left behind whom the young recruit will dream of while fighting for his country; the sentimental notion of fighting for (and protecting) one's womenfolk manages to ennoble and justify to the home audience the actual brutalities occurring in the faraway land.

Stephen chooses instead to advocate pacifism: "Struggle for life is the law of existence but but human philirenists, notably the tsar and the king of England, have invented arbitration"; Czar Nicholas II and Edward VII had both at times advocated world peace and disarmament (it was the Czar's petition for peace that Stephen refused to sign in *A Portrait*). But all Carr can understand or hear is the sound of his own xenophobia: "What's that you're saying about my king?" (*U* 15.4434–48) At this point "*Edward the Seventh*" appears, sucking (as in Bloom's earlier image of him in *U* 8.3–4) red and white jujubes (British colors), and wearing royal insignias such as that of "*Skinner's and Probyn's horse*" – thus revealing the hypocrisy of an English imperial monarch advocating world peace, for Skinner's Horse and Probyn's Horse were both cavalry regiments famed for their campaigns against India; appropriately, the monarch's spoken words are hardly those of a peacemaker: "We have come here to witness a clean straight fight and we heartily wish both men the best of good luck" (*U* 15.4449–62). Rather, it is Bloom who is trying to intervene and play peacemaker.

Like Bloom with the Citizen, Stephen refuses to be provoked by

Private Carr: "You die for your country. Suppose ... Not that I wish it for you. But I say: Let my country die for me. Up to the present it has done so. I didn't want it to die. Damn death. Long live life!" (*U* 15.4471–74). Stephen's attitude here coincides both with Bloom's advocacy of life-giving forces over violence, as well as with Joyce's repeated depiction of an Ireland that self-destructs and eats her own. The drunken soldiers are no doubt baffled by Stephen's drunken pronouncements, and Private Compton goads Private Carr: "Eh, Harry, give him a kick in the knackers. Stick one into Jerry"; in calling Stephen here "Jerry" (slang for both penis and for any German – especially in view of the Great War during which *Ulysses* was being written), Carr is exhibiting the masculist, xenophobic, racist tendency to essentialize everything foreign in terms of a single binarized pole, the hated enemy Other (in which place Irish, German, Boer, black, Jew, and so on, are interchangeable). Stephen mutters that somehow "I seem to annoy them. Green rag to a bull" – like a red flag provoking a bull, but here a kellygreen flag to John Bull (recall also that "shoneen" comes from *seoninism*, named after the Gaelic version of "Seon" Bull); appropriately, the wild goose patriot "KEVIN EGAN" appears now, deriding Queen Victoria ("The *vieille ogresse* with the *dents jaunes*"), while his son Patrice calls Stephen a "*Socialiste!*" On cue, the bystanders begin arguing among themselves: "Green above the red, says he. Wolfe Tone"; versus "The red's as good as the green. And better. Up the soldiers! Up King Edward!"; and then "Hands up to De Wet" (Christian R. De Wet was a distinguished commander for the Boers in defeat). "THE CITIZEN" shows up to curse "the English dogs"; "THE CROPPY BOY" appears to sing from the song about him ("But I love my country beyond the king"); "RUMBOLD" materializes to show off the ropes he used to hang Irish martyrs, while "EDWARD THE SEVENTH" sings "Coronation Day" (*U* 15.4483–564). This entire passage in "Circe" (the encounter between Stephen and Private Carr) proves to be a symptomatic, dialogic panoply of the colonial dynamics, struggles, and currents under the British Empire at the turn of the century.

When Carr keeps harping on the king ("What are you saying about my king?"), Stephen tires of the subject: "O, this is too monotonous! Nothing. He [the King] wants my money and my life, though want must be his master, for some brutish empire of his. Money I haven't." Stephen, so conscious of his servitude ("a server to a servant") to Haines and Mulligan and Deasy and the imperia of Rome and of England, understands that (like the appeal of the

Egyptian high priest to the Israelites in Fitzgibbon's speech), the Empire hails its colonial subjects to join and participate in its "brutish empire," an interpellation which the *non serviam*-wishing Stephen would reject. And now the British soldier, as if to prove the masculine "brutishness" (like "THE MALE BRUTES" in *U* 15.2019) of the Empire, is about to deck a defenseless and unresisting Irish bard. Appropriately, "OLD GUMMY GRANNY" now appears as the embodiment of Ireland, to complain, in the words of Yeats's Cathleen, of "Strangers in my house, bad manners to them … Ochone! Ochone! Silk of the kine! … You met with poor old Ireland and how does she stand?" (*U* 15.4568–88)

Meanwhile, Private Carr is still harping on his king: "I'll wring the neck of any fucker says a word against my fucking king" while Private Compton keeps goading him: "Go at it, Harry. Do him one in the eye. He's a proBoer." Bloom, trying to calm them down, reminds them that "We fought for you in South Africa, Irish missile troops"; on cue, Major Tweedy (Molly's father) shows up to yell "Rorke's Drift! Up, guards, and at them!" as the Citizen yells *"Erin go bragh!"* Tweedy and the Citizen then *"exhibit to each other medals, decorations, trophies of war, wounds. Both salute with fierce hostility."* There is great irony in the mirrored images here, for the Irish fought on both sides of the Boer War; the echoed battle slogans of Major Tweedy and the Citizen, as well as the mirrored images of their war decorations and salutes, suggest that xenophobic patriotisms are but interchangeable images caught in a binary mirroring: both Wellington's battle cry of "Up, guards, and at them" and the Celtic "Erin go bragh" result in the same brutish irrationality. This point is underscored in the simultaneous and indistinguishable playing by *"Massed bands"* of two patriotic national anthems "Garryowen *and* God save the king" ("Garryowen" is appropriately both the xenophobic Citizen's dog, and a rollicking Irish drinking song). The ambivalent split of Irish response to Bloom's comment about fighting "for you in South Africa," exemplified by Tweedy and the Citizen, also reflects the colonial ambivalence between the poles of shoneen appeasement and outright rebellion. And the disputed space is, of course, Hibernia herself – both the Poor Old Woman (Cathleen, Old Gummy Granny) and her younger incarnation here in the person of Cissy Caffrey: "They're going to fight. For me!" (*U* 15.4597–632) It is a paradigmatic moment.

As Carr once more repeats that "I'll wring the neck of any fucking bastard says a word against my bleeding fucking king," Bloom urges

Cissy, who is dallying with the soldiers, to speak the truth and admit that Stephen had not insulted her: "Speak, you! Are you struck dumb? You are the link between nations and generations. Speak, woman, sacred lifegiver!"[3] Cissy here represents Joyce's feminized Hibernia as a figure who repeatedly betrays her own, who (like the milkwoman in "Telemachus") cannot recognize the true patriot trying to create the conscience of his race but instead chooses to dally with the Saxon invader. (Stephen meanwhile obliviously sings the gypsy cant [first cited in *U* 3.381–84] about "White thy fambles, red thy gan / And thy quarrons dainty is," appropriately invoking English colors.) As the fantasy approaches its holocaustic moment, the stage directions describe, as Dublin burns, an image of Irish civil enmity, duels of brother against brother: "*Wolfe Tone against Henry Grattan, Smith O'Brien against Daniel O'Connell, Michael Davitt against Isaac Butt*" and so on. All of this binary enmity prepares for the moment of violence between Carr and Stephen, reinscribing the curve of, at once, the confrontation between the Citizen and Bloom, the boxing fight between Bennett and Keogh, and the strife between England and Ireland. Thus, at this moment "*In strident discord peasants and townsmen of Orange and Green factions sing* Kick the Pope *and* Daily, daily sing to Mary" (*U* 15.4644–718).

Private Carr is no longer to be restrained, and so "Old Gummy Granny" begins to pray for Stephen. Cissy's half-hearted attempt to stop the fight ("He insulted me but I forgive him ... I forgive him for insulting me") comes too late, as Carr rushes towards Stephen and punches him in the face; "*Stephen totters, collapses, falls, stunned. He lies prone, his face to the sky, his hat rolling to the wall.*" The brutal redcoat violence against the helpless and unresisting Irishman replicates in microcosm the hopelessness of Irish insurrections in a colonial history marked by the extreme power imbalance between the most powerful country in the world, ruler of the waves on whose empire the sun never sets, and an island whose only real hope of successful resistance has always depended on the unreliable support of foreign military help – from France, Spain, or America. As the police arrive on the scene, the two redcoats slip away ("Bugger off, Harry. Here's the cops! ... bugger off, Harry. Or Bennett'll shove you in the lockup") unmolested and scot-free, while "A HAG" yells out poignantly over the unconscious Stephen: "What call had the redcoat to strike the gentleman and he under the influence. Let them go and fight the Boers!" (*U* 15.4737–94) It is left to Bloom to save Stephen now from the clutches of the police.

"Nostos": unmasking name and essence

In the discourse of nation formation, as we have seen, a community is imagined along the logic of "unisonance," "that progressive metaphor of modern social cohesion – *the many as one* – shared by organic theories of the holism of culture and community" (Bhabha, *Nation*, 294); "Finally, the imagined community ... thinks of the representative body, not the personal life" (Anderson, *Imagined Communities*, 32). Such a totalizing logic posits a nation as the universal-particular, as imagined collectivity, in a process which universalizes particularity of difference and character, homogenizing heterogeneity (both individual and cultural) into frozen, static essences. Such essentialism means that someone (like Bloom) who does not conform to the constructed image – wherever he/she was born, or is actually like, or chooses to live as – is typed forever as an outsider (as Jew, Italian, black, and so on) within the term's essentialist connotations. While the national Self is thus homogenized from irreconcilable differences into an essentialized national character, so also the same process leads to the naming/typing/classifying/colonizing of Others as counter-types, according to the ethnographic mentality which Anderson calls the "museumizing imagination" (*Imagined Communities*, 178):

Interlinked with one another, then, the census, the map and the museum illuminate the late colonial state's style of thinking about its domain. The "warp" of this thinking was a totalizing classificatory grid, which could be applied with endless flexibility to anything under the state's real or contemplated control: peoples, regions, religions, languages, products, monuments, and so forth. The effect of the grid was always to be able to say of anything that it was this, not that; it belonged here, not there. It was bounded, determinate, and therefore – in principle – countable.

(*Imagined Communities*, 184)

So also Leopold Bloom is, to the other Dubliners, eminently determinate, countable, essentializable, typable, namable – and thus he is constantly being slurred according to "type." But Bloom, like each of us, is at once universal/representative in certain homogeneous respects but very particular/unique in many other heterogeneous respects, defying essentialist categorization and namability; as we are told in "Ithaca" ("What universal binomial denominations would be his as entity and nonentity?"), he is "Everyman or Noman" (*U* 17.2006–8).

In the *Odyssey*, the "Nostos" involves Odysseus returning home to

Ithaca, disguised and unrecognized, treated as a stranger and foreigner, culminating in a recognition scene in which he is finally unmasked and identified by Euryclea and Penelope so as to reveal who/what he truly is. Similarly, the "Nostos" of *Ulysses* (the novel's last three episodes), poses the issue of identity through the problematics of essence, nominalism, stereotype, and disguise – before Bloom, finally returned to "Ithaca," can be fully and finally revealed as what he is, and not what his fellow Irish have made him out to be.

"Eumaeus" is an episode full of unclear, indeterminate, or mistaken identities and essences. The keeper of the cab shelter, for example, is "said to be the once famous Skin-the-Goat, Fitzharris, the invincible" (*U* 16.323–24) – though it is not clear to Bloom and the others there if this is true, if the Fitzharris involved in the Phoenix Park Murders was actually working in the cab shelter (in fact, the issue is also a matter of continuing scholarly debate; see Gifford, *"Ulysses" Annotated*, 538). Bloom and Stephen overhear some Italians in heated altercation in their own language, which leads Bloom to essentialize them with Mediterranean romanticism: " – A beautiful language. I mean for singing purposes ... so melodious and full." But then, when Stephen, who *knows* Italian – for it is often a lack of actual familiarity which encourages the imagination to stereotype – deflates Bloom's romanticized image by pointing out the actually mundane nature of their conversation (the Italians are haggling over money), Bloom – typically both the product of cultural constructions and their skeptic – also questions such typing: "Of course, he subjoined pensively, at the inward reflection ... [that] it may be only the southern glamour that surrounds it" (*U* 16.345–53).

In fact, it seems to me that this particular episode is suffused with a very interesting linguistic effect: we witness many things that have been named or identified repeatedly undergoing a process in which those very "names" and essential identities get questioned (e.g., is Skin-the-Goat really Fitzharris the Invincible?) and problematized. Since we can only know reality through the names and words we give it, the supposed identity and reality of everything are rendered problematic by the ultimately discursive nature of all language. Joyce renders "Eumaeus" into a self-conscious playground of linguistic deconstruction, revealing the inherent instability of words as mere language and constructed essences: thus, the language of the episode is a thick jungle of self-conscious qualifications, such as: "a choice concoction labelled coffee"; a "specimen of a bun, or so it seemed";

"the cup of what was temporarily supposed to be called coffee"; "Our *soi-disant* sailor"; "the *soi-disant* townclerk"; and so on (*U* 16.355–64, 620, 1354). As Stephen says at this point: "Sounds are impostures ... like names. Shakespeares were as common as Murphies. What's in a name?" What indeed? So also with essences: what's in a "Murphy" (slang for both Irishman and potato)? What's the difference between an Irish Murphy (like D. B. Murphy, the "sailor" in this episode whose real identity is a mystery to everyone), and an English Shakespeare? Between an Irish essence and an English essence? What does the name "Ireland" or the word "nation" really mean, beyond what the constructed cultural discourse tells us it means? Bloom acknowledges Stephen's point: " – Yes, to be sure, Mr Bloom unaffectedly concurred ... pushing *the socalled roll* across" (*U* 16.365–66; my emphasis).

We may wish to believe, with logocentric confidence in nominalist linguistic powers, that if we can name – and define, circumscribe, classify – something "objectively," we can understand it and thus capture its essence (or at least put it in a museum). But since all those essences and words are themselves social constructions based on the collective desire of the culture and on the particular needs of the interpreting individual, those names can never accurately pin down the actual difference/*différance* of the particular. It is through collective versions of such linguistic slippage that people(s) get stereotyped, without careful accounting for actual and specific differences.

And so Stephen and Bloom at this point engage in amicable discussion and disagreement (in spite of their significant, particular differences: "poles apart as they were both in schooling and everything else with the marked differences in their respective ages") about unknowables and unknown identities – such as the existence of God or who wrote Shakespeare; everything in the episode keeps returning to the problematics of forgery, disguise, essence, reality, difference: "And take a piece of that bun. It's like one of our skipper's bricks disguised" (*U* 16.786–77). The others present in the cab shelter now start talking about the Italians, essentializing their nature as hotblooded Southern passion: Italians are "great for the cold steel ... That was why they thought the park murders of the invincibles was done by foreigners on account of them using knives" (*U* 16.589–91). And now the sailor, claiming to have been all over the world, shows them a postcard of "maneaters in Peru that eats corpses and the livers of horses" (*U* 16.511–12): his postcard is not so different from what often passes as ethnography or anthropology, images of absolute otherness which result in a projection of typed identities and characteristics onto the savage "primitives." Thus, Bloom now launches into descriptions of essentialized museum ethnographies about different peoples which he has seen (" – Mind you, I'm not saying that it's all a pure invention"): giants; midgets; waxwork "Aztecs, as they are called, sitting bowlegged" and so on. Once more, though, Bloom admits that the stereotyped reality is "probably not a bit like it really," as he thinks of the actual Italians he has personally experienced (selling ice cream or fish and chips – not to speak of Nannetti):

On the contrary that stab in the back touch was quite in keeping with those italianos though candidly he was none the less free to admit those icecreamers and friers in the fish way not to mention the chip potato variety and so forth over in little Italy there near the Coombe were sober thrifty hardworking fellows.

(*U* 16.865–69)

Once again, actual experience and personal knowledge of specific individuals ("sober thrifty hardworking fellows") can mitigate the power of the essentialist discourse. Nonetheless, Bloom, always also a receptacle and product of the culture, goes on now to essentialize Spaniards as "passionate temperaments ... It comes from the great heat, climate generally" – for that Mediterranean stereotype corresponds here to his personal experience: "My wife is, so to speak, Spanish, half that is ... She has the Spanish type. Quite dark, regular brunette, black ... It's in the blood" (*U* 16.877–99). But even Bloom's classification of Molly as "the Spanish type" is undermined by the episode's ubiquitous linguistic qualifiers ("so to speak" and "half that is"). Perhaps one reason that "Eumaeus" is so ridden with euphemistic clichés and linguistic qualifiers – as commentators have often noted – is precisely because the narrative language (constantly qualifying and questioning identity and essence) mirrors the episode's ongoing discussion about the very problematics (and imprecision) of language, the presumed ability of cultures to name and control accurately through discursive and verbal typing of essences and differences (e.g., the "Italians" or "Spaniards" as passionate and hot-blooded).

Thus, we return to the national Irish identity and essence posited by militant Celticist nationalism, here in a lengthy Fenian argument by Skin-the-Goat that "the natural resources of Ireland ... [render it] the richest country bar none" for "You could grow any mortal thing in Irish soil" and that, in sum, Ireland is the greatest nation on earth. Another man asks: "Who's the best troops in the army ... And best jumpers and racers? And the best admirals and generals we've got? Tell me that?" The others answer, of course: "The Irish, for choice ... The Irish catholic peasant. He's the backbone of our empire" (*U* 16.984–1022). This is the same binary logic posited earlier by the Citizen, in which a polarizing of absolute difference whitewashes every other specificity between the poles of absolute wonderfulness and absolute depravity, between "Irish" and "English" (or vice versa, depending on which you are), refusing to acknowledge any possible shared characters and similarities. Bloom, arguing instead (to Stephen) that "it was highly advisable in the interim to try to make the most of both countries even though poles apart," recognizes the xenophobic logic of the Citizen: "he had heard not so long before the same identical lingo as he told Stephen how he simply but effectually silenced the offender"; Bloom now narrates the events in "Cyclops" culminating in his pointing out that Christ was a Jew (*U* 16.1079–87). But again Bloom (unlike the one-eyed Citizen) is willing to look at all sides, even where he is personally involved:

– Of course, Mr B. proceeded to stipulate, you must look at both sides of the question. It is hard to lay down any hard and fast rules as to the right and wrong but room for improvement all round there certainly is ... It's all very fine to boast of mutual superiority but what about mutual equality. I resent violence and intolerance in any shape or form. It never reaches anything or stops anything. A revolution must come on the due instalments plan. It's a patent absurdity on the face of it to hate people because they live round the corner and speak another vernacular, in the next house so to speak.

(*U* 16.1094–1103)

This important passage seems to me to get to the heart of some of the ideological positions Joyce advocates via Bloom: the need to look at more than one side in each question; the vigilance required to combat any moral smugness or essentialist confidence in a world in which nothing is actually simple or onesided, for "it is hard to lay down hard and fast rules as to the right and wrong but room for improvement all round there certainly is"; the absurdity of the Citizen's binary logic of exclusive national/ethnic greatness ("all very fine to boast of mutual superiority but what about mutual equality"); anti-violence and pacifism; and the need to refute the binary stereotypes of absolute difference which generate hatred for a constructed Other: "It's a patent absurdity on the face of it to hate people because they live round the corner and speak another vernacular, in the next house so to speak."

Nothing in this particular episode is "on the face of it" and every notion or name may be a false identity. Bloom goes on now to note that one such "patent absurdity" is to hate Jews – for, while Jews are accused of ruining national economies, Bloom points out the fact that countries with large Jewish populations have actually prospered. And then he questions the meanings of the terms "Irishman" and "patriotism":

I'm, he resumed with dramatic force, as good an Irishman as that rude person I told you about at the outset and I want everyone, concluded he, all creeds and classes *pro rata* having a comfortable tidysized income, in no niggard fashion either, something in the neighbourhood of [LL] 300 per annum. That's the vital issue at stake and it's feasible and would be provocative of friendlier intercourse between man and man. At least that's my idea for what it's worth. I call that patriotism.

(*U* 16.1131–38)

This passage makes it clear that Bloom's idealistic platform of social reform in "Circe" was not just a fantasy (in that episode's phantasmagoric feast of fantasies) but a deeply-held personal belief, for here he repeats his neo-Marxist belief that it's "very largely a question of the money question which was at the back of everything" (*U* 16.1114–15) and that real patriotism lies in improving the lot of the masses and not in bloodshed and hatred of others. *That*, for Bloom, is what it really means to be a "patriot" and a good Irish "citizen." As he tells Stephen, reasserting his belief in a nation willing to accommodate heterogeneity and difference ("all creeds and classes") without imposed hierarchies or exclusions: "You have every bit as much right to live by your pen in pursuit of your philosophy as the peasant [typed and glorified by the Celtic Revival] has. What? You both belong to Ireland, the brain and the brawn. Each is equally important" (*U* 16.1157–59).

In a revealing passage (despite the episode's typically circuitous language), Bloom now traces his political history:

At his [Stephen's] age when dabbling in politics roughly some score of years previously when he [Bloom] had been a *quasi* aspirant to parliamentary honours ... he had a sneaking regard for those same ultra ideas ... For instance when the evicted tenants question ... [he] was in thorough sympathy with peasant possession ... and even was twitted with going a step farther than Michael Davitt in the striking views he at one time inculcated as a backtothelander, which was one reason he strongly resented the innuendo put upon him in so barefaced a fashion by our friend at the gathering of the clans in Barney Kiernan's so that he, though often considerably misunderstood and the least pugnacious of mortals, be it repeated, departed from his customary habit to give him (metaphorically) the gizzard though, so far as politics themselves were concerned, he was only too conscious of the casualties invariably resulting from propaganda and displays of mutual animosity and the misery and suffering it entailed as a foregone conclusion on fine young fellows, chiefly, destruction of the fittest, in a word.

(*U* 16.1581–1601)

What I would posit as "Eumaeus"'s larger argument about naming, unrepresentability, and the essentializing of specific difference – is precisely what Bloom is getting at here: while he again laments the results of martial violence (i.e., that young men get killed), he particularly resents the Citizen's attack precisely because Bloom was being judged on the basis of a name/word – "Jew" – which endows him with a "socalled" or "*soi-disant*" character (the stage Jew) of absolute Otherness – which has nothing to do with Bloom's actual ("considerably misunderstood") self, revealed here rather as containing a politics (and history) of radical and activist Irish Nationalism ("those same ultra ideas"), including Land League activism. Bloom is clearly much more patriotic and much better an Irishman, patriot, and "citizen" than the bloodthirsty Citizen himself could have imagined. "At the same time he inwardly chuckled over his gentle repartee to the blood and ouns champion about his god being a jew. People could put up with being bitten by a wolf but what properly riled them was a bite from a sheep" (*U* 16.1637–40). This comment, too, is to the point, in invoking the amusing image of Bloom as a wolf in sheep's clothing: for names and labels and stereotypes create imagined "clothing" which does not reflect the actual specificities of individual and cultural differences.

As an episode of homecoming, "Ithaca" plays the same role as Euryclea and Penelope do when Odysseus returns to his island of Ithaca – that is to say, the "Ithaca" narrative unmasks the unanswered mysteries and reveals to us true identities. Thus, we have the question-and-answer objectivity of what Joyce called the episode's "mathematical catechism" (cf. *JJII*, 501); it is an episode that refuses to "imagine" false identities, revealing instead a plethora of specific facts and objective details which are thus cleared of the suspicion that they might be either slanted by an individual stream of consciousness (in subjective indirect monologue), or exaggerated through stylistic parody or fantasy. Thus, for example, the Ithacan

241

narration repeatedly makes clear that Stephen and Bloom are at once similar and different in a number of specific (and Joycean) ways, such as:

Both preferred a continental to an insular manner of life, a cisatlantic to a transatlantic place of residence. Both indurated by early domestic training and an inherited tenacity of heterodox resistance professed their disbelief in many orthodox religious, national, social, and ethical doctrines ...

Did he find four separating forces between his temporary guest and him?
Name, age, race, creed.

(*U* 17.21–26, 402–3)

Stephen and Bloom then share with each other their respective knowledge of Gaelic and Hebrew; the narrator asks for "points of contact ... between these languages and between the peoples who spoke them," and the question is answered with a lengthy list of similarities – including each people's sacred books and "the restoration in Chanah David of Zion and the possibility of Irish political autonomy or devolution" (*U* 17.745–60), for both the Irish and the Jews are peoples still denied Home Rule and their promised land.[4]

And now we get "objective" narrative proof (i.e., the Ithacan narrator, and neither stream of consciousness nor interior monologue) of Bloom's socialistic idealism and conscience:

Why would a recurrent frustration the more depress him?

Because at the critical turning point of human existence he desired to amend many social conditions, the product of inequality and avarice and international animosity.

(*U* 17.989–92)

And, even in "Ithaca," we get a version of the New Bloomusalem as the "course of action" Bloom favors:

A course that lay between undue clemency and excessive rigour: the dispensation in a heterogeneous society of arbitrary classes, incessantly rearranged in terms of greater and lesser social inequality, of unbiassed homogeneous indisputable justice ... the repression of many abuses ... [and the suppression of] all orotund instigators of international persecution, all perpetuators of international animosities, all menial molestors of domestic conviviality, all recalcitrant violators of domestic connubiality.

(*U* 17.1617–33)

This Bloomian agenda includes not only the day's specific concerns – the Citizen ("orotund instigators of international persecution"),

242

Private Carr ("perpetuators of international animosities"), Blazes Boylan ("violators of domestic connubiality") – but, more strikingly, a clearly and objectively stated expression of Bloom's opposition to class structures and hierarchies, arguing against the imposition of "arbitrary classes" and "social inequality" upon a "heterogeneous society." The New Bloomusalem was clearly not just a momentary fantasy in "Circe."

With the objective unmasking of Bloom's true identity come the objective details of his patriotic activism, for which we have already had scattered evidence in earlier chapters. Earlier we had been presented, either through Bloom's subjective perspective or through narrative parody and fantasy, with some hints that Bloom is most likely every bit as active a "patriot" as the barspongers in "Cyclops" who type him with the false identity of being anti-Irish and "a stranger in the house": whereas John Wyse Nolan and Martin Cunningham "tell[] the citizen about Bloom and the Sinn Fein" (*U* 12.1624–25; the apocryphal tale about Bloom being Arthur Griffith's secret mastermind); and whereas Bloom himself tells Stephen the story (starting at *U* 16.1495) of how he once met Parnell and "enjoyed the distinction of being close to Erin's uncrowned king in the flesh," retrieving the Chief's hat for him in a moment of riot and confusion (in the process sustaining "a minor injury from a nasty prod"); we have also had hints of more significant patriotic political activity.

In "Oxen of the Sun" the parodic narrator had questioned:

But with what fitness ... has this alien, whom the concession of a gracious prince has admitted to civic rights, constituted himself the lord paramount of our internal polity? ... During the recent war whenever the enemy had a temporary advantage with his granados did this traitor to his kind not seize that moment to discharge his piece against the empire of which he is a tenant at will while he trembled for the security of his four per cents?

(*U* 14.905–12)

While the "Oxen" narrator (and the other men in the episode) may question Bloom's right to speak as an Irishman (the Jews, expelled from the British Isles in 1290, were readmitted under Cromwell but only gradually granted any civil rights), we can read between the lines: that, whereas Bloom as a Jew is denied many civic rights and is constantly mistreated by his countrymen, he was still patriotically willing to speak up and criticize the British Empire during the Boer War, even against his own financial interests (Bloom has invested in "four per cent" government stock [see *U* 17.1864–65] whose security would have been threatened if the English had lost; Gifford, *"Ulysses" Annotated*, 429). We had earlier heard of Bloom's participation in a pro-Boer, anti-English demonstration on the occasion of Joseph Chamberlain's visit to Dublin, again risking personal injury and arrest by the police (e.g., *U* 8.420–36 and 15.791). Now Bloom has just told Stephen of his "ultra ideas," even "going a step farther than Michael Davitt" in his views as a "backtothelander" in the times of the Land League agitation (*U* 16.1579–602).

In "Penelope" Molly, too, will tell us about Bloom's politics: that Bloom had upset her by arguing about "Our Lord being a carpenter ... and the first socialist he said" and by his socialist ideas (*U* 18.175–78); she confirms that at one point he "said he was going to stand for a member of Parliament" though she herself is unconvinced by "all his blather about home rule and the land league ... explaining and rigmaroling about religion and persecution" (*U* 18.1184–91). We are less skeptical of Bloom's convictions than Molly is – especially as it becomes clear that Molly's politics are very different from Bloom's: the daughter of a major in the British army, she worries that Irish nationalists may be discriminating against her career "on account of father being in the army and my singing the absentminded beggar and wearing a brooch for Lord Roberts ... and Poldy not Irish enough" (*U* 18.376–79); but the fact that she wears an anti-Boer brooch and sings Kipling's "The Absent Minded Beggar" in concerts, would seem by itself both sufficiently indicative and incendiary, regardless of whom she was married to. Molly's anti-Boer politics might be partly explained by her father's British sympathies and by the memory of Lieutenant Gardner, the former beau to whom she gave a Claddagh ring for luck when he went "to south Africa where those Boers killed him" (*U* 18.866–67). Furthermore, we learn through Molly that Bloom's political concerns were not just a matter of youthful idealism but are still an ongoing concern: "he was going about with some of them Sinner Fein lately or whatever they call themselves talking his usual trash and nonsense he says that little man he showed me without the neck is very intelligent the coming man Griffiths" (*U* 18.383–87); and she worries that Bloom might get fired from his job "on account of those Sinner Fin or the freemasons then well see if the little man he showed me [Griffith] dribbling along in the wet will give him much consolation that he says is so capable and sincerely Irish" (*U* 18.1227–30; one wonders if all this linking of Bloom with Griffith is a Joycean hint that there may be some truth to Nolan's and Cunningham's story after all).

And now, in the "mathematical catechism" of "Ithaca," we have a finally "objective" recognition scene, in which Bloom (despite all the false identities posited upon him) is at last unmasked as a political animal. This is suggested – not only in the passages of "Ithaca" already cited above (such as Bloom's "course of action" for "a heterogeneous society") – but now in a catalogue that suggests that his nationalist politics were perhaps no less vigorous than those of Simon Dedalus and other Irishmen, and probably much more carefully considered in terms of specific policies:

> In 1885 he had publicly expressed his adherence to the collective and national economic programme advocated by James Fintan Lalor, John Fisher Murray, John Mitchel, J.F.X. O'Brien and others, the agrarian policy of Michael Davitt, the constitutional agitation of Charles Stewart Parnell (M.P. for Cork city), the programme of peace, retrenchment and reform of William Ewart Gladstone.

We are further told that "in support of his political conviction, [he] had climbed up into a secure position" in a tree "to see the entrance (2 February 1888) into the capital of a demonstrative torchlight procession ... in escort of the marquess of Ripon and (honest) John Morley" (*U* 17.1645–56); the Marquess of Ripon and John Morley were both English statesmen who strongly supported Irish Home Rule and who were consequently popular with the Irish – thus, unlike the violent 1889 demonstration against Chamberlain that Bloom was also involved in, this one (on Joyce's sixth birthday) would have been a peaceful demonstration in support of the English politicians involved.

In sum, "Ithaca"'s factual/mathematical narrative provides "objective" narrative evidence, both of Bloom's political support for the Irish cause, and for his idealistic views and socialist sympathies. Near the end of the episode, we get a long list of Bloom's "schemes of wider scope," practical ideas (such as to connect the cattle market and the quays by tramline) to bolster his (perhaps impractical) utopian visions. Then, among a catalogue of items contained in his locked drawer, we find "a sealed prophecy (never unsealed) written by Leopold Bloom in 1886 concerning the consequences of the passing into law of William Ewart Gladstone's Home Rule bill of 1886 (never passed into law)" (*U* 17.1788–90). Alas, this is one of *Ulysses*'s *un*revealed mysteries: I would dearly love to know what

Bloom had prophesied for an Ireland finally granted Home Rule and a promised land freed from the house of bondage.

Coda: *Ulysses,* nation, and narrative

While nationalism and national pride are certainly essential to any liberation movement and to the formation of a new nation, the particular *forms* of national consciousness and discourse of Nation a society chooses to articulate (from among nationalisms in the plural) are crucial, a matter demanding self-aware cultural scrutiny. It is narratives that, over time, construct the particular forms of national discourses. As Homi Bhabha points out, "Without such an understanding of the performativity of language in the narratives of the nation, it would be difficult to understand why Edward Said prescribes a kind of 'analytic pluralism' as the *form* of critical attention appropriate to the cultural effects of the nation" (*Nation*, 3). Frantz Fanon has argued that "National consciousness, which is not nationalism, is the only thing that will give us an international dimension" (*Wretched*, 247), in contrast to what he calls a "tribal dictatorship" and an "ethnic dictatorship" which "claims to speak in the name of the totality of the people"[5]; and Bhabha elaborates that it is "this *inter*national dimension both within the margins of the nation-space and in the boundaries *in-between* nations and peoples" that our efforts and narratives should be directed at, in our explorations of "the problematic unity of the nation" and in "the articulation of cultural difference in the construction of an *inter*national perspective." This requires an awareness of cultural and geographical spaces as "contact zones," for "The 'other' is never outside or beyond us; it emerges forcefully, within cultural discourse, when we *think* we speak most intimately and indigenously 'between ourselves'" (*Nation*, 4–5).

Bhabha, in his essay on "DissemiNation: Time, Narrative, and the Margins of the Modern Nation," theorizes how the "imagined community" is simultaneously linked to the issues of essentialism, difference, and narration/narrative – a process which, as we have seen, *Ulysses* illustrates and symptomatizes. Bhabha argues for "Counter-narratives of the nation that continually evoke and erase its totalizing boundaries – both actual and conceptual" so as to "disturb those ideological manoeuvres through which 'imagined communities' are given essentialist identities." For the "nation," he notes, "reveals, in its ambivalent and vacillating representation, the ethnography of its own historicity and opens up the possibility of other narratives of the people and their difference" ("DissemiNation," 300). *Ulysses* seems to me just this sort of narrative, which – in its cultural specificity and detailed historicity, set as it is in the concrete and material specificities of turn-of-the-century Dublin – enacts symptomatically and voices all the diverse discourses and ideological positions of 1904 Dublin; in its precision of concrete detail and specific representation (each person, each street, each building drawn in such particularized detail, distinct and different, so as to avoid the "the narrative of national cohesions" signified by "the many as one"), it attempts to avoid the homogenizing of difference; in its presentation of analogies and similarities between those differences and peoples, it suggests possible lines of solidarity and refutes the binary essentialisms of absolute difference.[6] It is thus both universal and particular at the same time, allowing for solidarity/ likeness while accepting and respecting heterogeneous difference; it is (perhaps along with *Finnegans Wake*) at once the most materially concrete/specific, *and* the most analogically universal, work imaginable – covering Ireland both vertically and horizontally in its dialogical re-presentation of the conscience of a race as a pluralistic contact zone. Thus, it illustrates what Bhabha advocates (in taking up Abdul JanMohamed and David Lloyd's term) as "minority discourse":

Minority discourse ... contests genealogies of "origin" that lead to claims for cultural supremacy and historical priority. Minority discourse acknowledges the status of national culture – and the people – as a contentious, performative space of the perplexity of the living in the midst of the pedagogical representations of the fullness of life.

("DissemiNation," 307)

That seems to me a fair description of *Ulysses*.

In quoting Walter Benjamin's contention that "To write a novel means to carry the incommensurable to extremes in the representation of human life. In the midst of life's fullness, and through the representation of this fullness, the novel gives evidence of the profound perplexity of the living" (cited in "DissemiNation," 311) – Bhabha argues for novels of discursive resistance:

It is from this incommensurability in the midst of the everyday that the nation speaks its disjunctive narrative. It begins ... from that anterior space within the arbitrary sign which disturbs the homogenizing myth of cultural anonymity. From the margins of modernity, at the insurmountable extremes of storytelling, we encounter the question of cultural difference as the perplexity of living, and writing, the nation.

("DissemiNation," 311)

Ulysses, a novel steeped "in the midst of the everyday," displays in its cultural specificity and representational fullness what Seamus Deane calls a "mirror held up to Culture" ("Joyce," 41), disturbing the homogenizing myths of a racial/national essence through its representations of a heterogeneous and inevitably pluralistic culture, a narrative space charting, through its detailed representations of the perplexity of living, both the discursive processes of "writing the nation" and the conscience of a "race."

Claude Lévi-Strauss had understood "the unconscious as providing the common and specific character of social facts ... not because it harbours our most secret selves but because ... it enables us to coincide with forms of activity which are both *at once ours and other*" (cited in "DissemiNation," 313). Joyce's own study of the unconscious evokes much the same discursive awareness of the interpenetrated nature of the Same/Self and the Other – for, as Foucault argued, "the history of the order imposed on things would be the history of the Same" (*Order*, xxiv). *Ulysses*, through the images revealed in its "nicely polished looking-glass" of the cultural contact zone that was Dublin in 1904, advocates an acceptance simultaneously of heterogeneity and difference, on the one hand, and, on the other hand, of a potential sameness and solidarity of shared similarities-in-difference – between Irish, Jewish, black, Oriental, Indian, English, Boer, paleface, redskin, jewgreek and greekjew – within a multivalent, inter-nationalist perspective, rather than within a binary polarization that freezes essences into poles of absolute and unbridgeable difference.

Finnegans Wake: **forays**

9.

White horse, dark horse: Joyce's allhorse of another color

The present study originated with an investigation into tropes of race and empire in *Finnegans Wake*, and expanded into a study of issues of race and empire in Joyce's works as a whole. In the process, I have discovered that the ideological issues of race and empire are overtly and consciously layered into each page of *Finnegans Wake* to an astonishing degree, from the very first lines of the book – with their references to Wellington and Napoleon's "penisolate war" (*FW* 3.06); to the competing factions in Phoenix Park "where oranges have been laid to rust upon the green" (*FW* 3.23); to the "Whoyteboyce of Hoodie Head" and the "Sod's brood!" (*FW* 4.05–6) – referring not only to Irish insurrectionists but, in the context of Dublin, Georgia and of competing factions, also invoking the white boys (with hooded heads) in the Ku Klux Klan ("Kekkek Kekkek Kekkek! Koax Koax Koax!" and "Killykillkilly" in *FW* 4.02, 4.07–8) and the racial competition between whites and blacks in the Southern United States.[1]

The issues I have been discussing (in the preceding chapters) concerning Joyce's earlier works are vibrantly present in *Finnegans Wake* with an even more startling, ubiquitous, and fundamental insistence (once one starts *looking* for them), so that – in due course, as Joyce scholars begin to look for and pay attention more carefully to these matters within the pages of *Finnegans Wake* (a number are beginning to do so already) – I am confident that representations of racial and imperial/colonial relationships will eventually be recognized as one of the central and structuring topics of *Finnegans Wake*, alongside such fundamental Wakean building blocks (and influences) as Vico, Egyptology, the topography of Dublin, the sleeping body, Shakespeare, and so on. Joyce's own political commentary, within the Wakean representations, will thus also be recognized as even more insistent and consistent than in his previous works. There is, I have discovered, enough material on these matters within *Finnegans Wake* for a whole separate book, perhaps for several, to be eventually written on this topic. In the end there was no way, consequently, given the limitations of length and time, for this single volume on *Joyce, race, and empire* to include within its scope a comprehensive study of *Finnegans Wake* along these lines; the full investigation of these issues in *Finnegans Wake* will remain a project both for others and for myself to continue to pursue in co-operative and accumulating awareness.

For the purposes of this current volume, I would like to provide two forays, as case studies into both the nature and the dense texture of such issues within the *Wake* – issues that are deadly serious in content and conception but, as with all of *Finnegans Wake*, playfully and "jocoseriously" (one might say Joyceanly) presented. I do so, in these two chapters, through two quite different modes of analysis: this first chapter, "White horse, dark horse: Joyce's allhorse of another color," is a case study of how Joyce takes a particularly emphatic and repeated trope – horses and horse races – to elucidate, negotiate, and intertextually elaborate his developing positions and politics about races, empires, and essences through the course of the entire Joyce corpus (but especially in *Finnegans Wake*). If this can thus be thought of as a study of a "thematic" development through the whole of the Wakean text, the following (shorter) chapter – "The general and the sepoy: imperialism and power in the Museyroom" – is a demonstration of the powerfully dense texture (page by page) of such concerns within *Finnegans Wake*, by performing a close reading and focused analysis of a single, short *Wake* passage (of only three pages) which nevertheless yields a careful and complex ideological argument concerning the dynamics of imperialism and power. Both sorts of approaches to these issues – macrocosmic and microcosmic – could be (and should be) applied with good effect and rich results to much of *Finnegans Wake*. These two chapters mean to stand as illustrative forays and exempla of the possibilities for the study of such topics in the complex and challenging but wonderful and moving text that is *Finnegans Wake*.

Joyce's horses could fill up a multitude of stables. From Johnny the horse in "The Dead" to Trojan horses to equine Buck Mulligan to Swift's Houyhnhnms to Throwaway to the turd-happy horse in

"Eumaeus" to Copenhagen the "big wide harse," Joyce's texts are a mare's nest of "all sorts of horsehappy values and masses of meltwhile horse" (*FW* 111.28–29). It is intriguing to think of the uncanny number of central and significant passages in Joyce that have to do with horses – for example, "Scylla and Charybdis"; the discovery in "Cyclops" of Throwaway's victory in the Gold Cup; the climax of "Circe," where Bloom himself becomes a horse; *Finnegans Wake*'s most self-reflexive chapter ("The Mamafesta"), where the photograph of a horse unearthed from the dungheap receives elaborate commentary; the passage describing St. Patrick's debate with the Archdruid Berkeley near the end of the *Wake*, which is introduced by a description of the two as competing racehorses; and so on. From those many possibilities, I would like selectively to foreground Joyce's multi-faceted discussion of horseness in terms of essences and the essential Self: a discussion which both inscribes and problematizes the binary and dialogic opposition between knowable essences and indeterminate subjectivities; between monologism and multiplicity; between centralized authority and the destabilizing of authority; between day and night worlds; between the conscious Self and the repressed Other that cannot be erased; between the empire of Whiteness/Light and the colonies of invisible darkness on the peripheries.

A horse is a horse (of course, of course) – but what exactly *is* a horse? What do we mean by that term? Stephen Dedalus, thinking of Plato and Aristotle in the Library episode (" – Which of the two ... would have banished me from his commonwealth?" [*U* 9.82–83]), challenges himself to a definition: "Unsheathe your dagger definitions. Horseness is the whatness of allhorse" (*U* 9.84–85). Stephen is cerebrating on the nature of empirical realities and the nature of essences, positing here an essentialist argument about natural objects: all horses have an essential whatness, or horseness. Such a Platonic proposition would have it that all individual horses are but imperfect approximations, even aberrations, of the authoritative centralized ideal, essential horseness, the idea of Horse. A horse is a particularly appropriate example for Stephen to use, for he is echoing a remark traditionally attributed to Antisthenes speaking to Plato: "O Plato, I see a horse, but I do not see horseness" (Gifford, *"Ulysses" Annotated*, 199). However, Stephen is less concerned with (and less enamored by) Plato than Aristotle (who would not have banished poets from his commonwealth) and with Aristotle's arguments about the nature of an essential, undeniable reality ("Space: what you damn well have to see" [*U* 9.86]). Even Stephen's metaphorical challenge to himself – "Unsheathe your dagger definitions" – assumes a sharp, phallic hardness to its logocentricity, a belief in the definable/knowable "real"; and refers to Aristotle's distinctions between "nominal definitions" and "essential definitions" (*Posterior Analytics*, 2:8; Gifford, *"Ulysses" Annotated*, 199). Earlier, in the "Proteus" episode on the strand, he had tried to understand the ineluctable modalities of the visible and audible. In the "signatures of all things I am here to read ... coloured signs ... in bodies" (*U* 3.02–4), Stephen carried on a mental debate between Aristotle's reality and Bishop Berkeley's metaphysics. Aristotle, suggesting that color is the "peculiar object" of sight (as sound is of hearing) in *De Sensu et Sensibilita* and *De Anima*, had tried to prove the physical existence of "bodies"; while Bishop Berkeley, by suggesting that we do not "see" objects but only "coloured signs," had cast doubt on the reality and existence of concrete matter (see Gifford, *"Ulysses" Annotated*, 45).

In Stephen's mind, this opposition is not only between hard "reality" and indeterminate illusoriness, but between authoritative knowability and indeterminate multiplicity, between essentialist logocentrism and subversive plurability. For his notion of essence – "whatness" – is in part derived from still another philosopher, St. Thomas Aquinas. In *A Portrait of the Artist as a Young Man* Stephen had discussed Aquinas' trio of aesthetic principles, *integritas*, *consonantia*, and *claritas*. Stephen chooses to equate that third step – *claritas* or "radiance" – with yet another Thomistic term, *quidditas* or the "whatness of a thing." Stephen makes the argument more clearly and fully in the earlier *Stephen Hero* manuscript (*SH* 213):

Claritas is *quidditas* ... This is the moment which I call epiphany. First we recognize that the object is *one* integral thing, then we recognize that it is an organized composite structure, a *thing* in fact: finally ... we recognize that it is *that* which it is. Its soul, its whatness, leaps to us from the vestment of its appearance.

In positing the radiant presence of an object's *quidditas*, what Irene Hendry Chayes describes as "the *essential* identifying quality of the thing" ("Joyce's Epiphanies," 360; my emphasis), Stephen in *A Portrait* was also voicing his belief in an essentialist, logocentric certainty; in an authoritative, unitary, and knowable reality. As he puts it in *A Portrait*: "You see that it is that thing which it is and no other. The radiance of which [St. Thomas] speaks is the scholastic *quidditas*, the *whatness* of a thing" (*P* 213). In *Ulysses*, by using the example of Antisthenes' horseness as "the whatness of all horse," Stephen is tying his essentialist version of St. Thomas (perhaps this is why the latter is "tumass equinous" in *FW* 93.09) with the Plato/Aristotle/Berkeley discussion on the nature of knowable reality. Stephen's dagger definition presupposes an authorized ideal, an essence of Horse.

But Stephen himself is, in actuality, afraid of horses. As he says in *A Portrait*: "I fear many things: dogs, horses, firearms, the sea, thunderstorms, machinery, the country roads at night" (*P* 243). In Stephen's analogic mind, these fears are related: the sea is our great sweet mother and all the nightmares of history she represents to Stephen; dogs suggest God, as do Nobodaddy's thunderstorms; firearms suggest power, Haines's gun, and the black panther; country roads at night suggest Davin's story about the lonely farmwife and thus the provincialism of the old sow that eats her farrow; and so on. But horses?

For Stephen, horses represent not only logocentric authority and essentialist certainty (whatness of all horse) – but also a generalized Authority, all that he would oppose with his *non serviam*. Such equestrian symbolism was natural enough throughout history, in which the status of achieved power *was*, literally and symbolically, represented by the possession and rule by horses: a *chevalier* was one who rode a *cheval*; it was the distinguishing status symbol of the cavalier, the gentleman, the legitimized figure of respectability and authority – all the things which Stephen, a pedestrian in borrowed boots, is not.

In general terms, the horse has been a traditional symbol of power and the ruling class (in Ireland, the Penal Laws had long forbidden Catholics from owning a horse worth more than five pounds[2]); specifically for Stephen, it denotes the rule of authority, especially "the imperial British state" (*U* 1.643), exemplified particularly by the power of the "light horse" (*U* 15.1529) of the British cavalry. This is a rule and authority which is brought home pointedly to the Dubliners on June 16, 1904 – by the mounted cavalcade of the viceregal procession winding its way through the city's streets, reminding them of their subordinance to the British Crown: the Viceroy's horses become a metonymy for the power of Empire, as the viceregal parade's "horses pass Parliament street – harness and glossy pasterns in sunlight shimmering" (*U* 10.1034–35), and then "the glossy horses pranced by Merrion Square" (*U* 10.1265), and so on –

their bright trappings and clanking hooves dominating the streets of Dublin. When the horses go by, Martin Cunningham asks, " – What was it?"; as John Wyse Nolan replies: " – the lord lieutenantgeneral and general governor of Ireland" (*U* 10.1038–40).

White horses in particular are symbols of empire and authority, reflecting the popularity of equestrian paintings and statues of monarchs and generals (status = statues[3]) on white horses. When Leopold Bloom has a megalomaniac fantasy in "Circe" and imagines himself to be Emperor Leopold I, he is – like Napoleon on his milk-white charger Marengo – emblematically atop a white horse: "*Under an arch of triumph Bloom appears, bareheaded, in a crimson velvet mantle trimmed with ermine, bearing Saint Edward's staff, the orb and sceptre with the dove, the curtana. He is seated on a milkwhite horse with long flowing crimson tail, richly caparisoned, with golden headstall*" (*U* 15.1441–45).

Such an emblem of empire is especially appropriate if we remember that the "white horse" was the specific emblem of the House of Hanover, the English ruling dynasty (later the Windsors) – and was thus already the essential ideal of authorized horseness. Furthermore, the white horse was a personal symbol of William III, King Billy, the Protestant Prince of Orange, winner of the Battle of the Boyne and the scourge of Irish Catholics. As Adaline Glasheen points out (citing Gilbert's *History of Dublin*, III. 40–56):

In Dublin (before the Free State) the Ulstermen's brazen calf was a lead equestrian statue of King Billy on College Green which, on Williamite holy days, was painted white (a white horse in a fanlight is still a sign of Protestant sympathies) and decorated with orange lilies ... and green and white ribbons 'symbolically placed beneath its uplifted foot.' Catholics retorted by vandalizing the statue, tarring, etc., and in 1836 succeeded in blowing the figure of the king off the horse.

(*Third Census*, 309)[4]

The particular symbolism of the uplifted foot of King Billy's white horse, ready to crush rebellious Irish Catholics, appears in "Wandering Rocks," when the viceregal parade rounds College Green: "Where the foreleg of King Billy's horse pawed the air Mrs Breen plucked her hastening husband back from under the hoofs of the outriders" (*U* 10.1231–33). The effectively ambiguous syntax here suggests an equal danger to Dubliners of being crushed by King Billy's horse and by the viceregal hooves – for they are both metonymies for the same thing, Imperial (and Protestant) England.

No wonder then that Stephen, at the end of "Telemachus," warns himself to beware of the "Horn of a bull, hoof of a horse, smile of a Saxon" (*U* 1.732): for Irish Catholics, the latter two amount symbolically to the same thing. Stephen distrusts both the smile of Saxon Haines, who was just that moment "smiling at wild Irish" (*U* 1.731), and his Irish collaborator, Buck Mulligan, whose treachery – like Greeks bearing gifts – Stephen relates to the wooden horse of Troy, for Buck is "equine ... grained and hued like pale oak" (*U* 1.15–16).[5] For Stephen, the horses of authority and power are not to be trusted.

He certainly does not trust Garrett Deasy, thrice a symbol of empire and English authority for Stephen: Deasy is an Ulsterman, a Protestant, and Stephen's employer. Appropriately, Deasy is a defender of the very hooves Stephen fears, an activist against hoof and mouth disease, having drafted a letter expressing concern over "Foot and mouth disease ... Emperor's horses at Murzsteg" (*U* 2.332–34). In his office, Deasy hangs over the mantelpiece a picture of the Prince of Wales, while "Framed around the walls images of vanished horses stood in homage ... lord Hastings' *Repulse*, the duke of Westminster's *Shotover*, the duke of Beaufort's *Ceylon*, *prix de Paris*, 1866" (*U* 2.300–3); the very names of these horses, owned by English royalty, suggest military violence and the British Empire. Amid such symbols of an equestrian royalty, Stephen can only look at Deasy and see, as he had also done with the Englishman Haines, "The seas' ruler ... on [whose] empire ... the sun never sets" (*U* 2.246–48). When a bit later that morning Stephen walks on the beach and the crackling shells remind him of Deasy's coins (another symbol of English power and authority), he thinks: "Wild sea money. Dominie Deasy kens them a'. *Won't you come to Sandymount,* / *Madeline the mare?* ... *deline the mare*" (*U* 3.19–22). For Stephen, the polyvalent "mare" combines to suggest *mère* (mother); *mer* and Latin *mare* (sea: "she is our great sweet mother"); and those equine authorities represented by his mother, by the night-*mare* of history, and by Deasy's horses of authority. No wonder Stephen is afraid of horses and would like to "deline the mare."

Leopold Bloom (to use one of his own terms, straight from the horse's mouth) is "a horse of quite another colour" (*U* 16.770). Hippophilic rather than hippophobic, he has no problems getting along with horses. Bloom has no fear of horses because he is not concerned with their ideal or symbolic value, or with essentializing them – he is able to see horses as real entities and individual animals within a spectrum of multiplicity, each one a horse of another color amid the concrete reality of the streets of Dublin. Thus, repeatedly during the day we witness his horse sense and sensitivity to, and compassion for, the creatures. In "Lotos Eaters," he "passed the drooping nags of the hazard" at "Nosebag time ... a crunching of gilded oats, the gently champing teeth. Their full buck eyes regarded him as he went by, amid the sweet oaken reek of horsepiss ... Poor jugginses! Damn all they know or care about anything with their long noses stuck in nosebags ... Good poor brutes they look" (*U* 5.211–19). At the funeral he empathizes with a "team of horses," especially one with a "Dull eye: collar tight on his neck, pressing on a bloodvessel or something" (*U* 6.511–12). When Bloom helps the blind stripling cross the street, he notices a "drooping" horse and makes sure to "keep [the stripling's] cane clear of the horse's legs" (*U* 8.1099). Late in the evening he tells Stephen that "I scolded that tramdriver on Harold's cross bridge for illusing the poorhorse with his harness scab. Bad French I got for my pains" (*U* 15.699–701); and in "Eumaeus" he looks at the cabdriver's horse, a "horse not worth anything ... a noodly kind of horse" and "was sorry he hadn't a lump of sugar" (*U* 16.1782–89, 1787) to give him. (Molly, too, in her thought proves to be a horse-lover, bemoaning bullfights with bulls "ripping all the whole insides out of those poor horses I never heard of such a thing"; *U* 18.633–34).

While Bloom actually imagines becoming a horse in the fantasies of "Circe,"[6] there is a significant way in which horse lover Bloom is himself "equinous" in *Ulysses*. Not that he indulges in the races – for, unlike most Irish men, he is not a bettor. For Irish men, however, horse-racing is a national pastime second only perhaps to drinking – and June 16, 1904 is distinguished by the running of the Ascot Gold Cup. Earlier in the morning, Bloom had given Bantam Lyons his newspaper ("I was just going to throw it away"; *U* 5.534), an act which Lyons interprets as a sly tip by Ikey Moses Bloom on Throwaway, a dark horse at twenty to one, a "bloody horse" that (in Lenehan's words and in the general opinion) "hasn't an earthly" (*U* 10.518–20) – in a race which, significantly, is a social event notoriously associated with the English ruling classes. The favorites touted by the papers that day are Sceptre and Zinfandel (Gifford, *"Ulysses" Annotated*, 98). Lenehan and Boylan, like many of the other men in *Ulysses*, have put their money on Sceptre – a horse whose very name and whose status as the favorite both signify the power of

13. *Throwaway.* Winner of the 1904 Ascot Gold Cup. Painting now at the Joyce Tower, Sandycove.

phallic and imperial authority, like King Billy's white horse. As with the domination of the English white horse and of phallogocentric authority, the authoritarian sceptre/structure would like to suppress or deny the value of difference, to mark and bracket difference as dark, or invisible, even non-existent – to, as it were, throw it away. But, as we know, it is Throwaway who (in both Joyce's novel and in the 1904 Ascot) wins the Gold Cup on June 16: "[Sceptre] was leading the field ... But in the straight on the run home when all were in close order the dark horse Throwaway drew level, reached, outstripped her" (*U* 14.1129–32). As Lenehan complains bitterly: " – *Throwaway* ... at twenty to one. A rank outsider. And the rest nowhere" (*U* 12.1219–20).

When, in "Cyclops," the men suspect that Bloom has "gone to gather in the shekels" on Throwaway (*U* 12.1551), on "A dark horse," Joe Hynes remarks that " – He's a bloody dark horse himself" (*U* 12.1557–58). This frequently repeated term is doubly significant because, in *Ulysses*, the dark horse is not only a metaphor for the underdog but also literally a *dark* horse (just as Throwaway – see picture – was literally a dark horse), a horse of a darker color.

259

Dark horses and horses of another color combine in Joyce to suggest both race (ethnicity and color) and races (horse-racing). Thus, the white horse of English authority and Eurocentric rule (over the darker races of its far-flung empire) is contrasted to the dark horses on the margins, those throwaway races who haven't got an earthly, the rank outsiders. Bloom, himself a Jew and rank outsider and symbolic member of the darker races suffering at the hands of white Aryan male authoritarian domination, is throughout *Ulysses* represented as a dark horse, the silenced Other/double (literally, the *alter ego*) of the ruling white horse (the "Sceptre"). "A bloody dark horse himself," Bloom emerges in the novel – like Throwaway – unconquered, a tenacious testament to the futility of authority's attempts to erase and silence the marks of difference.

In the world of horses and horseness,[7] we have actual white horses and dark horses; we have powerful favorites and unempowered underdogs. The literal and the metaphorical become (like everything else) mixed and indistinguishable within the fantasies of "Circe," where the Gold Cup horse-race is replayed in fantasy:

(*A dark horse, riderless, bolts like a phantom past the winningpost, his mane moonfoaming, his eyeballs stars. The field follows, a bunch of bucking mounts. Skeleton horses, Sceptre, Maximum the Second, Zinfandel, the duke of Westminster's Shotover, Repulse, the duke of Beaufort's Ceylon, prix de Paris. Dwarfs ride them ... Last in a drizzle of rain on a brokenwinded isabelle nag, Cock of the North, the favourite, honey cap, green jacket, orange sleeves, Garrett Deasy up, gripping the reins, a hockeystick at the ready. His nag on spavined whitegaitered feet jogs along the rocky road.*)

(*U* 15.3974–83)

Running in this phantom race are not only the preferred favorites for the Gold Cup – Sceptre, Maximum the Second (the "French horse" Lyons was originally going to bet on; *U* 5.26), and Zinfandel – but also the historical horses over Deasy's mantelpiece (Shotover, Repulse, Ceylon), owned by nobility and representing the English empire. Once again, the "favourite" here is (like "Sceptre") a symbol of phallic power ("Cock of the North"), like King Billy's white horse of Protestant allegiance, ridden here by Garrett Deasy himself (as Ulsterman and horse lover). Appropriately, "Cock of the North" was also "a nickname for the Scot George Gordon (1770–1836), the fifth and last Duke of Gordon, whose Gordon Highlanders were instrumental in the suppression of the Catholic peasant insurrection in Wexford during the Rebellion of 1798" (Gifford, *"Ulysses" Annotated,* 515). But this race (both equine and ethnic) favorite is a sorry old nag who comes in last – while, once again, it is *"A dark horse"* which *"bolts ... past the winningpost."* In the night world of the Circean carnivalesque, the "white horses" of monologic authority can be upended by the dark horses of the night and of the margins. "Circe" 's night world forecasts the night world of *Finnegans Wake*, in which daytime consciousness and univocal authority will much more ubiquitously be destabilized by the multi-vocal voices from the darker margins.

For *Finnegans Wake* is a night-book, giving voice to the night world repressed and marginalized during the day within the authorized consciousness of the ego: thus, the book is more openly subversive, full of dark insurgencies challenging the clean ("white") authority of Anglocentric (and Eurocentric) empire. As *Finnegans Wake* critics have well argued (and I have particularly Margot Norris and John Bishop in mind here), the *Wake* is a night world/text which defies and decenters the authorized grammars of language, psyche, systems, power, empires, and daytime consciousness.

So also Stephen's confidence in Greek rationalism and logocentrism, in the monologic reality of Aristotle's universe and Aquinas' *quidditas*, is more frequently challenged and unseated in *Finnegans Wake*. Julia Kristeva, in *Desire in Language*, elaborates a distinction between "symbolic" discourse and "semiotic" discourse: the former attempts repressively to fix meaning and is associated with the authoritarian Father, while the latter is "a disposition that is definitely heterogeneous to meaning but always in sight of it or in either a negative or surplus relationship to it" (a description remarkably applicable to Wakean discourse; Kristeva, *Desire*, 133) and is the province of the Mother and of the feminine. *Finnegans Wake*'s own unnamable, unfixable play of textual desire marks it as approaching "semiotic" discourse. For any notion of essentialist whatness, of symbolic horseness, is shown in *Finnegans Wake* to be by nature unstable, multiplicitous, heterogeneous, full of plurabilities, anti-essentialist in nature, a horse of an-Other color(s). As Giordano Bruno argued, anything is a composite of opposites; as Yeats noted, fair and foul are near of kin, and fair needs foul. In equine terms, white horses are dependent on (and are but consubstantial doubles/ negatives/inversions of) dark horses – which "wild horses shall not drag" apart (*U* 256). This is the point of the key passage, discussing the letter discovered by the hen (111); the passage harkens back to Stephen's debate in *Ulysses* and *A Portrait* on horseness and whatness/essence:

261

Well, almost any photoist worth his chemicots will tip anyone asking him the teaser that if a negative of a horse happens to melt enough while drying, well, what you do get is, well, a positively grotesquely distorted macromass of all sorts of horsehappy values and masses of meltwhile horse. Tip. Well, this freely is what must have occurred to our missive (there's a sod of a turb for you! please wisp off the grass!) unfilthed from the boucher by the sagacity of a lookmelittle likemelong hen. Heated residence in the heart of the orangeflavoured mudmound had partly obliterated the negative to start with, causing some features palpably nearer your pecker to be swollen up most grossly while the farther back we manage to wiggle the more we need the loan of a lens to see as much as the hen saw. Tip.

(*FW* 111.25–112.02)

In this passage, the letter becomes equated with (or indistinguishable from) a photograph, a portrait of a horse (like the two equine portraits in the illustrations) – so that once again horse becomes equated metaphorically with art, text, *Wake*, and the world. In the "darkroom" of the night, a photographer with his chemicals ("photoist worth his chemicots"), like an artist or a dreamer, *can* develop his pictures and portraits of the nightworld. The repeated "Tip" in this passage is Joyce's tip that we should have in mind both the Museyroom passage (with its many "Tip"s) housing Wellington's big white horse, as well as the dark horse Throwaway which was Bloom's unwitting racing "tip" for the Gold Cup. For, sure enough, the passage is full of white horse and dark horse in its discussion of horseness (and the nature of the *Wake*/world). Let me paraphrase the passage: Any photographer worth his chemicals will "tip" this answer to anyone asking him the question ("the teaser") about the essential nature and whatness of "allhorse" and of the world: that if a negative of a horse (a photo-negative of a white horse would be a dark horse) happens to melt enough to show its true colors, what you get is a distortion of the "positive" image ("positively ... distorted"), a mass of all sorts of horsehappy values and masses of melted horse (the repetition of "mass" and "masses" in the passage suggests the eucharistic transformation and consubstantiality of the opposing essences), revealing that within the horseness of the "milkwhite horse" is a pluralistic and multiple set of horses of another color, a "meltwhile horse." This is what must have occurred to the "missive" (letter, portrait, photo: text, horse, *Wake*, World) unearthed from the filthy midden pile by the hen; for heated residence in the heart of the orangeflavoured mudmound had partly obliterated the negative to start with, causing some distortion in what can only thus be considered an indeterminately relativistic approximation of any essentialist quiddity. (The "orangeflavoured mudmound" also hints that perhaps the dark horse [the negative] of Catholic Ireland [the mudmound, the Old Sod] has been distorted by the ruling influence of the Anglo-Protestant Ascendancy [Orange flavoring].)

In other words, when the true colors of a horse are allowed to run together, we see that a positive (milk-white) image is but a "negative" combination of dark horses of other colors; and that logocentric clarity (radiance, *claritas*, *quidditas*) is destabilized into pluralism, indeterminacy, and relativity. The portrait of a horse, like the letter, thus becomes a broad metaphor for the world: a midden dump containing the accumulated crap (and horse dung) of the past, pluralistic and multiple and dark (and often filthy) in nature in spite of the clear and clean (milk-white) portraits of authorized photographs (the official story), the "positives" that bleach out (and suppress/ repress) the true colors of the negatives revealed only in the "dark room" of history, those dark horses in the horseness of allhorse.

This is an extension of the Brunonian synthesis of multiple opposites as an answer to rational logocentrism, of the unerasable, unrepressible existence of the other: "from each equinoxious points of view, the one fellow's fetch being the other follow's person" (*FW* 85.28). One fellow's meat may be another person's noxious poison/person/*poisson*/fish/fetch. Appropriately, a "fetch" is an apparition, the double of a person, a *doppelgänger*. The passage suggests that, in the night world ("nox") the multiple points of view may be "noxious" (filthy, dark, and poisonous), for they include within a person a person's "fetch," in a multiplicity of meat and man and fish and fetch. Horseness is actually a diverse set of pluralistic essences – and thus these are "equinoxious points of view," nauseously ("noxious") unhorsing the monologic quiddity of St. Thomas Aquinas "as would turn the latten stomach even of a tumass equinous" (*FW* 93.09).

Appropriately, this "equinous" sentence also includes "Arthre jennyrosy" and "firewaterloover," for perhaps the largest number of horse references in *Finnegans Wake* suggest Arthur, Duke of Well-ington, the Iron Duke (whose nemesis was Jenny, or the *Wake*'s "jinnies"), victor over Napoleon at Waterloo, mounted on his famed horse Copenhagen: "This is the Willingdone on his same white harse, the Cokenhape ... his big wide harse" (*FW* 8.17, 21). Wellington and his big white horse are the *Wake*'s prime symbols for the authority and empire of white over black: white races, black races; day, night; essentialism, pluralism. However, as Glasheen (303) notes, "Arthur Duke of Wellington is scarcely to be distinguished" from King Arthur (certainly a symbol of British rule), William the Conqueror, and William III (the Orange King Billy on his Protestant "white horse") – among others (such as Viscount Wolseley, Napoleon on Marengo, and so on), all mounted figures denoting imperial and colonial rule. There are a legion of examples in *Finnegans Wake* of imperial rulers seated on the white horse of authority.

To begin with, horses are naturally linked to monarchs, as symbols of royal authority and power, through the repeated refrain from the Humpty Dumpty (HCE) rhyme, "All the King's horses and all the King's men": "And not all the king's men nor his horses / Will resurrect his corpus" (*FW* 47.26); "Of all the Wide Torsos in all the Wide Glen" (*FW* 106.01); "Before all the King's Hoarsers with all the Queen's Mum" (*FW* 219.15); "*Arthurgink's hussies and Everguin's men*" (285.L2, combining King Arthur, Queen Guinevere, Arthur Wellington's white horse, and Arthur Guinness), and so on. Most suggestive of the English empire is perhaps this reference: "the queen lying abroad ... her liege of lateenth dignisties shall come on their bay tomorrow, Michalsmas, ... there to all the king's aussies and all their king's men" (*FW* 567.13–17; "come on their bay" echoes "Camptown Races," a song about horse-racing) – in which the dynastic queen (perhaps Victoria?) in her full dignity ("dignisties"; we have "hangover"/Hanover in the previous sentence) visits on horse (on a "bay") her colonies, all the King's "Aussies."

More specifically, the king's white horse is a precise symbol of the authority of empire. The great arch-father (HCE/Finnegan/King Arthur/Arthur Wellington, and so on) is presented as "the great Finnleader himself ... on his statue riding the high horse ... Father of Otters [Arthurs] ... to the ghostwhite horse" (*FW* 214.12–15). Or, again, we find "Lapoleon, the equestrian, on his whuite hourse of Hunover," in a passage about invasion, empire, and colonialism: "the Flemish Armada ... Clunkthurf ... General Bonaboche (noo poopery!)" (*FW* 388.13–18). We have here Napoleon (Bonaparte) on his white horse, the Spanish Armada, the Flemish armada which invaded Ireland in 1169, the Battle of Clontarf, and the invading Huns (Hunover). Most importantly, we have the "whuite hourse of Hunover" that is both the "emblem of House of Hanover" (McHugh, 388) and King Billy's white horse, both equestrian symbols of British imperial domination over Catholic Ireland (no popery).

On *FW* page 135 HCE as Mr Porter ("missed a porter") is again described as a king: "Dutchlord, Dutchlord, overawes us ... like the prince of Orange and Nassau" with his "great wide cloak ... and his little white horse" (*FW* 135.08–22). The "Dutchlord" is both Protestant King William III (King Billy), the Dutch Prince of Orange and Nassau who overawed Catholic Ireland at the Boyne and who ruled on the white horse of Protestant sympathies – and another empire-mongering King William, Kaiser Wilhelm (*Deutschland, Deutschland über alles*). In another passage about battles and empire-building (including references to Hittites, Bulgars, and many battles), we learn that "Hittit was of another time, a white horsday ... along about the first equinarx" (*FW* 347.02); McHugh glosses this equine "White Horse Day" as "12 July in Ulster: King Billy on a White Horse," celebrated by Ulster Protestants as the victory at the Boyne over the papists. That equestrian statue of King Billy's white horse, which Catholics repeatedly tried to deface, returns in the description of HCE as "*he*, conscious of *e*nemies, a kingbilly whitehorsed in a finglas mill" (*FW* 75.15, my emphasis; McHugh notes that William III stayed at Finglas after the Battle of the Boyne).

But the greatest cluster of horse images centers around the "Museyroom" passage, around the museum's wax figure of "Willingdone" sitting on his big white horse, Copenhagen. Arthur, Duke of Wellington, is certainly an ideal prototype to represent British imperial authority and the Law of the Father: the most successful British general in the nineteenth century, he fought brilliantly for the Empire in battlefields ranging from India to Portugal to Waterloo – and was instrumental in foreign conquest, in stretching and defending that empire on which the sun never set. His horse Copenhagen was named after one of those battles, in which Wellington defeated the Danes – and so both its name and its white-horse symbolism make Copenhagen an emblem of British domination. Copenhagen was Wellington's most beloved horse, the one he rode all through the Peninsular War and at Waterloo.[8] Later, Wellington became Prime Minister of the realm – and so, seated atop his white horse, he melds in *Finnegans Wake* into King Billy ("Willingdone" combines William and Wellington) as a composite figure of patriarchal English domination. Significantly, the "Iron Duke"'s authority is memorialized in Dublin by the phallic ("Willingdone git the band up" in *FW* 8.34) Wellington Memorial in Phoenix Park, representing the brute power of masculine erection, conquest, and imperial authority. Appropriately, "iron panels at the base depict the duke in India [and] at Waterloo" (Glasheen, *Third Census*, 302), and its four sides are engraved with the names of all the Duke's battles.

The Museyroom passage (8–10) is one of the *Wake's* richest, most resonant, and most admired (and most studied) set pieces. I can hardly do it full justice here, but have devoted a separate chapter (see chapter 10, "The general and the sepoy: imperialism and power in the Museyroom") to a specific analysis of this passage – in which the Museyroom becomes a Joycean case study of colonial power politics and of the responses that such politics engender from the margins of empire, in which the white horse (as an authorized horseness) is itself the symbolic site for this battle of politics, ideology, and power.

But even as the symbolic white horse may claim for itself an authorized, essential horseness, it is already being unhorsed in the process, destabilized in spite of itself by the perilous modality of the very lie of monologic essence and superiority it claims. Just as words inevitably reflect that repressed (but ultimately unrepressible) double-reality in the gaps and slippages we call Freudian slips (and just as dreams are the ruptures and fissures through which the night world consciousness slips out to mock the day), so also the equine terminology in *Finnegans Wake* is already self-decentered through revealing puns. That majestic white horse of empire on which Wellington/HCE/King Billy ride is "his same white harse ... his big wide harse ... his big white harse ... his big wihte harse ... his big wide harse" (*FW* 8.17–10.21). The multiple punning going on mocks the monologic authority through the indeterminate nature of the white horse: it is at once a big white horse, a big white arse, a big wide arse, and a big white ass (donkey). The emblematically royal white horse is indistinguishable from the less imposing, less impressive possibilities that it is not a horse at all but a donkey (a comic caricature, or "negative," of a stallion) or even a man on his big white/wide arse (HCE as a horse's ass). For this Museyroom passage about Duke Wellington echoes a well-known joke in Freud's *Jokes and Their Relation to the Unconscious* (Leipzig and Vienna, 1905), related by Von Falke after a trip to Ireland, about a child who asks the guide in a waxworks museum (presumably the very museum at the base of the Wellington Memorial), in response to the guide's comment that "This is the Duke of Wellington and his horse": "Which is the Duke of Wellington and which is his horse?" – to which the guide answers, "Just as you like, my pretty child. You

14. *Copenhagen.* Wellington praised this portrait of his chestnut charger, painted by B. R. Haydon (n.d.), as a good likeness. Clearly Copenhagen is *not* a white horse. Reproduction by permission of His Grace the Duke of Wellington, KG, LVO, OBE, MC, DL.

pays your money and you takes your choice" (see also Tindall, 52; and Glasheen, 302). Invoking Freud's own study of the "joking" unconscious, Joyce's puns already reveal that the nature of a horse's reality is inherently unstable (de-stabled), decentered into man and horse and arse and ass.

The inherent doubleness in the "harse" (horse/arse) on which the Father sits is implicit in the very concept of a ruler sitting on a high horse – for what goes up must come down, as HCE's own name (Humpty) suggests: sitting on a wall results in a great fall. He is "The old man on his ars. Great Scrapp!" (*FW* 514.34): in the midst of a great scrap, the Old Man on his horse is unhorsed, and becomes the old man on his ass, the deposed king – like Richard III – wishing for his high horse again: "Roger. Thuthud. Heigh hohse, heigh hohse, our kingdome from an orse" (*FW* 373.16). Without the horse which upholds his authority, the king thuds to his fall. One position implies (and depends on) its opposite: for pride goeth necessarily with a fall.

The indivisibility of the "positive" official version from its photo-negative inversion is suggested even in the official portraiture of

15. *Wellington Musing on the Field of Waterloo.* 1839 painting
by B. R. Haydon of the Duke and Copenhagen. Reproduction
courtesy of The Board of Trustees of the National Museums and
Galleries on Merseyside (Walker Art Gallery, Liverpool).

equestrian power, Copenhagen the big white horse. Please notice the
attached painting of Duke. Wellington's horse, which the Duke
himself praised as a remarkable likeness: Wellington's beloved
Copenhagen was *not* a white horse at all, but "a strong chestnut"
(Longford, *Years*, 136), a dark horse! Surely Joyce, who in *Finnegans
Wake* repeatedly shows that he knew all about Wellington and his
career, had seen some of the many paintings and representations of
Copenhagen at Waterloo (as in the sample illustration) and knew
that Copenhagen was not white.[9] Rather, in his depiction of "Willingdone"'s Copenhagen as King Billy's white horse of empire and
authority, Joyce – like a Freudian slip or a Wakean pun – is revealing
the repressed lie behind the official story, the uncertainty and
absurdity of any essentialist or monologic claim to authority and
Horseness (and genetic purity), in which the whiteness of the
Emperor's horse has the same indubitable authoritativeness as the
Emperor's new clothes.

268

In fact, it is the very nature of *Finnegans Wake* to call into question all monologic claims to a unitary authority, revealing all essences to be multiple, dependent on their opposites/doubles/twins/fetches, the "negatives" of a horse in the *Wake*'s darkroom of horseness. For "When Lapac walks backwords he's darkest horse in Capalisoot. You knew me once but you won't know me twice" (*FW* 487.32–33). But in the doubleness of the night world we *can* "know twice," for we can read words "backwords": and so the white horse of the day (*Capal*, Irish for horse) in Dublin's Chapelizod is unmasked at night as "Lapac," the "darkest horse in Capalisoot" (the sooty darkness of Capal). In the dark room it is hard to tell dark from white, Negroid from Aryan, like "fight niggers with whilde roarses" (*FW* 40.13): while the Empire fights the "nigger" Others with its white horses (both literally and symbolically), the very notion of the enemy Other is itself questioned (in the echo of "white niggers" – and of "white Negroes," as the English had labeled the Irish), for "wild horses" couldn't really separate the interdependent doubleness of black and white.

All attempts to assert the Self by denying the Other are problematized as unstable in the multipleness of *Finnegans Wake*, a point underscored by the doubleness of everything in the book, the omnipresence of "twins" – Shem and Shaun, Ondt and Gracehoper, Mutt and Jute, Jacob and Esau, Cain and Abel, Brutus and Cassius, and so on. One frequent version of the vying brothers is Hengest and Horsa, equine by the nature of the latter's name – e.g., "too much hanguest or hoshoe" (*FW* 63.22). Hengest (aka Hengist) and Horsa were the legendary brothers who led the Saxon invasion of England (in the fifth century AD). In the *Wake* the great Father on his high horse is a Brunonian synthesis of the two twins, Hengest and Horsa, both contained in the "horse" which upholds him: "Is that the great Finnleader himself on his joakimono on his statue riding the high horse there forehengist?" (*FW* 214.12). This doubleness is not only undeniable and unrepressible but overdetermined, for in the rivalry between Horsa and Hengest the clarity of essence and difference is clouded, veiled, perhaps missing. Horsa suggests "horse," but *Hengest* is the Old English term for "horse" (McHugh, *Annotations*) – and so the two competing essences are basically indistinguishable.[10] As usual with Joyce, as with Vico, etymology is destiny/history. Horseness becomes an equivalent of the pluralistic indeterminacy of the midden heap and melting pot of history, in which horse and horsesauce are indistinguishable: "Here, Hengest and Horsesauce, take your heads out of that taletub! And leave your hinnyhennyhindyou! It's haunted. The chamber. Of errings. Whoan, tug, trace, stirrup!" (*FW* 272.17–21; appropriately, a "hinny" is the hybrid offspring of a stallion and a female donkey). The horse here seems to belong to the brothers, walking behind them and neighing like Swift's whinnying Houyhnhnms ("taletub" and "hinnyhennyhindyou," a Museyroom combination of Hinnessy-Jenny-jinny-hinny-and-Hindu). But the Museyroom wax figure of Willingdone on a horse is really an equine HCE ("haunted ... chamber ... errings") as an amalgam encompassing both his sons (Hengest and Horsa) in a four-part Vico-equine cycle (Whoa! tug, trace, and stirrup; or one, two, three, up – the cadence for mounting a horse) in the waxworks chamber of horrors; as such, *Finnegans Wake* and the Wellington Museyroom are both a Chamber of Horse, and this lovely passage is a microcosm of Joycean/Viconian/Brunonian history.

In a much more familiar passage, the wonderful Question 9 of Book I, chapter 6 (the "collideorscape" question), a passage about the nature of reality and dreams (and Hamlet's fear of the afterworld, perchance to dream), one of the many things at issue is the nature of horses ("old hopeinhaven" – both Copenhagen and Hamlet's Denmark – is here in *FW* 143.10):

> ... but Heng's got a bit of Horsa's nose and Jeff's got the signs of Ham round his mouth and the beau that spun beautiful as it palls, what roserude and oragious grows gelb and greem, blue out of the ind of it! Violet's dyed! then *what* would that fargazer seem to seemself to seem seeming of, dimm it all?
>
> Answer: A collideorscape!
>
> (*FW* 143.22–28)

In the "dimm" and "dinmurk" (143.07) of the Wakean night (as in Copenhagen and Hamlet's Denmark), Hengest and Horsa are – by their very names and etymologies and genes – indistinguishable, each one looking like a horse's nose. So also Jeff appears to be Ham: the reference is not only to Hamlet, but – more importantly in this context – to another set of brothers, Ham and Japheth, sons (along with Shem) of Noah. This is a passage about horses (Hengest and Horsa) and about colors (all the colors of the rain "beau" are mentioned), about the unseparability of white horses and dark horses in horse "races" and racial colors; differences in these photo-finishes are not even discernible by a "horse's nose." So also Japheth has the signs of Ham round his mouth. As Shem is the putative originator of the Semitic race, so Ham is the putative source of the black (Hemitic) race and Japheth of the white/Aryan race. The

Western characterization of Africans as "the sons of Ham" has long been useful in the rationalization of the oppression of blacks, since blackness – "the signs of Ham" – was conveniently interpreted as the literal sign of the curse that Noah placed on Ham.[11] Yet, in Joyce's pluralistic world, those convenient and discursive distinctions of race and color simply do not obtain, for "Jeff's [Japheth] got the signs of Ham round his mouth." Color is very much the point, for the new world promised to Noah and inherited by his sons was sealed with a beautiful rainbow, and this "beau that spun beautiful" includes all the colors of the spectrum (here: rose, red, orange, yellow [G. *gelb*], green, blue, indigo, violet). While Hamlet may lament ("I know not seems") living in a "dimm" world in which there is no clear black and white (Hemitic and Japhetic) and all acts of "seeing" are perspectival acts of "seeming" ("seem to seemself to seem seeming"), of rainbows and kaleidoscopes – Joyce on the other hand revels in the colorful pluralism and indeterminacy. In the "collide-orscape" of *Finnegans Wake*, there are a multitude of colors, none of which can claim an essential or distinguishing authority (not even by a horse's nose) over any other.

What is true of competing brothers – Shem and Shaun, Ham and Japheth, Hengest and Horsa, Cain and Abel – is true of the Duke himself, Wellington seated on Copenhagen:

With is the winker for the muckwits of willesly and nith is the nod for the umproar napollyon and hitheris poorblond piebold hoerse. Huirse. With its tricuspidal hauberkehelm coverchaf emblem on. For the man that broke the ranks at Monte Sinjon.

(FW 273.25–274.02)

In this passage, Wellington/HCE – as the man who broke Napoleon's ranks at Mont St. Jean, the geographical center of Napoleon's forces at Waterloo – is hardly to be distinguished from his rival Other, for he is wearing the Lipoleums' tricolored hat (the "tricuspidal h ... c ... emblem"), an amalgamated figure seated on Copenhagen/Marengo the "poorblond piebold hoerse" (the horse itself is at once white/ blond and piebald). Moreover, Wellington is also not to be distin-guished from his own *actual* brother–Other, Richard Wesley, the Marquess of Wellesley ("muckwits of Willesley"). In the "winker" and the "nod" of the "poorblond" horse, all possibilities are possible – for, as the old proverb goes, "A nod is as good as a wink to a blind horse." The Marquess of Wellesley, the Duke of Wellington's older brother, had himself a distinguished diplomatic career and became

Viceroy and Lord Lieutenant to Ireland. But, unlike his younger brother who grew to symbolize the power of the English empire, Wellesley defended the Irish and advocated Catholic emancipation, so angering not only the anti-Catholic King George IV but also the Orange factions that there was a riot in 1822 in which Orangemen threw bottles at him. As the Eleventh (1911) *Encyclopaedia Britannica* (the edition Joyce sometimes consulted) noted: "From early life Wellesley had, unlike his brother, been an advocate of Catholic emancipation, and with the claim of the Irish Catholics to justice he henceforward identified himself" (506). When in 1828 his brother Arthur, who opposed Catholic emancipation, became Prime Minister, Wellesley resigned the Lord-Lieutenancy. Thus, Wellesley as Irish-Catholic dark horse becomes the twin-Other, the "negative," of Anglo-Protestant Wellington/William III (Willingdone) on his big white horse.

As conqueror for the English empire while his brother Richard defended the Irish Catholics, Arthur Wellington would have liked – like Cain from Abel – to separate himself and ask: "Am I my brother's keeper?" But he cannot: just as the chestnut Copenhagen can only claim white-horse status by denying his own basic darkness, so also Wellington would have liked to deny the fact that he was *in fact Irish*, born and raised in Ireland. In the Museyroom, on his big white horse, he is described thus: "This is the Willingdone, bornstable ghentleman, tinders his matchbox to the cursigan Shimar Shin" (*FW* 10.17–18). Those who seize authority repeatedly wish to claim longstanding noble origins, to the manor born of stable gentlemanly families, repudiating their interdependent relationship (genetic – as with brother Richard; economic; colonial; racial) from those on the margins, those born of "lower" origins, like the Corsican ("cursigan") Napoleon or the "hinndoo" Shimar Shin. Willingdone as "bornstable ghentleman" refers directly to Wellington's infamous answer (so much like Cain's) when he was asked if he were Irish: "If a gentleman happens to be born in a stable, it does not follow that he should be called a horse" (McHugh, *Annotations*, 10). In denying his own Irishness, Wellington was – like Cain – trying to deny the humanity and allhorseness in all of us. For, as in Copenhagen the chestnut "big white horse" or in the imperial stable-born Duke or in the humble stable-born Jesus in Bethlehem, our true quiddities are, as in Hopkins's "inscape," an unexpected explosion of repressed colors: for "blue-bleak embers, ah my dear, fall, gall themselves, and gash gold-vermilion" ("The Windhover").

In the "stable" world of *Finnegans Wake*'s equine values, all horsenesses are essentially un-stable, for "From each equinoxious points of view [even the pronoun 'each' is rendered plural here], the one fellow's fetch [is] the other follow's person" (*FW* 85.28). The multipleness of the "fetch" as double and other (meat/fish/fetch/ *poisson*/poison/person) suggests that the "whatness of allhorse" is not a single horseness, but an "allness" that encompasses Everybody (as in "Here Comes"): "Ear! Ear! Weakear! [HC Earwicker] An allness eversides! We but miss that horse elder yet cherchant of the wise graveleek in cabbuchin garden. That his be foison, old Caubeenhauben!" (*FW* 568.26–28) Old Copenhagen's foison/fetch/ poison/person is a "horse elder" whose quiddity is an "allness eversides" which is multitudinous and all-inclusive. Like Ahab's white whale, the white horse is a "poorblond piebold hoerse," a blind horse and blank text[12] in which nothing is clear but in which all inscriptions and equinoxious viewpoints are not only possible but already encoded. Thus the *claritas* (which Stephen equates with *quidditas*) of a clear, univocal *parole* breaks down into garbled, unclear, indeterminate hoarseness: "And this is ... the funst man in Danelagh, willingtoned ... that born appalled [Bonaparte] ... And thisens his speak quite hoarse. Dip" (*FW* 334.12–16; this "willingtoned" seems Danish, so perhaps Copenhagen here is quite literal). The clarity of the "big white horse" of authority here is rendered, within the realm of linguistic utterance, as the de-stabilized, decentered murkiness of unclear "speech" – as "speak quite hoarse," as garbled and unclarified texts (like the *Wake*) containing multiple inscriptions full of surplus traces which we supplement with our own equine-nox-ious viewpoints. Thus, the peculiar language of Joyce's Wakean text defies the possibility of a "correct" reading in order to demonstrate how impoverishingly reductive any "authoritative" interpretation is.

All of these connections between horses and races (ethnic races and horse races), colors (racial colors and horse colors), and the nature of reality (Bishop Berkeley's colors versus monochromatic quidditas) are invoked near the end of the book in "the whorse proceedings" (*FW* 610.02) between the Archdruid Bulkily and St. Patrick, on *FW* 609–13. As the insurgent Buckley who shoots the Russian General (in the Crimean War which resulted from the clash between British and Russian imperialistic aspirations) or as the philosopher Berkeley whose relativistic pluralism (Stephen's "coloured signs" in "Proteus") challenged traditional metaphysics, Bulkily challenges the monologic authority symbolized by the dogmatic St. Patrick. The "whorse proceedings" are a horse-race spectated by commentators Muta and Juva: "Peredos Last in the Grand Natural" (*FW* 610.34) – the Grand National horserace/debate over the nature of the Natural (of Paradise Lost). In this race, Peredos (a famous racehorse; Glasheen, *Third Census*, 231; McHugh, *Annotations*, 610) comes in "Last" while "Velivision victor. Dubs newstage oldtime turftussle, recalling Winny Willy Widger" (*FW* 610.35–36). Muta and Juva take bets on this "turftussle":

Muta: Haven money on stablecert?
Juva: Tempt to wom Outsider!

(*FW* 610.17–18)[13]

The "stablecert" is St. Patrick, the favorite (a "dead cert") from the stable of Christian dogmatics (like Wellington, Christ was born in a stable) and textual stability/certainty. The challenger/temptor is a "tempt to wom" dark horse, like Throwaway a rank "Outsider." The favorite may be the great racehorse Peredos (who like Sceptre is not victorious), but the "victor" is "Velivision" ridden by "Winny Willy Widger" (*Veni, vidi, vici* – i.e., the *Victor*), coming and conquering – alias J. W. Widger (an "amateur rider" and the "most famous of [that] Waterford racing-associated family," according to McHugh, *Annotations*, 610). "Velivision," significantly, suggests not stable clarity but the indeterminacy of vision through a veil or vellum, a gauzy film or membrane.

For Bulkily stands for Berkeley's relativism and pluralism of color (in both racial and chromatic senses) while St. Patrick stands for the black-and-white color blindness of imperial authority.[14] It is suggestive in this context that throughout the passage Bulkily seems to speak in Chinese pidgin and Patrick in Japanese pidgin: during the writing of *Finnegans Wake* in the 1920s and 1930s, the Japanese empire was ruthlessly colonizing China. St. Patrick is described by Juva as "the Chrystanthemlander with his porters of bonzos, pompommy plonkyplonk, the ghariwallahs" (*FW* 609.32–33) – a Christian leader (doubtlessly on a white horse) leading his troop of native porters and "ghariwallahs" (Anglo-Indian: native horse-drawn ["plonkyplonk"] taxi drivers). The horse-race becomes a metaphysical debate about "colour," in which Berkeley argues for the "grand natural" as a "photoprismic velamina of hueful panepiphanal world spectacurum" (*FW* 611.13–14), a veiled spectrum of many colors and races. Stephen's *quidditas*/epiphany is displaced by a whole "panepiphanal" spectrum. Countering arguments about essential quiddities and the "inside true inwardness of reality, the Ding hvad in idself id est" (*FW* 611.20) – i.e., the Whatness of the Thing reveals in its punning slippage the veiled Id – Bulkily counter-proposes that "all objects ... allside showed themselves in trues coloribus resplendent with sextuple gloria of light" (*FW* 611.22–23), that objects contain a glorious "allsides" and "allness eversides" (*FW* 568.27). "Rumnant Patholic" (Roman Catholic Patrick), however, does not understand the complex argument ("no catch all that") for he is "stareotypopticus": his optical color-blindness is a stereotyping, essentializing urge to see everything in black and white, for he is a "niggerblonker" (*FW* 611.24–35). Appropriately, Bulkily's bulky and open-ended and complex argument begins with "Tunc" (*FW* 611.04), suggesting the Tunc page of the Book of Kells, full of color and light and interpretational possibility and multipleness. St. Patrick's re-buttal begins, conversely, with "Punc." (*FW* 12.16) – not only the voice of authority dismissing the "punk" but a terse and emphatic punc-tuational period (German *punkt*), closing off discussion in an aggressive imposition of traditional rule and grammar.

As with St. Patrick's rationalized and imposed clarity, the following is a passage from the *Wake* in which the speaker is trying to argue for logocentric clarity and certainty, for old-fashioned textual as well as political authority:

... while we in our wee free state, holding to that prestatute in our charter, may have our irremovable doubts as to the whole sense of the lot, the interpretation of any phrase in the whole, the meaning of every word of a phrase so far deciphered out of it, however unfettered our Irish daily independence, we must vaunt no idle dubiosity as to its genuine authorship and holusbolus authoritativeness. And let us bring-theecease to beakerings on that clink, olmond bottler! On the face of it, to volt back to our desultory horses, and for your roughshod mind, bafflelost bull, the affair is a thing once for all done and there you are somewhere and finished in a certain time, be it a day or a year or even supposing, it should eventually turn out to be a serial number of goodness gracious alone knows how many days or years.

(*FW* 117.34–118.11)

In a passage referring in part to the heated debates over constitutional charters regarding "our Irish daily independence" which resulted in the creation (in 1922) of the Irish "free state," the speaker here expresses his nostalgic desire for a pre-lapsarian (pre-structuralist!) logocentrism still confident in "irremovable doubts as to the whole sense of the lot [the world, the *Wake*, the Free State of Ireland and of the universe], the interpretation of any phrase ... the meaning of every word" – eschewing all "dubiosity" so as to accept "holusbolus authoritativeness." But this certainty is, as the speaker admits, merely "on the face of it" – and in *Finnegans Wake* nothing is "on the face of it," for we "volt back to our desultory horses." To "volt back" is literally to re-volt, and the sentence admits the insurgent otherness of multiplicity, for despite the speaker's confident bravado we are still "bafflelost" in the many-sidedness of our "desultory horses": Rabelais's Gargantua learned, while riding, to jump from horse to horse, and these horses were called *chevaux desultoires*, desultory horses – as in a rodeo (Buffalo Bill is here in "bafflelost bull"). This is the nature of horseness – of the world and of the *Wake*: that we never know for sure, but that we're changing horses (in midstream) all the time, that the reality we are riding on is changing beneath us all the time in "the chaosmos of Alle ... moving and changing every part of the time" (*FW* 118.21–23). The desultoriness of horseness thus becomes a universal metaphor for the ineluctable modality of all modalities in this anti-stable world of ours.

What, finally, *is* it to be a "bequined torse" (*FW* 607.33)? Big, white, equine, and horsey? What is it to be "truly torse" (*FW* 165.18)? What is the essential picture/representation of horseness? An important passage (602) invokes the "negative of a horse" passage (111) to help answer the teaser:

The Games funeral at Valleytemple. Saturnights pomps, exhabiting that corricatore of a harss, revealled by Oscur Camerad. The last of Dutch Schulds, perhumps. Pipe in Dream Cluse. Uncovers Pub History.

(*FW* 602.21–24)

The "funeral games" (that is, the wakes) of the *Wake* are a night world of the Rabelaisian carnivalesque ("Saturnights" and saturnalia) in which the official photographic portrait of the royal equestrian presence, the big white horse, is – in the "dark room" of the *Wake*'s pub history as revealed by our *camera obscura* (literally, dark room) of photographic/cinematic film (Oscars) – actually the "negative of a horse," a caricature: "that corricatore of a harss," the horse as dark horse/arse/ass. What it reveals is a subversively dark horse that presages perhaps ("perhumps") the overthrow of the Hump-Father by the insurgent commies (Oscar Comrade), and the last of Dutch Schulz (perhaps an Oscar-winning gangster film?), and last of the "Dutch" House of Orange: a pipe dream perhaps, but also a pre-lapsarian dream closed by the bolshevik-insurrectionist Cad with his pipe/gun/bomb ("Pipe in Dream Cluse"). In the "Saturnights pomps" of wakes and *Wake*, the "negatives" of otherness are allowed a saturnalia of carnivalesque play repressed by our daytime cameras. "Negatives of a horse" and "corricatores of a harss" define a Joycean style of photography: "This genre of portraiture of changes of mind in order to be truly torse should evoke the bush soul of females" (*FW* 165.18). Among "the Negroes of Calabar," a "bush soul" was only the "external soul embodied" (McHugh, *Annotations*, 165). How to be "truly torse"? In this Joycean genre, not essentialist or logocentric but full of "changes of mind in order to be truly torse" – jumping from one desultory horse to another in midstream – portraits of a horse are like the pictures of the dark horse Throwaway or of the "big white" chestnut Copenhagen: Wakean portraits are not exclusive, but rather "allnesses eversides" that also include the bush souls of females, of "Negroes," of bush men – of all those dark mares and horses and Others maginalized by the daytime empire of the world's Sceptres and Cocks of the North.

In Joyce's works, the nature of authority has less to do with "white horses" than with "desultory horses," all the dark horses and rank outsiders and throwaways silenced into the dark room of the repressed Other. Joyce's pluralistic world – of many horses (white horse, dark horse, chestnuts, piebalds, isabelle nags, and so on), of many races, many colors, many languages, many discourses – belies the repressive authority of a monologic, essentializing "horseness." In the kaleidoscopic anti-stable of horses of many colors, "allness" is the whatness of allhorse: in the dark room of the unrepressed consciousness, the "negative of a horse" yields up, not a single or solid milk-white horse, but a "macromass of all sorts of horsehappy values and masses of meltwhile horse" (*FW* 111.28–29).

10

The general and the sepoy: imperialism and power in the Museyroom

Colin MacCabe has suggested, as previously cited, that "*Finnegans Wake*, with its sustained dismemberment of the English linguistic and literary heritage, is perhaps best understood in relation to the struggle against imperialism" ("Finnegans," 4). With its polyglot multiphonics displacing the centrality of English, the *Wake*, like Shem, "would wipe alley english spooker, or multiphoniaksically spuking, off the face of the erse" (*FW* 178.06–7);[1] Joyce himself had said (as earlier quoted) that "I'd like a language which is above all languages ... I cannot express myself in English without closing myself in a tradition" (Zweig, 275). McCabe's claim, while somewhat reductive, seems to me nevertheless suggestive since the struggle against imperialism and the structures of colonial authority is itself already such a major and overt topic in *Finnegans Wake*. I wish here to re-present the *Wake*'s Willingdone Museyroom as a site, and a case study, of colonial power dynamics; and as an example of the dense texture of Joyce's ideological commentary on such dynamics, layered and compressed into the textual topography of *Finnegans Wake*. The Museyroom passage (pages 8–10) is a deservedly celebrated passage, wonderful and rich and full of resonant meanings to pursue. Henriette Power has previously investigated, in her essay on "Shahrazahde" in *Finnegans Wake*, the intricacies of the Museyroom's "hinndoo seeboy" as a "hidden," "seeing" boy within the contexts of voyeurism and concealment. I would like to focus on his identification as a "Hindu sepoy" reacting to the great British general, the Iron Duke of Wellington.

Dominating the wax museum that is the "Willingdone Museyroom" (*FW* 8.10) is Arthur, Duke of Wellington on his big white horse,

Copenhagen. Around him are the Lipoleum(s), the three young insurgents who sometimes seem one and are collectively represented by their "triplewon [three-in-one] hat," the "Lipoleumhat" (*FW* 8.15–16); they are aided by the female "jinnies" (Jenny was a blackmailer of Wellington). Thus, the Duke of Wellington is presented as an archetypal patriarch and wielder of authority and power, sitting on his high horse over the children who try – in the universal power struggle – to unhorse the Father and the Law of the Father, and make Humpty have a great fall. Appropriately, the passage is peppered with hundreds of references to famous battles and martial conflicts, especially those from Wellington's own life, which Joyce obviously knew in intimate detail. For example, in these three pages we find not only many references to Wellington's celebrated horse Copenhagen (the "Cokenhape," and so on) but to Wellington's many battles: "inimyskilling" (Inniskilling dragoons at Waterloo), "Belchum" (Waterloo, Belgium), "Dispatch ... Dispitch" (*The Dispatches of the Duke of Wellington during his Various Campaigns, 1834–9*), "thin red lines" (Wellington's famed Thin Red Line), "Salamangra" (Salamanca, 1812), "hundred days'," "Tarra's widdars" (Torres Vedras, 1810), "blooches" (General Blücher), "solphereens" (Solferino, 1859), "Almeidagad!" (Almeida, 1811), "Arthiz too loose!" (Orthez, 1814; Toulouse, 1814), "Cumbrum!" (General Cambronne at Waterloo), "ousterlists" (Austerlitz, 1805), "Dalaveras fimmieras" (Talavera, 1809; Vimeiro, 1808), "hiena" (Jena, 1806), "lipsyg" (Leipzig, 1815), "insoult" (French Marshal Soult, Waterloo's nemesis all through the Peninsular War), "Hney, hney, hney!" (French Marshall Ney), "upjump and pumpim" (Wellington's famed "Up, guards, and at them!"), "cursigan" (Corsican Napoleon), "Basucker" (Bussaco, 1810), and so on.[2] I would like, however, to concentrate on the lesser-known Wellington references – the numerous allusions here to his military campaigns in India (prior to battling Napoleon in the Peninsular War), in which he was instrumental in expanding England's Oriental empire.

"This is the Willingdone on his same white harse, the Cokenhape ... his big wide harse" (*FW* 8.17, 21). The Iron Duke of Wellington seated on his big white horse is, like all such equestrian statues, a stylized symbol of the power of authority over those it rules. Wellington himself is an ideal embodiment of such imperial power – having been first a general who fought brilliantly in India during the Mahratta War and expanded England's colonial power in the Orient; who then defeated Napoleon in the Peninsular War and again at

16. *Portrait of Wellington* by Sir Thomas Lawrence. Writes
Elizabeth Longford about this painting: "The artist began by
putting a watch in the Duke's hand, as if waiting for his
Prussian allies, but the Duke expostulated, 'That will never do. I
was *not* waiting for the Prussians at Waterloo. Put a telescope in
my hand, if you please.'" (Longford, *Wellington: Pillar of State*,
illustration 14.) Reproduction courtesy of Wellington College,
Crowthorne, Berkshire, England.

Waterloo; and who later became England's Prime Minister. As such, he is a symbol of domination by patriarchal power and violence; it is appropriate that in Dublin he is represented by the phallic Wellington Memorial in Phoenix Park, embodied in the Museyroom by Willingdone's erection ("Willingdone git the band up" in *FW* 8.34 and 9.09) and by his phallic "mormorial tallowscoop Wounderworker" of "Sexcaliber hrosspower" (*FW* 8.35–36), combining phallic telescope, candle (tallow), obelisk memorial (marble "mormorial"), sex, power, and violence (six-caliber and Excalibur). (In fact, I suspect that Joyce's "tallowscoop" comes from a story associated with a painting of Wellington [see illustration] in which he was originally depicted with a watch in his hand, but – in truly militaristic fashion [notice the phallic sword hanging from his legs] – expostulated: "That will never do. I was *not* 'waiting' for the Prussians at Waterloo. Put a telescope in my hand, if you please" [Longford, *Pillar*].)

Wellington on his white horse is only the most prominent and frequent of many references in *Finnegans Wake* to rulers on white horses (including Napoleon on his white charger Marengo), all figures denoting imperial and colonial rule. Such an emblem of empire is especially appropriate if we remember that the "white horse" was the specific emblem of the House of Hanover, the English ruling dynasty (later the Windsors), and was the personal symbol of King William III, the "King Billy" whose equestrian statue dominated College Green; see also chapter 9 of this study for a detailed analysis of the equine/imperial symbolism in Joyce's works.

In the Museyroom, the description of Wellington on Copenhagen is indistinguishable from King Billy, for he is "the big Sraughter Willingdone [combining William and Wellington], grand and magentic [like His Majesty] in his goldtin spurs and his ironed dux [Iron Duke] and his quarter brass woodyshoes and his magnate's gharters" (*FW* 8.17–19). McHugh (8) notes that "brass money and wooden shoes" was an "Orange Toast to William III." And, sure enough, two lines later we find the lipoleums described as "the three lipoleum boyne grouching down in the living detch" (*FW* 8.21–22): three rebellious Irish boys crouching down on the ground in a living ditch (i.e., Ireland, the peat bog and old sod; as opposed to the Orange King on his high horse) waiting for King Billy at the Boyne. Thus, Wellington on his white horse (as conqueror of India and defender of the empire against challengers like Napoleon) and King Billy (as conqueror/oppressor of Catholic Ireland) unite into a collective figure (in which Ireland and India are correspondingly united as a collective victim of English imperialism), a symbol of colonial domination and power politics. The centerpiece of the Museyroom is but a wax version of at least three famous equestrian statues that all symbolize the imperial, Protestant, English rule: the statue of King Billy on College Green, Dublin; the giant Wyatt equestrian memorial to Wellington in London (see illustration); and an equestrian statue of Wellington in the center of Madras.[3]

After all, as we learn, the lipoleum "boyne" in the ditch, living like dogs, are not merely Irish colonials, but include those of the Empire's darker "Oriental" races. The Museyroom tour guide goes on to point out the three: "This is the bog lipoleum mordering the lipoleum beg. A Gallawghurs argaumunt. This is the petty lipoleum boy that was nayther bag nor bug. Assaye, assaye!" (*FW* 8.24–26) While the first two boys are similar (like bog and beg, with perhaps an echo of "murdering Irish"), it is the third boy who is neither "bag nor bug" and is perhaps the most rebellious ("*nay*ther"). While the first two are Irish rivals "mordering" each other or holding an argument among Irishmen (Gallaghers' argument), the identity of the third boy, who is neither "bag nor bug," is hinted at quite obliquely and Orientally: for "Galwilgarh" and "Argaum" were both battles in the Mahratta War (1803) Wellington conducted in India; they followed upon the heels of the most decisive and bloodiest battle of that war, Wellington's great victory at Assaye. These three battles broke the powers of the Mahrattas, and treaties were agreed to forthwith (*Britannica XI*, 1911, vol. 28, 507). (The museum visitor's startled reaction to the discovery of this hidden identity is "I say! I say!") Confirmation of the Indian identity of the third lipoleum occurs three lines later: "This is Mont Tivel, this is Mont Tipsey, this is the Grand Mons Injun" (*FW* 8.28–29) – in which the third lipoleum is pegged as an "Injun."[4]

These identifications all occur on the first of the three Museyroom pages (8). After much description of Willingdone's skirmishes with the jinnies (9), the Museyroom episode concludes (10) with the lipoleums' attack on Willingdone. Again, these "nice young bachelors" (like Willingdone with his "tallowscoop," they are quite nicely "hung" themselves) are identified by the tour guide: "Lipoleums is nice hung bushellors. This is the hiena hinnessy laughing alout at the Willingdone. This is lipsyg dooley krieging the funk from the hinnessy. This is the hinndoo Shimar Shin between the dooley boy and the hinnessy" (*FW* 10.03–7). The first two appear to be Irish – Hennessey and Dooley – or perhaps Irish and American, since Irish-

17. *Wyatt's equestrian statue.* Illustration of Wellington's
London funeral procession, as it passes Apsley House and
Matthew Cotes Wyatt's colossal bronze equestrian statue of the
Duke. Reproduction courtesy of The Victoria and Albert
Museum, London.

American comic P. F. Dunne wrote a book called *The Dooley
Philosophy*, featuring two Irish-Americans named Dooley and Hennessey (Glasheen, *Third Census*, 76, 127). The third is a Hindu named
Shimar Shin. Standing "between the dooley boy and the hinnessy,"
"hinndoo" as the third is a combination of the other two
("Hinnessy" plus Dooley) – one ("hinn") plus two ("doo") equals
"hinndoo." Whether Irish, American, or Hindu, all are English
colonials. Their three-in-one solidarity is again symbolized by "the
threefoiled hat of lipoleums" (*FW* 10.08) – not only Napoleon's
tricornered hat but a "trefoil," suggesting the Irish shamrock, St.
Patrick's emblem of Ireland's trinitarian Catholic faith. In Joyce's
pencil sketch (in *First-Draft*, 50) of Waterloo, the signs "∧ ⌐ ⌐ "
show Shaun (∧), Shem (⌐), and standing between them ⌐ as their
composite substance (see McHugh, *Annotations*, ix; Glasheen, 127) –
suggesting a religious mystery in this holy trinity of the collective
"hinndoo." Furthermore, as Brendan O Hehir (also McHugh,

Annotations, 10) points out, *siomar sin* is Irish for "that fair-dark trefoil (or shamrock)" (Glasheen, *Third Census*, 127). Thus, the "hinndoo Shimar Shin" is a combination of the fair Irish and the dark Hindu in a tripartite unity, joined in a religion of rebellion from subservience (motto: *non serviam*) whose religious symbolism is a shamrock-like trefoil, the "threefoiled hat." Just as the figure of Willingdone on a white horse unites William III (who conquered and tyrannized the Irish and whose symbol was a white horse) and Wellington (who conquered the Hindus in the Mahratta War, and was himself notorious for opposing Irish Catholic Emancipation) on Copenhagen, so also the three lipoleums unite into a collective archetype (Irish, American, Hindu) and united cause of colonial insurrection against the imperial power.

As so frequently happens in colonial uprisings, the immediate cause of conflict is the colonizer's religious arrogance or intolerance. Just as the Orange faction's repression of Catholic Ireland led to terrorist acts (such as blowing up King Billy's horse), so also the incident in the Museyroom is precipitated by Willingdone's arrogance toward the lipoleums' religious icon: "This the wixy old Willingdone picket up the half of the threefoiled hat of lipoleums fromoud of the bluddle filth ... This is the Willingdone hanking the half of the hat of lipoleums up the tail on the buckside of his big white harse" (*FW* 10.07–11). Not only does Willingdone yank the mystically-joined, sacred trefoil-icon in half, but he then uses it to wipe his horse's ass. "That was the last joke of Willingdone. [by the First Duke of Wellington, and it was a direct] Hit, hit, hit! This is the same white harse of the Willingdone, Culpenhelp, waggling his tailoscrupp with the half of a hat of lipoleums to insoult on the hinndoo seeboy. Hney, hney, hney! (Bullsrag! Foul!)" (*FW* 10.11–15). Stung by the direct hit of Willingdone's cruel "insoult" to their religion, the colonial "hinndoo" (Irish and Indian) can only cry "Foul!" – but even that cry is a marginalized discourse silenced and bracketed by an authoritative grammar of brackets and parentheses: "(Bullsrag! Foul!)" – in contrast to the loud and uncontained laughter (ha, ha, ha) of Willingdone ("Hit, hit, hit!") and his horse ("Hney, hney, hney!" – the neigh and "insoult" also mock Napoleon's marshals, Ney and Soult).

Can the subaltern speak?[5] Silenced into the bracketed margins of official discourse, but angered by the insult to his religion and thus moved by a cultural desire to represent himself, the Irish-Hindu colonial "hinndoo" responds in the only effective discourse available to him, violence – the bomb: "This is the hinndoo waxing ranjymad for a bombshoob" (*FW* 10.09; "Ranji," aka "Jam Sahib" [Glasheen, *Third Census*, 243], was a popular Rajput cricketer who played for England and made over 3,000 runs, thus a princely Hindu who can make "hits" of his own). Mad as a hatter in his anger, the "hinndoo" responds to Wellington's famed rallying cry ("Up, guards, and at 'em") with a Hindu war cry of his own: "This is the seeboy, madrashattaras, upjump and pumpim, cry to the Willingdone: Ap Pukkaru! Pukka yurap!" (*FW* 10.15–17).[6] "Madrashattaras" combines Madras (a Mahratta city, dominated by an equestrian statue of Wellington) and the Mahratta War won by Wellington; the "hinndoo"'s war cry suggests that things are no longer *pukka* for Willingdone, and sounds suspiciously like either "Bugger Europe!" or "Bugger your arse!" (the "harse" is, after all, the seat of Willingdone's power). "This is the Willingdone, bornstable ghentleman, tinders his maxbotch to the cursigan Shimar Shin. Basucker youstead!" (*FW* 10.17–19). Wellington's verbal response to the cursing Hindu (also Corsican/Napoleonic) upstart is one offering ("tinder"-ing) battle (Wellington's victory over Napoleon at Bussaco, Portugal), massacre ("Basucker youstead" sounds like "Massacre *usted*"), and firepower ("tinders" and "matchbox" ["maxbotch"]).

It is significant that our "hinndoo" lipoleum, both Irish and Indian, becomes newly identified three times at this point as a "seeboy" – a term that has very interesting connotations in this context. A "sepoy" (who is literally and militaristically a colonial "subaltern") is "a native of India employed as a soldier by a European power, esp. Great Britain" (*Webster's*), and is a term derived from the Hindi and Persian words for "cavalryman." In other words, a sepoy is a native imitation of a British dragoon – playing at being British (for the British) in the European war games that involve cavalry charges and so on – a native attempt to mimic the "horsepower" of Wellington mounted on Copenhagen. Indian sepoy brigades were famous for their ferocious effectiveness and loyalty in fighting for the Crown, just as Ranji became a star for the British at their own game of cricket. But, as Homi Bhabha has incisively noted in "Of Mimicry and Man: The Ambivalence of Colonial Discourse," one of the distinguishing qualities of a colonial relationship is what he calls the "colonial mimicry" induced in (and expected of) the subject race taught to imitate (resemble, and *almost* become) the dominant race, in a form of cultural desire, but – in the dilemma of being "almost the same" but "not quite/not white" –

never being actually granted the privileges and freedoms that come with sovereignty, dominion, and citizenship. The object of such colonial mimicry, from the colonizer's viewpoint, is, as Bhabha puts it, to "ensure its [own] strategic failure, so that mimicry is at once resemblance and menace" ("Mimicry," 126–27, 132) — menace, that is, if the mimicry is too successful (as in the case of Paul Scott's Hari Kumar in *The Raj Quartet*). The sepoys can be proud, like British Tommies, of serving the Crown; but since they must not claim the other rights and privileges accorded to the Crown's own citizens and soldiers, rebellion – once the sepoys have been insulted to the point of being "ranjymad" and "madrashattaras" – is inevitable, as eventually happened in the bloody Sepoy Mutiny of 1857–58.

"Sepoy" is a particularly interesting term in relation to the Duke of Wellington. When he first took on Napoleon in the Peninsular War, he was known only for his very successful Indian campaigns, and Napoleon foolhardily wrote him off as merely a "Sepoy General" (*Britannica* xv, vol. 29, 735); Wellington was subsequently and frequently referred to as "The Sepoy General" or even just "The Sepoy." The label of "sepoy" is doubly ironic because, in a sense, he *was*: born in Dublin and raised Irish, Wellington was himself one of the dark horses that, in this ambivalent discourse of colonial desire, trains to become a white horse in a whitehorse world, as does a Hindu sepoy or a Rajput cricketer – going to Eton and then fighting for England, becoming its leading military figure and eventually Prime Minister (in the process opposing Irish Catholic Emancipation as long as he could). In Wellington, the mimicry was so authentic that it became authoritative (even in his own mind), and he himself grew to symbolize (to both himself and the world) the dominant, not the subject, race. This is an irony Joyce shows us he is quite aware of in describing Willingdone as "bornstable ghentleman" (also referring to Wellington's role in the Treaty of Ghent), for, when asked if he was Irish, Wellington's infamous reply, disowning his own native heritage as one of the colonized (in the stables, in the living ditch) in favor of the colonizer (in the ducal manor/manner), was: "If a gentleman happens to be born in a stable, it does not follow that he should be called a horse" (McHugh, *Annotations*, 10).

Furthermore, in calling our insurgent "hinndoo" a Hindu and a sepoy, Joyce is invoking the notorious "Sepoy Mutiny" of 1857, thus forecasting the eventual results of Wellington's aggressive campaigns in India. As with Irish Catholic uprisings against Orange forces and as with the lipoleum's bomb response to the attack on their trefoiled icon, the Sepoy Rebellion had its origin in the Empire's religious insensitivity and was sparked by a religious "insoult": to load the new Enfield rifles, "lubricated cartridges had to have their ends bitten off by the sepoys" but "the grease used for this purpose was a mixture of pigs' and cows' lard, an insult to both Muslims and Hindus." (This is perhaps why the Hindu "seeboy"'s pained cry at Willingdone's insult is "[*Bull*srag! Foul!]"). The sepoys at Meerut refused the Enfield cartridges; "as punishment, they were given long prison terms, fettered, and put in jail." Incensed at this injustice, numerous sepoy companies mutinied and marched on Delhi – and thus began the Sepoy Rebellion. Unfortunately, the English response, like Willingdone's, was precisely massacre, "tinders," and "max-botch": "In the end the reprisals far outweighed the original excesses. Hundreds of sepoys were shot from cannons in a frenzy of British vengeance" (*Britannica XV*, vol. 6, 289).[7]

In *Finnegans Wake*, the Museyroom episode climaxes with the lipoleum's response to the religious "insoult" by Willingdone and his horse. Driven "ranjymad" and "madrashattaras," the "dooforhim seeboy" (two-for-one, Irish and Indian, Hinnessy and Dooley; Dufferin was the "first marquess" and ruler of annexed Burma[8]) picks up his "bombshoob" and uses it to close the episode: "This is the dooforhim seeboy blow the whole of the half of the hat of lipoleums off the top of the tail on the back of his big wide harse. Tip (Bullseye! Game!) How Copenhagen ended" (*FW* 10.19–22). Like the Sepoy Mutineers, the incensed "seeboy" ("madrashattaras") rebels and blows the big white horse, emblem of imperial authority, to bits ("How Copenhagen ended"). The cry of "Bullsrag! Foul!" is now replaced by the children's glee at their own bull's eye, which ends the game and literally unhorses HCE (and the Law of the Father) by destroying his horse ("*How* Copenhagen *e*nded").

Thus, in *Finnegans Wake* Indian colonial domination by, and resistance to, English imperial rule is re-presented (or co-presented) by Joyce as parallel to and synonymous with Catholic Ireland's subservient relationship to Protestant England – for the "hinndoo" sepoy blowing up Willingdone's big white horse is but another version of Irish Catholic Hennesseys and Dooleys tarring, defacing, and then (in 1836) blowing up King Billy's white horse on Dublin's College Green. (I understand that the Wellington equestrian statue in Madras has had a similarly perilous history.) The Museyroom thus becomes a collective case study of colonial politics and the dynamics of power. In suggesting that *Finnegans Wake* is "best understood in relation to the struggle against imperialism," MacCabe ruefully concludes that "*Finnegans Wake* is a primer for a failed revolution, one that would have allied Ireland to Europe rather than simply separating twenty-six counties from Britain" ("Finnegans," 5). Perhaps the *Wake*'s pluralistic vision of a polylogic, universal discourse, displacing the monologic discourses of nationalism, is as yet "failed," even hopelessly utopian. But I would add that, even in 1939 (long before the independence of India and Pakistan), Joyce seems at least to have known that – whether in the twenty-six counties of Ireland or in the many provinces and princedoms of England's Oriental colonies – failed revolutions are a tragic and bomb-laden reality that only temporarily derails, but does not finally deny, the inevitability of sovereignty and Home Rule.

11.

Conclusion

This study has been engaged in presenting Joyce's texts as a strikingly sustained and systematic commentary on the ideologies of racial and imperial politics in Joyce's Ireland, written by a highly self-conscious Irish writer who was hardly apolitical but who was, rather, deeply steeped, like the dyer's hand, in the very hues and textures of the complex political fabrics of a racialized and colonized Irish state. Woven into the very texture and fabric of Joyce's works are the discourses and issues of British imperialism and of colonial resistance, in very specific detail – whether about Ireland, Africa, India, and so on. These are the precise and historicized building materials from which Joyce's texts, like Joyce's cities themselves, are erected. The degree and complexity of the ideological presence and details in Joyce's texts underscore his complicated awareness of such issues; they also reveal a writer with very strong Nationalist sympathies (who subscribed to much of the Irish Nationalist agenda but who decried its insistence on "the old pap of racial hatred") but who nevertheless undertook a systematic critique of the repressiveness of both English imperialism and certain forms of Irish Nationalist consciousness.

This is a Joyce who (whether or not one agrees with his particular positions) took very strong stances – a fact which becomes clearer when we look at their representations in his books in both detail and collectively – on such matters as: nationalism and especially Irish Nationalism; internationalism and multicultural politics; cultural stereotypes and racism; essentialism, whether racial, cultural, or linguistic; and alternatives to the problematics of all the above. This is a Joyce who also, as we have seen, argued these positions repeatedly and consistently in his books.

This study has attempted to demonstrate that Joyce's works house a carefully constructed, highly textured representation of the various ideological positions on issues of race and empire in turn-of-century Ireland; given their representation of these issues through a characteristically Joycean immersion in concrete and localized detail (culturally and historically specific), the Joyce corpus can thus be collectively read as a dialogic representation of the disparate, historically based voices and social discourses within the various hegemonic and social blocs of turn-of-century Ireland.

Furthermore, Joyce's works, as a whole, constitute an insistent and consistent critique of such ideological discourses and of the resulting, systemic colonial dynamics – dynamics that can be usefully understood by our own contemporary culture through the social theories of, among others, Frantz Fanon, Antonio Gramsci, and Edward Said. As part of these critiques, Joyce also elaborates some of the complex psychological, linguistic, and philosophical implications embedded in a racialized discourse of an imperial Self and a colonized Other. Finally, within the fictional (and often parodic or fantastic) representations in which these ideological commentaries are couched, Joyce consistently articulates a number of alternatives – some practical, some utopian – to the complex system of racial/colonial pathology that he depicts repeatedly in his writings, from the early essays to *Finnegans Wake*.

As early as 1907, Joyce voiced his awareness that nations participate in the dynamics of Self and Other, resulting in the essentialized negative stereotypes of races, including the British conception of the Irish race. Atempting to break the pattern and represent one's own "race" and conscience, Joyce urges his compatriots to cease to be provincial and to stop trying to define themselves within English constructions of empire, race, and nationhood – a closed system of binary opposition in which the rules have already been constructed always to favor the dominant culture. In his fiction, Joyce repeatedly reverses the racialized and derogatory analogies of the Irish as racial others by re-presenting them as enabling bonds of shared ethnicity, re-functioning and activating them to suggest a solidarity and positivity in the racialized analogies – suggesting an implied equation of otherness with the self, of Oriental/Jew with West/Greek, thus denying the convenient, constructed essentialisms of binary distinctions based on absolute and inherent difference.

Joyce argued in his essays, and then represented repeatedly in his works, his understanding that peoples and populations depend not on static essences and absolute differences but rather contain pluralistic and heterogeneous characteristics (of both individual and cultural difference) that cannot be so conveniently named and essentialized. While Joyce's writings are arguably "nationalist" in intention, they repeatedly remind us to be vigilant about forms of national consciousness that simply reproduce the same binary, essentialist hierarchies inherited from Anglo-Saxonist racism.[1] Joyce did not forget the actual racial differences and heterogeneities within the Irish contact zone, for Ireland herself was "a vast fabric, in which the most diverse elements are mingled" and in which "it is useless to look for a thread that may have remained pure and virgin without having undergone the influence of a neighbouring thread" (*CW* 165–66). Joyce's texts repeatedly represent these various intersecting and competing threads/grains/voices in Irish culture, within a symptomatic representation of turn-of-century Dublin; in representing the dominant cultural discourses and the competing voices and hegemonic blocs within the social fabric, Joyce's texts thus constitute an attempt to be a "mirror held up to Culture."

Within Joyce's depictions of English/Irish colonial and racial symptomatics are elaborated highly-textured awarenesses of the connections between a dominant discourse – based on essentialism, racism, and forms of cultural othering – and: Orientalism and the cultural daydream of the Exotic East; English imperialism and racism; Irish colonialism and the various, fluid hegemonic blocs and positions within the colonial system; international imperialism and colonialism; patriarchy and sexual politics; family politics; class politics. All of these types of cultural politics are represented by Joyce as, in part, counterparts and endlessly replicable extensions, results, and mirrors of a racial/colonial dynamics and pathology, internalizing and propagating the received values of an oppressive colonizer – dynamics that we can theorize today in terms of a Gramscian politics of class and of the fluid but consensual processes of social-discursive formations characteristic of "hegemony"; as well as in terms of an ethnographic or anthropological dynamics of racial othering, cultural desire, and colonial ambivalence.

In response to such ethnocentric dynamics, Joyce's texts argue for a cultural relativism (outside any single, fixed system of binarized polarities) implicit in an awareness and acceptance of different cultures, internationalism, and multiple perspectives;[2] as Stephen Daedalus points out: "What we symbolise in black the Chinaman may symbolise in yellow: each has his own tradition. Greek beauty laughs at Coptic beauty and the American Indian derides them both" (*SH* 212). Leopold Bloom, inevitably (like every member of the culture) both a consumer and a propagator of the dominant and racist cultural discourse about Otherness, is able nevertheless to be repeatedly skeptical of essentialized constructions, and sensitive to the cultural processes by which they are erected. Bloom, always interested in cultural difference and parallactic perspectives, is able to hold simultaneous vantage points, to imagine being other, and thus to go beyond the monologic limitations of a cycloptic myopia, to "see ourselves as others see us."

Although some of Bloom's as well as Stephen's ideals (such as the fantasized New Bloomusalem) are highly fantastic, parodic, utopian, or self-contradicting, yet there are woven throughout these ideals certain coherent consistencies of vision recognizable in all Joyce's texts – combining humanitarian concerns, socialistic agenda, practical reform, non-violence, and a redefinition of Irish nationhood. Like Bloom, Joyce seems to advocate a tolerant society of "universal brotherhood" not fractured by exclusive or polarized allegiances to language, religion, or nationality – a contact zone willing to acknowledge and accept its own ethnic and racial heterogeneities, both the reality and the tolerance of "Mixed races and mixed marriage." Repeatedly the texts advocate (even as they engage in self-mockery or parody) certain ideological positions: the necessity of learning to look at more than one side in each question; the self-conscious vigilance required to resist moral smugness or essentialist certainty in a complex, pluralistic, un-simple universe; opposition to the hierarchized imposition of "arbitrary classes" and "social inequality" upon a "heterogeneous society" (*U* 17.1617–20); the absurdities of xenophobia and of forms of national/ethnic pride based on racist or religious exclusivity; anti-violence and pacificism; and the general project of refuting the binary stereotypes of absolute difference which generate a discursive hatred for a culturally reified Other.

Seamus Deane has voiced concern that "it could be argued" that "the pluralism of [Joyce's] styles and languages" provides "the harmony of indifference, one in which everything is a version of something else, where sameness rules over diversity, where contradiction is finally and disquietingly written out" (*Heroic*, 15). In the end, it seems to me, such a concern can be addressed, to large degree, by the careful precision of Joyce's narrative representations as (again in Deane's words) "a mirror held up to Culture." For Joyce's texts try to negotiate the simultaneous presence of individual difference and particularity, on the one hand, and of shared solidarity and similarity on the other. As narratives, Joyce's works play out symptomatically, in their cultural specificities and historicized detail, all the diverse discourses and ideological positions of Joyce's Ireland, thus attempting to avoid the homogenization of difference (and the "harmony of indifference"). But, simultaneously, these narratives suggest – by presenting analogies and similarities between these differences and between various cultures/peoples – possible lines of solidarity that refute the simplistic, binary essentialisms of absolute difference. Thus, they negotiate the complexities of the "universal" and of the "particular" at the same time. These narratives strike me as at once the most materially concrete (steeped in, say, the most minute details of Dublin on June 16, 1904) and the most analogically universal fictional works imaginable. They re-present Ireland in both vertical and horizontal dimensions, as a dialogical site in which the conscience of a race is depicted as at once a pluralistic contact zone full of vibrantly particular heterogeneities, and as a model for analogous dynamics of power and culture within other peoples and populations. Joyce's *material* specificity fights against totalization, homogenization, and essentialism; but his simultaneous and ubiquitous metaphoricity allows for a celebration of shared bonds and similarities, without denying specificity and difference.[3] *Ulysses* especially, as a novel immersed "in the midst of the everyday" and functioning (in its cultural specificity and representational fullness) as "a mirror held up to Culture," manages to displace the homogenizing myths of racist or xenophobic essentialism through its depictions of a pluralistic and heterogeneous Ireland; *Ulysses's* Dublin is a lively narrative space of cultural multivocality, charting the various discourses involved in "writing the nation" and in creating the conscience of a "race." Joyce's texts, finally, advocate and allow for a simultaneous acceptance of (on the one hand) heterogeneity and difference, and (on the other) a potential sameness and solidarity of similarities-in-difference shared by different peoples, within an inter-cultural, inter-national perspective that tries both to respect difference and to recognize shared bonds of similarity.

In analyzing the ideological dimensions of any "literary" text (a notion in itself problematic), especially one that appears to manifest a particular politics, we should perhaps consider the effectiveness of that text's mode of ideological argumentation. As narratives of resistance to repressive ideologies, Joyce's texts – especially *Finnegans Wake* – do seem both utopian and hopelessly esoteric as agents for a pluralistic vision of a polylogic, universal discourse which can displace the monologic discourses of both nationalism and imperialism. Certainly it is hard to imagine that texts as difficult as *Ulysses* and *Finnegans Wake*, however wonderful they may be as literary artefacts, can be very useful vehicles for *direct* political influence or change. This is, of course, true of most works of what we would call European High Modernism, steeped as they are in a modernist style and poetics of complexity and difficulty, thus limiting themselves to a narrow reading audience composed of the educated or privileged. This is an unfortunate paradox for a writer like Joyce (less so for more reactionary writers like Eliot or Pound), whose socialistically democratic ideas and ideological subversiveness can seldom directly reach the readers he is trying to empower as part of that "spiritual liberation" involved in attempting to represent the "conscience" of his "race."[4]

On the other hand, readers seldom read "fiction" in conscious search of ideological messages anyway, and what we call "literary" texts seldom function directly in the same way as political tracts; their effectiveness in political terms, while real, is largely indirect. In the case of Joyce's narratives, they can function effectively in different ways: (1) as fictional correspondences to cultural or social theories for a progressive literary art form – as in my argument that *Ulysses* (and Joyce's fiction in general) answers to Homi Bhabha's call for "Counter-narratives of the nation that continually evoke and erase its totalizing boundaries – both actual and conceptual" and thus "disturb those ideological manoeuvres through which 'imagined communities' are given essentialist identities" by allowing for "the possibility of other narratives of the people and their difference" (*Nation*, 300); (2) and they can function as practical applications of theoretical arguments for certain ideological positions and theories, such as those voiced by Said, Anderson, Spivak, Bakhtin, and Derrida, whose positions Joyce's texts (as I have argued) both illustrate and advocate, within an anti-essentialist and anti-imperialist politics.

The effectiveness of such applications upon readers can be direct enough, whether conscious or unconscious: someone reading *Dubliners* or *Ulysses* is likely to carry away and store (and at some level be influenced by) some of the ideological implications embedded in the texts, even if that influence is unconscious and unexamined. More alert and self-conscious readers may grasp directly and mull over some of the political or ideological implications of the texts they have been reading.

But the ideological power of internationally widespread and influential works like Joyce's is perhaps just as effectively spread *indirectly* – by the influences they have on various other sources, who then propagate those influences in their own ways: (1) more overtly politicized writers, such as Salman Rushdie or Ralph Ellison, who have themselves been directly influenced by both Joyce's styles and his ideologies, and whose writings do play a more direct role in shaping cultural or racial positions and ideologies; (2) the literary Academy, specifically university teachers, whose classrooms are the most common source for the continued existence of a Joyce reader-ship: the nature of how Joyce is taught and the particular classroom analyses of his texts certainly shape the ideological reception of those works, and consequently influence the politics of the student readers themselves; (3) and finally, the indirect influence propagated by works of criticism (such as, I hope, this one), which can help shape the reception and interpretation of particular literary texts, as well as contribute to both the influence and the nature of ideologically purposive intellectual disciplines, such as minority discourse and cultural studies.

In *Stephen Hero* young Stephen Daedalus refers self-importantly to one of his essays as "the first of my explosives" (*SH* 81), suggesting that it is his own contribution to the arena of revolutionary and nationalist activism. Joyce's own works can hardly be characterized as "explosives" in that sense. However, as is abundantly clear from the influence Joyce has had on both modern and contemporary literature worldwide, his works are far from un-influential. Perhaps the potential ideological power of Joyce's texts might be character-ized, more accurately, not as "explosives" but as time-release capsules: because – as with the ideas of Bakhtin or Gramsci whose ideological potencies had to wait to be discovered/recovered in a later, different cultural environment more receptive and ready to understand or apply them – so also Joyce's political ideologies perhaps can be more clearly understood and analyzed and received *now*, at a cultural moment (and discursive space) in which the tools and political climate of multiculturalism, minority studies, cultural politics, and our more complex understandings of the dynamics of cultural discourses and political power, can allow us more clearly and fully not only to interpret and theorize the discursive practices within literary texts, but also to recognize in Joyce an important modernist figure who can hardly be justly characterized any longer as an apolitical writer. The exploration of Joyce's texts on these terms – well under way now by a number of literary scholars – holds rich possibilities for literary and cultural analysis.

Notes

1 Introduction

1. As Joyce said: "I'd like a language which is above all languages ... I cannot express myself in English without closing myself in a tradition." Joyce to Stefan Zweig, in Zweig, *The World of Yesterday*, 275.
2. As Deane notes in an essay on "Joyce the Irishman": "Subversion is part of the Joycean enterprise ... There is nothing of political or social significance which Joyce does not undermine and restructure." In *The Cambridge Companion to James Joyce*, ed. Derek Attridge, 44.
3. I have in mind most particularly the work of, among others, Dominic Manganiello, Seamus Deane, Cheryl Herr, Margot Norris, Vicki Mahaffey, R. B. Kershner, Colin MacCabe, and Franco Moretti. For example, Manganiello's work on Joyce's politics helps to dismantle the long-held illusion that Joyce's works are apolitical by demonstrating how his writings not only are shaped by contemporary politics but argue a significant political ideology. MacCabe has gone on to suggest that *Finnegans Wake* "is perhaps best understood in relation to the struggle against imperialism" ("Finnegans," 4). Herr, in her continuing analyses and placement of Joyce's works within a contemporary Irish popular culture, repeatedly shows how "in Joyce's works, culture is the space in which ideologies perform" – as when Joyce "uses the newspaper, the play, and the sermon as signifying forms" (*Joyce's Anatomy*, 12). Kershner, in his investigations of the early works delineates "the degrees to which [Joyce's characters'] conversation and thoughts are dialogical participants in – or even products of – a series of culturally mandated discourses of his time" (*Joyce/Bakhtin*, 228). Moretti has even suggested that *Ulysses* in its very structure reflects the "crisis of ... liberal capitalism" itself (*Signs*, 186).

   Furthermore, there has been of late a good deal of strong scholarship on the related issues of Joyce and feminism; and Joyce and Jewishness.
4. Vincent J. Cheng: *Shakespeare and Joyce: A Study of "Finnegans Wake"*; *"Le Cid": A Translation in Rhymed Couplets*.

2 Catching the conscience of a race

1. Cited in *Anglo-Saxons*, 22. Curtis adds: "So persistent has been this theme of English cultural and racial superiority over the Irish that one begins to suspect the existence among those who tried to subdue and rule the Irish of a deep-seated need to justify their confiscatory and homicidal habits in that country" (18).

2. Curtis (*Anglo-Saxons*, 65) goes on to suggest that perhaps the English were "trying to discharge their own anxieties about feelings of violence, indolence, emotional incontinence, and even femininity onto another people who seemed to bear these stigma. Paddy served as a convenient scapegoat for the frustrations which arose out of a code of civilized and gentlemanly conduct that regulated the public lives of countless Englishmen ... thus really the Irish Question is an English Question, that is to say, a by-product of the social and emotional pressure under which many middle and upper class Victorians lived and suffered."

3. We know that Joyce read both Renan and Michelet: in *Stephen Hero*, Stephen Dedalus cites Renan three times (*SH* 175, 189, 190), and in *Ulysses* he thinks of Michelet several times (e.g., *U* 3.167). Joyce had also visited Renan's birthplace in France.

4. In this engaging Alan Parker film (based on a novel by Roddy Doyle), a young man named Jimmy Rabbitte organizes a rock-and-roll band in Dublin which he trains to perform black "soul music." When one of the skeptical band members asks, "D'ya think maybe we're a little white for that kind of thing?" – Jimmy points out: "You don't get it, lads. The Irish are the blacks of Europe. And Dubliners are the blacks of Ireland." The poor Dublin youngsters in the band then take on as their motto, "I'm black and I'm proud." At another point, standing in a dole queue and finding another band member also on the dole, Jimmy notes that, "We're a Third World country, what can you do?" Finally, in a comment suggestive of the racialized discourse of the Irish as apes, Jimmy describes his band thus: "We're the guerillas of soul. That's guerilla with a 'u,' not an 'o.'"

5. Curtis comments in *Anglo-Saxons* (18): "Having little or no awareness of the unsettling effects which the forceful and armed English presence had upon Irish society, English observers jumped to the conclusion that the Irish people were a turbulent semi-nomadic, treacherous, idle, dirty, and belligerent lot who reminded them of the 'savages' or Indians of North America."

6. "The stereotype of the primitive, melancholic, and prognathous Irish Celt was documented by anthropologists and ethnologists who constructed impressive typologies of the physiognomies of the British and Irish peoples" (Curtis, *Apes*, 94).

7. As Trinh Minh-ha puts it in *Woman Native Other* (80): "You who understand the dehumanization of forced removal-relocation-reeducation-redefinition, the humiliation of having to falsify your own reality, your voice – you know. And often cannot say it, you try and

keep on trying to say it, for if you don't, they will not fail to fill in the blanks on your behalf, and you will be said."

8. Gibbons goes on to suggest that "The racial mode is, moveover, the version of Irish nationalism which has passed into general academic circulation in recent years through the 'revisionist' writings of Conor Cruise O'Brien and F. S. L. Lyons (among others) – largely, one suspects, because it redefines even resistance within the colonial frame and thus neutralizes the very idea of anti-colonial discourse" (Gibbons, 104).

9. As Seamus Deane points out: "Nationalism, as preached by Yeats or by Pearse [and by Hyde], was a crusade for decontamination. The Irish essence was to be freed of the infecting Anglicising virus and thus restored to its primal purity and vigour" (*Celtic*, 94).

David Lloyd reminds us of the extent to which Gaelic language and culture were already a distant past for most Irish people: "Simultaneously, the emergence of an increasingly politically con- scious middle class coincides with the critical decline of the Irish language as the medium of daily life for the people, a decline that had already passed the 50 percent mark by the mid 1840s. Irish nationalism thus emerges at the moment of virtual eclipse of what would have been its 'natural' language and primarily among a class that was, already, necessarily, estranged from that language" ("Writing," 74).

10. Theresa O'Connor's essay on "Demythologizing Nationalism: Joyce's Dialogized Grail Myth" (in Cheng and Martin, eds., *Joyce in Context*, 100–21) demonstrates how Joyce subverts such a Celtic mythological discourse of war and blood by replacing it with a mythos of life, birth, and renewal.

11. As Frantz Fanon writes: "To the saying 'All natives are the same' the colonized person replies, 'All settlers are the same.' ... On the logical plane, the Manicheism of the settler produces a Manicheism of the native. To the theory of the 'absolute evil of the native' the theory of the 'absolute evil of the settler' replies" (*Wretched*, 92–93).

12. As David Lloyd notes in a parallel discussion: "Paradoxically, in adopting such a model of cultural identification ... Irish nationalists reproduce in their very opposition to the Empire a narrative of universal development that is fundamental to the legitimation of imperialism" ("Writing," 76).

13. Pratt defines "contact zone" in this way: "I use this term to refer to the social spaces where cultures meet, clash, and grapple with each other, often in contexts of highly asymmetrical relations of power, such as colonialism, slavery, or their aftermaths as they are lived out in many parts of the world today" ("Arts," 34).

14. Stephen had already tried his hand, unsuccessfully, at a sort of government, playing at empire and familial "home rule" with the money from his scholastic awards: he "*marshalled* his books up and down their shelves, pored upon all kinds of price lists, drew up a form of *commonwealth* for the household by which every member of it held some *office*, opened a loan bank for his family [but soon] The

commonwealth fell, the loan bank closed its coffers" (*P* 98; my emphases).

15. Stephen's "intelligence, moreover, persuaded him that the tomahawk, as an effective instrument of warfare, had become obsolete" (*SH* 146).

3 *Dubliners*: The exoticized and Orientalized Other

1. As Lisa Lowe puts it in *Critical Terrains: French and British Orientalisms*: "binary constructions of difference – whether Occident and Orient, male and female, or a static concept of dominant and emergent – embody a logic that gives priority to the first term of the dyad while subordinating the second" (24).

2. As Robert Young has argued (in noting that "Orientalism represents the West's own internal dislocation" and reflects a deep ambivalence towards the desired "otherness"), "colonial discourse is founded on an anxiety, and ... colonial power itself is subject to the effects of a conflictual economy" (*White Mythologies*, 142).

3. See also R. B. Kershner's study of *Dubliners*, aptly titled *Joyce, Bakhtin, and Popular Literature: Chronicles of Disorder*.

4. See especially Harry Stone, "'Araby' and the Writings of James Joyce" (in Scholes and Litz); Robert M. Adams, *Surface and Symbol: The Consistency of James Joyce's "Ulysses"*; Cheryl Herr, *Joyce's Anatomy of Culture*; and R. B. Kershner, *Joyce, Bakhtin, and Popular Literature: Chronicles of Disorder*.

5. Key critics here include Julia Kristeva on Desire and Edward Said on Orientalism. Hélène Cixous, Robert Young points out, reminds us that Western politics and knowledge have long "worked according to the same Hegelian dialectic ... whether it be Marxism's History, Europe's colonial annexations and accompanying racism or orientalism, Freud's characterization of femininity as the dark unexplored continent" (*White Mythologies*, 3).

6. Said thus concludes forcefully: "In the system of knowledge about the Orient, the Orient is less a place than a *topos*, a set of references, a congeries of characteristics, that seems to have its origin in a quotation, or a fragment of a text, or a citation from someone's work on the Orient, or some bit of previous imagining, or an amalgam of all these" (*Orientalism*, 177).

7. As Lowe points out: "The [actual, occluded] heterogeneity is borne out most simply in the different meanings of 'the Orient' over time. In many eighteenth-century texts the Orient signifies Turkey, the Levant, and the Arabian peninsula occupied by the Ottoman Empire, now known as the Middle East; in nineteenth-century literature the notion of the Orient additionally refers to North Africa, and in the twentieth century more often to Central and Southeast Asia" (*Critical Terrains*, 7).

8. So also Oriental bazaars grew to suggest immorality or wrongdoing: in *A Portrait* (76) Heron comments about Stephen, "Dedalus is a model youth. He doesn't smoke and he doesn't go the bazaars and he doesn't flirt and he doesn't damn anything or damn all."

9. This is also the first instance of the frequent later usage by Joyce of the image of the "dark horse" as a symbol for the marginalized Other under British imperial rule (see chapter 9), as well as for the connection between "horse" and "whores" (here, between the dark Arab horse equated with both Dark Rosaleen and Caroline Norton as symbols of Ireland prostituted to the English masters).

4 The gratefully oppressed: Joyce's Dubliners

1. While Michael Balfe's *The Bohemian Girl* is about a girl from Bohemia, I am invoking the meaning of the adjective "bohemian" – a meaning I suspect Joyce also intended to invoke, as he clearly later does in "After the Race": "They drank ... it was Bohemian" (*D* 47).

2. Lisa Lowe describes the term thus: "in Gramsci's thought hegemony ... also includes the complex interconnected relations between social, cultural, and ideological practices through which a ruling group exercises domination. Hegemony is Gramsci's way of describing the entire process of negotiation, dissent, and compromise whereby a particular group or ideological formation gains the consent of the larger body to lead" (*Critical*, 16).

3. See the last endnote of chapter 5 (on "The Dead") in reference to Joyce's use of the key term "generous" – as kind (generous), kin (*genus*), societal, socialistic.

4. This "thumbnail sketch of Irish history" is elaborated further by Zack Bowen, who has suggested that the story is "a sort of allegory of Irish history and international relations":

> The hope that Segouin and the French will provide this emancipation is reflected in the "oppressed" Irish sightseers cheering on "the cars of their friends, the French." The liberation of the Irish by the French is, of course, not exactly a new idea. The Irish, since the time of the Stuarts and particularly during the days of Wolfe Tone, have regarded the French as prospective emancipators. The failure of the French to free the Irish in the 1690's and in the 1790's leads up to the suspicion that still one hundred years later history will again repeat itself in "After the Race."

> As Bowen concludes: "Young Doyle finally comes to understand that the last 'great' game lies between Routh and Segouin, as history repeats itself in the struggle between France and England. Jimmy, Ireland, as in the days of Tone, having been an unimportant but involved bystander in the struggle, understands that 'he would lose, of course'" ("After," 54, 57, 59).

5. Gramsci identifies two functions, "social hegemony and political government," comprising, in his words:

> (1) The "spontaneous" consent given by the great masses of the population to the general direction imposed on social life by the dominant fundamental group; this consent is "historically" caused by the prestige (and consequent confidence) which the

dominant group enjoys because of its position and function in the world of production.

(2) The apparatus of state coercive power which "legally" enforces discipline on those groups who do not "consent" either actively or passively. This apparatus is, however, constituted for the whole of society in anticipation of moments of crisis of command and direction when spontaneous consent has weakened. (*Selections*, 12)

6. "On the turf" is another example of Joyce's horse/whores pun, as something sexual, to be ridden and exploited.

7. For example, Thomas Moore wrote a well-known song based on the harp as a national symbol, "The Harp that Once Through Tara's Halls," which Bloom recalls in *Ulysses*: "The harp that once did starve us all" (8.606–7) and "Only the harp. Lovely ... Erin. The harp that once or twice" (11.580–820).

8. William York Tindall refers to Polly Mooney in "The Boarding House" as "Corley's female counterpart" (*Reader's Guide to James Joyce*, 26). Like "Two Gallants," "The Boarding House" is a story of seduction and conquest – in which the seducer-conquerors are female, Polly Mooney and her mother. Although this story does not directly concern racial or imperial politics, it does reinforce the depiction and metaphor, already carefully delineated (as we have seen) in "Araby," "After the Race," and "Two Gallants," of an Ireland hegemonically prostituted to England. Mrs. Mooney runs a "boarding house" – a term perhaps containing an echo of "bawdy house," an implication Joyce would substantiate years later when, in a passage of *Finnegans Wake* listing the *Dubliners* stories, this story gets punned on as the "boardelhouse" (*FW* 186.31), with its clearer echo of both brothel and bordello. Appropriately, the boarders of this "house" refer to its proprietress as "*The Madam*" (*D* 62).

Although not literally a house of ill repute, the "house" already seems rather disreputable, with its "floating population made up of tourists ... and *artistes* from the music halls" (*D* 62), entertainers who were generally considered promiscuous and disreputable. Indeed, Jack Mooney "was always sure to be on to a good thing – that is to say, a likely horse or a likely *artiste*" (*D* 62): this line again suggests a verbal correspondence of "horse" and "whores" as good bets and good lays. As Bob Doran himself realizes, the "boarding house was beginning to get a certain fame" (*D* 66). After all, Polly herself was being shopped around by her mother like a horse, having been "given the run of the young men in the house" (*D* 63). Significantly, the boarders seem to be largely English: "Her house had a floating population made up of tourists from Liverpool and the Isle of Man and, occasionally, *artistes* from the music halls" (*D* 62). There is a hint that one of these English *artistes* might already have had "the run" of Polly, even before Bob Doran (so that she would be literally a "perverse madonna" [*D* 63], an inverted virgin) – for Doran remembers a night "when one of the music-hall *artistes*, a little blond Londoner, had made a rather free allusion to Polly" (*D* 68), for which comment Polly's brother almost starts a fight with the Londoner. Polly herself sings: " *'I'm a ... naughty girl ... You know I am"* (*D* 62).

Although the male victim of Mrs. Mooney's manipulative designs as a whorehouse madam turns out to be Bob Doran, an Irishman, in any event it is clear that this is so in part because the other alternatives had already been exhausted and Mrs. Mooney was unable to sell her daughter successfully to the English foreigners: "Mrs Mooney, who was a shrewd judge, knew that the young men were only passing the time away; none of them meant business" (*D* 63). For Mrs. Mooney, young men are business: as a Madam and as a "butcher's daughter" (*D* 61) who "dealt with moral problems as a cleaver deals with meat" (*D* 63), she is a whore-mistress trying to sell her daughter's Irish flesh to both English and Irish buyers on the open meat market. The psychological damage effected by the prostitution of Ireland is suggested by Polly's reappearance later in *Ulysses* as a pathetic exhibitionist, parading herself "without a stitch on her, exposing her person, open to all comers" (*U* 12.401–02). Such are the wages of prostitution.

9. See Brian W. Shaffer's essay on " Joyce and Freud: Discontent and Its Civilizations" for a persuasive elaboration of this concept of a culturally constructed "narcissism" as applied to Joyce.

10. In Spivak's words, an imperial Europe has become consolidated as "sovereign subject, indeed sovereign and subject" – such that the colonized have been constituted (as the "self-consolidating other") according to the colonizer's self-image: "[Europe] consolidated itself as sovereign subject by defining its colonies as 'Others,' even as it constituted them, for purposes of administration and the expansion of markets, into programmed near-images of that very sovereign self" ("Rani," 128).

11. Cf. *FW* 479.14: "Do not flingamejig to the twolves!"

5 Empire and patriarchy in "The Dead"

1. See also Robert Scholes's excellent essay on "Joyce and Modernist Ideology." Scholes argues the intriguing possibility (among other points) that both "scrupulous meanness" and the "conscience of my race" were terms Joyce picked up and translated from Ferrero's *L'Europa giovane*.

2. In August 1904 Joyce wrote to Nora the memorable lines: "My mind rejects the whole present social order and Christianity – home, the recognised virtues, classes of life, and religious doctrines ... When I looked on [my mother's] face as she lay in the coffin – a face grey and wasted with cancer – I understood that I was looking at the face of a victim and I cursed the system which had made her a victim ... I cannot enter the social order except as a vagabond" (*Letters II*, 48). As early as 1904 Joyce recognized all the marginalized (including himself) as confederated members of victimization by a social system that encompassed colonial politics, sexual politics, familial politics, class politics, and religious hierarchies. As he wrote further to Nora,

"It seemed to me that I was a fighting a battle with every religious and social force in Ireland" (see Manganiello, *Joyce's Politics*, 218).

3. I share with critics like Spivak and Homi Bhabha the assumption that "imperialism was not only a territorial and economic but inevitably also a subject-constituting project" (Young, *White Mythologies*, 159). Spivak has argued that Europe has been constituted and consolidated as "sovereign subject, indeed sovereign and subject," while constructing the colonized in its own self-image, "consolidated itself as sovereign subject by defining its colonies as 'Others,' even as it constituted them, for purposes of administration and the expansion of markets, into programmed near-images of that very sovereign self." ("Rani," 128).

4. Such correspondences by Joyce thus anticipate not only a broader sense of the word "politics" (as I am using it), but also our correspondingly broader sense of the terms "imperialism" and "empire" – in the sense, as Fredric Jameson puts it, "which is now very precisely what the word 'imperialism' means for us – ... one of necessary subordination or dependency ... it now designates the relationship between a generalized imperial subject ... and its various others or objects" ("Modernism," 48). Imperialism, in other words, is tied into – as are all these forms of "politics" – subject–object dynamics.

5. Nor do I intend to undermine the validity of the persuasive characterizations of Gabriel which previous critics have presented us – but rather to explore some of the further subtleties and dynamics of such characterizations as Joyce has encoded them.

6. Gabriel tries to speak in what Kimberle Crenshaw calls "the authoritative universal voice": "The authoritative universal voice – usually white male subjectivity masquerading as nonracial, nongendered objectivity – is merely transferred to those who, but for gender, share many of the same cultural, economic, and social characteristics" ("Black," 204). I am suggesting that this story cumulatively evinces an encoded transferral of that authoritative voice from the British imperium to the Irish male, who in turn imposes it on the Irish female – in an act (on Gabriel's part) of consensual (if unconscious) servitude and submission to an imposed hegemonic system.

7. As Frantz Fanon puts it, the imperial power is "a mother who unceasingly restrains her fundamentally perverse offspring from managing to commit suicide and from giving free rein to its evil instincts. The colonial mother protects her child from itself" (*Wretched*, 211).

8. In the "Aeolus" section of *Ulysses*, Joyce describes mailcars under the appropriately royal headline (and metonymy) "THE WEARER OF THE CROWN": "Under the porch of the general post office shoeblacks called and polished. Parked in North Prince's street His Majesty's vermilion mailcars, bearing on their sides the royal initials, E. R. [Edward Rex] ..." (*U* 7.14–18).

9. Said notes: "it is the first principle of imperialism that there is a clear-

cut and absolute hierarchical distinction between ruler and ruled" ("Yeats and Decolonization," 82).

As Robert Young writes: "The creation of man as centre was effected by defining him against other, now marginalized groups, such as women, the mad, or, we would add, the allegedly sub-human 'native'" (*White Mythologies*, 74).

10. Writes Fanon: "This European opulence is literally scandalous, for it has been founded on slavery"; "For in a very concrete way Europe has stuffed herself inordinately with the gold and raw materials of the colonial countries ... Europe is literally the creation of the Third World" (*Wretched*, 96, 102).

   In *Ulysses* the Dubliners would likewise discuss the recent international uproar about "those Belgians in the Congo Free State ... raping the women and girls and flogging the natives on the belly to squeeze all the red rubber they can out of them" [*U* 12. 1542–47].) The report was filed by Roger Casement. As Gifford (366) notes: "In February 1904, while serving as a consul in the Congo, Casement filed a report on the forced labor in rubber plantations and other cruelties to natives under the Belgian administration there. The report was published, and the public reaction led in January to a reconvening of the Conference of Powers that had originally established Belgian control of the Congo; the conference resulted in a measure of reform." Casement, of course, was hanged in 1916 for treason as a Sinn Feiner. Joyce owned a book of his in his Trieste library.

   In *A Portrait* Stephen Dedalus thinks of India and ivory: "ivory sawn from the mottled tusks of elephants. *Ivory, ivoire, avorio, ebur ... India mittit ebur*" (India sends ivory; *P* 179).

11. Robert Spoo has also suggested that the word "goloshes" may remind Gretta of black or blackface figures through the missing verbal link of "golliwog," "the popular term for a grotesque black doll inspired by a series of children's books" ("Uncanny," 107); in *Ulysses*, Cissy Caffrey has "golliwog curls" (*U* 13.270).

12. I am invoking here a Joycean critical history that has frequently contrasted Gabriel and Michael Furey along the qualities suggested by the gentility of the archangel Gabriel in contrast to the fiery power and "fury" of the archangel Michael.

13. Jameson notes: "When the other speaks, he or she becomes another subject, which must be consciously registered as a problem by the imperial or metropolitan subject" ("Modernism," 49).

14. One recalls the symbolic significances of the gold sovereign in "Two Gallants," another story in which brutal sexual conquest is presented by Joyce as analogous to England's equally brutal conquest of Ireland. As Manganiello notes, commenting on the influence of Guglielmo Ferrero on "Two Gallants": "For Joyce [as for Ferrero] ... the brutalism of love and politics were interconnected" (52).

15. As we are told in the narrative of *Stephen Hero* (181), "About this time there was some agitation in the political world concerning the working of the Royal University."

16. See Manganiello, 24, on the derogatory designations of "shoneen" and "West Briton."

17. Certainly such a view would ally Gabriel closely with Joyce himself, who it is supposed similarly wanted nothing to do with Irish Nationalism, who had moved abroad into exile on the continent, and who also wrote paid reviews for *The Daily Express*. On the other hand, Joyce knew quite well that literature was certainly not above politics, and his exploration of Gabriel here strikes me as, in part, a very complex exorcism of some of his own guilt and feelings of anti-Irish complicity. After all, Joyce was writing this story in exile but at a time when he felt that his judgments of Ireland had been too harsh and was thus having second thoughts about his homeland; "The Dead" was itself expressly conceived with the intent to recuperate some of the attractions of Ireland in the wake of the other *Dubliners* stories – thus he was trying *not* to forget his distinctly Irish heritage. As Joyce wrote to Stanislaus: "it seems to me that I have been unnecessarily harsh. I have reproduced (in *Dubliners* at least) none of the attraction of the city … I have not reproduced its ingenuous insularity and its hospitality. The latter 'virtue' so far as I can see does not exist elsewhere in Europe. I have not been just to its beauty: for it is more beautiful naturally in my opinion than what I have seen of England, Switzerland, France, Austria or Italy." Letter to Stanislaus Joyce, September 25, 1906, *Letters II*, 164.

    Furthermore, it is interesting to note that in 1902 Joyce had reviewed for *The Daily Express* William Rooney's patriotic poems, published by Arthur Griffith, founder of Sinn Fein. In *The Consciousness of Joyce*, Richard Ellmann argues convincingly that by 1906 (at the time when Joyce was conceiving "The Dead") Joyce had been won over by Griffith's non-extremist brand of nationalism and "approved Griffith's moderate programme" (86–88). Stanislaus claimed that Joyce read Griffith's newspaper *United Irishman* every week and Joyce himself wrote that it was the only policy of any benefit to Ireland (*Letters II*, 158; Manganiello, 118). Both Ellmann and Manganiello further document not only Joyce's own Irish Nationalist leanings at this time, but his intense interest and readings in socialism and his identification of himself as a "socialist."

18. A comment by Terry Eagleton applies incisively in this context: "This bankrupt Irish Arnoldianism is particularly ironic when one considers that the title of Arnold's own major work, *Culture and Anarchy*, might well have been rewritten as *Britain and Ireland*. The liberal humanist notion of Culture was constituted, among other things, to marginalize such peoples as the Irish, so that it is particularly intriguing to find this sectarian gesture being rehearsed by a few of the Irish themselves" ("Nationalism," 33).

    This sectarian gesture reflects Frantz Fanon's elaboration of the complicity in values between the colonialist intelligentsia and the colonizer: "The colonialist bourgeoisie, in its narcissistic dialogue, expounded by the members of its universities, had in fact deeply implanted in the minds of the colonized intellectual that the essential qualities remain eternal in spite of all the blunders men may make: the essential qualities of the [colonizing] West, of course" (*Wretched*, 36).

19. See also Norris ("Stifled" 500–1) on Freddy Malins.

20. This connection between horses and British economic collaboration and patriarchy will be extended in *Ulysses* to sexist Blazes Boylan, who – just as Gabriel is grandson to Patrick Morkan – is the son of a man who unpatriotically sold horses to the British during the Boer War. Boylan seems one extreme of Joyce's representation of the effects of the collusion between patriarchal imperial politics and patriarchal sexual politics.

   Owning horses was, through much of Irish history, itself a material and literal manifestation of British imperial/class politics and status. Under the Penal Laws, Catholics in Ireland were not only barred from Parliament, from the professions, and from public schools, but they were also forbidden to own a horse worth more than five pounds. See also chapter 9 of this study.

21. It is interesting to note that, on the cab ride home, Miss O'Callaghan comments as they pass O'Connell Bridge, " – They say you never cross O'Connell Bridge without seeing a white horse" – to which Gabriel replies that " – I see a white man this time" (214). In the white horse and the "white man" (the snow-capped statue of Daniel O'Connell) we have here, emblematically represented, the opposing forces of the British Empire (King Billy's white horse) and the Irish-Catholic resistance ("The Liberator").

22. Most recently, for example, Norris writes ("Stifled," 482): "In this superb staging of the aestheticizing act, Joyce displays his acute awareness that in their genderized form, in the male artist's representation of the female, the politics of representation are expressed in doubly brutal gestures of occlusion, oppression, and exploitation: doubly brutal, because these acts are masked as love. The very form of Gabriel's gesture toward woman – the rhetorical question ('He asked himself what is a woman ... a symbol of') that proclaims its disinterest in what woman is in favor of parading its own profundity – masks artistic conceit as gyneolatry. The generality of the question implies an answer of indeterminacy and over-determination, that woman is a symbol of anything and everything man wants her to represent – except her own sense of who or what she is."

23. See 124–25 of Bauerle ("Date Rape") for the words to this version of the song.

24. Bauerle writes: "Joyce would have felt little trouble calling the Lass of Aughrim's situation what feminists today call it: date rape ... It seems very likely that [Gretta] now identifies with the Lass of Aughrim, a victim of date rape, and sees herself as having been, too often, a victim of unwanted and perhaps forced sexual attention – that is, of mate rape by her hypereducated, though shallow, husband" ("Date Rape," 115, 118).

25. "Generous" as a key word in "The Dead" is given a much more

ironic interpretation by Vincent P. Pecora in " 'The Dead' and the Generosity of the Word." In my own reading of "generosity" (as derived from *genus, generis* just as "kindness" is derived from "kind" and "kin") as a desirable, socialistic breaking-down of hierarchy and individualistic status-formation, I am conscious of the phrase Joyce himself had used (in his essay "A Portrait of the Artist") in describing socialism as "the generous idea," within a passage arguing for the leveling of hierarchies (see Manganiello, *Joyce's Politics*, 68–69):

Already the messages of citizens were flashed along the wires of the world, already the generous idea had emerged from a thirty years' war in Germany and was directing the councils of the Latins. To those multitudes, not as yet in the wombs of humanity but surely engenderable there, he would give the word: Man and woman, out of you comes the nation that is to come, the lightening of your masses in travail; the competitive order is employed against itself, the aristocracies are supplanted; and amid the general paralysis of an insane society, the confederate will issues in action.

6 Imagining selves

1. Like all current scholars working on *Ulysses*, I am greatly indebted to the wealth of annotated information found in Don Gifford and Robert J. Seidman's *"Ulysses" Annotated: Notes for James Joyce's "Ulysses"* – itself, of course, a compendium of scholarly research done by many Joyce scholars over the past few decades.
2. In *Primitive Art in Civilized Places*, Sally Price demonstrates that "Like its now aging parent, colonialism, and its somewhat younger cousins, travel journalism and tourism, Primitive Art collecting is based on the Western principle that 'the world is ours'" (79).
3. Frantz Fanon uses the same trope in *The Wretched of the Earth*, noting that "the national middle class" will "take on the role of manager for Western [colonial] enterprise, and it will in practice set up its country as the brothel of Europe" (154).
   Later on, this meaning of "kip" will be reinforced when we are told that Polly Mooney's mother ("The Madam" in "A Boarding House") "kept a kip in Hardwicke street" (*U* 12.399).
4. Admittedly, Stephen is following somewhat in the recent footsteps of Wilde and Shaw, whose verbal witticisms were themselves further contributing to the discursive constructions and expectations of "Irish" verbal wit and spiritedness.
5. As W. J. McCormack notes: "In 1904 'the death of the Irish language was already a cliché, and attempts to revive Gaelic were already under way." "Nightmares of History: James Joyce and the Phenomenon of Anglo-Irish Literature," in *James Joyce and Modern Literature*, eds. W. J. McCormack and Alistair Stead, 84.

6. As Edward Hirsch has noted: "This gap or disjunction between the imaginary peasant ... and the real country people illuminates the language that informed both Irish culture and, consequently, Irish literature ... In Ireland the conjunction of pastoralism and romantic nationalism – of projecting an ancient, national, and unchanging Irish peasant culture deep into the past – went arm in arm with the project to [in Yeats's words] '[c]all the Muses home' " ("Imaginary," 1118, 1120).

7. Haines's anti-Semitism is presumably shared by Mulligan. As Ira Nadel points out in *Joyce and the Jews*: "[Arthur] Griffith's journal *Sinn Fein* published Oliver St. John Gogarty's anti-Semitic racist views ... Extending Griffith's earlier views of Jewish control of England, Gogarty emphasised the English prejudices and anti-Semitism attributed to Jewish dominance. Jews in Ireland can only bring similar decay and economic ruin he concluded, a view similar to that of Haines, Mr. Deasy, and the Citizen in *Ulysses*. In a letter to Stanlislaus, Joyce referred to Gogarty's essays as 'stupid drivel' " (66).

8. "Hegemony" is a term Joyce used in both *Ulysses* and *Finnegans Wake* (if not necessarily in the Gramscian usage). In "Ithaca," Bloom contemplates water and "its indisputable hegemony extending in square leagues over all the region" (*U* 17.194). In *Finnegans Wake*, Joyce asks: "Has he hegemony and shall she submit?" (*FW* 573.32).

9. For example: "Wanderers, then, by nature ... [the Jews] never could acquire a fixed home or abode. Literature, science, and art they possess not. It is against their nature – they never seem to have had a country, nor have they any yet." Or: "two hundred years at least before Christ they were perambulating Italy and Europe precisely as they do now, following the same occupations – that is, no occupation at all; that the real Jew has no ear for music as a race, no love of science or literature; that he invents nothing, pursues no inquiry." And so on (*Races*, 138, 131).

10. Among Joyce's acquaintances in Paris was Paul Robeson, whose concerts Joyce helped to promote. An entry from Eslanda Goode Robeson's diary (at Harvard University) records a tea party at Sylvia Beach's that included, among others, Joyce, Nora, Lucia, Hemingway and Mrs. Hemingway, George Antheil, and the Schirmers (the music publishers). My thanks to Sterling Stuckey for this information.

11. See Gayatri Spivak's provocative treatise on the implications of *suttee* and the arguments surrounding it, in "Can the Subaltern Speak?"

12. Similarly, in his Trieste lecture on Defoe, Joyce had analogized Robinson Crusoe and Friday in the roles of colonizing and colonized races: "The true symbol of the British conquest is Robinson Crusoe ... He is the true prototype of the British colonist, as Friday (the trusty savage who arrives on an unlucky day) is the symbol of the subject races. The whole Anglo-Saxon spirit is in Crusoe" (in Manganiello, *Joyce's Politics*, 109).

13. "The term 'whiteeyed kaffir' is a phrase Joyce has taken from one of Kipling's Boer War poems, 'Columns,' and refers to a traitorous

black African who alerts the Boers to the British presence. By means of this insult (the equivalent of 'nigger'), Joyce extends the Irish discrimination ... to include not only anti-Semitism, but the black/white issue as well." Barbara Temple-Thurston, "The Reader as Absentminded Beggar: Recovering South Africa in *Ulysses*" (252).

7 Imagining nations

1. Even in listening to such language, Stephen thinks of the rhetoric in terms of national history: "Gone with the wind. Hosts at Mullagh-mast and Tara" (*U* 7.880–81) – recalling Daniel O'Connell's "monster meetings" at Tara and Mullaghmast to protest against English mistreatment (Gifford, *"Ulysses" Annotated*, 150) – and perhaps an uncanny premonition of Margaret Mitchell's Tara in *Gone with the Wind*?

2. Cf. *FW* 260.R3: "THE PARTICULAR UNIVERSAL."

3. G. J. Watson goes so far as to suggest that "The politics of Joyce's *Ulysses* may be seen as a characteristically massive attempt to deconstruct the mythology of Romantic Ireland" ("Politics," 41).

4. "Patrick W. Shakespeare" is also a Joycean joke, equating his own name to that of Shakespeare's, since Patrick W. Joyce was a well-known Irish historian, some of whose reference works Joyce owned and used in writing his books. Patrick W. Joyce's *Irish Names of Places* had been named by Joyce in his poem "Gas from a Burner" (*JJII*, 336).

5. Emmet's attempt to seize Dublin Castle had been farcically botched – as was subsequently his public execution. Gifford, 124, notes: "But the mystery remains: how and why did this disastrous farce get transformed into one of the most potent Irish-hero myths?" He cites Robert Kee's *The Green Flag* (1972): "Why was it Robert Emmet's portrait above all others that was to go up along with the crucifix in countless small homes in Ireland for over a century and may even be seen there still? ... The proximity of the crucifix may provide a clue. The success of the Emmet myth lay in the very need to ennoble failure. For tragic failure was to become part of Ireland's identity, something almost indistinguishable from 'the cause' itself" (Gifford, *"Ulysses" Annotated*, 124).

6. See chapter 10 of this study, on "The general and the sepoy: imperialism and power in the Museyroom."

7. Joyce deflates the Citizen's advocacy for the Irish language by the latter's use of it in the episode – such as telling his dog Garryowen to " – *Bi i dho husht*" (*U* 12.265; shut up).

8. A recent episode of the CBS-TV sitcom "Brooklyn Bridge" showed the patriarch of an Irish family in Brooklyn, a policeman who wanted to have nothing to do with Brooklyn Jews, appropriately preparing to meet the Jewish family portrayed in the series, by militaristically and xenophobically playing "A Nation Once Again" on his record player.

The song reappears in *Finnegans Wake* as "Innition wons agame" (*FW* 614.17–18).

9. This anachronistic lynching (it took place in Omaha, Nebraska on September 28, 1919) became international news: the victim had been accused of raping a young white woman; the lynch mob hanged him, "riddled his body with bullets, and burned it"; they tried to lynch the mayor, who tried to stop the rampage against blacks which ensued. It was the London *Times* that mistakenly reported Omaha as being in Georgia. Cf. Timothy Weiss, "The 'Black Beast' Headline: The Key to an Allusion in *Ulysses*," 183–86; and Gifford, *"Ulysses" Annotated*, 357.

10. As Watson points out, for Fenians such as Padraic Pearse (or Michael Cusack), "to be Irish meant to be a hater of England, a Gaelic speaker, a Catholic, and a believer in physical force" ("Politics," 43).

11. Erwin R. Steinberg has shown that in the months preceding June 1904, Jews were being massacred in Morocco; the reports made headlines in both the London *Times* and *The New York Times*. Steinberg, "'Persecuted ... sold ... in Morocco like slaves'," 615–22.

12. One could argue, even after 1922, that "Ireland" still has not existed as a sovereign nation – for the Republic continues to claim Northern Ireland as part of its national sovereignty and thus as part of the "imagined" community of "Ireland." Such an "Ireland" – which is to say, the entire island as one sovereign community – has never existed in history.

13. As Seamus Deane points out: "In revealing the essentially fictive nature of political imagining, Joyce did not repudiate Irish nationalism. Instead he understood it as a potent example of a rhetoric which imagined as true structures that did not and were never to exist outside language" (*Celtic*, 107).

14. David Lloyd writes: "Even in its oppositional stance, nationalism repeats the master narrative of imperialism, the narrative of development that is always applied with extreme rigor and priority to colonized peoples ... The nationalist desire to develop the race into authenticity, borrowed already from a universalist ideology, produces the hegemonic conditions for the ultimate perpetuation of imperial domination even after independence is achieved" ("Writing," 83–84).

   As G. J. Watson suggests, it was "perhaps inevitable that the tides of nationalism which swept all of Europe in the nineteenth century should have led, in Ireland, to the construction of a set of compensatory myths which would appropriate, shape, and glamorize the dismal story. This version of Irish history is powerfully teleological, even apocalyptic" ("Politics," 51). *Ulysses*, Watson agrees, "presents a powerful critique of this unholy alliance of romanticism, nationalism, and aestheticized history" (52).

   On the other hand, Terry Eagleton has argued in an essay on "Joyce and Mythology" (310) that:

   If colonialism tends to deprive those it subjugates not only of their land, language, and culture but of their very history ... then it is arguable that the mythological image of Ireland ... is itself a markedly historical phenomenon. A people robbed of their sense of agency and autonomy, unable to decipher the social institutions around them as expressions of their own life-practice, may tend quite reasonably to read their collective experience through the deterministic optic of mythology, with its sense of human life as shaped by the mighty forces of some process quite hidden to consciousness. Myth is in this sense less some regrettable, primitive irrationalism than a kind of historical truth.

8 Imagining futures: nations, narratives, selves

1. Joyce himself had, in his essays, spoken of "the new Ireland in the near future" (CW 228).
2. The autobiographical resonances and sources concerning Joyce, Carr, and Percy Bennett of the consular staff in Zurich are well known.
3. Laura Doyle has posited an interesting reading of these lines, placing Cissy Caffrey (as well as Molly Bloom) – as "woman, sacred lifegiver" and "link between nations and generations" – in the context of a "deeply embedded cultural matrix in which feuds over race or nationality and claims on 'sacred' motherhood depend on each other" ("Races," 149).
4. Ellmann has suggested that "The central action of *Ulysses* is to bring together Stephen Dedalus and Leopold Bloom by displaying their underlying agreement on political views which the author thereby underwrites" (*Consciousness*, 90).
5. When "the so-called national party behaves as a party based on ethnic differences," Fanon argues, it "becomes, in fact, the tribe which ... claims to speak in the name of the totality of the people ... [and] organizes an authentic ethnic dictatorship. We no longer see the rise of a bourgeois dictatorship, but a tribal dictatorship" (*Wretched*, 183).
6. As David Lloyd argues in *Anomalous States: Irish Writing and the Post-Colonial Moment*: "*Ulysses*'s most radical movement is in its refusal to fulfil either of these demands [i.e., individual and stylistic totalizations] and its correspondent refusal to subordinate itself to the socializing functions of identity formation. It insists instead on a deliberate stylization of dependence and inauthenticity, a stylization of the hybrid status of the colonized subject as of the colonized culture, their internal adulteration and the strictly parodic modes that they produce in every sphere" (110).

9 White horse, dark horse: Joyce's allhorse of another color

1. I might add that I have very recently learned from Karl Reisman that he has been working on African, African American, and West Indian references in *Finnegans Wake*, including allusions to W. E. B. DuBois and Marcus Garvey.
2. As Joyce noted in his essay on "Ireland, Island of Saints and Sages": "Today, a Catholic in Ireland can vote, can become a government

employee, can practise a trade or profession, can teach in a public school, can sit in parliament, can own his own land for longer than thirty years, can keep in his stalls a horse worth more than five pounds sterling, and can attend a Catholic mass, without running the risk of being hanged, drawn, and quartered by the common hangman. But these laws have been revoked such a short time ago ...'' (*CW* 168).

3. As Frantz Fanon has noted, the colonial world is a "world of statues" – of monuments everywhere to the imperial conquerors (*Black Skin, White Masks*, 51–52).

4. This is the same equestrian statue which, in "The Dead," Patrick Morkan's horse Johnny had been enamored of: "... Johnny came in sight of King Billy's statue: and whether he fell in love with the horse King Billy sits on or whether he thought he was back again in the mill, anyhow he began to walk round the statue ...' " (*D* 208).

5. Stephen uses this metaphor for treachery again in "Scylla and Charybdis," combining it with a metaphor of promiscuous and treacherous women as mares that many men ride: "Argive Helen, the wooden mare of Troy in whom a score of heroes slept" (*U* 9.622–23) and Mistress Mary Fitton, "the bay where all men ride, a maid of honour with a scandalous girlhood" (*U* 9.452–53).

6. In his sexual fantasies Bloom even imagines himself becoming a horse ridden by dominating women ("Strong as a brood mare some of those horsey women. Swagger around livery stables" – *U* 8.345–46), reversing the usual male/macho imperative, willing to see himself dominated (ridden) as much as dominating (riding): in "Circe," Mrs. Talboys, Mrs. Bellingham, and Mrs. Barry accuse Bloom of writing letters in which he "implored [them] ... to chastise him as he richly deserves, to bestride him and ride him, to give him a most vicious horsewhipping" (*U* 15.1070–73). In a reversal of both domination and gender, Bloom then *does* become a horse which Bello rides roughly and cruelly (see *U* 15.2950–60).

7. In "Eumaeus," when the cabman's horse drops "three smoking globes of turds" on the street (*U* 16.1876–77), there is a hint that the crapping horse may be for Joyce even a general metaphor for the "chaosmos" of both world and text – for the cabdriver, supervising his horse, is described thus: "the lord of his creation [who] sat on the perch ... [and] never said a word, good, bad, or indifferent, but merely watched" (*U* 16.1785–86) – like Stephen's "artist," "the God of the creation ... above his handiwork, ... indifferent, paring his fingernails" (*P* 215).

8. Upon Copenhagen's death, Wellington remarked: "There have been many faster horses, no doubt many handsomer, but for bottom and endurance I never saw his fellow" (Bryant, *The Great Duke*, 451; Longford, *Years*, 484).

9. James Atherton assumes that Copenhagen and Napoleon's Marengo are "both white horses" (155), but Glasheen has pointed out that Copenhagen "was not white – Marengo was" (62). Copenhagen was "a strong chestnut" born to a mare named Lady Catherine:

"Copenhagen had Arab blood from his dam and was a grandson of the famous race-horse Eclipse, whose son, Young Eclipse, was the second horse to win the Derby" (Longford, *Years*, 484).

10. So it doesn't really matter if we are "pudding the carp before d'oevre hors" (*FW* 164.18).
11. I would like to thank Richard Yarborough for helping me to clarify this point.
12. As Henriette Lazaridis Power notes, Wakean narrative "is a form of *de-scription*, the unwriting of any particular text" ("Shahrazade," 256). By encoding a surplus of pluralistic significations and inscriptions, Wakese de-scripts the "symbolic" discourse of the Father by removing the possibilities of a monologic signification, rendering the *Wake*'s "semiotic" discourse "heterogeneous of meaning but always in sight of it, or in either a negative or surplus relationship to it" (Kristeva, *Desire*, 133).
13. The "whorse proceedings" here also have overtones of sexual politics and sexual dynamics: "turftussle" recalls "on the turf" (from "Two Gallants") as slang for prostitution, within the metaphor of sexual "riding" (horse/whores/whorse); and the ten-to-one outsider seems also to involve temptation and women ("Tempt to wom Outsider").
14. Joyce had written (in his notes to *Exiles*) that "All Celtic philosophers seemed to have inclined towards incertitude or scepticism – Hume, Berkeley, Balfour, Bergson" (*E* 159).

10 The general and the sepoy: imperialism and power in the Museyroom

1. As Manganiello (183) has noted, both Stannie and Gogarty had referred to *Finnegans Wake* as "literary bolshevism."
2. Among the references in this passage to battles *not* connected to Wellington are "Saloos" (Salo, Loos), "magentic" (Magenta), "goldtin spurs" (Golden Spurs), "pulluponeasyan wartrews" (Pelopponesian War), "boyne," "Mons," "crimealine," "phillippy," "hastings," "fontannoy," "agincourting," "stampforth" (Stamford), "camelry" (Camel), "floodens" (Floddens Field), "action" (Actium), "their mobbily" (Thermopylae), "panickburns" (Bannockburn), "bunkersheels" (Bunker Hill), "marathon," "spy on" (Spion Kop). Some of these are listed in McHugh, *Annotations*, 8–10.
3. I am indebted to Hemalatha Chari for telling me about the Wellington statue in Madras. As Fanon puts it, the colonial world is a "world of statues" (*Black Skin*, 51–52).
4. "Mons Injun" is also Mont St. Jean, where Napoleon's troops were centered at Waterloo.
5. I am of course again invoking Gayatri Spivak's complex and cogent treatment of the intricacies in positing subaltern discourses, "Can the Subaltern Speak?"
6. McHugh notes that "pukkaroo" is Anglo-Indian for "seize!" (10).
7. Joyce had earlier referred to this outrage in *Ulysses*, when one of the British officers presiding at Robert Emmet's hanging (in a parodic

section of "Cyclops") is identified as "he who had blown a considerable number of sepoys from the cannonmouth without flinching" (*U* 12.671–72).

8. Glasheen, *Third Census*, 79. The veiled Irish presence within the hegemonic structure of English imperialism (as in Wellington himself) is again suggested here, since – as Joyce himself noted in 1907 (in "Ireland, Island of Saints and Sages"): "the Marquess of Dufferin, Governor of Canada and Viceroy of India, like Charles Gavin [sic] Duffy, and Hennessey, colonial governors" (Hennessey was Deputy Surveyor-General of India) were all Irish (*CW* 172).

Joyce noted further that "the three most renowned generals of the English army – Lord Wolseley, the commander-in-chief, Lord Kitchener, victor of the Sudan campaign and at present commanding general of the army in India, and Lord Roberts, victor of the war in Afghanistan and South Africa" – were also Irish: "if Ireland has been able to give all this practical talent to the service of others, it means that there must be something inimical, unpropitious, and despotic in its own present conditions, since her sons cannot give their efforts to their own native land" (*CW* 172).

11 Conclusion

1. Edward Said has recently argued (in his essay on "Yeats and Decolonization") for "*liberation*, and not nationalist independence, [as] the new alternative, liberation which by its very nature involves, in Fanon's words, a transformation of social consciousness beyond national consciousness"; Said argues for such "liberation" as a mode of getting beyond the nativist impasse of "Imagined community, Benedict Anderson's fine phrase for emergent nationalism": "You don't give in to the rigidity and interdictions of those self-imposed limitations that come with race, moment, or milieu; instead, you move through them to an animated and expanded sense of 'le rendez-vous de la conquête,' which necessarily involves more than your Ireland, your Martinique, your Pakistan, etc." ("Yeats," 83, 86, 85).

2. Joyce aspired to be, like Shem, a "Europasianised Afferyank" (*FW* 191.04).

3. As Terry Eagleton notes in his recent essay on "Nationalism: Irony and Commitment" (30): "Ironically, then, a politics of difference or specificity is in the first place in the cause of sameness and universal identity – the right of a group victimized in its particularity to be on equal terms with others as far as their self-determination is concerned … In a further dialectical twist, however, this truth itself must be left behind as soon as seized; for the only point of enjoying such universal abstract equality is to discover and live one's own particular difference. The *telos* of the entire process is not, as the Enlightenment believed, universal truth, right and identity, but concrete particularity." In this sense, I feel, Joyce's texts satisfy both urges simultaneously.

4. As David Pierce asks pointedly in his essay on "The Politics of *Finnegans Wake*" (252): "Put differently, could the time needed to understand *Finnegans Wake* be better spent changing the world? Is there not a tyranny on Joyce's part in requiring so much time and attention from the reader? Have all the words written by the professors in interpreting the text contributed to anything significant beyond the Joyce confederacy? Has *Finnegans Wake*, in Brecht's words, shortened 'the age of exploitation'?"

Works cited

Adams, Robert M. "A Study in Weakness and Humiliation." In Baker and Staley, eds., *James Joyce's "Dubliners": A Critical Handbook*. 101–04.

Surface and Symbol: The Consistency of James Joyce's "Ulysses." New York: Oxford University Press, 1962.

Anderson, Benedict. *Imagined Communities: Reflections on the Origin and Spread of Nationalism*, revised edition. London: Verso, 1991.

Anzaldúa, Gloria. *Borderlands/La Frontera: The New Mestiza*. San Francisco: Spinsters/Aunt Lute, 1987.

Atherton, James S. *The Books at the Wake*. Carbondale: Southern Illinois University Press, 1959.

Attridge, Derek, ed. *The Cambridge Companion to James Joyce*. Cambridge: Cambridge University Press, 1990.

Axtell, James. *The European and the Indian: Essays in the Ethnohistory of Colonial North America*. New York: Oxford University Press, 1981.

Baker, James R. and Thomas F. Staley, eds. *James Joyce's "Dubliners": A Critical Handbook*. Belmont, CA: Wadsworth, 1969.

Banton, Michael. *Racial Theories*. Cambridge: Cambridge University Press, 1987.

Bauerle, Ruth. "Date Rape, Mate Rape: A Liturgical Interpretation of 'The Dead.'" In *New Alliances in Joyce Studies*, ed. Bonnie Kime Scott. Newark: University of Delaware Press, 1988. 113–25.

The James Joyce Songbook. New York: Garland, 1982.

Beja, Morris, and Shari Benstock, eds. *Coping with Joyce: Essays from the Copenhagen Symposium*. Columbus: Ohio State University Press, 1989.

Bhabha, Homi K. "Difference, Discrimination, and the Discourse of Colonialism." In *The Politics of Theory*, ed. Francis Barker et al. Colchester: University of Essex, 1983.

"DissemiNation: Time, Narrative, and the Margins of the Modern Nation." In Bhabha, ed., *Nation and Narration*. 291–322.

"Of Mimicry and Man: The Ambivalence of Colonial Discourse." *October*, 28 (Spring 1984), 125–33.

Works cited

"The Other Question." *Screen*, 24.6 (1983), 18–35.
Bhabha, Homi K., ed. *Nation and Narration*. London: Routledge, 1990.
Bishop, John. *Joyce's Book of the Dark*. Madison: University of Wisconsin Press, 1987.
Bloom, Harold, ed. *James Joyce's "Dubliners": Modern Critical Interpretations*. New York: Chelsea, 1988.
Bowen, Zack. "After the Race." In Hart, ed., *James Joyce's "Dubliners": Critical Essays*. 53–61.
The Encyclopaedia Britannica, eleventh edition. Cambridge: Cambridge University Press, 1911.
The New Encyclopaedia Britannica, fifteenth edition, *Micropaedia* vol. 2 (448: "Boyne, Battle of the"). Chicago: Encyclopaedia Britannica Inc., 1992.
Bryant, Arthur. *The Great Duke*. New York: William Morrow, 1972.
Carlyle, Thomas. *The Works of Thomas Carlyle*, vol. 29. London, 1989.
Chayes, Irene Hendry. "Joyce's Epiphanies." In *A Portrait of the Artist as a Young Man: Text, Criticism, Notes*, ed. Chester A. Anderson. New York: Viking Critical Library, 1968.
Cheng, Vincent J. "Empire and Patriarchy in 'The Dead.' " In *Joyce Studies Annual 1993*, ed. Thomas F. Staley. Austin: University of Texas Press, 1993. 16–42.
"The General and the Sepoy: Imperialism and Power in Joyce's Museyroom." In Patrick McCarthy, ed., *Critical Essays on "Finnegans Wake."* 258–68.
"Le Cid": A Translation in Rhymed Couplets. Newark: University of Delaware Press, 1987.
Shakespeare and Joyce: A Study of "Finnegans Wake." University Park: Pennsylvania State University Press, 1984.
"White Horse, Dark Horse: Joyce's Allhorse of Another Color." In *Joyce Studies Annual 1991*, ed. Thomas F. Staley. Austin: University of Texas Press, 1991. 101–28.
Cheng, Vincent J. and Timothy Martin, eds. *Joyce in Context*. Cambridge: Cambridge University Press, 1992.
Cheyette, Bryan. " 'Jewgreek is greekjew': The Disturbing Ambivalence of Joyce's Semitic Discourse in *Ulysses*." *Joyce Studies Annual 1992*, ed. Thomas F. Staley. Austin: University of Texas, 1992. 32–56.
Cixous, Hélène and Catherine Clément. *The Newly Born Woman*, trans. Betsy Wing. Manchester: Manchester University Press, 1986.
Clifford, James. "Four Northwest Coast Museums: Travel Reflections." In *Exhibiting Cultures: The Poetics and Politics of Museum Display*, eds. Ivan Karp and Steven D. Lavine. Washington, DC: Smithsonian Institution Press, 1991. 212–54.
"Traveling Cultures." In *Cultural Studies*, eds. Lawrence Grossberg, Cary Nelson, Paula Treichler. London: Routledge, 1991. 96–116.
The Commitments. Film. Alan Parker, director.
Crenshaw, Kimberle. "A Black Feminist Critique of Antidiscrimination Law and Politics." In *The Politics of Law: A Progressive Critique*, revised edition, ed. David Kairys. New York: Pantheon, 1990.

Curtis, L. P., Jr. *Anglo-Saxons and Celts: A Study of Anti-Irish Prejudice in Victorian England.* Bridgeport, CT: University of Bridgeport, 1968.

Apes and Angels: The Irishman in Victorian Caricature. Washington: Smithsonian Institution Press, 1971.

Dahl, Robert. *Modern Political Analysis.* Englewood Cliffs, NJ: Prentice-Hall, 1970.

Darwin, Charles. *The Descent of Man and Selection in Relation to Sex.* London: John Murray, 1882.

Deane, Seamus. *Celtic Revivals: Essays in Modern Irish Literature 1880–1980.* London: Faber and Faber, 1985.

Heroic Styles: The Tradition of an Idea. Derry: Field Day pamphlet no. 4, 1984.

"Introduction" to *Nationalism, Colonialism, and Literature,* by Terry Eagleton, Fredric Jameson, and Edward W. Said. Minneapolis: University of Minnesota Press, 1990. 3–19.

"Joyce the Irishman." In *The Cambridge Companion to James Joyce,* ed. Derek Attridge. 31–53.

"'Masked with Matthew Arnold's Face': Joyce and Liberalism." In *James Joyce: The Centennial Symposium,* eds. Morris Beja, Philip Herring, Maurice Harmon, and David Norris. Urbana: Univeristy of Illinois Press, 1986. 9–20.

"National Character and National Audience: Races, Crowds and Readers." In *Critical Approaches to Anglo-Irish Literature,* eds. Michael Allen and Angela Wilcox. Totowa, NJ: Barnes & Noble, 1989. 40–52.

Derrida, Jacques. *Margins of Philosophy,* trans. Alan Bass. Chicago: University of Chicago Press, 1982.

Writing and Difference, trans. Alan Bass. Chicago: University of Chicago Press, 1978.

Devlin, Kimberly J. *Wandering and Return in "Finnegans Wake": An Integrative Approach to Joyce's Fictions.* Princeton: Princeton University Press, 1991.

Doyle, Laura. "Races and Chains: The Sexuo-Racial Matrix in *Ulysses.*" In Friedman, ed., *Joyce: The Return of the Repressed.* 149–89.

Eagleton, Terry. "Joyce and Mythology." In *Omnium Gatherum: Essays for Richard Ellmann,* eds. Susan Dick, Declan Kiberd, Dougald McMillan, and Joseph Ronsley. Gerrards Cross: Colin Smythe, 1989. 310–19.

"Nationalism: Irony and Commitment." In *Nationalism, Colonialism, and Literature* by Eagleton, Fredric Jameson, Edward W. Said (intro. by Seamus Deane). 23–39.

Eagleton, Terry, Fredric Jameson, and Edward W. Said. *Nationalism, Colonialism, and Literature* (intro. by Seamus Deane). A Field Day Company Book. Minneapolis: University of Minnesota Press, 1990.

Ellmann, Richard. *The Consciousness of Joyce.* New York: Oxford University Press, 1977.

James Joyce, first edition. Oxford: Oxford University Press, 1959.

James Joyce, revised edition. Oxford: Oxford University Press, 1982.

Works cited

Fairhall, James. "Big Power Politics and Colonial Economics: The Gordon Bennett Cup Race and 'After the Race.'" *James Joyce Quarterly*, 28.2 (Winter 1991), 387–97.

Fanon, Frantz. *Black Skin, White Masks*, trans. Charles Lam Markmann. New York: Grove Weidenfeld, 1967.

The Wretched of the Earth, trans. Constance Farrington. New York: Grove Weidenfeld, 1968.

Flood, Jeanne A. "Joyce and the Maamtrasna Murders." *James Joyce Quarterly*, 28.4 (Summer 1991), 879–88.

Ford, Charles. "Dante's Other Brush: *Ulysses* and the Irish Revolution." *James Joyce Quarterly*, 29.4 (Summer 1992), 751–61.

Forster, E. M. *A Passage to India*. New York: Harcourt, Brace, and World, 1952.

Foster, R. F. *Modern Ireland 1600–1972*. London: Penguin, 1988.

Foucault, Michel. *The Order of Things: An Archaeology of the Human Sciences*. London: Tavistock Publications, 1970.

Freud, Sigmund. *The Future of an Illusion*, trans. James Strachey. New York: Norton, 1961.

Jokes and their Relation to the Unconscious, trans. James Strachey. New York: Norton, 1989.

Friedman, Susan Stanford, ed. *Joyce: The Return of the Repressed*. Ithaca: Cornell University Press, 1993.

Gates, Henry Louis, Jr., ed. *"Race," Writing, and Difference*. Chicago: University of Chicago Press, 1986.

Gibbons, Luke. "Race Against Time: Racial Discourse and Irish History." In *The Oxford Literary Review*, 13: 1–2 (1991): *Neocolonialism*, ed. Robert Young. 95–117.

Gifford, Don. *Joyce Annotated: Notes for "Dubliners" and "A Portrait of the Artist as a Young Man."* Berkeley: University of California Press, 1982.

Gifford, Don, and Robert J. Seidman. *"Ulysses" Annotated: Notes for James Joyce's "Ulysses,"* revised edition. Berkeley: University of California Press, 1988.

Glasheen, Adaline. *Third Census of "Finnegans Wake."* Berkeley: University of California Press, 1977.

Gramsci, Antonio. *Selections from the Prison Notebooks*, ed. G. Nowell Smith and Q. Hoare. New York: International Publications, 1971.

Hall, Stuart. "Gramsci's Relevance for the Study of Race and Ethnicity." *Journal of Communication Inquiry*, 10.2 (1986), 5–27.

Hart, Clive, ed. *James Joyce's "Dubliners": Critical Essays*. New York: Viking, 1969.

Hawthorn, Jeremy. "*Ulysses*, Modernism, and Marxist Criticism." In McCormack and Stead, eds., *James Joyce and Modern Literature*. 112–25.

Herr, Cheryl. *Joyce's Anatomy of Culture*. Urbana: University of Illinois Press, 1986.

Hirsch, Edward. "The Imaginary Irish Peasant." *PMLA*, 106.5 (October 1991), 1116–33.

Hume, David. *A History of England*, new edition, vol. 5. London, 1796.

Hyde, Douglas. "The Necessity for De-Anglicising Ireland." In *Language, Lore and Lyrics: Essays and Lectures* by Douglas Hyde, ed. Breandan O Conaire. Dublin: Irish Academic Press, 1986. 153–70.

Jameson, Fredric. "Modernism and Imperialism." In Eagleton et al., *Nationalism, Colonialism, and Literature.* 43–66.

"*Ulysses* and History." In *James Joyce and Modern Literature*, eds. W. J. McCormack and Alistair Stead. 126–41.

JanMohamed, Abdul R. and David Lloyd. "Introduction: Toward a Theory of Minority Discourse: What Is To Be Done?" In *The Nature and Context of Minority Discourse*, eds. Abdul R. JanMohamed and David Lloyd. Oxford: Oxford University Press, 1990. 1–16.

Jones, Ellen Carol, ed. *Feminist Readings of Joyce.* Special Issue of *Modern Fiction Studies*, 35.3 (Autumn 1989).

Joyce, James. *The Critical Writings of James Joyce*, eds. Ellsworth Mason and Richard Ellmann. New York: Viking, 1964.

Dubliners: Text, Criticism, and Notes, eds. Robert Scholes and A. Walton Litz. New York: Viking, 1969.

Exiles: A Play in Three Acts. New York: Viking, 1951.

Finnegans Wake. New York: Viking, 1939.

A First-Draft Version of "Finnegans Wake," ed. David Hayman. Austin: University of Texas Press, 1963.

Letters of James Joyce, II and III, ed. Richard Ellmann. New York: Viking, 1966.

A Portrait of the Artist as a Young Man: Text, Criticism, and Notes, ed. Chester G. Anderson. New York: Viking, 1968.

Stephen Hero, eds. John J. Slocum and Herbert Cahoon. Norfolk, CT: New Directions, 1959.

Ulysses, eds. Hans Walter Gabler et al. New York: Vintage, 1986.

Kershner, R. B. *Joyce, Bakhtin, and Popular Literature: Chronicles of Disorder.* Chapel Hill: University of North Carolina Press, 1989.

"*Ulysses* and the Orient." Unpublished essay.

Knox, Robert, MD. *The Races of Men: A Fragment.* Philadelphia: Lea & Blanchard, 1850. Reprinted Miami: Mnemosyne Publishing, 1969.

Kristeva, Julia. *Desire in Language: A Semiotic Approach to Literature and Art.* New York: Columbia University Press, 1980.

Lebow, Richard Ned. *White Britain and Black Ireland: The Influence of Stereotypes on Colonial Policy.* Philadelphia: Institute for the Study of Human Issues, 1976.

Litz, A. Walton. "Two Gallants." In Scholes and Litz, eds., *"Dubliners": Text, Criticism, and Notes.* 368–78.

Lloyd, David. *Anomalous States: Irish Writing and the Post-Colonial Moment.* Durham: Duke University Press, 1993.

Nationalism and Minor Literature: James Clarence Mangan and the Emergence of Irish Cultural Nationalism. Berkeley: University of California Press, 1987.

"Writing in the Shit: Beckett, Nationalism, and the Colonial Subject." *Modern Fiction Studies*, 35.1 (Spring 1989); (special issue on *Narratives of Colonial Resistance*, guest editor Timothy Brennan), 71–86.

Works cited

Longford, Elizabeth. *Wellington: Pillar of State*. New York: Harper & Row, 1972.
   Wellington: The Years of the Sword. New York: Harper & Row, 1969.
Lowe, Lisa. *Critical Terrains: French and British Orientalisms*. Ithaca: Cornell University Press, 1991.
Lowe-Evans, Mary. *Crimes Against Fecundity: Joyce and Population Control*. Syracuse: Syracuse University Press, 1989.
Luedtke, Luther. "Julian Hawthorne's Passage to India." Unpublished essay.
Lyons, F. S. L. *Culture and Anarchy in Ireland 1890–1939*. Oxford: Clarendon Press, 1979.
MacCabe, Colin. "*Finnegans Wake* at Fifty." *Critical Quarterly*, 31.4, 3–5.
   James Joyce and the Revolution of the Word. New York: Barnes & Noble, 1979.
Mahaffey, Vicki. *Reauthorizing Joyce*. Cambridge: Cambridge University Press, 1988.
Manganiello, Dominic. *Joyce's Politics*. London: Routledge and Kegan Paul, 1980.
   "The Politics of the Unpolitical in Joyce's Fictions." *James Joyce Quarterly*, 29.2 (Winter 1992), 241–58.
McCarthy, Patrick A., ed. *Critical Essays on James Joyce's "Finnegans Wake."* New York: G. K. Hall, 1992.
McCormack, W. J. "Nightmares of History: James Joyce and the Phenomenon of Anglo-Irish Literature," in McCormack and Stead, eds., *James Joyce and Modern Literature*. 77–107.
McCormack, W. J., and Alistair Stead, eds. *James Joyce and Modern Literature*. London: Routledge & Kegan Paul, 1982.
McGee, Patrick. *Telling the Other: The Question of Value in Modern and Postcolonial Writing*. Ithaca: Cornell University Press, 1992.
McHugh, Roland. *Annotations to "Finnegans Wake."* Baltimore: Johns Hopkins University Press, 1980.
Mohanty, Chandra Talpade. "Under Western Eyes: Feminist Scholarship and Colonial Discourses." *Boundary 2*, 12.3/13.1 (1984), 333–358.
Moretti, Franco. *Signs Taken For Wonders: Essays in the Sociology of Literary Forms*, trans. Susan Fischer, David Forgacs, and David Miller. London: Verso, 1983.
Nadel, Ira B. *Joyce and the Jews: Culture and Texts*. Iowa City: University of Iowa Press, 1989.
Norris, Margot. *The Decentered Universe of "Finnegans Wake."* Baltimore: Johns Hopkins University Press, 1980.
   Joyce's Web: The Social Unraveling of Modernism. Austin: University of Texas Press, 1992.
   "Narration Under a Blindfold: Reading Joyce's 'Clay.'" *PMLA*, 102.2 (March 1987), 206–15.
   "Stifled Back Answers: The Gender Politics of Art in Joyce's 'The Dead.'" *Modern Fiction Studies*, 35.3 (Autumn 1989), 479–506.
O'Brien, Maire and Conor Cruise O'Brien. *A Concise History of Ireland*, third edition. New York: Thames & Hudson, 1985.

O'Connor, Theresa. "Demythologizing Nationalism: Joyce's Dialogized Grail Myth." In *Joyce in Context*, eds. Cheng and Martin. 100–21.

O'Farrell, Patrick. *England and Ireland Since 1800*. Oxford: Oxford University Press, 1975.

O'Grady, Thomas B. " 'Ivy Day in the Committee Room': The Use and Abuse of Parnell." In Harold Bloom, ed., *James Joyce's "Dubliners": Modern Critical Interpretations*. 131–42.

O Hehir, Brendan. *A Gaelic Lexicon for "Finnegans Wake."* Berkeley: University of California Press, 1967.

Pecora, Vincent P. " 'The Dead' and the Generosity of the Word." *PMLA*, 101.2 (March 1986), 233–45.

Pierce, David. "The Politics of *Finnegans Wake*." In *Critical Essays on James Joyce's "Finnegans Wake"*, ed. Patrick A. McCarthy. 243–57.

Potts, Willard. "The Catholic Revival and 'The Dead'." *Joyce Studies Annual 1991*, ed. Thomas F. Staley. Austin: University of Texas, 1991. 3–26.

Power, Henriette Lazaridis. "Shahrazade, Turko the Terrible, and Shem: The Reader as Voyeur in *Finnegans Wake*." In Beja and Benstock, eds., *Coping with Joyce: Essays from the Copenhagen Symposium*. 248–61.

Pratt, Mary Louise. "Arts of the Contact Zone." In *Profession 91*, ed. Phyllis Franklin. New York: MLA, 1991. 33–40.

Price, Sally. *Primitive Art in Civilized Places*. Chicago: University of Chicago Press, 1989.

Renan, Ernest. "What is a Nation?" In *Nation and Narration*, ed. Bhabha. 8–22.

Rushdie, Salman. "The Book Burning." *New York Review of Books*, 36.3 (March 2, 1989), 26.

Ruskin, John. *The Works of John Ruskin*. London: G. Allen, 1908.

Said, Edward W. *Orientalism*. New York: Vintage, 1979.

"Yeats and Decolonization." In Eagleton et al., *Nationalism, Colonialism, and Literature*. 69–95.

Sartre, Jean-Paul. "Preface" to Frantz Fanon, *The Wretched of the Earth*. 7–34.

Scholes, Robert. "Counterparts." In Scholes and Litz, eds., *"Dubliners": Text, Criticism, and Notes*. 379–87.

"Joyce and Modernist Ideology." In Beja and Benstock, eds., *Coping with Joyce: Essays from the Copenhagen Symposium*. 91–107.

Scholes, Robert and A. Walton Litz, eds. *Dubliners: Text, Criticism, and Notes*. New York: Viking, 1969.

Scott, Paul. *The Raj Quartet*. New York: Avon, 1979.

Senn, Fritz. "An Encounter." In Hart, ed., *James Joyce's "Dubliners": Critical Essays*. 26–38.

Shaffer, Brian W. *The Blinding Torch: Modern British Fiction and the Discourse of Civilization*. Amherst: University of Massachusetts Press, 1993.

"Joyce and Freud: Discontent and Its Civilizations." In Cheng and Martin, eds., *Joyce in Context*. 73–88.

Shloss, Carol. "Molly's Resistance to the Union: Marriage and Colonialism in Dublin, 1904." *Modern Fiction Studies*, 35.3 (Autumn 1989), 529–41.

Simmons, William S. "Culture Theory in Contemporary Ethnohistory." *Ethnohistory*, 35.1 (1988), 1–14.

Spivak, Gayatri Chakravorty. "Can the Subaltern Speak?" *Marxism and the Interpretation of Culture*, eds. Cary Nelson and Lawrence Grossberg. Champaign: University of Illinois Press, 1988. 271–313.

"The Rani of Sirmur." In *Europe and Its Others*, vol. I, eds. Francis Barker et al. Colchester: University of Essex, 1985. 128–51.

Spoo, Robert. "Uncanny Returns in 'The Dead': Ibsenian Intertexts and the Estranged Infant." In Friedman, ed., *Joyce: The Return of the Repressed*. 89–113.

Steinberg, Erwin R. "'Persecuted ... Sold ... in Morocco like Slaves'." *James Joyce Quarterly*, 29.3 (Spring 1992), 615–22.

Stone, Harry. "'Araby' and the Writings of James Joyce." In Scholes and Litz, eds., *Dubliners: Text, Criticism, and Notes*. 344–67.

Temple-Thurston, Barbara. "The Reader as Absentminded Beggar: Recovering South Africa in *Ulysses*." *James Joyce Quarterly*, 28.1 (Fall 1990), 247–56.

Tindall, William York. *A Reader's Guide to "Finnegans Wake."* New York: Farrar, Straus, and Giroux, 1969.

A Reader's Guide to James Joyce. New York: Farrar, Straus, and Giroux, 1959.

Trinh, T. Minh-ha. *Woman Native Other*. Bloomington: Indiana University Press, 1989.

Vizenor, Gerald. *Crossbloods*. Minneapolis: University of Minnesota Press, 1990.

Watson, G. J. "The Politics of *Ulysses*." In *Joyce's "Ulysses": The Larger Perspective*, eds. Robert D. Newman and Weldon Thornton. Newark: University of Delaware Press, 1987.

Webb, Virginia-Lee. "Manipulated Images: European Photographs of Pacific Peoples." In *Prehistories of the Future*, eds. Elazar Barkan and Ronald Bush. Stanford, CA: Stanford University Press, 1994.

Weiss, Timothy. "The 'Black Beast' Headline: The Key to an Allusion in *Ulysses*." *James Joyce Quarterly*, 19.2 (1982), 183–86.

Werner, Craig Hansen. *"Dubliners": A Pluralistic World*. Boston: Twayne, 1988.

Wollaeger, Mark. "Bloom's Coronation and the Subjection of the Subject." *James Joyce Quarterly*, 28.4 (Summer 1991), 799–808.

Woolf, Virginia. *A Room of One's Own*. New York: Harcourt, Brace, & World, 1929.

Yeats, William Butler. *The Collected Plays of W. B. Yeats*. New York: Macmillan, 1935.

Young, Robert. *White Mythologies: Writing History and the West*. London: Routledge, 1990.

Zweig, Stefan. *The World of Yesterday*. New York: n.p., 1943.

Index

Index

Index